5.4.71

FRANCE IN CRISIS, 1620–1675

FRANCE IN CRISIS
1620-1675

Selected, translated and introduced by

P. J. COVENEY

Lecturer in European History
University of Nottingham

ROWMAN AND LITTLEFIELD
Totowa, New Jersey

First published in the United States 1977
by Rowman and Littlefield, Totowa, N.J.

Selection, introduction, editorial matter and translation
© P. J. Coveney 1977

Library of Congress Cataloging in Publication Data
Main entry under title:
France in crisis, 1620–1675

   Bibliography: p.
   Includes index.
   CONTENTS: Méthivier, H. A century of conflict.—Porshnev, B.
Popular uprisings in France before the Fronde, 1623–1648.—Porshnev,
B. The Bourgeoisie and feudal-absolutism in seventeenth-century France.
[etc.]
   1. France—Politics and government—17th century—Addresses,
essays, lectures. I. Coveney, Peter.
DC121.3.F7   1977   944.032   76–41790
ISBN 0–87471–916–X

Printed and bound in Great Britain

Contents

Preface

The aim has been to make available in English major contributions to the historiography of seventeenth-century France, and to provide, in an introductory chapter, the general context of discussion within which they may be studied. The decision to include this article and to exclude that was not an easy one. From the outset, I decided that it was preferable to present a limited number of articles intact, and fairly extensive extracts from longer works, rather than a larger number of shorter fragments. The basis of my selection was that, taken separately, the articles and extracts should be important in themselves; that, taken together, they should raise, as far as possible, most of the essential considerations involved in the debate on the French seventeenth century which has been in process for over a generation; and that, both separately and together, they should contribute to the general theme of the whole work, which is clearly indicated in its title.

I have taken the fifty or so years which fall almost equally on either side of the Fronde as the chronological framework for this study. Everything suggests, and will I think increasingly suggest, the need to read these years as a continuous period, not divided as they so often have been at 1653 and 1661. The consolidation of the *ancien régime* in the later seventeenth century stems from the crisis and resolutions of these crucial decades. They are fundamental to the formation of French absolutism. They are by far the most important decades in modern French development before the era of the Revolution and Napoleon.

It has given me very great pleasure to translate and prepare these articles and extracts for publication in English. Their publication is of course only made possible by the generous permission given to me to undertake it. I am indeed grateful to Professor Roland Mousnier, Professor Pierre Deyon and M. Hubert Méthivier for their permission to translate and publish their work; and to Professor Fernand Braudel and Professor Robert Mandrou for their permission to translate and publish extracts from the French edition of Professor Boris Porshnev's work on popular uprisings in France before the Fronde. A major aim of this collection has indeed been achieved by my being able to draw together in one publication the work of Roland Mousnier and Boris Porshnev.

I wish also to record my thanks to Professor W. R. Fryer, who read an early draft of my introductory chapter and made many valuable comments upon it. I am grateful too for the awarenesses which have arisen from my teaching and learning from successive classes of final year students reading 'France under Louis XIV' in the History Department of the University of Nottingham.

I am grateful to my publishers for their providing me with space to include the authors' notes to their work virtually intact, as collected notes at the end of the chapters. My own interpolated notes, wherever they occur, are clearly indicated as editorial material.

I have appended a glossary of French terms which have been left untranslated, and whose meaning is not immediately clarified in their context. Technical terms are always I think best left untranslated, even when they may seem to have approximate equivalents. I do not like rendering *bailliage*, for example, as 'bailiwick', or *officier* as 'official'. A word given in the glossary is indicated by the glossary mark (†) on the first occasion when it occurs in any chapter.

The bibliography is intended to assist any further reading which this work may encourage.

P. J. COVENEY

University of Nottingham,
July 1976

Acknowledgements

The editor and publishers wish to thank the following for their permission to translate and publish extracts and articles included in this collection:
M. Hubert Méthivier and the *Presses Universitaires de France* for the extract from M. Méthivier's *L'Ancien Régime, 6e édition*, Paris, 1974, pp. 63–78; Professor Fernand Braudel and Professor Robert Mandrou and the *Centre de Recherches Historiques de la VIe Section de l'Ecole Pratique des Hautes Etudes* for the extracts from Professor Boris Porshnev's *Les Soulèvements populaires en France de 1623 à 1648*, S.E.V.P.E.N., Paris, 1963, pp. 17–44, 539–61 and 574–82; Professor Roland Mousnier and the *Revue d'Histoire moderne et contemporaine* for 'Recherches sur les soulèvements populaires en France avant la Fronde', *Revue d'histoire moderne et contemporaine*, 1958, pp. 81–113; Professor Roland Mousnier and the *Société d'Etude du XVIIe Siècle* for 'Quelques raisons de la Fronde: les causes des journées révolutionnaires parisiennes de 1648', *XVIIe Siècle*, 1949, pp. 33–78, and for 'Recherches sur les syndicats d'officiers pendant la Fronde: Trésoriers Généraux de France et Elus dans la Révolution', *XVIIe Siècle*, 1959, pp. 76–117; and Professor Pierre Deyon and the *Presses Universitaires de France* for 'A propos des rapports entre la noblesse française et la monarchie absolue pendant la première moitié du XVIIe siècle', *Revue Historique*, ccxxxi, 1964, pp. 341–56.

1 Introduction: France in Crisis, 1620-1675

P. J. COVENEY

I

The French seventeenth century has been a major interest among European historians since the Second World War. The reason for this, at least in part, is that the seventeenth century saw the formation of the French *ancien régime* and occupies therefore a determining position in the transformation of the late-medieval constitution in France into the political society we term absolutism. Much of the history, however, remains controversial, even in its widest and deepest issues. Are we indeed justified in speaking in terms of 'crisis' in relation to any part of the century? Did the economic expansion of the 'long sixteenth century' come to a close in France in the 1630s and 1640s, giving way to a period of economic contraction? What was the relation of the monarchy to the dominant elements within the French state, and what were the relationships between those elements themselves, especially between 'sword' and 'robe'? What was the nature of the constant popular unrest which disturbed France for so long? Was seventeenth-century France still a 'feudal' society, in which the political state was merely the instrument of a 'feudal' élite in achieving the defeat of the popular masses? Or, conversely, had the monarchy become associated with elements of the bourgeoisie, either through venality or mercantilism, thereby transforming the late-feudal character of the monarchical state by ending the political monopoly of a traditional feudal class? Was the French seventeenth century a society about which it is possible to talk usefully in terms of modern class-conflict, as Boris Porshnev has, or was it a society still meaningfully contained within the framework of late-medieval 'orders', as Roland Mousnier sees it? These are some of the major issues involved in the modern historiography of seventeenth-century France, and which form the basis of much of the discussion of the various chapters of this work.

I have used the word 'crisis' in my title very deliberately, since it still seems to me the word which best approximates to a description of the experience through which the French monarchical state passed in the middle decades of the seventeenth century; and I have, equally deliberately, extended the period of crisis beyond the Fronde, to include the first period of Louis XIV's personal reign itself, since important elements of that crisis continued until well beyond Louis' assumption of personal power in 1661. Royal policy in the crucial period of the early personal reign was largely a response to the mid-century crisis as it had revealed itself in the Fronde, a repetition of which the monarchy was intent at all costs to avoid; not solely by the blunt response of a simplifying 'reduction to obedience', in Lavisse's celebrated phrase, but by something altogether more acutely attuned to the nature of the crisis within the monarchical state and to its solution. This, more than anything perhaps, was the major legacy of the Fronde.

Students of the early modern period will be well aware of the whole corpus of 'crisis' literature which has grown up since Roland Mousnier's synthesising account of the sixteenth and seventeenth centuries in 1954[1] and E. J. Hobsbawm's essay on 'The Crisis of the Seventeenth Century', which appeared the same year,[2] followed by H. J. Trevor-Roper's 'The General Crisis of the Seventeenth Century' some five years later.[3] Just as they will be aware of the disagreements and caveats expressed by, among others, J. H. Elliott,[4] I. Schöffer,[5] A. D. Lublinskaya[6] and P. Goubert[7] regarding the whole concept of seventeenth-century crisis. Some historians have perhaps tended to use the word crisis to suggest explanations where in fact no explanation is, and the word has certainly tended to subsume historical phenomena, especially economic, into generalisations which are often highly controversial and conjectural. The idea of 'crisis' has, equally, derived sometimes from *a priori* assumptions, where the concept anticipates the reasons adduced to explain it, which is a common enough enemy of all historical wisdom.

Even so, it would be an arid excursion into the meaning of words to propose that the word crisis should be limited to a strictly medical analogy and therefore to its short-term meaning only; thus denying the historian access to the concept that political societies do indeed experience crises, sometimes of fairly long duration, which reach their climax and find resolution only very slowly. Such semantic nicety would much reduce the historian's access to a word which, by figurative extension, has had a long and largely meaningful usage. It does not strain semantic proprieties to propose that the English state was in a condition of crisis in the late Tudor and early Stuart periods until the Civil War and beyond. Spanish history has been usefully written of in terms of 'crisis' at the close of the sixteenth and during the early seventeenth centuries.[8] It is a common acceptance that Muscovy succumbed to a period of accumulating and prolonged crisis following the death of Ivan IV in 1584 until the restoration of stable monarchy from the accession of Michael Romanov in 1613. Crisis seems the only word which usefully defines the condition of a political society which experiences chronic or closely recurring periods of instability and tension, caused most often by pressures arising from conflict between legally constituted authority and major social interests, testified to most frequently, though not always, by varying degrees of violence, which may or may not resolve itself through revolution. Such was indeed the experience of France from the 1620s until the initial period of Louis XIV's personal reign.

In using the term crisis, I had better be entirely precise, that I am of course talking of the French state at a particular time and at a particular stage in its development. I am not suggesting that there was a 'seventeenth-century crisis' in Europe as a whole, whether over the total length of the century or in its middle decades, and that this was in some way part of it; nor – even less indeed – that there was a 'crisis in capitalism'; nor even that there was a general 'economic crisis' in the middle seventeenth century, even though the '*conjoncture*' of French economic circumstances in the mid-century was almost certainly adverse and a major concomitant of French difficulty. I have no wish to generalise on the European situation in the seventeenth century in terms of crisis, even though it becomes increasingly clear that comparative studies in the early modern period enrich not only an understanding of European studies as a whole, but the understanding of each particular society of the age. Much of what the authors of the extracts and articles in this collection are concerned with has relevance to the history of many other European states in their early modern development. Even so, it is no part of the thinking of this work to propose even common 'preconditions of revolution in early modern Europe' – valuable and perhaps mandatory as comparative studies in the early modern period may be.[9]

II

In its clearest manifestation, the crisis of my title was a crisis in the French political state, occasioned in the short-term by the fiscal pressures imposed upon it in the period of the Thirty Years War. Many immediately apparent factors combined to create the instability of the French monarchical state in the mid-seventeenth century. A powerful late-medieval nobility was still able and willing to inflame and raise the provinces against the Crown in a period of royal minority. An alienated official class was prepared to withdraw support from and ultimately to challenge the Crown at a time of great international crisis for the monarchy; and a wholly unprecedented level of taxation burdened an already depressed peasantry to the point of revolution, in a context of rising economic and monetary difficulty. Indeed, it seems not so much whether there was a crisis in the French state in these central decades of the seven-

teenth century as a question of its origins, its depth and duration.

The seriousness of the crisis, however, lay in its long-term development
and multiplicity. The 'administrative revolution' undertaken by Richelieu
and Mazarin to raise the finances necessary to contain and then defeat
the Habsburgs in Europe, together with the political and economic contin-
gencies of the middle century, aggravated tensions within the whole
French monarchical structure to the point of insupportability, which
ultimately culminated in the Fronde.

A. Lloyd Moote has recently stressed the long-term nature of the
mounting crisis within the French state and speaks of France's 'unique
potential for widespread upheaval' in the early seventeenth century and of
a 'growing crisis'. He suggests that 'Louis XIII's reign would have been a
critical period for France', even 'without the intrusion of disputes between the monarchy and the *officiers*'†; it was possible that 'a few false
steps, such as an unwillingness to compromise or military indecision,
could well have brought a major upheaval to France by 1640, as it did
to Spain and England'.[10] For Mousnier, the Fronde resulted from 'fundamental tensions and clashes of social and political interests' in the French
state, which 'can be traced back through the first half of the seventeenth
century', and which 'seem almost permanent features of French society'.
They were, he says, manifestations 'of a deeply troubled society and
state'.[11] In his review-article of the Porshnev-Mousnier controversy,
J. H. M. Salmon stresses that for both Porshnev and Mousnier 'French
society in the seventeenth century experienced a critical change of direction which foreshadowed, if it did not predetermine the subsequent
history of the *ancien régime*'.[12] For him, indeed, the crisis may not be
entirely comprehensible by reference to the seventeenth-century situation alone. Its origins may 'lie further back in time . . . in a period of
even greater anarchy, the concluding phases of the Wars of Religion'.[13]
Even if we take the time-scale of a historian more dubious than most
of concepts of seventeenth-century 'crisis', A. D. Lublinskaya herself
accepts that in the first half of the seventeenth century 'the time was out
of joint and the whole of society in ferment' – a description which bears
little relationship to the political society which coheres in France from
the 1670s.[14]

These decades of the middle seventeenth century were the formative
phase in the development of French absolutism. They are the hinge on
one side of which lies the late-medieval constitution of France in its
long-term condition of instability, and on the other the stabilisation and
consolidation of the *ancien régime*. The political society which emerges
from the 1670s and 1680s, and which was to carry France through to
the second half of the eighteenth century, quite evidently differs very
materially from the century of almost uninterrupted internal conflict

which preceded it, from the France of the League and the *Seize*, of the *Jour des Dupes* and the Fronde – just as, in England, for all the continuities, there seems almost a difference in kind between the political society of the England of Queen Anne and that of the early Stuarts. It is very evident that considerable political transformations have occurred in both societies.

The image of the early seventeenth century as one of monarchical consolidation in France, after Richelieu's brilliant disposal of the difficulties stemming from the death of Henry IV and the minority of Louis XIII, has given place in post-war historiography to the image of a France in deep economic, social and political difficulty. France in the first half of the seventeenth century seems to have had at least some affinities with the incoherent particularism of the German Empire and with the financial instability and rural depression of Habsburg Spain. Under de Luynes, France indeed suffered all of Spain's disastrous encystment of the political state within the Court and all of its consequent trivialisation. J. H. Elliott has remarked on the similarities between the France of Louis XIII and the Castille of Philip IV;[15] even though in the end it is the differences between them which make for all the historical significance. It seems improbable that France was in so much difficulty that she might have been permanently defeated by Spain, if only Olivares had had a few crucial regiments to throw into the military scale against her, bringing about a lasting reversal in Spanish and French comparative fortunes.[16] The greater movements of history, such as the formation and nature of the European states, are scarcely ever a matter of short-term touch and go. There were most probably organic processes directing France toward the social and military resolutions of her monarchical *ancien régime*, just as there were most probably those pointing England toward the Hanoverians and limited 'parliamentary' monarchy, and the Spanish Habsburgs toward European oblivion. It seems likely that long-term development made it probable that the late-medieval crisis in the English political state would produce both a monarchical *and* a parliamentary resolution, just as the French state would resolve into an *ancien régime* which would be above all monarchical. But this is not to talk in terms of inevitabilities. It was by no means clear in the early seventeenth century how matters would resolve in France; whether there would be some coalescence of oppositional interests, even some revolutionary focus, which might impose significant and lasting limitations upon the development of 'sovereign monarchy'.[17]

It is the deep organic monarchical constant in French development which leads J. H. Shennan, however, to discount altogether the idea of 'crisis' in the French seventeenth century, laying his emphasis instead on the 'fundamental stability' of 'French government and society' from the mid-fifteenth century. He accepts that there was 'constant tension, constant pressure and counter-pressure, poise and equipoise, between the crown and the various component parts of the state', but, in the end, he stresses the stability and continuity of French constitutional development 'founded on monarchy'.[18] Viewed from the lengthy time-scale and institutional emphasis of his extended essay, from 1461 to 1661, this might seem the ultimate pattern of French development. But to stress the element of continuity and stability is to be in danger of losing the matching reality of dynamic change and risk in French development during this major transformational period. There were periods when the 'tensions and pressures' were manifestly not, in Shennan's phrase, 'for the most part contained'.[19] Between the mid-sixteenth century to the post-Fronde, they were scarcely ever contained in any exact or useful sense of that word, except very briefly under Henry IV. There were indeed times, in the late 1580s, say, or again during the Fronde, when the feeling of Paris cannot have been entirely unlike that of Brussels in the mid-1560s. There was the same sense of political dissolution and submergence. In the age of Richelieu and Mazarin the role of monarchy was not to create political stability, but its reverse, and, in so doing, it almost brought about the collapse of the political state. French political development in the sixteenth and seventeenth centuries was not a matter of foregone conclusions, whatever the inner probabilities of organic time. Nor was it a matter of 'pressure and counter-pressure, poise and equipoise' cancelling each other out, in a monarchical continuum, in a 'cyclical' movement, to use Shennan's term,[20] but a dynamic process, developmental, producing change. It is not that the seventeenth-century constitution ended up, in any significant sense, as the fifteenth-century constitution began, because of an omnipresent and easily distinguishable monarchy. It is a question of a quite different balance becoming established between traditional and 'absolutist' elements. It is often one of the complexities and deceptions of political development that institutions and nomenclature remain, the institutional grammar remains, while a quite different language of power is being expressed through it. Sometimes the more it seems, as in Shennan's analysis, constitutionally the same thing, the more in fact it has changed.

There was indeed little challenge to the idea of monarchy as such in France in the early modern period. This was for the most part the case throughout western Europe at this time. Only in the Northern Netherlands, and for a brief period in England, did monarchy itself succumb and give way to republican forms. Most often, as in France, the challenge was not whether monarchy itself should survive, but what *kind* of monarchy should develop and what its prerogatives should be; in what sense and to what extent should it be answerable to law, whether fundamental or customary; how binding were the 'liberties' conceded in the past in face of the exigencies of a current and pressing *raison d'Etat*;

and to what extent should the policies and legislation of the state be the product of a dialogue between a prince and his Estates? These were the major references of seventeenth-century European political debate, and, although it was largely contained within the framework of monarchical forms, fundamental issues were nevertheless involved regarding the nature of monarchy. There is a very real sense in which the challenge of the *Parlementaires* in the summer of 1648 may be said to have been, in Mousnier's word, 'revolutionary': in the sense that, if the challenge had been sustained, the direction of French monarchical development would have been fundamentally changed, to a degree far beyond the 'victory in defeat' which some historians see as the lasting outcome of the Fronde; the balance between the 'traditional' and 'absolutist' constitutions would have reached a new adjustment quite different from that of the 1670s.

Conflict concerning the prerogatives of monarchy lay at the heart of most political disorder in late-medieval Europe; and in this the French experience is representative. Conflict between centralising monarchs and traditional constitutional structures was the point of major political incidence. It was the point at issue, initially, in Philip II's political failure in the Netherlands, as it was in the early Stuarts' failure with their English 'medieval' Estates. There was endemic friction between the traditional or late-medieval and the absolutist or modern constitutions in most western European states in that long transformational period we term early modern Europe. It is the chronic instability of the late-medieval states which constantly enforces itself, manifested in long periods of social and political crisis and recurring internal violence.

The concept of 'two' French 'monarchies' in coexistence, which John Stoye talks of in relation to the period of the Fronde, has relevance to the development of the French monarchical state in the whole early modern period.[21] From the time when the unitary state strengthens in the late medieval period, areas of potential friction develop at the 'interface' of these two kinds of monarchy – the one the product of decentralisation and structured diffusion of authority, the political embodiment of the economic and social devolution of the medieval state; the other the embodiment of monarchical concentration. Throughout most of the early modern period it was unresolved what degree of monarchical control would develop in France, what compromises would ultimately need to be effected between continuing particularist and newer centralising forces, what the comparative weighting, the balance between the 'two monarchies' would ultimately be; how far the monarchy of France would remain dual; what *modus vivendi* would underwrite the stability of the French *ancien régime* – even if it indeed seems to us likely that in the event the balance would be more monarchical than devolutionary.

There were constant factors in the situation weighting the balance against monarchical concentration. Geography produced its own inherent regionalism. Poor communications imposed constant restraints upon governmental initiative, which were to affect the whole history of the *ancien régime* and were to continue until the communications revolution of the nineteenth century. It is difficult to appreciate the vastnesses of seventeenth-century France. It was a society of very intense social contiguities in the towns; but the rural interstices were continental in their scale for the few who needed to move among them, even though the administrative correspondence of the period reveals the remarkable speed with which the turn-round in correspondence was in fact achieved.

So, too, the 'federal' nature of the monarchy in its fundamental constitutional relationship with the provinces created a political structure which was inherently particularist and a sure recourse for separatism and provincial non-cooperation. The French monarchy in its relationship with certain of the *pays d'états*† was as 'federal' as the crown of Castile with its Aragonese territories. Particularism was institutionalised in the *pays d'états*, in the municipal corporations, in all the secular and ecclesiastical corporations whose franchises and privileges were the product and sanction of a continuing medieval constitutionalism. And omnipresent, whether in the *pays d'états* or in the *pays d'élections*†, that central core of monarchical France, there was the underlying structure of seigneurial France, the varying patchwork of social and economic power which covered the realm and which, in a very real though minor sense, still judged, administered and taxed within the major sovereignty of the monarchical state. This was the immemorial France deriving from the medieval period which survived until the close of the *ancien régime* itself; a France consisting of multitudinous enclaves of social power divided vertically each from the other, and all, in varying degrees, entrenched opponents of the levelling interests and unifying ambitions of the monarchical state.

The successive means by which the monarchy had attempted to achieve control and give coherence to these late-medieval elements were in themselves a major element in maintaining incoherence. The organic proliferation of royal officials established in the provinces over the centuries, superimposed one upon the other, with no group ever cleared away – the initial *baillis*† and *sénéchaux*, the subsequent *gouverneurs* and the *lieutenants-généraux*†, the whole body of *officiers* which the process of venality created in the course of the sixteenth century in the law courts and finance *bureaux* of Valois France, the *commissaires départis*† of late Valois and early Bourbon France – everything generated confusion of function and jurisdiction, and a recourse for the use of procedural device to impede and circumvent the royal will. This could make for local independence, or rather the independence of local oligarchy; but it also made for debilitating rivalries between the different groups of officials, and worked, in times of political challenge, to the advantage of a monarchy which wished to be master by a process of divide and rule.

The centralising performance and reality of the Renaissance monarchy of France is not however to be underestimated. The growth of the monarchical idea, the rising concept of the self-sufficient political and economic state, above all the extension of the royal administration itself led to the formation of the French monarchical armature on an unprecedented scale in the first half of the sixteenth century. Although the late-medieval constitution in France was to remain intensely multiple, containing within it major elements working for the limitation of royal power, such as the judicial review of royal legislation through the registration of edicts by the *Parlements*, it nevertheless distorts both the ambitions and the performance of the Renaissance monarchy to emphasise its overriding 'constitutional' and 'representative' character.[22] It is not really a question of alternative readings of the sixteenth-century monarchy, to decide whether it was 'constitutional' or 'absolutist', but of its inherent ambivalence, based as it was on the coexistence of two kinds of monarchy, the one conceding and guaranteeing 'liberties' of itself, the other eroding and retrieving the same in endless counterpoint. It is indeed this central ambivalence at the constitutional heart of early modern France which more than anything made for tension and disorder.

It was in the sixteenth century that the whole apparatus of the 'administrative monarchy' was constructed, in the two areas of primary state interest, justice and finance, and this was to have fundamental repercussions on the relationship between the monarchy and the traditional constitution. To meet the bureaucratic needs of the monarchy the system of venality of office developed; at first *ad hoc* and then 'institutionalised', from the third decade of the sixteenth century by Francis I, through the *bureau* of the *parties casuelles*† which administered the sale of his bureaucratic merchandise. It was a development of the greatest importance. Venality made the formation of the administrative monarchy possible. It attracted into the service of the monarchy a cadre of *officiers* from the law schools of Renaissance France, who were not members of the feudal class. There seems little doubt that the feudal class, at least initially, attempted to contain the situation by acquiring offices put up for sale, especially those conferring 'nobility' in the upper reaches of the *Parlements*.[23] But whatever the subsequent relationship between the traditional nobility of the 'sword' and the nobility of the 'robe', venality created a bureaucratic structure staffed for the most part by *officiers* who were not thereby ennobled. This most certainly created tension between the monarchy and a feudal class which saw itself increasingly endangered in its monopoly of the public function which it still considered its own essential patrimony, and this was to be of the greatest importance for the future.

Venality staffed the great judicial service of the Renaissance monarchy. The provision of justice remained the primary social responsibility of the monarchy; and this was as true in the sixteenth and seventeenth centuries as it had been in the thirteenth. A whole apparatus of royal justice ascended from the courts of the medieval *bailliages* and *sénéchaussées*, through the intermediate level of the *présidiaux*† formed by Henry II, up to the high courts of appeal, the *Parlement de Paris*† and the provincial *Parlements*†. With the *Cours des Aides*†, the *Chambres des Comptes*† and certain minor courts, the *Parlements* formed the 'sovereign courts' of the realm. It was to become part of the seventeenth-century constitutional conflict between the Crown and the *Parlement de Paris* whether the judgments of the 'sovereign courts' were in fact 'sovereign' and 'without appeal', or whether cases could be regularly evoked away from them to the special tribunals of specially appointed *commissaires*, or to the *Conseil* itself as the ultimate expression of royal sovereignty. It is worth insisting here, since it was to become in time of the greatest importance, that financial litigation in the courts closely affected the financial interests of the Crown. This was indeed a major reason inducing the monarchy to circumvent judicial impediments to its financial interests by the use of *commissaires* and their tribunals in the financial crisis of the Thirty Years War, in order to break through the integuments and delays involved in the normal processes of financial justice.

Venality was in itself a product of the growing financial needs of the monarchy, and it rapidly became and remained an important element in the revenues of the Crown. The fiscal structure of the *ancien régime* was largely the construct of the sixteenth-century monarchy. It was then that the provincial *bureaux* of the *Trésoriers de France*† were formed, together with the fiscal unit of the *généralité*†.[24] The *généralités* as the seventeenth century knew them had their origin in the reign of Francis I. They were to become the basic administrative unit of the *ancien régime*, the basis of the *intendances*, with which they were virtually synonymous in the seventeenth-century governmental mind. The apotheosis of the *généralité*, a basically fiscal unit, as the basic administrative unit of the monarchical state is evidence indeed of the central transference of emphasis, in the mind of its rulers, from justice to finance, which was the irreversible dynamic of the age.

The growing financial needs of the monarchy in part resulted from the Court's increasing consumption and from the cost of its own bureaucratic development. But increased military expenditure was by far the most important factor. The territorial vulnerability of the French kingdom is central to French development in the early modern period and to the formation of French absolutism. It generated, more than anything else perhaps, the ethos of the aristocratic military culture of the French *ancien régime* and sustained the values of the late-medieval military aristocracy into the sixteenth and seventeenth centuries. The financial demands it created enforced the consolidation of the administrative monarchy, and, ironically, was the source of its chronic financial instability. It was to be a major factor in generating the crisis of the mid-seventeenth century, when the financial demands of the foreign situation became most acute, in a context of intense internal difficulty and disruption. The crisis of the Fronde was the product of a harsh counterpoint between the most adverse external and internal factors.

From 1494, with Charles VIII's invasion of Italy, the French monarchy was involved in constantly recurring wars until the close of Louis XIV's reign. Charles's invasion broached France's modern dynastic involvement in Italy. The situation was then compounded, almost immediately afterwards, by a sudden and overwhelming increase in Habsburg power in western Europe, arising from the entirely fortuitous results of dynastic marriages, which brought about the union of the German and Spanish crowns in the empire of Charles V (1519–56) and all its celebrated consequence of 'encirclement' for France. This 'encirclement' was not to cease when the German and Spanish components of Charles's empire were divided at his abdication in 1556, but was to remain the central reference of French dynastic and financial policy from then until the eighteenth century.

The sixteenth-century military costs of the French monarchy were continuously compounded by inflation. It was the military commitment of the Valois state under Francis I and Henry II which led it to over-extend its credit resources in the middle century. This more than anything brought the collapse of the Lyons credit-market at the end of Henry II's reign, from which, in the almost immediately ensuing disturbances of the religious wars, it was slow to recover.[25] This may well have given the Habsburgs, for all their financial difficulties, an edge over the late Valois and Bourbon dynasties in raising military credit and thus served to increase the problems of the French state during the military-financial crisis of the Thirty Years War. The fiscal pressure on the French peasantry at that time and the administrative measures which the financial interests of the monarchy led Richelieu to introduce were all intensified by the urgency with which the taxes had to be brought in to nourish the credit-worthiness of the French monarchy on the French finance-market, by which alone the day-to-day military expenditure could be met. The French monarchy had immense resources in comparison with the English monarchy of Elizabeth or Charles I, but those resources were nevertheless chronically inadequate to the scale of diplomatic and military operation that had to be mounted. The French Crown needed very considerable revenues in face of an enemy with direct access to the mines of Peru and the American trade. The dynastic situation forced the French monarchical state to become a machine for levying taxes, not only to defend the frontiers of a chronically vulnerable kingdom, but also, increasingly, and as importantly, to sustain itself internally. The problem of the internal security of the monarchy was indeed annexed to the external, since it was to be one of the constant and major weaknesses of the French Crown in the sixteenth and seventeenth centuries that internal subversion could always find ready support among the monarchy's European enemies.

III

The instability of the French late-medieval state revealed itself continuously from the mid-sixteenth century. Seventeenth-century difficulties were in fact merely to compound an already exceedingly deteriorated situation. The accelerating collapse of the monarchy following the accidental death of Henry II in 1559 thrust the late-medieval state into a major political crisis, from which it was not to recover until the close of the century, and then only temporarily under Henry IV. The Wars of Religion resulted from difficulties within the political state which it was the function of religious conflict to compound. The bankruptcy of the Valois Crown and the consequent weakening of its hold over its own bureaucracy were already creating a major crisis in the state before the reception of Calvinism in France. The combination of a weak Crown and mounting doctrinal conflict brought the late-medieval state to collapse, exposing the most powerful factor militating against political stability, the desire on the part of the late-medieval nobility to sustain itself at the centre of government, which was to remain a constant factor in the difficulties of the state until the personal reign of Louis XIV. It is indicative of the tenuousness of the stabilities provided by monarchy that so much depended upon the person, even the actual existence, of an adult king, without whom, at successive royal minorities, the whole edifice tended toward rapid disintegration. If for no other reason, this alone would suggest the unwisdom of laying too great a stress on the continuities and stability of monarchical tradition in France, and lends weight to the inverse proposal that, for all the strength of the French Renaissance monarchy, the continuing factor in the late-medieval French political situation was one of very marked potential instability, which was punctuated by periods when the potentialities for strengthened government were realised.

The discontinuity in the development of the monarchy following the death of Henry II and the simultaneous politicising of the Calvinist Reformation constitute perhaps the most significant event in the history of early modern France. It had a decisive effect far beyond the history of the later sixteenth century. France succumbed to the nightmare which haunted the Tudor mind, of a weak succession in a context of radical doctrinal conflict, with a factious high nobility competing for control of the state. It is arguable that had the discontinuity not been so deep in the later sixteenth century, the restoration of continuity would not have been so difficult to achieve in the seventeenth.

The wars were important also in that they almost certainly retarded the development of the French rural economy. The recurring subsistence crises of the French seventeenth century may in part have stemmed from the fact that an increased population from the sixteenth century was left to be supported in the seventeenth on an under-developed agrarian economy, chronically susceptible to adverse climatic conditions. In this, the disruption of the religious wars and the military preoccupations of the landed class, especially during the last and most furious phase of the wars following the death of Anjou in 1584, must have contributed to the subsistence problems of the seventeenth century, which could perhaps only have been solved, in the absence of major agrarian advance, by a malthusian adjustment in the form of recurring *'mortalités'*.

It is important too that intense inflation in the last decades of the sixteenth century, combined with increased taxation arising from the wars, created a chronic indebtedness among sections of the peasantry. The despair and social turbulence which reveals itself among the French peasantry in the period before the Fronde almost certainly had its origins among the inflation, the heavy taxation and the rural indebtedness of the final phases of the religious wars. Chronic debt and consequent expropriation by active urban classes became a phenomenon among the rural poor by the close of the sixteenth century. Already, by 1600, there were victors and vanquished among the French rural classes, both seigneurial and peasant, and this, perhaps more than anything, was the social heritage the seventeenth century acquired from the sixteenth. The mounting difficulties of the age of Louis XIII occurred in a society still suffering the adverse effects of an earlier period, which the brief reign of Henry IV had done little to alleviate.

Most importantly, for future political development, the religious wars exposed the instability of the late-medieval constitution and seemed therefore to enforce the need for sovereign monarchy in France. In a remarkable way, the whole problem of the late-medieval constitution was conceptualised by Bodin, out of the circumstances of the wars, in his *Six Livres de la République* (1576). Bodin's concept of *'souveraineté'*, which he asserted as the *sine qua non* of all political societies, was to become central to the restoration of the monarchy in the last decade of the sixteenth century and to the ultimate establishment of sovereign monarchy under Louis XIV.

The reign of Henry IV was not however one of really major achievement. It foreshadowed what monarchy might achieve, and Henry IV was to occupy, not surprisingly, an essential place in the personal 'myth' of

Louis XIV, as the mentor of seventeenth-century monarchy; but much of the concentration on monarchy during the closing stages of the wars derived from military and political exhaustion rather than from any really meaningful desire to accept 'monarchical' solutions. The social revolution of the period of the League had impelled the Catholic nobility back to the side of legitimate monarchy, very much as Calvinist radicalism had done in the southern Netherlands in the middle 1570s. The Huguenot nobility increasingly recognised that it had fought itself into a political impasse; and it was this which held its allegiance to Henry in face of his apostasy of 1593. Much indeed of what Henry achieved was made possible by the European *détente* which followed the peace with Spain at Vervins in 1598, the Anglo-Spanish peace of 1604 and the Twelve Years Truce in the Netherlands some five years later. There was no guarantee, nor likelihood even, that this pacification would last. It was Henry's good fortune that Spain was, for the moment, as exhausted by her European policies as France was by her internal wars. In the event, Vervins was to prove, not unexpectedly, a truce, and the temporary pacification of the early seventeenth century proved merely the prelude to a renewal of European conflict.

Fundamentally, Henry's reign solved little. His religious peace was based on the compromise of underwriting Huguenot separatism to the point of establishing a lasting risk to the military integrity of the state. The Huguenot problem was not solved so much as shelved and the Huguenot wars renewed themselves only four years after Henry's death. His economic policies were no more than broached;[26] and, most importantly, nothing was done to reform the structure of the administrative monarchy. The pragmatic emphasis of the monarchy was, for compelling enough reasons no doubt, sustained. The monarchy resumed, in a sense, where it had left off. The system of the *taille*†, the farming of the indirect taxes, the provincial array of *officiers* superimposed and juxtaposed, with the regulating use of *commissaires* working among them – this had been and was to remain the pattern of the monarchy, and the *ancien régime* was never really to move outside it, even though the total 'balance' was ultimately to swing more strongly in favour of the Crown.

The central political problem for the monarchy lay in its relationship with the politically dominant elements in the state. The nobility was by no means stabilised and Henry faced noble conspiracy in the provinces during almost every year of his reign. More important, however, were the Crown's relations with its own *officiers*. During the wars, these had fallen increasingly outside the control of the monarchy, into the control of either Catholic or Huguenot nobility. In this, the essentially ambiguous position of the *officiers* was already exposed, in that they lay between the 'two monarchies', the two constitutions. On the one hand, they were agents of the centralising monarchy; they were in a sense the administrative monarchy itself. On the other hand, however, through the nature of provincial things, they were already in process of becoming moulded into the mass of traditional France, into the social realities of the other constitution. There was always the danger for the monarchy that their allegiances would become localised and that they would become a new kind of 'administrative feudalism' in the provinces, another 'estate' within the realm, asserting their corporate rights *vis-à-vis* the Crown which, they could claim, it was the function of monarchy to sustain and respect. There was the danger indeed that the Crown's own bureaucracy would in fact become spokesmen and defenders of particularist rights in general, of 'constitutionalism' against the Crown itself. It was a danger that was to materialise in the seventeenth century. This indeterminacy and ambiguity in the position of the *officiers* was indeed to play a major role in the political confusion of the first half of the seventeenth century.

Henry IV sought initially to resume control over the *officiers* by an increased use of *commissaires* to inspect them and to correct abuses. The introduction of the *paulette* in 1604, however, was a more subtle move to re-establish confidence between the monarchy and its own bureaucracy. Beyond the fiscal motive of the measure, which was real enough, lay a desire to engage the allegiance of these vital corporations for the Crown, by providing them with the opportunity to pay an 'insurance premium', in Mousnier's phrase, to secure the inheritance of their offices to their families. The principle of hereditary tenure of office was not in any way new. The *paulette* institutionalised the principle and facilitated inheritance by making it less precarious. It simply abolished the 'forty day' rule, by which in the past any bequest of office had been nullified and the office had automatically fallen into the Crown for resale if the office-holder died within forty days of making the settlement. In a period of acute epidemic disease, this had made inheritance of office exceedingly precarious. The rule was now abolished in return for the payment of an annual tax, the *annuel*, of approximately one-sixtieth of the value of the office.

It was a pragmatic measure, as much fiscal in intent as political. It was however to have repercussions of the greatest political importance. By institutionalising hereditary office it increased the danger of creating a new 'administrative feudalism', of entrenching the *officiers* behind the barricades of seventeenth-century constitutionalism. In this, it was important that an element of insecurity was introduced by the decision that the *paulette* was to be renegotiated between the Crown and its *officiers* every nine years. The renewal of the *paulette* became an inbuilt friction-point between the monarchy and the *officiers* on each successive occasion of its renegotiation. It was to be an important element indeed in provoking the final crisis leading to the Fronde. The *paulette* also aggravated relations between the Crown and the traditional nobility. There was already widespread concern among elements of the traditional nobility that venality had created an administrative state outside the control of the feudal class. By institutionalising the principle of hereditary office, the *paulette* in effect entrenched still further the position of the *noblesse de robe*.

We reach here a difficult and controversial area. It is central to the analysis of the French seventeenth century made by Pagès and Mousnier[27] that venality enabled the monarchy to erode the political supremacy of the feudal class during the course of the sixteenth century by attracting elements of the bourgeoisie into its service. In this sense, venality retrieved the administration of the state from the hands of the feudal class and secured it to the monarchy. Pagès and Mousnier find it equally significant that some *officiers* acquired 'nobility' through office and formed what is termed the '*noblesse de robe*', especially in the higher ranks of the *Parlements*. This was, for them, a new, secondary nobility, secondary indeed in Mousnier's analysis to the old nobility of the 'sword'. Venality therefore created inherent conflict between the monarchy and the traditional nobility, and also between the traditional nobility and *officiers* who became members of the *noblesse de robe*. For Mousnier this inherent discord between the Crown and the traditional *noblesse d'épée* and these rivalries within the ruling élite are central to an understanding of the crisis within the seventeenth-century monarchical state, as also to an explanation of the origins of the Fronde, and, perhaps most importantly, to an understanding of its failure. Venality and the consequent formation of the *noblesse de robe* created a central conflict between 'orders', between 'robe' and 'sword', which was to be played out in the Fronde. The danger to the monarchy in the Fronde lay most especially indeed in the opportunistic alignment of sword and robe against their *common* enemy, the Crown, during the period 1648–9.

It is important to clarify the Pagès and Mousnier schema and its division of the *noblesse* into two meaningfully identifiable categories, because its validity has been denied. J. H. Shennan suggests that it is of 'dubious validity' to distinguish 'sword' from 'robe'. 'An idea persists', he says, 'that there was . . . a division between *noblesse de robe* and *noblesse d'épée*, robe and sword, with the implication of the latter's social superiority over the former, but that idea is of dubious validity.'[28] For Shennan, 'sword' and 'robe' stand for different 'professions', not different social levels. If members of each group possessed nobility, he says, they were as 'indistinguishably a part of the *noblesse de race* as the Great Condé himself'.[29] Then, by reference to the work of Sutherland[30] and Orest Ranum,[31] he shows the indisputable nobility of the secretaries of state under the late Valois and Louis XIII. But this is not indeed the real point of Mousnier's analysis. No one could doubt the fact of Villeroy's or Bouthillier's 'nobility'. The *fact* of their 'nobility' is not in question. The question resides in the more subtle area of social acceptability and regard. It is also important that the examples Shennan gives from Orest Ranum's work on the *conseillers d'Etat* under Louis XIII were early members of a rising ministerial élite, a *noblesse d'Etat*, which was to reach its apogee under Louis XIV. This élite most certainly rose through nobility conferred by office, from within the *parlementaire* robe; but by attaining the highest offices in the state its members were recruited to what Goubert calls the '*robe du conseil*', and cannot therefore be taken as in any real sense members of the ordinary 'robe'.

Goubert, however, in his own *Ancien Régime*,[32] suggests an identification of 'sword' and 'robe', from evidence that the traditional families of the 'sword' did in fact acquire offices conferring nobility. His dependence, however, upon evidence from the *Parlement* of Rennes, in which the 'sword' most certainly maintained its position, tells us nothing of the general position. Brittany was very much a *pays* apart in the *ancien régime* and it would be exceedingly unwise, as Goubert himself of course accepts, to generalise from its evidence. Also, and it is of the greatest significance, Goubert accepts the 'newness' of the robe families of the *Parlement de Paris* – 'the parlementary nobility was "newer" in Paris than elsewhere'.[33] It is an important caveat, since the essence of the robe lay in the *Parlement de Paris*; its prestige lay there and the *parlementaire* leadership of the Fronde lay there. In this, it is to be remembered that the title *Parlement de Paris* is entirely misleading, in that the area of its jurisdiction, its '*ressort*', extended through half of the French kingdom, from Picardy in the north-east to the border of Guyenne in the south-west, and from the Breton frontier in the north-west to the Lyonnais in the south-east, and contained indeed the majority of the central core of monarchical France, the *pays d'élections*.[34] When Goubert asserts that 'the majority of seats in the provincial *Parlements*' (as distinct from the *Parlement de Paris*) were 'held by the Grands and the old nobility', it is crucial to distinguish that he is really talking of the provinces of the *pays d'états*, since the majority of the 'provincial *Parlements*' were situated in *pays d'états*, or, as in the case of Normandy, *pays d'états* recently demoted. There was another 'provincial' France, a half of the realm, which fell within the *ressort* of a court, the most important court indeed of the realm, in which 'robe' and 'sword' were not identical. There is nothing in Goubert's analysis which sustains any blanket suggestion that the *noblesse de robe* as such and the *noblesse d'épée* were one.

Shennan cites in support of his case sections from Labatut and Durand's edition of the *cahiers* of the order of the nobility of Troyes and Angoumois, drawn up for the Estates General mooted but not convoked during the crisis of the Fronde.[35] In his introduction to the edition,

Mousnier returns again to the conflict between 'sword' and 'robe', and to *gentilshommes* grievance against the whole process of venality and the principle of hereditary office enshrined in the system of the *paulette*, which he sees clearly reflected in the *cahiers*.[36] Shennan, however, reads this grievance as merely the expression of frustration on the part of the *gentilshommes* at their inability to acquire office by reason of the inflated price of the seventeenth-century merchandise.[37] He reads their desire to acquire office as evidence of their social acceptance of it. For them it was not an act of social *dérogeance* to purchase office. But the urgent point is not how *gentilshommes* would regard office if they continued to acquire it, but what their opinion was of *officiers* who had acquired office and consequently nobility, but who were not of the 'sword', even though they had 'robe nobility' in their families for several generations. In the first instance, there would clearly have been, in terms of social acceptance, a complete identification of 'sword' and 'robe'. The cause for *gentilshommes* grievance, however, lay in the second. Their grievance was that power and influence lay in office, which some other group was increasingly acquiring and they were not, and that this nobility of the robe considered *themselves* the social equals, in their nobility, of the 'sword'. If one is to accept the validity of their complaint, which Shennan does, from its very nature, the inference must be that by the middle of the seventeenth century there was an identifiable 'robe' which was not of the *gentilshommes* and the *noblesse de race*, whatever the situation had been in some golden age when office had been purchasable by old nobility at reasonable prices.

Shennan suggests that Mousnier would have had great difficulty in convincing the 'robe' of its membership of and identity with the 'bourgeoisie'.[38] But again it is important not to mistake the point that Mousnier is making. He entirely accepts the *de jure* nobility of the 'robe'. Their own social appraisal of their own social status, the fact that they themselves considered themselves members of the *noblesse de race*, is not really of very great significance, except in so far as it was apparently a cause for *gentilshommes* grievance. Mousnier's whole position is that the important distinctions were made the other way round. It was the social pretension of the 'bourgeois' robe which was most complained of. It is of course undeniable that 'robe' offices were bought by 'sword' families, and that marriage often formed an alliance between the two. It may well have been the consequent blurring of distinctions and the narrowness of distinctions, and therefore the difficulty of establishing and enforcing them, which made them seem all the more important to those able and wishing to sustain them. There is every indication of a confusion of status within the *noblesse* which may have led to the extravagant response expressed in the eighteenth century in Saint-Simon's famous castigation of the whole reign of Louis XIV as a 'long reign of low-born bourgeois'. To take Shennan's point as to how the great *Parlementaires* would have responded to the suggestion that they were 'bourgeois', one might reasonably feel that the greater difficulty would have been in persuading the hero of Rocroi and the *Passage du Rhin* of his social identity with the *Parlementaires*, no matter how nobly the *Parlementaires* thought of themselves. The *Parlementaires* were not Condés – as the Grand Condé himself was to find to his political cost in the crux of the Fronde itself.[39] It seems impossible to comprehend the complex realities of seventeenth-century French society without an acceptance of the importance of the distinctions to be made between families considering themselves 'sword' and those who were considered 'robe'. The military essence of the feudal families remained, and was to be further entrenched by the wars, both civil and international, of the seventeenth century. The social aspirations of certain members of the highest 'robe', inside the *Conseil* itself, were symbolised in their intense desire to create genealogies for themselves. This was not by any means a figment of Saint-Simon's distorting imagination, and is surely suggestive that only in that way could ennoblement by office really attain the status of the *noblesse de race*. Even membership of the *robe du conseil* was evidently not enough without real genealogical validation. Colbert's ambitions in this direction are well enough known. Less well known perhaps is the fact that Chancellor Séguier harboured an identical ambition. Why, if everyone were uniformly noble, did Séguier, a man who held the highest office in the realm, have an entirely fictitious genealogy for himself printed in Paris in 1642, seven years after assuming office, in which his family was traced back 'to a certain Arnaud Séguier, *seigneur* of Saint-Geniers in 1129'?[40] Why, if 'sword' and 'robe' were one, did the secret registers of the *Parlements* contain so many disputes over precedence between the *robins* and the traditional nobility, to which Mandrou has so interestingly drawn our attention;[41] and why was it that members of the *noblesse de robe* were for the most part excluded from the sessions of the second order of the nobility at the meetings of the Estates General in 1614, to which Mousnier has equally interestingly drawn our attention?[42]

It is indeed reasonable to ask whether things might not have gone very differently if the French seventeenth-century monarchy had been confronted by a homogeneous ruling élite, a nobility of 'robe' and 'sword,' divided perhaps in professional occupation, but jointly determined to see major modifications in the monarchical state. In such a situation it might at least be reasonable to wonder whether, in the event, the boy Louis XIV would have fared very much better than his uncle, Charles I. Although the pattern of relationships between 'sword' and 'robe' may have been more various, more *nuancé*, than was once supposed, to propose a blunt identification of 'sword' and 'robe' in the seventeenth century is to confuse important realities of the early *ancien régime* and is surely in danger of obfuscating more than it clarifies. Much work has yet to be done on the French seventeenth-century nobility, but in the direction perhaps of formulating distinctions rather than toward defining it in monolithic terms. Mousnier's theory of tensions within the *noblesse* accords with a great deal of the evidence we have and suggests the importance, in the history of social hierarchies, of psychology over legal, and perhaps even social, fact. Scorn for the *robins* and resentment toward the monarchy that had created them may well have been of great importance as a defensively aggressive posture for at least certain elements within an insecure 'order' in French political society.

Mandrou, in a recent work of synthesis, sees the 'robe' as an 'intermediate body' between the nobility and the bourgeoisie, a nobility of 'second rank':

> For a very long time the monarchy exercised to its own profit the position of arbiter between the different groups which it employed to maintain the social structure; on the one hand, the traditional nobility, confined now to its military function, but sustained in all its social and financial privilege, and, on the other, the new nobility issuing from the bourgeoisie, which administers, judges and directs affairs in its name and which has acquired since the beginning of the century through the principle of hereditary office an independence equivalent to that of the traditional nobility. A coming together of these two forces (against the monarchy) could only be ephemeral. The Fronde showed that.[43]

It may be, however, that a blurring indeed occurred, where families of the traditional nobility acquired office or married into the robe; and in face of this a too strict distinction may therefore be 'misleading', as R. Mettam has suggested. But, he continues: 'many members of the *épée* . . . did indeed despise the professional bureaucrats of the *robe*, and lived by the traditional landed wealth and military talents of their class. Others, whose financial position was more precarious, resented that they could not afford to compete with middle class men in purchasing these posts in the bureaucracy themselves.'[44]

If indeed this were not so and were not a major point of incidence in the social and political structure of seventeenth-century France, then much of the social and political history of the century would be largely incomprehensible.

IV

In 1610 there were, therefore, only unresolved problems for the future; the Huguenots, the nobility and the great corporations of the *officiers*, already ambitious under Sully of establishing their voice in the legislation and policy of the state, confident in the newly-reinforced hereditary tenure of their offices through the *paulette*. The future stability of the state lay in the fundamental relationships between the Crown and 'both nobilities', to use Mandrou's phrase, and between the Crown and the *officiers* in general, who most certainly numbered many thousands by the middle of the century. There was nothing on this bureaucratic scale in any other of the European states.

A combination of the most adverse circumstances activated the instability of the state into crisis. The assassination of Henry IV in 1610 renewed the situation of 1559. In the absence of an adult king, the *grands* attempted once again to reassert their position at the centre of public affairs. Faced with the loss of their patron, and increasingly alarmed at the energies and success of a reformed French Catholicism, the Huguenot nobility felt their only recourse lay in military separatism. It is conceivable that a continuation of Henry's reign and a continuing *détente* in Europe would have enabled pragmatic resolutions of the pressures within the governmental structure. A continuously applied mercantilism might have provided the requisite stimulus to the French economy, at the crucial time when the Dutch were establishing their European economic supremacy. Had the European *détente* lasted, enabling fiscal pressures to be more than temporarily lifted, then even the *commissaires* might have continued to be moulded into the provincial mass of the royal bureaucracy without aggravating resentments to the point of revolt. The pragmatic accommodations upon which the stability of the *ancien régime* was ultimately to reside might have been achieved earlier.

It was the international crisis of the Thirty Years War and the fiscal and administrative pressures arising from it which precipitated the French crisis. It so happened that the international situation deteriorated dramatically, against the French monarchical interest, in the 1620s, at the very time when the consequences of chronic provincial distress were already beginning to express themselves in popular uprisings, even before the financial burdens of the war made their appalling impact. The German and European situation had already become tense enough by the last years of Henry IV's reign to initiate renewed conflict. The disputed succession to the crucially placed duchies of Cleves-Jülich in the lower Rhineland in 1610 might well have triggered the German and western European conflict, which was in fact to unfold from the Bohemian revolt nine years later. In the event, the Cleves-Jülich dispute was negotiated out by the settlement of Xanten in 1614, but the prospect at the time of Henry's assassination was already ominous for the European and French future.

When the first main crisis of the Thirty Years War came, with a decade of Protestant collapse in Germany, from the battle of the White

Mountain (1620), through the unfortunate intervention of Denmark (1625–6) to the triumphs of Wallenstein in 1629 which carried Catholicism and the Habsburgs to the shores of the Baltic, France was in a condition of great internal difficulty. Throughout the first six years of Richelieu's ministry (1624–30), France was torn by religious faction, social distress and endemic insurrection, in a context of rising disaffection among the *officiers*, and with aristocratic conspiracy reaching up to the royal family itself. The monarchy's external problems were indeed compounded by a most adverse internal situation. The 'Protestant' posture of French policy in Europe, initiated in the age of the German Reformation and tentatively restored by Henry IV, now came under the growing disapproval of the French Counter-Reformation Church, as did the Crown's internal policy of conceding toleration to the Huguenots. With the French monarchical interest crumbling in Europe in the 1620s, in the North, on the Rhine and in Northern Italy, it was crucial to Richelieu that he should be denied the support of Marie, the queen-mother, and Gaston d'Orléans, the king's brother. He was confronted by a party of royal *dévots*, with Marillac their political protagonist in the *Conseil*, advocating a policy of *rapprochement* with Spain in Europe, in opposition to Richelieu's advocacy of support for the Habsburgs' enemies to the extent of actually forming a French system in Europe based on German and Scandinavian Protestantism. In this way, aristocratic intrigue and overt sedition, right up to the nearest of the *princes du sang*†, could assume a moral posture against Louis XIII's chief minister, urging peace in Europe and a policy of internal restoration and reform, and that at a moment of the most acute international crisis in the period 1629–30.[45]

In this context of extreme European difficulty, which could only be met by increased expenditure on the part of the French monarchy, either indirectly through diplomatic subsidies or ultimately by direct involvement in the war, the social situation in France deteriorated to the point where widespread popular insurrection unleashed itself almost continuously among the peasantry and urban lower classes. These uprisings, which continued for over fifty years, from the early 1620s to the mid-1670s, have been the centre of a major historical controversy between the Soviet historian, Boris Porshnev, and the French historian, Roland Mousnier. The controversy was slow to come to the notice of English historians. Porshnev's work on the uprisings before the Fronde, which was in conscious disagreement with the interpretations of Mousnier's major thesis published in 1945 on venality under Henry IV and Louis XIII, was published in Russia in 1948[46] and in an East German edition in 1954. Mousnier responded in an article published in the *Revue d'histoire moderne et contemporaine* in 1958,[47] and Porshnev's work was published in French in 1963 under the direction of Braudel and Mandrou. It was only then that it was noticed, in the *English Historical Review*[48] in 1966, and in 1967 J. H. M. Salmon provided his valuable review-article in *Past and Present*.[49] This volume is the first in which any significant amount of Porshnev's work will have been made available to readers in English.

Porshnev's study of the popular uprisings in France before the Fronde remains an important study, even though its central thesis has for the most part failed to substantiate itself. Using the correspondence between Chancellor Séguier and the *intendants* available to him in the Séguier archive in Leningrad, Porshnev proposed that a class-front existed in the France of the pre-Fronde, of the ruling classes against the peasants and the urban poor, within a framework of 'feudal-absolutism'. Anxious to discover the reason for the failure of the Fronde, Porshnev finds it in venality and its ramifications. His central position is that major elements of the French bourgeoisie were deflected from their 'revolutionary' role in support of the peasantry through the process of venality, by which they became 'feudalised' through service and commitment to a 'feudal-absolutist order'. In face of the adamantine wall of the class-front of the nobility and 'feudalised' *officiers*, the 'revolutionary' peasants and urban poor could only struggle in vain and meet with terrible retribution.

Subsequent research by Mousnier into the sections of the Séguier archive remaining in Paris[50] and publication of further papers from the Leningrad Séguier archive by A. D. Lublinskaya,[51] some of them supplementing papers selectively edited by Porshnev, have not substantiated the Porshnev thesis; and research undertaken by both Mousnier and his pupils at the *Centre de Recherches sur la civilisation de l'Europe moderne* has likewise done nothing to justify Porshnev's analysis of the pre-Fronde.[52] It seems clear that for the period Porshnev discusses, the period from 1623 to the Fronde, the Pagès-Mousnier model of French seventeenth-century development lies closer to the evidence we have. The provincial situation diagnosed by Mousnier, in which he sees a highly multiple interaction of forces operating a provincial opposition to the fiscalism and revolutionary administrative methods of the Crown, seems to emerge more consistently from the evidence. An alienated nobility, competing with the Crown for the limited amount of surplus money available in the provinces, can be seen taking its political opportunity in the social disintegration of the popular seditions (in a manner not un-reminiscent of the way in which certain elements of the Netherlands aristocracy behaved, if for different reasons, in the initial stages of the Netherlands Revolt); and disaffected *officiers* can frequently be seen in tacit support of rebellious elements against the fiscal exactions of the Crown. The situation was indeed essentially multiple; a kaleidoscope of grievance, conflict and sedition; but most often a basic pattern emerges of a combined provincial resistance to the financial policies of the Crown.

B

It seems unmistakable that the fiscal and administrative policies of the monarchy, in the period of Richelieu and then Mazarin, had so alienated powerful elements within the dominant social groups as to create an endemic insurrectionary situation, which the monarchy found difficult to contain. The pressure of royal policy had thrust the tenuous stability and frail allegiances of the late-medieval constitution into acute disequilibrium and disturbance.

Porshnev's major error was perhaps one of over-anticipation. Generalising from a comparatively limited documentary base, he perhaps expected his ingenious and intelligent perceptions about the nature and structure of the *ancien régime* in its final formation to be corroborated by the papers in the Séguier archive. Almost certainly, in the short-term, in the pre-Fronde at least, they were not. In this connection I have included Pierre Deyon's valuable study of the attempts on the part of the monarchy to erode the fiscal immunities of the 'feudal' class. Deyon's study forcefully sustains Mousnier's concept of a monarchy operating above class, representing the interests of none in its harsh pursuit of its own dynastic financial purposes. The article in no way corroborates Porshnev's concept of a 'feudal-absolutism' in formation in the first half of the French seventeenth century. The fiscal policies of the Crown during the pre-Fronde seem indeed from Deyon's evidence to have been, to a significant degree, adverse to the interests of the seigneurial class.[53]

The great merit of Mousnier's diagnosis of the disorders is that it is firmly based in the actual financial and administrative situation – in the increased taxation and the use of *commissaires* to usurp the functions of the regular *officiers*. It was this, for Mousnier, which thrust into opposition and alliance against the Crown groups which, in Porshnev's diagnosis, sixteenth-century developments might have been thought likely to consolidate in support of the monarchical state. The question remains, however, whether Porshnev's perceptions may well have validity in terms of the long-term movement of society within the *ancien régime*; whether the ultimate effect of venality was not indeed to bring elements of the bourgeoisie into the service of a state which was still essentially aristocratic, or, in Porshnev's terminology, 'feudal'.

In this, it is interesting to have L. Bernard's suggestion, in his article on the popular uprisings in France during the first part of the personal reign of Louis XIV, that preliminary investigation of the revolts after 1661 inclines him toward a 'Porshnev' analysis of the situation, in that they seem 'popular uprisings' as such, rather than movements initiated or manipulated by disaffected groups among the nobility or bourgeoisie.[54] This indeed inclines Bernard toward a 'Porshnev' analysis of the popular uprisings as a whole. It should be clear however that, whatever the situation after 1661, this has no necessary relevance to the situation of the pre-Fronde. It would indeed be exceedingly unwise to generalise about the total seventeenth-century situation backward from the evidence of the revolts of the 1660s and 1670s. It could well be that Mousnier was entirely right about the pre-Fronde and the influences of venality as they revealed themselves then, from the evidence of what was actually happening in the provinces; but that from 1661 a new situation gradually emerged, with a growing consolidation of the dominant social groups toward the monarchy and a consequent isolation of the peasants in their opposition to the 'feudal' régime, such as Porshnev talks of. Bernard's evidence does not therefore so much justify a 'Porshnev' interpretation of the pre-Fronde as perhaps point toward the growing realities of the period from 1661, which, for Porshnev, were always there in gestation, in the long-term development of the *ancien régime*, in the social and political consequences of venality. Mousnier's analysis rests essentially upon the collaboration of noble and *officier* with popular elements in a provincial front against the royal fisc and the *commissaires*. This indeed constituted the seriousness of the mid-century crisis for the French monarchy. Could it be, however, that this collaboration fades from 1661, and that without it, by the 1670s, the popular uprisings cease to have the significance and opportunity they had had in the mid-century, and accordingly fade as major social movements?

In his case against Porshnev's theory of seventeenth-century French 'feudal-absolutism', Mousnier vigorously rejects Porshnev's use of the term 'feudal' in relation to seventeenth-century France. While Porshnev's response that this is largely a matter of terminology does have some force, as also does his suggestion that the word 'capitalism' is likewise used to cover social and economic developments over a very extended time-scale, without evidently creating confusion,[55] even so it is difficult not to be persuaded by Mousnier that the term 'feudal' does indeed confuse important economic and social realities of the period. It fails to take into account the essentially non-feudal nature of the French rural economy in the seventeenth century, in relation to any strict definition of feudalism. Serfdom as such was almost entirely dissolved, and the term 'feudal' scarcely reflects the degree of security which the peasants had in the holding of their tenures. Equally, to stress the 'feudal' identity of the seventeenth-century French nobility is to underestimate the non-feudal elements in the values underlying the aristocratic and monarchical state. French seventeenth-century aristocratic culture was an amalgam of 'sword', chivalric elements, commingled with concepts, such as *'gloire'*, deriving from the courtly values of the Italian Renaissance. The 'militarism' of the French seventeenth-century nobility was not solely the militarism of a 'feudal class' – though it was the residue of that class who were accorded the privilege of sustaining it. It was the militarism of the dynastic state; and in this we are again aware of a monarchy, in Mousnier's terms, subjecting all classes, or rather 'orders', to its own interest and power. To use the word 'feudal' to describe either the seventeenth-century monarchy or its attendant aristocracy is to discount centuries of economic, social and political transformation and development.

V

It is also central to Mousnier's analysis that the increased taxation of the period of Richelieu and Mazarin bore especially heavily on a peasantry whose generally adverse condition was being aggravated by the effects of an economic *conjoncture* which in the middle seventeenth century became recessionary. Dearth, epidemic disease, vagrancy and *mortalités* were of course the constants of early modern France, whatever the *conjoncture*, as indeed they were of the under-developed social economy of Europe generally in the early modern period. Smallness of tenures, a primitive agricultural technology, the over-specialisation over large areas on the production of one, cereal, crop – especially on the corn lands of the north of France – were all important factors keeping large sections of the rural population on the edge of a precarious subsistence; to which the isolation and limited scale of the rural grain markets, together with the impediments imposed by poor communications and the ubiquitous tolls on the movement of corn, added their own adverse effects. In very large areas of the French provinces, as Goubert suggests, the majority of peasants were unable to provide sufficient food for their families from their tenures alone, and had to purchase corn from the proceeds of domestic labour, often in textiles, combined with day-labouring for the large-scale farmer. Both Goubert and Mandrou stress the dual components of social crisis in times of dearth and high corn prices: in that the demand for textiles and day-labouring fell away at the very moment when supplementation of income was most needed.[56] The consequent turning-off of hands added to the already pitiful situation of the French peasant-artisan.

To these elemental constants of the rural economy must be added the equally constant factor of the social effects of the seigneurial system. It is likely that some ninety per cent of the population lived within the framework of the *seigneurie*†. The work of Meuvret, Goubert and Saint-Jacob, among others, suggests that the average loss of the peasants in 'dues' to the *seigneur* and in ecclesiastical tithe could amount to some thirty to forty per cent of their gross product.[57] Although Le Roy-Ladurie has shown that the scale of seigneurial demand could be very much lower in Languedoc, it is likely that in these instances the scale of rent itself quite often reached the scale of exploitation of the peasantry in the north.[58] The proceeds of this exploitation, whether in dues, rents or tithes, passed for the most part from the countryside into the towns, where they were spent on consumption by the owning classes. The rural economy itself was seldom really stimulated by its own surplus, by re-investment in agricultural improvement. Even the 'bourgeois' *seigneurs* of the Paris region, producing for the comparatively large-scale Parisian market, were only partially interested as entrepreneurs in the improvement of their estates.[59]

Recurring food crises initiated the demographic problems of the early *ancien régime*. The work of Goubert and Meuvret[60] gives the fundamental aspects of French seventeenth-century demography, and their essays remain the central entries to the subject. Their work largely informs Méthivier's chapter from his *Ancien Régime* which is included in this work. Goubert's recent synthesis of current demographic findings for the century has largely endorsed what has become the classic schema as given by Méthivier.[61] He still proposes the elemental progression from poor harvests, perhaps two or three in succession, to acute shortage, to high corn prices, malnutrition, disease and widespread *mortalité*. A really serious *cherté* could lead to the loss of from a third to three-quarters of the children in a local population, which in turn could lead to a lost generation in the population some twenty-five to thirty years later. Subsistence crises seem to have occurred on a 'thirty year cycle' (in 1597, 1630, 1662 and 1694), with an intermediate smaller-scale cycle between (1622, 1651 and 1681). Poor harvests, as distinct from major crises, probably occurred in most regions every twelve or so years. It is possible that seventeenth-century food crises throughout western Europe were associated with especially adverse climatic conditions. The great food crisis surrounding the Fronde was certainly climatic, in that it was initiated by the appallingly heavy precipitations for the seven successive years from 1646 to 1652.[62]

Disease was not of course always related to dearth. Plague was endemic in Europe throughout the early seventeenth century and took its toll of the French population among the rest. It was widespread throughout the continent in the 1620s. In 1626, it ravaged Burgundy and the Loire valley. From 1628 to 1629 it affected the south-west, reaching an appalling peak in 1631, which happened to coincide with one of the three greatest dearths of the century. It recurred widely in the period 1636–9, and again from 1642 to 1651, and yet again from 1660 to 1665, both of these last periods being also affected by acute food crises. Plague reappeared again in the north of France from 1665 to 1667, but partly through effective administrative action – 'a remarkable human success', in Goubert's phrase – it was this time contained.[63]

Taking the period from 1500 to 1715, the evidence is that the number of marriages and baptisms in France reached their peak in the early modern period in and around 1580, although the whole pattern was of course subject to very wide regional variation. Numbers then fell heavily in the last decades of the sixteenth century, until expansion stopped, by 1630 in some areas and in others by 1645. It may have been as late as 1660–80 in Lower Languedoc. Then almost everywhere, from whichever date, a stagnation or decline in numbers ensued. Except for Brittany, the phenomenon was most probably general; and, after a period of stagnation or slow decline, numbers fell again at the close of Louis XIV's reign.[64]

If this evidence is correct, it seems likely that a stagnating or declining seventeenth-century population had an inverse economic effect to that of the population growth of the sixteenth century, when it is generally accepted that population growth increased general economic demand and provided at least part of the general stimulus for the sixteenth-century expansion of the European economy, as well as its chronic inflationary tendency. The rise and fall of a population is so intimately related to the level of its economic demand that a stagnation or fall in the French seventeenth-century population may well have acted as a major brake on the total economy, and have been a factor therefore in creating the general recessionary tendency from about 1630.

The general consensus among historians as to the recessionary tendency of the French economic *conjoncture* in the mid-seventeenth century for the most part holds. Mousnier has talked recently of the 'prolonged economic recession of the seventeenth century',[65] and Mandrou speaks of the 'sombre colours of the seventeenth-century depression'. For him, at least, 'the economic difficulties of the seventeenth century are now no longer in question':

> In the eyes of all historians of the age, the long seventeenth-century depression saw its moments of respite, and also its moments of greatest intensity . . . The depression, however, did not really retreat for the best part of a century, from the period 1630–40 to the corresponding years of the eighteenth century. It is no doubt more perceptible, in the present state of research, in its social repercussions rather than in the detail of its economic fluctuations. This long-term depression is assuredly the framework, within which we must place the efforts which Colbert made to surmount it, as well as the wars and *bâtiments* of Louis XIV.[66]

Goubert has been slightly more circumspect. In 1965, he spoke of a phase of 'difficulty and maladjustment', which 'clearly' began, 'which we call a recession, or a period of stagnation, or at the very least a slowing-down in the rate of growth'.[67] Although, in a more recent analysis, he proposes that the term 'tragic' is an 'excessive formula', when applied to the seventeenth century,[68] the whole section of the work on the French economy from 1660 to which he contributes is entitled 'From an economy in contraction to an economy in expansion', and Goubert's own title to his chapter for the section is 'Le "Tragique" XVIIe Siècle', the first part of which deals with 'the economic depression of the second half of the seventeenth century', and the second with 'the two periods of the depression'. He states that it is 'generally accepted that the second half of the seventeenth century, at least in the part of Europe of which France herself was a part, evolved under the unfavourable sign of a *conjoncture* of contraction', and, later, he goes further. 'In the French case, with certain exceptions, it is no longer open to doubt: the recession, the depression, at least the stagnation of the economy is blindingly clear.'[69] Although in an immediate footnote he records the doubts and qualifications expressed by Le Roy-Ladurie and Morineau as to the totality of the phenomenon, he proceeds to itemise the numerous indices leading him to his general conclusion; and, from the evidence, in the French case there seems little likelihood that the general model of economic 'recession', 'depression', or 'at least stagnation' affecting the central mass of France from some point toward the middle seventeenth century could be acceptably overturned.

The collapse of American silver imports into Europe led to a shortage of specie, which, in combination with the primitive state of French credit development, served as a brake on economic growth. Silver imports began to decline from 1600, followed by a sharper contraction from 1630, until they finally collapsed in the years 1656–60, by which time Europe was importing perhaps a tenth of the amount of silver coming in during the last years of the sixteenth century. The sharpened emphasis on bullionism in Colbert's mercantilist prospectus may well have derived from this contraction, as indeed the whole recessionary tendency may account for his conviction that there was only a fixed amount of trade in the world. Hauser, in criticism of Colbert, and in unfavourable comparison with Richelieu, considered this last the only new concept which Colbert added to the whole canon of French mercantilist thought, which, in the event, was in any case in error. This symbolised for Hauser the difference between the statesman Richelieu and the *commis* Colbert.[70] More recent economic evidence, however, suggests that Colbert's perceptions may well have been every bit as acute, as statesmanlike, as those of his mentor Richelieu.

Goubert relates the monetary difficulties of the mid-century to the general lowering of prices which became a phenomenon from the period 1630–5. In the south, it seems likely that the fall started from soon after the turn of the century and developed very perceptibly from 1620. From 1630 to 1650 the fall was essentially gradual. It was not until after 1650, and especially from 1660, that it became generalised. And then for some seventy to eighty years there was to be no sustained rise in prices, only rises of short duration. Cereal prices did not cease falling between 1662 and 1688: 'the years 1667 to 1673 and then again from 1685 to 1688 were in a sense record years for low cereal prices'.[71] It was not until the fourth decade of the eighteenth century that a sustained rise in agrarian prices was to recur. There were exceptions within the pattern: the price of wood, both for heating and construction, continued to rise, though more slowly; and the pastoral sector of the rural economy sustained itself through to the mid-century and then levelled out without actually receding.

The evidence from trading volume seems similarly adverse. The history of the Sound tolls shows conclusively that the Baltic trade collapsed from 1660 (though not earlier, as had previously been supposed).[72] Chaunu's work on Seville shows that the American trade passed into recession from 1600 and collapsed from 1622. The long depression in the Seville trade established itself from 1623 to 1650, and may well have been a major factor causing French economic difficulty in the second half of the seventeenth century.[73] The volume of textile production also contracted, and not only in France. Production in the main Italian centres contracted from 1600 and declined vigorously from 1630 to 1650, until it collapsed virtually entirely. By 1665 Venetian production was falling by a cumulative rate of three per cent per annum; by 1700 its production was only one-tenth of what it had been at the beginning of the seventeenth century. Deyon's work on Amiens and the textile centres of the French north-east, such as Reims, Valenciennes and Lille, shows a comparable experience. These industries peaked by 1635 and, except for a brief period from 1660 to 1670 under Colbert, failed to reach these levels again throughout the reign of Louis XIV.[74] The production of luxury textiles fell most dramatically. At Beauvais, fine-textile production fell by some fifty per cent from the level of the decade 1624–34, and this decline was to continue until the second decade of the eighteenth century. The falling away in the French and European production of textiles is suggested by the contraction in the sale of alum from the papal deposits at Tolfa, since alum was a vital element in all textile-finishing processes. The trade in alum through St. Malo contracted from 1614 and declined rapidly from 1650. This, perhaps more than any other single factor, leads Goubert to sustain the general validity of a recessionary Phase B.[75] The Dutch and, to some extent, the English economies were however exceptions. Leyden indeed continued to expand its textile production from the beginning of the century until 1672, and maintained that level until at least the second decade of the eighteenth century. Between Venice and Holland, France seems to have occupied an economically intermediate position.

The evidence suggests that the European economy underwent a process of shift in the seventeenth century, from its Mediterranean and Sevillian centres toward Holland and England, and that this adversely affected at least the relative position of France in the total European economy. A. D. Lublinskaya's inclusion of France among the economies which made a decisive advance toward capitalism in the seventeenth century seems to overestimate French economic performance.[76] It seems unlikely that the 1620s saw the formation of an alliance between the monarchy and the towns, following the defeat of the Huguenots and the feudal nobility during that decade. French mercantilist policies were doubtless intended, as Lublinskaya suggests, to extricate France from her economic disadvantage in face of Dutch and English competition; but they do not represent in any significant sense the formation of an alliance between the monarchy and the bourgeoisie. Mercantilism was an instrument of French dynastic power. The economy, even under Colbert – one might well say especially under Colbert – was merely a means toward a fiscal end. Mercantilist policies never reflected an alliance between the monarchy and the entrepreneurial class *qua* entrepreneurs.

Although France experienced economic difficulty throughout the period with which we are concerned, it is not possible to propose any direct causal relationship between economic recession, the popular uprisings and the general crisis in the state. Few would claim that the uprisings and the subsequent Fronde were the product of a social distress stemming from economic contraction. Even so, the reduction in monetary resources came at a time when the fiscal demands of the state climbed to unparalleled levels; and the fall in land values and rents from the midcentury must have reacted adversely on the interests of the *seigneurs* and must have increased the possibility of 'feudal reaction' creating further distress. It would indeed be unlikely that the adverse economic *conjoncture* did not serve as a contributory factor to the general *malaise* of the French state in the middle century.

There were perhaps even more important long-term consequences for the development of the French *ancien régime*. The rural depression of the second half of the seventeenth century may well have contributed to France's failure to achieve an agricultural revolution, which alone in the long-term could solve her subsistence problems. The most important consequence of the economic recession may however lie in the reduced stimulus it provided for the development of the French seventeenth-century bourgeoisie, with all the consequent entrenchment of the seigneurial idea within the French *ancien régime* that this involved. If France did indeed lie in her economic development mid-way between seventeenth-century Venice and Holland, as Goubert suggests,[77] or mid-way between Spain and Holland, as Hobsbawm suggests,[78] we can well understand the important effect this may have had on the formation and nature of the French *ancien régime*. There was assuredly a seventeenth-century France that was half seventeenth-century Spanish; with its '*gentilhomme*' tradition, and the attendant retreat of the bourgeoisie into the possession of *seigneuries*, the purchase of *rentes* and of office in the state. Bourgeois neglect of entrepreneurial opportunity, which seems to have been a major characteristic of the age, may well have been in part a contingent response to adverse economic risk. In this, the adverse economic *conjoncture* may have compounded, at a most crucial time, the already very deeply entrenched aristocratic and landed ethos of late-medieval France. If we also remember the continuous military involvement of the French nobility from the late fifteenth century, both internally and in Europe, it is not perhaps difficult to comprehend how it came about that the 'sword' tradition survived so tenaciously and was able to imprint itself so deeply upon the aristocratic 'myth' of the French *ancien régime*.

VI

Internal difficulties and the European diplomatic crisis combined to create a situation of intense challenge to the French monarchy at the close of the 1620s. At the heart of the immediate internal crisis lay the climatic attempt on the part of the queen-mother and Gaston d'Orléans to destroy the political leadership of Richelieu. The celebrated *Jour des Dupes* of November 1630, in which Richelieu 'duped' his rivals, is in many ways rightly considered as at least the beginning of Richelieu's triumph over the feudal nobility, even though noble conspiracy was to remain a major concomitant of French political disturbance until the Fronde.

The period of the *Jour des Dupes* coincided with the most intense international crisis of early modern Europe. The military triumph of the Counter-Reformation in Germany and the Emperor's attempt to reduce North German Protestantism by the Edict of Restitution initiated a period which, in the event, was to prove a major crux in the history of European power. From 1629 to 1631 the diplomatic front was stretched almost unmanageably wide. The political crisis between the Emperor and the German Princes, which was of central importance to the French monarchy in its containment of the Habsburgs, coincided with the formidable prospect of imminent, unilateral Swedish intervention in the German conflict. This was at the precise moment when French interests became critically involved with those of the Habsburgs in northern Italy in the problem of the succession to Mantua and Montferrat, the possession of which closely affected the security of the Spanish military road into central Europe via Genoa and the Duchy of Milan. Everything indeed conspired to compound the difficulty of everything else in these major years. Yet at the very moment when the international challenge to French monarchical interests was more acute than it had been at any time since the formation of the empire of Charles V, the French state was involved in conspiracy and subversion within the Court itself, in a rapidly deteriorating social situation, under the combined influence of dearth, plague and widespread provincial sedition – in face of which there were already alarming signs of a 'strike' on the part of those most closely concerned with bringing sedition to justice, the *Parlementaires*.

In the event, the most serious internal challenge to the monarchy came from the *officiers*. The *Parlementaires*, in Marillac's analysis, were already alienated from royal policy by 1630. It was significant for the future that, during the crisis of the *Jour des Dupes* and the crucial European negotiations of the period of the Diet of Regensburg, relations between the Crown and its *officiers* were soured by the internal negotiations then in process for the renewal of the *paulette*, during which the Crown had attempted the not entirely subtle manœuvre of dividing the *Trésoriers de France* from the *Parlementaires* by according renewal to the former while withholding it from the latter, and at the same time making renewal to the *Trésoriers* conditional upon payment of a forced loan. At this most critical juncture in French and European affairs, the *Parlement de Paris* was prepared to coerce the monarchy by dragging its feet, not only over sedition, but, more crucially, over the registration of royal edicts and *déclarations*, even those condemning the followers of the arch-conspirators, Marie and Gaston d'Orléans. Of all the difficulties confronting the Crown in 1630, this was perhaps the most menacing for future political stability.[79]

Richelieu did not seek confrontation with the *Parlementaires* from any ideological position, that monarchical government required the creation of *intendants*, to enforce the sovereignty of the Crown against the *Parlements* in the provinces. His approach to the use of *intendants*, which lay at the heart of *Parlementaire* grievance, was wholly pragmatic. His administrative policies were entirely related to financial needs. He would have liked, says Mousnier, to have used the *intendants* to the least possible extent.[80] His *Political Testament* makes it clear that his ideal *intendant* remained the *inspecteur*, the *commissaire*, acting within the constitutional framework and accepting the prerogatives of the bureaucracy which venality had constructed during the course of the sixteenth and early seventeenth centuries. The years from 1634 were the most crucial, following the Swedish defeat at Nördlingen and the achievement of peace between the Emperor and the German Princes at Prague in 1636. With Denmark and Sweden defeated and the Empire stabilised, there were no longer any surrogates to fight France's dynastic wars for her. Richelieu was forced into open warfare from 1635, and therefore into adopting the administrative techniques which alone could ensure the financial resources which the military situation demanded. It was the international situation and its financial corollary which alone enforced the abrupt creation of the Crown's immediate sovereignty in the provinces through the use of *commissaires* on an unprecedented scale, armed with powers to withdraw financial and judicial business from the hands of the regular *officiers* into their own.

The most direct weapon in the hands of the *officiers* in defence of their position lay in the power of the *Parlements* to obstruct government by the delaying use of their right of judicial review of royal legislation. Nothing on this scale of importance lay to the hand of the *Trésoriers*. Non-registration by the *Parlements* represented a very serious practical threat to the monarchy, since it could make government itself virtually impossible, especially in the critical financial sphere, which was always a matter of governmental hand-to-mouth, unless the Crown were prepared to invoke its most extreme constitutional prerogatives by way of habitual recourse. Initially, in face of obstruction, the *Conseil* could issue a *lettre de jussion* to the 'sovereign court', informing it that the king desired the registration of his legislation forthwith. Further delay could lead to the king's own attendance in the *Grand'Chambre*, the highest chamber of the *Parlement de Paris*, and there, in a *lit de justice*, resume the sovereignty he had delegated and exercise it in his own favour. In cases of registration by *lit de justice* in the provincial *Parlements*, it was most often the convention to dispatch members of the royal family rather than for the king himself to attend.

The controversy over judicial review involved however, more than a practical threat. The whole process of registration focused the ideological problems of the constitution and raised the issue between the Crown and the *Parlementaires* above the level of vested corporate interest onto that of serious political controversy involving the nature of monarchy itself. In defence of its right of judicial review and remonstrance, the *Parlement de Paris* was led to formulate a theory of delegated sovereignty and, by extension, of constitutional monarchy. The *Parlement de Paris* asserted its descent from the medieval *Curia Regis*, whose function and obligation was to advise the king. The *Parlement* was, in this sense, part of the king's *conseil* in its most ancient form, and its registration of legislation was therefore no formal duty, but part of its right to counsel the king and to participate in his legislative function, by considering the edicts presented to it and by remonstrating with the king for amendments when they were deemed necessary in the public interest.

In order to increase the weight of its corporate identity, the *Parlement de Paris* could summon all ten of its constituent chambers together in plenary session, which the *ducs et pairs* of the realm could attend at will. It could go further and give body to the collective identity of the *officiers* by issuing *arrêts d'union* in support of legal positions adopted by the other sovereign courts, as a first move toward the convening of a joint session with them. Through these procedures, the *Parlement de Paris* was able to extend its identity and become the representative and protagonist of constitutionality against arbitrary government. In the absence of viable Estates General, to which in any case it considered itself superior, as being in permanent session and not dependent therefore upon the king's will to convoke it, the *Parlement de Paris* attempted to assert its own version of the traditional constitution, which at this point of crisis in the 1630s and 1640s became embodied in the constitutional debate of the pre-Fronde and Fronde. In this way, the traditional constitution materialised, sometimes by way of wishful constitutional remembrance, in face of the ever-hardening outline of Richelieu's and Mazarin's sovereign monarchy.

In a normal period, the king was prepared to undertake and sustain a constitutional dialogue with these most powerful and impressive of his *officiers*. Constitutional legality lay at the heart of the French traditional monarchy and was to remain, notably so, within the 'absolutism' of Louis XIV. 'Absolutism' itself was a theory of legality. Absolutism was consolidated by Louis XIV in order to sustain legality by providing checks upon usurpations of sovereignty by those whom he considered unentitled to claim or exercise it. For Louis XIV and Bossuet, sovereign monarchy was the *sine qua non* of justice in the context of the French seventeenth century. It was the fear of conceding part of its sovereignty and thereby contravening the political lesson of its indivisibility, so recently and so harshly taught by the anarchies of the religious wars and so firmly conceptualised by Bodin, which set the Crown so much against the claims of the *Parlement de Paris* to participate in its sovereignty. In a context of foreign menace and internal sedition, the *Parlement de Paris* seemed to be blackmailing the Crown into concessions which could only subvert its sovereignty and fatally weaken the realm. Within the tortuous manœuvres of the Fronde it is important to appreciate that not only the *Parlementaires* but both sides operated from positions of conscience, from alternative readings of the political ideal.

In the military and financial crisis of the late 1630s, the response of Louis XIII and Richelieu was to circumvent constitutional obstructionism by repeated use of *lits de justice*, as well as by the harsher methods of imprisonment or exile for their more recalcitrant opponents. Although there was subtlety and finesse compared with what was to come under Mazarin, Louis XIII and Richelieu nevertheless made the monarchy's intention abundantly clear, that it would deploy its sovereignty when reason of state required it and combat any attempt to impose restrictions upon it. They were determined to use the *lit de justice* and to endow the *commissaires* with powers to evoke cases away from the 'sovereign courts' to their own tribunals, and ultimately to the *Conseil* itself. They were equally determined to empower the *commissaires* to assume control over and at need undertake the administration of the finances itself, in the interest of the *traitants*†, of whom, in the last years of Richelieu's ministry, the state had become virtually the mortgaged property. In the major international crisis of the 1630s – when the power resolutions of the century were, after all, beginning to be determined – the *taille*, the *aides*† and the *traites*† were the collateral of the credit which the monarchy required, to contain and ultimately to defeat the Habsburgs; and as such they had to be brought in, by whatever means were needed to exact them from a distressed and rebellious peasantry.

Richelieu succeeded in containing the crisis in the French state, but bequeathed an exceedingly difficult situation on his death in 1642, which was followed, disastrously enough, by that of Louis XIII himself early in 1643. In the next five years, which brought the situation to breaking point, the factor of contingency was to be of great importance. The 'foreignness' of Mazarin; his inveterate approach to every political problem from the diplomatic level of duplicity and intrigue; the ready facility afforded to both the *Grands* and the *Parlementaires* to dispute the constitutional legalities of a royal minority, with the *Grands* demanding to participate in government, indeed to conduct the government, as of right, and the *Parlementaires* seizing their opportunity to call into question the power of a regent to enforce her legislation by *lit de justice* – all this increased the sense of political confusion and the heightening of tension, as did the mounting power of the financiers over the state. The *taille* itself was farmed to them in 1645. Everything contributed to undermine the sense of moral dignity in the management of the state and to increase the suffocating sense of chicanery and corruption, which may indeed have been the overriding cause for revolt in the minds of the great patrician class of the *Parlement de Paris*. The *officiers* were filched by all kinds of legalistic manœuvre. Notional increases of salary were conceded them in return for entirely real advances of capital to the Crown. Salaries were chronically allowed to fall into arrears, and state expenditure regularly came to be placed outside the audit of the *Chambre des Comptes* by the increased use of direct payments on *comptants* from the Treasury, which were immune from audit by the court.[81]

In the closing years of the Thirty Years War, state expenditure reached some 124 million *livres*, a scale of expenditure indeed which was not to be reached again until 1679. *Taille*, which had regularly amounted to less than 20 million *livres* in the later sixteenth century, now reached between 50 and 60 millions. This was altogether a new fiscal situation, a difference in fiscal kind rather than simply in degree. This scale of taxation would have created distress and savage resistance even if the techniques for raising it had been left in the hands of the *Trésoriers de France*. It is doubtful indeed whether such sums could have been raised without the use of *commissaires*, backed by military force, and the claims made by the *Trésoriers de France* during the Fronde, that, left alone, they could have funded the financial requirements of the state, seem not really very convincing.[82]

The ultimate crisis of 1648 issued from the breakdown of negotiations for the renewal of the *paulette*.[83] This was an area where vested interest and a sense of abuse of legality combined in the minds of the *officiers*. Once again, Mazarin attempted to divide the *officiers*, by this time offering the favour of renewal to the *Parlementaires* alone. The anger of the *Parlement de Paris* was expressed in its determination to maintain a front of *officier* solidarity against Mazarin and in a repeated refusal to register important financial legislation. On 15 January 1648 the boy Louis XIV, not yet ten years old, was taken to the *Parlement de Paris* to register the contentious edicts by *lit de justice*. From the moment of this challenge, events moved swiftly to the decision of the *Parlement de Paris* to convoke an assembly of all the sovereign courts, in order to confront the Crown with its illegalities and to demand redress by formulating and enforcing reforms. On 13 May 1648 an *arrêt d'union* was issued for a joint assembly, which the Crown could do nothing but accept, in spite of threats to withdraw the *paulette* from all *officiers* altogether. The assembly met at the end of June in the *Chambre Saint-Louis* and continued its debates through most of July 1648. On 22 October, immediately before the signature of the Treaty of Westphalia, events in Paris forced Anne and Mazarin to concede the reforms formulated by the *Parlementaires*. The victory over the German Habsburgs had been bought at the cost of the Fronde, and the rising political and social collapse of the next four years.

VII

The confused imbroglio-like quality of certain phases of the Fronde – the Parisian Fronde of de Retz for example – should not be taken as evidence of its triviality, but rather of the complexity and depth of the crisis in the state. Too close a concern with the actual period of the Fronde, with its incoherence and sporadic nature, suggests a crisis of comparatively short duration, fairly speedily concluded. It is no longer possible however to consider that anything came to a full close with Anne's and Louis' re-entry into Paris in the autumn of 1652 and the re-establishment of Mazarin in the spring of 1653. In time, the Fronde may have come to seem conclusive, but this was not the perspective of things in 1653. It is equally no longer possible to consider the Fronde to have finished in any simple sense with a royal victory. Fear of the recurrence of the Fronde and a determination to avoid its repetition underlay the policies of Louis XIV during the crucial initial period of his personal reign; and the attainment of political stability under Louis XIV was to be the product of a subtle response to the Fronde, as well as of dramatic assertions of authority undertaken in the wake of royal victory against the *Parlementaires* and the nobility. Just as the origins of the Fronde stemmed from developments over a very long period, so its consequences affected the consolidation of the monarchy and the whole future of the *ancien régime*. It is by far the most important single fact of the French seventeenth century.

In the simple sense of the term, the Fronde failed. At no time did a really homogeneous opposition party to the Crown consolidate, consisting of the *princes*, the nobility and the *Parlementaires*. The *officiers* themselves were never able to sustain a united front of opposition after their first coming together in the summer of 1648. More crucial however were the divisions between the *Parlementaires* and the *princes*. Except for a joint and entirely negative detestation of Mazarin, the years from 1649 to 1652 reveal how little they had in common. The world of the *Parlementaires* was not the world of Condé and the archduke Leopold, whom the *Grands* seriously thought of calling in from the Netherlands with Spanish support.[84] There was indeed a tragic confusion in the whole position of the *Parlementaires*, in that they were caught between their elemental support of the monarchy, whose authority they represented and shared, and their intense distaste for government by decree of the *Conseil*, enforced by provincial *commissaires* and conducted in an atmosphere of flagrant chicanery. Equally they were faced with the dilemma of discovering how to limit absolutism without at the same time stimulating and condoning aristocratic anarchy. It became increasingly patent that their opposition merely served the purposes of aristocratic reaction and popular revolt, both of which they feared and deplored. In the end, their failure lay in their inability to focus their opposition in the coherent and continuous way necessary if the constitutionalism of 1648 was to become a permanent part of the seventeenth-century resolution of the late-medieval crisis in the French state. It proved impossible, however, for them to form an effective middle of constitutional moderation and legitimacy among the aristocratic disintegration and popular sedition of the period of the Fronde. In this, it may be important that the Fronde did not find the kind of leadership which it was the function of William the Silent to provide in a not incomparable confusion of constitutionalism and late-feudal disintegration in the Netherlands. The *Parlementaires*, having made their challenge regarding sovereign monarchy, found themselves unable to sustain it without inviting the risk of the possible overthrow of the monarchy itself, or, more likely, its emasculation in a context of princely dissolution and aristocratic provincialism.

A. Lloyd Moote has recently laid great stress on the sustained 'constitutionalism' of the *Parlementaires*.[85] There is indeed no doubt of their meticulously preserving a posture of legality throughout the Fronde. It was both their moral justification and their strongest political weapon to oppose the monarchy from an unimpeachable position within it. Both Moote and Shennan have stressed that no one sought to question the framework of monarchy itself; and while this is so, it is nevertheless important to distinguish the realities involved in the legal challenge of the *Parlementaires*. It is important to insist that the serious debate of the Fronde involved a debate as to what *kind* of monarchy should develop in

France. The challenge was from the traditional 'medieval' monarchy to the monarchy which had operated its own direct sovereignty from a basis of *raison d'Etat* throughout the period of Richelieu and Mazarin. The challenge of the *Parlementaires* was 'revolutionary', in the sense that if the 'reforms' of 1648 had been sustained – which, importantly, they were not – then the whole direction of the monarchy's constitutional development would have been different. If the desire for permanent political involvement and legislative competence had been made good by a body claiming a representative function within the monarchical state, then the development of the French *ancien régime* would have been profoundly different from what it was. If the *Parlementaires* and the *princes* had been able to coalesce about a programme of 'medieval constitutionalism' – as indeed in some sense happened in England – then France would not have proceeded to the degree of sovereign monarchy which developed under Louis XIV. The demands of the *Chambre Saint-Louis* intended the containment of the jurisdictional and financial freedom of the monarchy within the consent of the *Parlement de Paris*. They intended the cessation of government by *intendants*, by regular use of the *lit de justice* and by special judicial tribunal. This was the scale of challenge within the 'constitutionalism' of the *Parlement de Paris*, and it is significant that this is entirely how Louis XIV and Colbert understood the Fronde. It was indeed the elemental challenge to sovereign monarchy from within the legalism of the *Parlementaires* which accounts for so strong a response and assertion of sovereignty under Louis XIV.

The challenge was for the most part contained within the legal dialogue which the *Parlementaires* sought to sustain with the monarchy. But at other times the realities were only thinly concealed, and the frontier between constitutional dialogue and 'revolution' became tenuously narrow, as when during December 1648 and January 1649 the *Parlement de Paris* refused the Crown's instruction to leave the city, and on 8 January 1649 resolved to find means for raising an army for the defence of Paris against the Crown and for forming a wartime government for the city.[86] Anne of Austria may have had an accurate enough perception of the challenge involved in the situation, when she commiserated with the exiled Henrietta Maria that she herself would be in the English queen's position if events continued to develop in Paris as they were;[87] even though, ambiguously enough, the English queen was to be granted a pension with the consent of the *Parlement de Paris*.[88] The *Conseil* itself expressed the issues between the Crown and the *Parlement de Paris* entirely unambiguously in the *arrêt* which was issued in response to the famous *arrêt d'union* of the *Parlement de Paris* of 13 May 1648, convoking the assembly of the *Chambre Saint-Louis*: '*Officiers*', the *Conseil* declared, had 'no authority beyond what is given them by kings to be exercised according to the strict rules prescribed for them . . . Royal authority cannot permit, without itself becoming undermined, *officiers* to exercise [their delegated authority] by means of violent usurpations opposed to the will of their king and master.'[89] On 23 May 1648, under instructions from the *Conseil*, the *Avocat-Général*, Omer Talon, advised the *Parlement de Paris*, in the light of its decision to form a joint assembly of the sovereign courts, that 'to make out of four sovereign companies a fifth without an order from the king and without legitimate authority is without precedent and without reason, being the introduction of a kind of republic in the monarchy, and the creation of a new power which could pose a dangerous threat to the established order of government.'[90]

The *Parlementaires* strove to sustain the reforms conceded in 1648 throughout the years of rising chaos from 1649 to 1652, but without ultimately any formal success. They were indeed singularly unsuccessful in establishing, so to say, the letter of the constitutional law which should be binding on the monarchy. Although it is acceptable to talk in terms of a 'victory' for the Fronde 'in defeat', and to ask, as Moote does, what we should term a revolution which fails, but which at the same time denies the other side total victory, nevertheless in the long term that 'victory in defeat' was essentially limited and was to have no sanction beyond the unwritten acceptance by the monarchy that things could not, without very grave risk, ever be the same again. Right of arbitrary arrest and of political exile without trial and the use of *intendants* were to become permanent; and the procedure of the *lit de justice* ceased to be important under Louis XIV, not because he could not but because he had no need to use it. If it is true, as Moote claims,[91] that, in comparison with the Fronde, the constitutionalism of the English Parliament became temporarily submerged in the republican extremism of the period of the Commonwealth – which the Fronde was to avoid – it is nevertheless of some comparative importance that the lasting results of the English and French seventeenth-century constitutional conflicts were to be significantly different. It is not excessively whig to point out which of the two states was in fact to proceed toward limited monarchy within a framework of constitutional law and institutional development, rather than by the processes of a particularist society which managed to thwart and circumvent absolutism in practice by procedural device and geographical distance from the ministerial wing at Versailles; or, again, which of the two states possessed by the eighteenth century a 'representative' body which was ultimately to be capable of democratic transformation.

It is possible to read the whole policy of the *Parlement de Paris* within an entirely different framework of reference from that of the partially successful constitutionalism suggested by Moote. It remains equally important to insist that by the irresponsible pursuit of its own interest, by its cynical use of popular revolt and aristocratic sedition to further its own political ends, by its seeking to make use of 'late-feudal chaos', it merely produced the chaos of the Fronde, which was to give absolutism both its opportunity and its justification. It is part of the abiding tragedy of seventeenth-century France that the instability of the late-medieval constitution and the international crisis of the Thirty Years War combined to submerge the constitutionalism of the *Parlementaires* in a confrontation with the Crown which resulted in the formation of a sovereign monarchy cut off from participation with a 'representative' body in the nation. If there is to be a count made against the activity of the *Parlement de Paris* in the whole period 1620–52, it is that it consorted with the forces of aristocratic chaos long beyond the time when it should; and thereby made the response of the monarchy toward a fuller sovereignty that much more justified and, in terms of the monarchical state, that much more necessary. This is indeed part of the 'tragic' dilemma confronting the *Parlementaires* and the *officiers* in general, of which Lucien Goldmann has written.[92]

It was however essentially a pragmatic absolutism which emerged under Louis XIV. The reasons for this are several. There was the sheer impossibility of practising absolutism in a country so divided by deep-seated provincialism and by the seigneurial structure of its society. The tenacity of the traditional constitution in seventeenth-century France derived initially from the devolutionary nature of the society from which it had evolved. The deeper tendency of the monarchy was also toward compromise and legality. By its nature, the French monarchy was always likely to remain to some degree '*tempérée*'. But, as importantly as all this, the experience of the Fronde directed the monarchy toward accommodation with the realities of seventeenth-century political society. Insubstantial as the 'victory in defeat' of the Fronde may have been in the long term, in the short term the Fronde was to be a major influence in moderating and in enforcing a degree of constitutional caution upon Louis XIV — which was to be the greatest 'victory in defeat' of the Fronde and of fundamental importance in the stabilisation of the monarchical regime. Within the assertions of sovereignty which Louis XIV considered the Fronde had made it necessary for him to make, the 'two monarchies' continued to coexist after 1653 and, indeed, after 1661. The balance may have swung irreversibly in the sovereign direction, but the traditional constitution survived; and not only from reasons of structural particularism and deeper concepts of legality within the monarchy, but from a supple political response. With every reason, the government after 1661 acted under the reasonable assumption that the state could dissolve again under the impact of the forces which had brought it to the confusions of the period of Richelieu and Mazarin. Rural distress and fiscal pressure in a deteriorating monetary situation, in combination with the alienation of powerful elements within the dominant groups, might once again cause French political society to rive open. Almost a century of civil disturbance lay behind Colbert's fear that the '*temps difficiles*', in his phrase, might return.[93] To understand the realities of the early personal reign of Louis XIV, it is important to work forward from the potentialities of the situation at the time rather than backward from our knowledge of what actually happened. No one in the 1660s could have foreseen either the longevity or the enduring capacity of Louis XIV. There is no indication whatever that a wand had been waved in and around 10 March 1661. Who knew then that Westphalia and the Pyrenees had brought a full close in the European power struggle between Bourbon and Habsburg? Who could then foresee the military expenditures of the next generation, or the social and political impact if the fiscal pressures had to be, albeit unwillingly, resumed? Although the period from 1653 had seen the tentative restoration of the *commissaires*, it had not been one of real stabilisation. It had been, in Moote's phrase, a 'miniature Fronde', involving 'strikes or threatened strikes by judges, lawyers, merchants, *rentiers* and peasants'.[94] Who knew what further Fronde might not be gestated, if it became necessary for the administrative and fiscal pressures to rise once more to the levels of unacceptability.

The sense of caution and moderation which influenced policy from 1661 must in some part have stemmed from the impossibility of the government's ever knowing very much at any time that was precise about the provincial situation; and this was perhaps especially so in a period of post-failed-revolution, when past records were held close to the chest, and in a period when the *intendants* were only ambiguously restored in the provinces. Even though, by 1679, Colbert was declaring the 'noise of *Parlements*' to be 'no longer in season', and that they were now 'so old one no longer remembers them',[95] this was not, significantly, his diagnosis of the priorities of the French political situation when, more than a decade after the Fronde, the '*instruction*' was drawn up for the 'general enquiry' of 1664. The priority given to the *maîtres des requêtes*† in their '*enquête générale*' was in fact to construct an inventory of the political reliability of the ruling class.

VIII

Amidst the legal debate of the *Fronde parlementaire*, it is easy enough to lose the sense of what was involved in practice for the monarchy, in its financial and legal sovereignty. Although it was of great importance that the *Parlementaires* were able to raise their challenge to the ideological level, the problem of the Fronde was in no sense a political abstraction. If it had been, it would not have disturbed the political stability of the state. The constitutional debate arose from and involved the realities of actual power. That this was so is suggested well enough by the disarray into which the reforms of 1648 immediately threw the finances of the monarchical state, following the suppression of the provincial *commissaires*. Once the guarantee of the *commissaires* was withdrawn, the *traitants* were at once dissuaded from making the advances of credit upon which the whole function and security of the monarchy depended.[96]

There is every indication that Louis XIV entirely understood the meaning of the Fronde: that, on the one hand, it exposed the political instability of the feudal class; and that, on the other, there was the ambition of the *Parlementaires* to contain the exercise of his sovereignty within clearly defined limits. The problem of the feudal class could be solved by firm political exclusion, combined with the concession of a continuing social and military primacy. The more crucial and complex problem lay with the *officiers* and the challenge of the *Parlementaires* over sovereignty. Louis XIV's *Mémoires pour l'instruction due dauphin* indicate the importance he attached to the seventeenth-century debate on sovereignty. The necessity to establish Bodin's '*souveraineté*' is the central political '*instruction*' for his son. It is important to remember that the *Mémoires* for the year 1661, which deal most especially with the theory and justification of monarchy, were not composed contemporaneously. It is not therefore a matter of Louis's being concerned with the challenge of the Fronde simply at the time of his assumption of personal power in 1661. The *Mémoires* for 1661 were in fact first assembled in 1666, were worked on again in 1670 and only assumed their final form as late as 1671, when, as a project, the *Mémoires* were discontinued.[97] The '*élévation*' of the *Parlements* which had been so 'dangerous' during Louis XIV's minority was still of importance to him, it seems, some fifteen years, perhaps indeed nearly twenty years, after the crisis of the Fronde:

> It was necessary, for a thousand reasons, in order to prepare for the reform of justice, which had so much need of reform indeed, to reduce the authority of the principal companies. Under the pretext that their judgments were without appeal and, as one says, sovereign and of last resort, and having gradually assumed the title of sovereign courts, they considered themselves as so many distinct and independent sovereignties. I let them understand that I would no longer tolerate their enterprises.[98]

Forbidding the 'sovereign courts' to contravene the judgments of his *Conseil*, he had, he declares, ordered them to have recourse to his own authority in matters in dispute between them, on the grounds that the authority he had 'confided to them was merely to administer justice' to his subjects, 'and not to make themselves into justice itself, which is a part of sovereignty so closely identified with the Crown and so much the possession of the king alone that it cannot be communicated to any other person.'[99] An institutionalised egotism – not the personal egotism with which it is so usually and misleadingly confused – informed the mind of Louis XIV, the egotism of '*La Grande Monarchie de France*', to use de Seyssel's sixteenth-century expression; and it was in part this which found it difficult to accept the prescriptions of professional bureaucrats and lawyers as to the exercise of its sovereignty. This, together with common-sense deductions from the actual seventeenth-century political situation, combined to form Louis XIV's determination to have done with fundamental conflicts with the *Parlementaires* over sovereignty. It was significantly apropos of the need to show the *Parlements* that he had 'no fear of them' that Louis XIV so famously declared that 'times were changed'.[100] The assertions of the *Mémoires* concerning the *Parlements* could indeed be brutally direct. In the *Mémoires* for 1666, Louis takes the occasion to record that in response to an attempt on the part of the *Parlement de Paris* to debate royal edicts relative to the price of certain offices, after his holding a *lit de justice*, he had 'ordered' the *premier président*† to convene the *Parlement de Paris*, and in order to 'let them understand that in my mind they passed as things of very little significance, I ordered him . . . to inform it that I wished it no longer to discuss edicts which had been registered in my presence, to see if it would dare to disobey me. I wanted to use this encounter to make a glaring example of the absolute subjection of this *compagnie* or of my just and severe intention to punish them.'[101]

The situation is indeed reminiscent of the celebrated assertion of his authority of eleven years earlier, when as a youth of seventeen Louis appeared in person to upbraid the *Parlement de Paris*: 'Everyone knows how much your assemblies have incited troubles in my state, and how many dangerous effects they have produced. I have learned that you presume to continue them again under the pretext of deliberating on my edicts which not long ago were read and published in my presence. I have come here expressly to forbid the continuation [of your debate] and to forbid you, M. *le premier président* to allow or to agree to it.'[102] Even though on this occasion Mazarin, fearful perhaps of a too forceful expression of royal determination, held out hopes of negotiation, in fact none took place and the *Parlement de Paris* accepted Louis's chastisement.

It would be misleading, however, to extrapolate from these assertions of Louis' authority a policy of brutal subjection of those who had disrupted the state. There was in fact no simplifying 'reduction to obedience', in Lavisse's famous and, in many ways, misleading phrase. The political practicalities of the period, at least in the short term, directed policy away from crude enforcements of royal authority. Louis XIV's *Mémoires* themselves indicate clearly enough that there was no intention of sustaining a vendetta against those who disrupted the stability of the state. It is manifest that an ambiguous policy was pursued in the solution of the central problems confronting the monarchy in the middle seven-teenth-century: on the one hand, an abrupt, even brutal, assertion of royal sovereignty; on the other, a pragmatic policy of wide accommoda-tions within the political practicalities. It was a formidable combination, a formidable ambiguity. It can be seen in Louis' relations with both the nobility and the *officiers*.

In face of the nobility, there was an unequivocal intention of showing them that, as with the *Parlements*, the 'times were changed'. The *princes du sang* and with them the *ducs et pairs* were excluded from the *Conseil* from 1661, and with certain exceptions were to remain excluded for the remainder of the reign. This exclusion of the nobility from the political centre of the state has been to some extent confused by an article, which has become well known, by F. Bluche.[103] Writing on the social origins of the secretaries of state under Louis XIV, he seeks to show their noble status, and that, contrary to received opinion, 'Louis XIV governed with-out recourse to the collaboration of a single bourgeois'.[104] His title suggests that he is concerned with the 'secretaries of state'. It is import-ant perhaps to note that by the end of the first decade of the personal reign, three of the four secretaryships were in the hands of ministers, Le Tellier, de Lionne and Colbert. Bluche is in fact also writing therefore of the great minister-secretaries of Louis XIV, and he has no difficulty in displaying their juridical nobility, acquired through three or four genera-tions of office in their families – with Colbert the very considerable ex-ception, of course, in all this. Mousnier, however, in his introduction to the issue of the journal in which Bluche is writing, makes the essential point that Bluche's article fails to take sufficient account of the social realities of the period; that these men were socially members of the highest reaches of the 'robe', but were not in any way to be confused with the *noblesse d'épée*, in whose eyes, for all their distinction in the service of the state, they were still merely *gentilshommes de plume et d'encre*.[105] Far from providing evidence of the oneness of 'sword' and 'robe', as has been suggested,[106] Bluche's article does no more than sub-stantiate the fact (never really perhaps very much in question) that the minister-secretaries of Louis XIV derived from the nobility of the high 'robe'. They were not 'bourgeois', indeed, in any sense, in legal fact; but, equally, they were not socially acceptable as members of the nobility to which Condé and Turenne belonged.

Louis XIV's *Mémoires* show clearly enough that he himself, not perhaps surprisingly, had an entirely accurate perception of the social realities of the origins of these ministers, whose 'nobility' Bluche wishes so much to stress. Ironically, in seeking to discount Louis' own testimony regarding them in his *Mémoires*, Bluche actually arrives at misquoting him. Suggest-ing that Louis himself erroneously proposed that his minister-secretaries were the bourgeois *'néants'* Saint-Simon was ultimately to write about,

Bluche quotes Louis XIV as saying: 'It was not in my interest to take for ministers men of eminent rank.'[107] We have, Bluche claims, been misled by Louis' misrepresentations. If Louis had in fact written that, we should indeed have been misled. In fact, Louis actually wrote: 'It was not in my interest to take for ministers men of more eminent rank.'[108] Bluche has omitted the crucial refinement Louis introduces by the word *'plus'*. The word indeed gives a precise indication, none could be clearer, of Louis' precise awareness of the gradations within the *noblesse*, between the *noblesse* of even the very highest 'robe' and the *noblesse* of 'high birth'. There is no indication whatever, in what he actually says, that Louis XIV is proposing that Le Tellier, de Lionne and Colbert were not *'éminent'*, that they were in some sense 'bourgeois'. They were *'éminent'* indeed, but there were those above them who were more so, men of 'high birth' whom he might have chosen in their place:

> To reveal everything I had in mind, it was not in my interest to take men of more eminent rank. It was above all necessary to establish my own reputation, and to let the public know by the rank I took them from that my intention was not to share my authority with them. It was important to me that they should not conceive for themselves higher expectations than those I wished to give them, which is difficult with men of high birth.[109]

Louis XIV is making here the very real distinctions that were to be made between the seventeenth-century 'sword' and 'robe', between the nobility deriving from *'une grande naissance'* and the highest members of his own ministerial élite, the *Robe d'Etat*.

There is further evidence in the *Mémoires* of Louis XIV regarding the true nobility within a distinctly traditional, 'medieval' framework of reference, when he refers to the problem of the *faux-noblesse*: 'the least of the defects of the order of the nobility', he declares,' was the infinite number of usurpers in its midst without any title, or who had acquired a title by purchase without any service . . .'[110] The word 'service' is resonant indeed of the feudal relationship of suzerain and fiefholder, and we may be sure that it would have been exceedingly unlikely that in Louis' mind the word contained any suggestion of the service of office in the state, even high ministerial office. Goubert suggests that Louis XIV conducted a policy of deliberate degradation of the *noblesse*, through cynical proliferation by sale of noble patents.[111] It seems more likely that this proliferation stemmed from financial motive rather than from any policy of conscious degradation. Chronic financial shortage more than anything determined the central transformation of the age of Louis XIV into the age of Samuel Bernard and the *financiers*. Louis XIV may have been self-deceived as to the effects of the adulteration of the nobility which financial necessity forced upon him; but there is no indication that this adulteration stemmed from a deliberate and coherent policy of malicious degradation of the principle of nobility itself. It stemmed from military extravagance, which drew everything in its wake, the traditional social hierarchies and the monarchy itself.

The evidence is that Louis' policy toward the nobility was far more plural than a policy of hostility and exclusion suggests. The pursuit of the, *faux-noblesse*, though essentially fiscal in intent, was done in part to please and purify the '*vraie noblesse*'. Mme de Sévigné's response to her cousin Bussy Rabutin, in talking of her own 'return' of nobility for the Sévigné in 1668, may well have been typical of those of the *noblesse d'épée* who had nothing to fear from investigation, but, on the contrary, welcomed the opportunity of 'displaying their merchandise', their true '*noblesse de race*'.[112] It was to some extent ironic in Mme de Sévigné's own case, since she herself, in her own origins, was the product of a *mésalliance*, between the 'sword' family of the Burgundian Rabutin-Chantal and the Coulanges family, who had made their fortune from farming the *gabelle*. She could only claim true lineage through her father's side, the Rabutin-Chantal, and through the impoverished Breton Sévigné, to whom the wealthy Coulanges, who raised her, managed to marry her.

It seems likely, as Deyon suggests, that the monarchy's attempt to erode the tax-immunity of the nobility, which had been a feature of the financial policies of the period of Louis XIII, was discontinued from the first years of the personal reign.[113] There had been a compelling logic, of course, in the monarchy's attempt to transform the old feudal obligation of service through the summons to arms, of the *ban et arrière-ban*†, into a tax to provide substitutes. The whole origin and rationale of tax-immunity was that it was granted in exchange for military service. With the emergence of 'national' armies in the seventeenth century it was entirely reasonable to update what had become a 'feudal' anachronism. The difficulty in this and other policies directed toward the curtailment of noble immunity was that they coincided with a period of growing rural depression and monetary shortage, and therefore contributed to noble grievance and to identification of interest between the nobility and other provincial classes against the Crown. Deyon's proposal that the pressure was lifted from the nobility in the early personal reign could well explain at least part of the stabilising of relationships between the Crown and nobility under Louis XIV. The problem of tax-immunity was not to re-emerge until the 1690s, when the financial situation once more thrust it forward, just as it had in the period of Richelieu and Mazarin, when, however, it became a more pressing matter than simply manipulating the *ban et arrière-ban*, or taxing the non-noble land held by the nobility in the Midi, or ensuring that the tenants of the nobility paid their *taille*, irrespective of the capacity of their *seigneurs* to protect them from it.

There was of course a fundamental ambiguity between a monarchy on the one hand denuding a traditional nobility of its political power and on the other sustaining it in all its social primacy. The sense of Versailles as the construct of a deliberate political cynicism, a calculated weapon of political emasculation, as a corral for subject nobility, is only one aspect of it. The iconography of the reign required an aristocratic galaxy in circulation about the king. The military function, the ever-increasing central reference of the reign, remained a monopoly of the 'sword' nobility. It would be naïve to suppose that the nobility, in all its political exclusion, was not fundamental to the 'myth' and therefore to the political system of Louis XIV. In the monarchy of Louis XIV it is important not to confuse the administration of politics, which is what the ministers – the Le Telliers and the Colberts – did, with the essence of politics, which is what Louis XIV and his attendant nobility symbolised and were.

IX

The same principle of contradiction and ambiguity prevailed in the Crown's relations with the *officiers*. Once again, there was a firm, unmistakable assertion of Louis's sovereignty. The registers of the Fronde debates of the *Parlement de Paris* were to be destroyed. In 1665 the *cours souveraines* were declared to be merely *cours supérieures*.[114] In a *lit de justice* of December of that same year, the *Parlements* were prohibited from the discussion of royal edicts subsequent to their registration in the royal presence;[115] and in 1673, but not earlier, came the finalisation of the position regarding judicial review of legislation, at virtually the vanishing point of permitting a 'humble remonstrance' only after the registration of edicts, within a very firm timetable of presentation for both the *Parlement de Paris* and the provincial *Parlements*.[116] Two years later, in 1675, the *Parlements* of both Rennes and Bordeaux were brutally exiled for their incapacity to sustain the Crown's position in the great Brittany and Bordeaux uprisings of that year.

But, within this framework of sovereign assertion, the regime adopted a policy of great administrative caution. The situation in the provinces during the last years of Mazarin's ministry and in the 1660s remained essentially confused, not least because of the continuing popular uprisings and the continuing indeterminacy surrounding the allegiance of the *officiers*. The popular uprisings were to continue through to the middle 1670s and indeed beyond. The year 1657 saw widespread uprisings in Anjou, Poitou, Angoumois and, unusually, as far east as Champagne. In 1658 uprisings spread into Sologne and Vendée, and the following year the Norman nobility rose and disaffection again spread to areas south of the Loire, into Anjou and Poitou. With every reason, writing in retrospect of the year 1661, Louis XIV declared 'disorder' to have been 'reigning everywhere'. And nothing ceased, in the matter of popular uprisings, in 1661. The early personal reign of Louis XIV was 'no more peaceful', Mandrou says,' than the preceding period'.[117] Revolt was endemic in the years 1662 to 1665, in the Boulonnais, Limousin, Velay, Poitou, Touraine and Béarn. In 1667 it was the turn of Limousin, again, and Berry. In 1669, Poitou was again convulsed. Vivarais, Guyenne and Roussillon were all affected by uprisings during the period 1668–70; and in 1670 the uprisings spread into Languedoc. In 1672 Brittany and Normandy were affected, and in 1674 disturbance spread through Tours, Guyenne and Angoumois. The whole series of uprisings which had affected France for more than half a century culminated in the great revolts of Brittany and Bordeaux in 1675. These were not, in fact, the full close of seventeenth-century French revolt. In 1677 uprisings occurred in Provence and Languedoc, and in the following year disturbance spread through Brie and Vivarais. Burgundy experienced uprisings as late as 1680. Everything indeed suggests continuing distress and tension in the provinces of Louis XIV's France, in spite of the fiscal relaxations which the period following the Peace of the Pyrenees enabled Colbert to pursue.

The personal reign of Louis XIV opened in the midst of very great social distress. Almost immediately, the realm was affected by the beginnings of what was to become the great *'disette'* of 1661–2, one of the three worst subsistence crises of the century. This was only one episode, however, in a context of continuing economic and social difficulty. The evidence is of a steepening recessionary curve, affecting the continental mass and interior of France, and there was to be no lasting respite throughout the period of Colbert. The early personal reign was not simply a matter of the great *Carousel*, of Louise de la Vallière and the *plaisirs de l'île enchantée* and of the first beginnings at Versailles, but of a government entirely conscious of governing in a situation of economic and social malaise. The work of the *Conseil de Commerce* established in 1664 was as much a response to the realities of a difficult economic situation as the reflection of the bureaucratic and mercantilist energies of Colbert. His constantly pessimistic analysis of the financial and economic situations cannot have seemed entirely unrelated to reality to those for whom his *memoranda* were prepared; and in this it is important to remember that he was in the closest contact with contemporary financial and commercial opinion. The establishment of La Reynie as *Lieutenant-général de police* for Paris in 1667, the formation of *hôpitaux-généraux* for the relief of pauperism in Paris and the major cities and towns of France between 1656 and 1680 testify to the reality of the French social crisis, as well as to the *dirigiste* preoccupations of royal administrators.

In this context of continuing difficulty, it is not surprising that the most important state paper of the early reign, the *instruction* drawn up under the direction of Colbert for the 'general enquiry' of 1664, should have been primarily concerned with the problem of order and the morale and reliability of the ruling class.[118] It is a paper of the greatest importance in revealing the priorities of the monarchy some twelve years after the Fronde; and those priorities are unequivocally political and financial. The *instruction* is most often seen as a reflection of the scale of royal initiative and ambition during the initial phase of the personal reign. The areas of policy, however, which have always been traditionally thought of such compelling interest to Colbert, in fact occupy only a tertiary place in the *instruction*. Political order and the revenues of the Crown are the first priorities, and in that order. The *maîtres des requêtes*, never as it happens called *intendants* at any point in the document, are clearly being sent out into very much the same realm as were those who had gone out and corresponded with Séguier during the reign of Louis XIII. It is a realm still troubled with the problems of potential disturbance arising from noble intrigue, *parlementaire* disaffection and peasant unrest and exploitation; a realm indeed in which 'difficult times' might well return. Accordingly, the initial section of the *instruction*, amounting to almost the first half of the document, requires the *maîtres des requêtes* to draw up an inventory of the dominant social groups, in their four traditional provincial '*gouvernemens*'. This is not a state paper of the France of the 1680s, of Versailles and the *Réunions*, of *intendants* permanently established in the provinces, but of a France in which the monarchy is still acutely aware of the potential for disturbance and subversion within the state. Instead of a 'Tudor peace', France had had only late Valois and early Bourbon disorder. The *instruction* may express an over-anxiety perhaps, and, in the event, an unnecessary anxiety, but there is nothing unreal in its awareness that the government operated within a society still fraught with the possibility of further upheaval.

The maps which were to be looked for, discovered or drawn up anew, which are so often referred to as symbols of Colbert's rationalising, 'geometric' spirit, were in fact to have drawn on them the internal frontiers of the late-medieval constitution of France, the frontiers of the traditional '*quatre gouvernemens*' – '*ecclésiastique, militaire, de justice et de finances*'.[119] There is a sense indeed of the monarchy confronted by the whole apparatus of the traditional socio-political constitution, in all the breadth and depth of its particularist presence. The *maîtres des requêtes* were ordered to begin their investigation, traditionally enough, with the ecclesiastical *gouvernement*. It was to be on the level of each individual personality, bishop or abbot, with the end of state security solely in mind. Each bishop was to be investigated as to the 'credit' he had in his own '*pays*' and what 'influence he might be expected to have in difficult times'.[120]

Moving to the *gouvernement militaire*, we find further and perhaps the most compelling evidence of the 'sword' identity of the *noblesse* in the mind of the monarchy. The *instruction* moves explicitly within a framework of medieval 'orders', and the 'second order', the '*noblesse*', is military in its profession and there is no ambiguity or nuance about it: 'pour le gouvernement militaire qui regarde la noblesse, qui est le second ordre de son royaume',[121] a similarly thorough investigation is to be mounted. The *maîtres des requêtes* are instructed to make a thorough investigation of the *gouverneurs*, in the first instance, taking into account their family connections and '*alliances*', their general credit and reputation and whether they oppress the people. Then, with the perspective of past difficulties and continuing political risks firmly in focus, the *maîtres des requêtes* are instructed that 'His Majesty wishes to be particularly informed of the past conduct of the said *gouverneurs*, in order to judge what can be expected as to the future.'[122] Similar investigations were to be made concerning the *lieutenants-généraux*, and 'everyone involved in the *noblesse*'. For the '*noblesse ordinaire*', it was especially important to 'discover whether they cultivated their estates or let them out to farmers', since this was always an indication of their '*humeur*', whether they were 'inclined to war or to remaining on their estates'.[123]

It is notable that in this entirely practical instrument of government, where we might assume that social and political realities were uppermost in the governmental mind, no professional associations are made regarding the *noblesse* other than those of war and landowning. There is no reference here, among the second order of the nobility, either to an equally highly regarded nobility or even to a secondary nobility, created by office. There is no reference whatever among the second order to the profession or existence of a *noblesse de robe*. In view of the unequivocal definition of the 'sword' identity of the second order in the *instruction* itself, it would be merely perverse to argue, from the omission, the indivisibility of the *noblesse*. It is indeed only in turning away from the second order, to the third *gouvernement*, the *gouvernement de justice*, that we reach the *Parlementaires*. With them, we also reach, significantly, 'the most important matter to examine in the province', their political reliability, if 'the same situation' of the king's minority should 'arise again':

Concerning justice, in the event of there being a *parlement* or some other sovereign court, in the province, the *maîtres des requêtes* must examine carefully, both in general and in particular, those who compose it. In general, its conduct during His Majesty's minority must be examined, by what motives did it determine its conduct, and what were the means employed by the principal members either to lead it into evil or good ways. If it behaved badly, to find out whether the reasons which have been able to change its mind since are strong enough to lead one to suppose that it would remain loyal if the same situation arose again, or whether there are grounds for fearing that it would fall into the same error. And since this is the most important matter to examine in the province, it will be good and very necessary indeed to know the detail of the interests and *qualités* of the principal *officiers* of these *compagnies*, and particularly whether those who led them into such conduct are still alive.[124]

Only in the word '*qualités*' is there any reference to rank among the *Parlementaires*; and there is no suggestion in the whole section of anyone's considering any among the *Parlementaires* as members of the *noblesse*.

We have seen that in their investigation of the *gouverneurs* the *maîtres des requêtes* are instructed to concern themselves with their '*alliances*'. It is the same with the *noblesse* in general: 'His Majesty desires to be particularly informed of everything concerning the *noblesse*, namely, the principal households in each province, their *alliances* . . .'[125] The indication is indeed of a society divided into enclaves of aristocratic power based on the clientage of the kind Mousnier describes and into which the monarchy clearly wishes to intrude. The *instruction* gives little support to Porshnev's theory of a monarchy sustaining a 'feudal-absolutist order' against the rural and urban masses. Something of the reverse is perhaps suggested. If the function of the monarchy was a collusive and mutual interchange of support between itself and the feudal class, it does not seem especially evident that it understood or particularly desired to perform its role. The *maîtres des requêtes* are especially instructed to discover whether the *gouverneurs*, members of the 'feudal class' indeed, 'are accused of taking money from the people or of vexing them in any way'. This was to be especially undertaken, the *instruction* continues, because 'the principal and most important thing which His Majesty wishes the provincial *gouverneurs* to apply themselves to is to uphold justice firmly and to prevent the oppression of the weak by the violence of the strong.'[126]

Even so, the *instruction* does suggest something of what Porshnev talks of. Although there is no sense of a monarchy in collusive support of a feudal class, there is constant reference to seigneurial exploitation and a polarisation between the socially dominant groups and the peasants. There is a significant awareness on the part of the Crown of collusion between the socially dominant in the oppression and distress of the poor. In turning to the *Parlements*, the *maîtres des requêtes* are especially asked to enquire whether they render equal justice, or 'whether there has been any manifest injustice done which has caused a stir in the province and caused the oppression of the weak in favour of friends or relatives.' The *instruction* continues: 'since the principal object of establishing these *compagnies* was that they should use the authority committed to them to protect the weak against the strong, they [the *maîtres des requêtes*] must inform themselves whether in any case of violence or murder . . . on the part of *gentilshommes* or other principal persons in the province, they have maintained that authority.'[127] The section on taxation also suggests an alliance between the socially dominant at the expense of the poor:

> There is a general rule to observe concerning all taxes levied on the people . . . which consists in being precisely informed about all those subject to pay them, as to whether each one bears what he is capable of bearing; since it is for sure that through inequality in taxation, that is to say when the most powerful and the most rich, through exploiting their position, relieve themselves of their own burden, the poor and weak find themselves overburdened; and this inequality in the provinces causes poverty, distress . . . and all sorts of evils . . . The *commissaires* in the provinces must therefore always have this fundamental and sure rule in mind, from which they must never depart, to know the exact capacity of all those who are liable to pay *aides*, *taille*, and *gabelle*, as much in the general sense, that is to say the capacity of the parishes and *communautés* concerned, as of the principal inhabitants of each, so as to prevent all the powerful members of all the orders in the province from obtaining relief for certain parishes and certain individuals, through their connections with *Trésoriers de France*, *élus* and even the *collecteurs* themselves.[128]

Concern for the eradication of flagrant oppression and tax evasion runs like a thread throughout the *instruction*, as indeed through so many comparable state *memoranda* of the period. We may not of course argue from these suspicions and implied accusations to the facts of the actual situation. Nevertheless, it is difficult to discount entirely the emphasis of this area of the *instruction*. We are of course a long way from the 'class-front' of Porshnev, supported by a 'feudal-absolutist order', since absolutism itself seems an obviously absent partner from the 'front'. If the function of the monarchy was to sustain feudal exploitation, it would seem to have adopted a somewhat roundabout and oblique way of achieving it. Even so, with the monarchy an absentee, we can discern in this something at least of what Porshnev talks of.

The initial section of the *instruction*, dealing with the investigation of the personnel of the provincial *gouvernemens*, which was to include the members of the *Cours des Aides*, the *Trésoriers de France* and 'all the *officiers de finances* in every province', occupies not quite one half of it. It is followed by an enumeration of the royal revenues and the problems associated with each element of them.[129] The third section of the *instruction*, dealing with what may be loosely termed 'economic' matters, occupies only a quarter of it,[130] and the sections on the state stud-farms and on counterfeiting occupy virtually one half of that. Within the wide-ranging interests of the monarchy – and in this sense it is important that the *instruction* became a blueprint for the administrative concerns of the *intendants* of the future – the initial priority of the Crown in 1664, some twelve years after the Fronde, very clearly lay in the area of state security.

Political stability in France could not reside permanently however, in the use of *maîtres des requêtes* as spies – though that is the word used of the *intendants* by John Locke in 1677.[131] It would, in the end, be determined by royal policy. There is every indication that in the period from 1661 Louis XIV attempted to restore the relationship of the Crown with its own *officiers*. The relaxation of financial pressure which the international situation permitted from 1659 made possible the development of an improved financial administration. Not only the above *instruction*, but the general correspondence with the *intendants* in the 1660s indicate that the main financial priority had moved toward rendering the system more equitable from simply aiding and abetting the extraction of the lion's share of whatever money was available for the king and tax-farmer. It was possible in the 1660s to undertake the general '*réforma-tion*', to use Louis XIV's own word, which the international crisis of the Thirty Years War had caused to be postponed *sine die* in the 1620s. Reduction in the amount of the *taille* became a major element of policy from 1661, when it was reduced from 42 million *livres* to 38 million for 1662. By 1665 it had fallen to 35·5 million *livres*, not three-fifths of what it had been in the worst years of the war under Richelieu and Mazarin. In spite of mounting military expenditure in the 1670s, the *taille* was kept firmly at an average of 38·7 million *livres* during the Dutch War and was reduced to an average of 34·9 millions between the Peace of Nymegen and Colbert's death in 1683.[132] It was equally important that the atmosphere of extortion and abuse should be promptly dissipated. The *Chambre de Justice* set up in 1661 to deal with Fouquet and his associates was part of the Crown's decision not only to break the overriding power of the *financiers*, but moreover to show that it was broken. A central grievance of the *officiers* both before and during the Fronde had been that the whole establishment of the offending *commissaires* in the provinces had been to serve the financial interests of the tax-farmers. During the Fronde, the *Parlement de Paris* had explicitly demanded the establishment of a special tribunal to deal with corruption, such as that which was actually established by Louis and Colbert in 1661. The tribunal was an important element in the policy of a minister whose expressed aim was to 'purge the age', as an act of discontinuity with what had gone before, under Mazarin and Fouquet.

The crucial issue, however, lay in the use of the revived *commissaires*.

There sometimes remains even now the erroneous idea that in some way Colbert developed the *commissaires* into *intendants* as a deliberate policy,[133] whereas the whole mass of his administrative correspondence suggests the reverse. In the levying of *taille*, it is clear from the outset that the Crown had no intention of allowing the *Trésoriers de France* and the *élus†* to resume control over its apportionment and collection. The *intendants*, in direct association with the *Conseil royal des finances*, remained in administrative control over it; not, this time, to extort the maximum possible amounts, but as the only means of ensuring a more equitable distribution of the tax. In all other respects, Colbert expressed constant irritation with *intendants* who were deemed to have exceeded the limits of their *commissions*; there were frequent reminders to them to read and reread the conditions of their appointments with the utmost care, and specific injunctions to them to allow the due administrative procedures to be pursued.[134] Everything indeed suggests the caution Mousnier has referred to: 'Louis XIV continued to use the *intendants*, but he wished to have them resume their role as simple inspectors . . . In no instance were they allowed to substitute themselves for the *officiers* and fulfil their offices for them.'[135] Colbert never went beyond the image of *intendants* continually out *en chevauchée* inspecting their *généralités*. They were to supervise and at need exercise such degree of direct authority as the situation required, but this was most often only to be set in motion after further reference back to the *Conseil*. The monarchy had no wish to disturb the fabric of provincial administration unnecessarily and thus risk engendering dangerous disaffection; nor had it any desire to create yet another cadre of *officiers* over whom it could so easily lose control. It was for this reason that the *commissions* of the *intendants* were always revocable at will and their offices uniquely outside the system of venality. It is true that they purchased their preparatory offices, almost always as *maîtres des requêtes*, and it has been suggested that their ultimate acceptance by the ordinary *officiers* in the provinces may have partly lain in the fact that they were thereby of the same official *genus* as the *officiers* themselves.[136] This may have been part of this crucial process. It is certain that a great deal depended upon the acceptance of the *intendants* by those who had previously resisted them to the point of revolution.

By the 1680s the *intendants* had become 'institutionalised'; they had become accepted as residential administrators throughout the *généralités*. Most important in this was the weight of business actually accorded them, especially in the areas of investigating communal debt and the administration of the *taille*. Ironically, it was most often Colbert himself who loaded them, adding indeed the supervision of his industrial policies to their competence – an area in which incidentally there was no danger of invading the vested interests of existing *officiers*. Colbert accommodated

C

himself to the pragmatic need for the office, but only with all the provisos and caveats his caution suggested.

So too the provinces accommodated themselves to the rise of the sovereign monarchy among them. They came to accept the consolidation of the 'absolutist' constitution to the partial eclipse of the 'traditional'. Somewhere a point of balance was reached between the two constitutions and a stabilisation emerged. As the monarchy moved progressively away from the Fronde into the second and third decades of the personal reign, it became clear that the crisis within the late-medieval constitution was over. The stability of the multiple constitution of the *ancien régime* was achieved; partly perhaps from the increasing military presence of the monarchy; more importantly, from accommodations in part enforced by immemorial political and social structures; but also achieved, perhaps most importantly, by a finer political appreciation on the part of the government of the limits within which the practice of absolutism was possible. It is not the brevity, which Lavisse stressed, of the regime bequeathed by Louis XIV in 1715 which should hold our attention, but the longevity of the regime which was consolidated in France in the 1670s and 1680s, of Louis XIV's personal reign. No regime of such multiple vitality and longevity can be supposed to have been founded upon the political sands of *lettres de cachet* and *dragonnades*, or to have survived for long in a condition of grievance and cold civil war.

In this, the role of the *intendants* was crucial. J. H. M. Salmon endorses the suggestion made by A. D. Lublinskaya that 'the monarchy had learnt from experience to associate them [the *intendants*] with local institutions and to provide them with subordinates'.[187] The appointment of subordinates, *sub-délégués*, for the *intendants* was perhaps the one crucial development which made the establishment of the *intendants* possible. But *sub-délégués* were not in any sense 'provided' by the government during the early years of the personal reign. Indeed, the reverse. It is entirely clear that the appointment of *sub-délégués* was the one process which Colbert most feared in the total development of the permanent *intendants*. Until the closing years of his life, he vigorously combated the appointment of *sub-délégués*, demanding that, if they were appointed, their competence should be specifically defined and be only of a temporary nature, to undertake the specific task delegated to them.[138] In Colbert's eyes, their appointment could only lead to the *intendants* becoming established as resident administrators in the chief towns of the *généralités*, neglecting their regular tours of inspection, and exposing themselves to corruption through the localisation of their interests and allegiances. It is significant, however, that *sub-délégués* continued to be appointed by *intendants* in spite of the constant prohibitions of Colbert and the *Conseil*. It seems possible that the *intendants* perceived quite early on that they might only gain the acceptance they required from local interests through the collaboration which the appointment of *sub-délégués* made possible. The weight of administrative business was certainly a major factor in the development of the *sub-délégués*, as was also the need for the *intendant* to work through and with those with intimate knowledge of the *généralité*, especially when newly appointed for purposes of continuity. It is equally possible, however, that awarenesses developed quite soon among the *intendants* as to the bridges which had to be built between the *intendances* and the alternative provincial infrastructure of local interest and power. It is perhaps a special irony that a development which Colbert so much disliked and feared should have played a major role in creating the *modus vivendi* between absolutism and provincialism, between royal and local interests, upon which the stability of the *ancien régime* was to depend. But it was probably at a cost Colbert would have continued to deplore and to have been unprepared to pay – in terms of provincialism, *'confusion'*: the *'dérèglement'* indeed of that amalgam of medieval and absolutist elements which constituted the French *ancien régime*.

Pagès perceived the seminal importance of the *sub-délégués*, in an analysis which deserves to be more widely known:

> For a long time, there was a continuing opposition from the *officiers* against the *intendants*, but it disappeared at the end of the seventeenth century. It seems that the proliferation of *sub-délégués*, definitively established in the provinces, contributed considerably to this; for only naturally the *intendant* wanted to attract about himself experienced administrators; he was led to choose *sub-délégués* from among the local *officiers* – *lieutenants de bailliage*, *Trésoriers de France*, *maires*. In this way, jealousy subsided and a collaboration established itself.[189]

'Une collaboration'? Was sub-delegation as important an administrative development as venality itself had been, in providing the essential link between the *intendants* and the *officiers*, and indeed with the whole spectrum of local interest, which was so vital to the consolidation of absolutism?

The mid-seventeenth-century crisis in the French monarchical state had lain in the factors which Mousnier diagnosed: the chronic erosion of the public power of the feudal class through the process of venality, combined with the subsequent invasion of the vested interest of the *officiers* by the use of *commissaires* by Richelieu and Mazarin, during the military-financial and social crisis of the Thirty Years War. These factors acted upon the inherent conflicts within the unstable late-medieval constitution and brought it to crisis.

It seems likely however that the deeper undertow of French society – and venality must have played its part in this – was toward the class-accommodations within an absolutist reference of the kind of which

Porshnev speaks, within which *lieutenants de bailliage, Trésoriers de France, maires* and the *intendants* and their *sub-délégués* 'collaborated' in the pragmatic business of sustaining a society which was seigneurial if not 'feudal'; in which, by the 1670s, the tensions between Crown and ruling class were becoming reduced, old animosities forgotten, at least for long enough to consolidate the collaboration, and exploitation, which was the French *ancien régime*.

NOTES

1 R. Mousnier, *Les XVIe et XVIIe siècles* (Paris, 1954).

2 E. J. Hobsbawm, 'The Crisis of the Seventeenth Century', in *Past and Present*, Nos. 5 and 6 (1954); reprinted in *Crisis in Europe, 1560–1660*, ed. T. Aston (London, 1965) pp. 5–58.

3 H. R. Trevor-Roper, 'The General Crisis of the Seventeenth Century', in *Past and Present*, No. 16 (1959); reprinted in *Crisis in Europe*, ed. T. Aston, pp. 59–95.

4 J. H. Elliott, 'Revolution and Continuity in Early Modern Europe', in *Past and Present*, No. 42 (1969) pp. 35–56.

5 I. Schöffer, 'Did Holland's Golden Age coincide with a period of crisis?', in *Acta Historiae Neerlandica*, I (1966) pp. 82–107.

6 A. D. Lublinskaya, *French Absolutism: the crucial phase, 1620–1629*, trans. B. Pearce (Cambridge, 1968) pp. 4–102.

7 P. Goubert, *L'Ancien Régime*, Vol. II (Paris, 1973) p. 83.

8 J. Lynch, *Spain under the Habsburgs*, Vol. II (London, 1969) p. 10; J. H. Elliott, 'The Crisis of the 1590s', in *Imperial Spain, 1469–1716* (London, 1963) pp. 279–95; also P. Vilar, 'Le temps de Quichotte', in *Europe*, XXXIV (1956) pp. 3–16.

9 See H. G. Koenigsberger's review-article of *Preconditions of Revolution in Early Modern Europe*, ed. R. Forster and J. P. Greene (London, 1970), in *History*, Vol. 57, No. 191 (Oct 1972) pp. 394–8.

10 A. Lloyd Moote, *The Revolt of the Judges: the Parlement de Paris and the Fronde, 1643–1652* (Princeton, 1971) p. 26 and pp. 36–40.

11 R. Mousnier, 'The Fronde', in *Preconditions of Revolution in Early Modern Europe*, ed. R. Forster and J. P. Greene (London, 1970) pp. 131–59.

12 J. H. M. Salmon, 'Venality of Office and Popular Sedition in Seventeenth-Century France', in *Past and Present*, No. 37 (July 1967) p. 40.

13 Ibid., p. 41; also *Society in Crisis. France in the Sixteenth Century* (London 1975), *passim*.

14 A. D. Lublinskaya, op. cit., p. 5.

15 J. H. Elliott, 'The Decline of Spain', in *Past and Present*, No. 20 (1961); reprinted in *Crisis in Europe*, ed. T. Aston, p. 168.

16 Ibid., p. 192: 'If France could be beaten swiftly, the future would be his [Olivares'] . . . in 1636, at Corbie, he very nearly achieved his aim. A little more money, a few more men, and French resistance might have crumbled.'

17 A. Lloyd Moote, op. cit., pp. 25–6. Although Moote declares a 'co-ordinated revolution against royal absolutism' an impossibility, he nevertheless suggests that 'simultaneous group protests' could cause 'such confusion throughout the realm that a decisive military repression . . . would be impossible'.

18 J. H. Shennan, *Government and Society in France, 1461–1661* (London, 1969) p. 73.

19 Ibid., p. 73.
20 Ibid., p. 71.
21 J. Stoye, *Europe Unfolding, 1648–1688* (London, 1969) pp. 80–7.
22 R. J. Knecht, *Francis I and Absolute Monarchy*, Historical Association Pamphlet, General series, No. 72 (London, 1969) p. 28.
It is important to note that the largely unnecessary debate on the 'representative' character of the French Renaissance monarchy, arising from J. Russell Major's *Representative Institutions in Renaissance France, 1421–1559*, is now firmly concluded against his 'view that the monarchy of Renaissance France was "popular and conservative" rather than absolute' (Knecht). Doucet's interpretation of the 'absolutist' tendencies of the sixteenth-century monarchy remains a primary reference.
23 See infra, pp. 16–20.
24 M. Marion, *Dictionnaire des Institutions de la France aux XVIIe et XVIIIe siècles* (Paris, 1923; reprinted 1968) p. 257 and pp. 60–1.
25 F. Mauro, *Le XVIe Siècle Européen, Aspects Economiques*, pp 199–200; R. Doucet, 'Le grand parti de Lyon au XVIe siècle', in *Revue Historique*, CLXXI–CLXXII (1923) pp. 473–513 and 1–41. G. Livet, *Les Guerres de Religion* (Paris, 1966) pp. 102–4 gives an account of the disastrous effects of the wars on the economic life of Lyons. The scale of financial decline in later sixteenth-century Lyons is suggested by the fact that in 1575 there were eleven Italian banking houses in the city and that by the end of the century there was only one.
26 C. W. Cole, *Colbert and a Century of French Mercantilism* (New York, 1939) Vol. I, pp. 27–82.
27 G. Pagès, *La Monarchie d'Ancien Régime en France* (Paris, 1928); R. Mousnier, *La Vénalité des offices sous Henri IV et Louis XIII* (Paris, 1945); also infra, Chapter 3, pp. 94–7.
28 J. H. Shennan, op. cit., p. 42.
29 Ibid., p. 43.
30 N. M. Sutherland, *The French Secretaries of State in the Age of Catherine de Medici* (London, 1962).
31 Orest Ranum, *Richelieu and the Councillors of Louis XIII* (Oxford, 1963).
32 P. Goubert, *The Ancien Régime* (London, 1973), being the translation of Vol. I only of the author's *L'Ancien Régime*, *'La Société'* (Paris, 1969). The second volume, *'Les Pouvoirs'*, has not yet been translated and no translation is as yet announced.
33 Ibid., p. 172.
34 See J. H. Shennan, *The Parlement de Paris* (London, 1968) p. 151, for map giving frontiers of the areas of jurisdiction, the *'ressorts'* of the *Parlement de Paris* and the provincial *Parlements*.
35 R. Mousnier, J.-P. Labatut, Y. Durand, *Deux Cahiers de la Noblesse, pour les Etats-Généraux de 1649–1651* (Paris, 1965).
36 Ibid., pp. 33–5 and pp. 41–2.
37 J. H. Shennan, op. cit., p. 154.
38 Ibid., p. 67.
39 A. Lloyd Moote, op. cit., Part III, 'The Noble Fronde, 1649–1652', passim and especially pp. 337–54.
40 R. Mousnier, *Lettres et Mémoires adressés au Chancelier Séguier, 1633–1649* (Paris, 1964) Vol. I, p. 27: 'Comme tous, les Séguier cherchaient á faire remonter très haut leur noblesse, dans une société où la meilleure noblesse est celle qui se perd dans la nuit du temps. En 1642, une généalogie imprimée

à Paris, chez P. Rocolet, imprimeur et libraire du Roi, rattachait les Séguier à un certain Arnaud Séguier, seigneur de Saint-Geniers en 1129.'

41 R. Mandrou, *La France aux XVIIe et XVIIIe siècles*, Nouvelle Clio (Paris, 1967) p. 120.

42 R. Mousnier, J.-P. Labatut, Y. Durand, op. cit., p. 35.

43 R. Mandrou, *Louis XIV en son temps, 1661–1715* (Paris, 1973) pp. 19–20.

44 R. Mettam, *French History and Society* (London, 1974) p. 5.

45 G. Pagès, 'Autour du "Grand Orage": Richelieu et Marillac, deux politiques', in *Revue Historique*, CLXXIX (1937) pp. 63–97.

46 See infra, Chapters 3 and 4, pp. 78–135.

47 See infra, Chapter 5, pp. 138–68.

48 M. Prestwich, *English Historical Review*, LXXXI (1966) pp. 565–72.

49 J. H. M. Salmon, 'Venality of Office and Popular Sedition in Seventeenth-Century France', *Past and Present*, No. 37 (July 1967) pp. 21–43.

50 R. Mousnier, *Lettres et Mémoires adressés au Chancelier Séguier, 1633–1649*, 2 vols. (Paris, 1964).

51 A. D. Lublinskaya, *Vnutrenniya Politika Frantsuzskogo Absolyutizma, 1633–1649 (The Internal Politics of French Absolutism, 1633–1649)* (Moscow, 1966).

52 See especially Degarne, 'Etudes sur les soulèvements provinciaux en France avant la Fronde', in *XVIIe Siècle* (1962) pp. 3–18; Pillorget, ' "Les Cascaveoux": l'insurrection aixoise de l'automne, 1630', in *XVIIe Siècle* (1964); also, 'Essai d'une typologie des mouvements insurrectionnels ruraux survenus en Provence de 1596 à 1715', in *Actes du Congrès National des Sociétés savantes, Strasbourg et Colmar* (1967); also, Foisil, *La Révolte des Nu-Pieds et les Révoltes Normandes de 1639* (Paris, 1970).

53 See infra, Chapter 8, pp. 231–46.

54 L. Bernard, 'French Society and Popular Uprisings under Louis XIV', in *French Historical Studies* (1964) pp. 454–74.

55 B. Porshnev, 'Préface de l'auteur pour l'édition française', *Les soulèvements populaires en France avant la Fronde, 1623–1648* (Paris, 1963) pp. 13–14.

56 P. Goubert, in *Histoire économique et sociale de la France*, Vol. 2 *1660–1789* (Paris, 1970) pp. 41–2; R. Mandrou, *La France aux XVIIe et XVIIIe siècles*, Nouvelle Clio (Paris, 1967) p. 103.

57 R. Mandrou, ibid., p. 65; J. Meuvret, 'Les crises de subsistance et la démographie de la France d'Ancien Régime', in *Population* (1946) pp. 643–50; P. Goubert, *Beauvais et le Beauvaisis de 1600 à 1730* (Paris, 1960); P. de Saint-Jacob, *Les Paysans de la Bourgogne du Nord au dernier siècle de l'Ancien Régime* (Paris, 1960).

58 R. Mandrou, ibid., p. 66; E. Le Roy-Ladurie, *Les Paysans de Languedoc*, 2 vols. (Paris, 1966).

59 R. Mandrou, ibid., p. 70; M. Venard, *Bourgeois et paysans au XVIIe siècle: recherches sur le rôle des bourgeois parisiens dans la vie agricole au sud de Paris au XVIIe siècle* (Paris, 1957).

60 See especially P. Goubert, 'Recent theories and research in French Population between 1500 and 1700', in *Population in History*, ed. D. V. Glass and D. E. C. Eversley (London, 1965) pp. 457–73; J. Meuvret, 'Demographic Crisis in France from the Sixteenth to the Eighteenth Century', in *Population in History*, pp. 507–22.

61 P. Goubert, 'Le régime démographique français au temps de Louis XIV', in *Histoire économique et sociale de la France*, pp. 23–54.

62 See E. Le Roy-Ladurie, 'History and Climate', in *Economy and Society in Early Modern Europe: Essays from Annales*, ed. P. Burke, pp. 134–69.

63 P. Goubert, op. cit., p. 45.

64 Ibid., p. 49.
65 R. Mousnier, 'The Fronde', p. 134.
66 R. Mandrou, op. cit., p. 113.
67 P. Goubert, 'Recent theories and research in French Population between 1500 and 1700', in *Population in History*, p. 467.
68 P. Goubert, in *Histoire économique et sociale de la France*, p. 46.
69 Ibid., pp. 329–30.
70 H. Hauser, 'Le Colbertisme avant Colbert', in *Revue bourguignonne de l'ens. sup.*, xiii pp. 3–69; also P. Goubert, *Louis XIV and Twenty Million Frenchmen* (London, 1970) p. 117.
71 P. Goubert, op. cit., p. 333.
72 The initial work, comparable in some ways to that of E. J. Hamilton on American bullion imports, was that of Nina Bang, *Tabellen over Skipsfart og Varetransport gennen oresund, 1497–1660* (Copenhagen, 1906–1922), which was followed by a second work on the period 1661–1783 completed by K. Horst (Copenhagen, 1930–1945). For subsequent research, see A. Christensen, *Dutch Trade and the Baltic about 1600* (1940); also, importantly, P. Jeannin, 'Les Comptes du Sund', in *Revue historique*, ccxxxi (1964) pp. 55–102 and pp. 307–40.
73 H. and P. Chaunu, *Séville et l'Atlantique, 1504–1650* (Paris, 1955–1960).
74 P. Deyon, *Amiens, capitale provinciale au XVIIe siècle* (Paris, 1967); also 'Variations de la production textile aux XVIe et XVIIe siècles', in *Annales* (1963) pp. 939–55.
75 P. Goubert, op. cit., p. 336; also J. Delumeau, *L'Alun de Rome (XVe–XIXe siècle)* (Paris, 1962).
76 A. D. Lublinskaya, *French Absolutism: the Crucial Phase, 1620–1629*, trans. B. Pearce (Cambridge, 1968) p. 329. See D. Parker, 'The Social Foundations of French Absolutism, 1610–1630', in *Past and Present* (Nov 1971) pp. 67–89, for an adverse critique of Lublinskaya's theories. In support of Porshnev, he claims that 'feudal social relations' remained 'dominant' in the seventeenth century and that therefore, in terms of Marxist theory, the bourgeoisie were 'feudalised'. He rejects both Mousnier and Lublinskaya for implying 'in different ways' that an 'embourgeoisement' of the monarchy resulted either from venality or from the economic policies of the absolutist state (p. 88).
77 P. Goubert, op. cit., p. 335.
78 E. J. Hobsbawm, op. cit., p. 7.
79 A. Lloyd Moote, op. cit., pp. 59–62.
80 R. Mousnier, 'L'évolution des institutions monarchiques en France et ses relations avec l'état social', in *XVIIe Siècle* (1963), p. 64; also, 'Etat et commissaire. Recherches sur la création des intendants des provinces (1634–1648)', in *Forschungen zu Staat und Verfassung: Festgabe für Fritz Hartung* (Berlin, 1958) pp. 325–44.
81 A. Lloyd Moote, op. cit., pp. 80 and 165.
82 See infra, Chapter 7, pp. 218–21.
83 A. Lloyd Moote, op. cit., pp. 125–41.
84 Ibid., pp. 215–17.
85 Ibid., Part iii, pp. 91–219, *passim*.
86 Ibid., pp. 186–190.
87 Ibid., p. 184.
88 Ibid., p. 194.
89 Ibid., p. 127.
90 J. H. Shennan, *The Parlement de Paris* (London, 1968) p. 264.
91 A. Lloyd Moote, op. cit., p. 172.

92   L. Goldmann, *Le Dieu Caché* (Paris, 1955); also R. Mandrou, *La France aux XVIIe et XVIIIe siècles*, Nouvelle Clio, p. 121.
93   See infra, p. 50–1.
94   A. Lloyd Moote, op. cit., p. 357.
95   Cited P. Goubert, *Louis XIV et Vingt Millions de Français* (Paris, 1965) p. 65.
96   A. Lloyd Moote, op. cit., p. 176.
97   P. Sonnino, 'The Dating and Authorship of Louis XIV's *Mémoires*', in *French Historical Studies* (1964) pp. 303–37. The rehabilitation of the *Mémoires* as a valid expression of Louis XIV's own mind, initiated by the work of J. Longnon in the 1920s, has been consolidated by Sonnino's research. See also his introduction to his edition and American translation of the work, *Mémoires for the Instruction of the Dauphin* (New York, 1970).
98   Translated from *Mémoires de Louis XIV*, ed. J. Longnon (Paris, 1927) p. 37.
99   Ibid., p. 39.
100   Ibid.
101   Ibid., p. 156.
102   Cited A. Lloyd Moote, op. cit., pp. 359–60.
103   F. Bluche, 'L'origine sociale des Secrétaires d'Etat de Louis XIV (1161–1715), in *XVIIe Siècle*, Nos. 42–43, pp. 8–22.
104   Ibid., p. 16.
105   R. Mousnier, 'Quelques aspects de la fonction publique dans la société française du XVIIe siècle', in *XVIIe Siècle*, Nos. 42–43, p. 5.
106   J. H. Shennan, *Government and Society in France, 1461–1661* (London, 1969), pp. 65–6.
107   F. Bluche, op. cit., p. 9.
108   Translated from J. Longnon, op. cit., p. 30.
109   Ibid.
110   Ibid., p. 17.
111   P. Goubert, op. cit., p. 90.
112   Mme de Sévigné, *Correspondance*, ed. R. Duchêne, Vol. I (Paris, 1972) p. 106.
113   See infra, Chapter 8, pp. 242–3.
114   M. Marion, *Dictionnaire des Institutions de la France aux XVIIe et XVIIIe siècles* (Paris, 1923; reprinted 1968) p. 522.
115   See supra, p. 44.
116   M. Marion, op. cit., p. 480.
117   R. Mandrou, *La France aux XVIIe et XVIIIe siècles*, p. 118, also the *tableaux chronologiques*, under 'société', pp. 32–57. See also, R. Mandrou, *Louis XIV en son temps*, pp. 156–7.
118   P. Clément, ed., *Lettres, instructions et mémoires de Colbert* (Paris, 1861–82) Vol. IV, pp. 27–43.
119   Ibid., p. 28.
120   Ibid., p. 29.
121   Ibid., p. 30.
122   Ibid.
123   Ibid., p. 31.
124   Ibid.
125   Ibid.
126   Ibid, p. 30.
127   Ibid., p. 32.
128   Ibid., p. 35.
129   Ibid., pp. 34–9.
130   Ibid., pp. 39–43.
131   J. Lough, ed., *Locke's Travels in France, 1675–1679* (London, 1953) p. 156.

132 E. Lavisse, *Histoire de France*, Vol. vii, Part i, p. 194.

133 e.g. H. G. Judge, *Louis XIV* (London, 1965) p. 89.

134 e.g. Letter of 15 April 1683 to M. de Bercy, *Intendant* at Riom: 'It is right that you should be advised that the *Cour des Aydes* at Clermont complains strongly about everything you do . . . you should act with a great deal of moderation, and, in executing the orders you receive from His Majesty, you must always regulate your conduct according to the *ordonnances* and the regulations. It will be very fitting and agreeable to the King if, when the *Cour des Aydes* wishes to enter into discussions with you, you explain to them the reasons for acting in the way you do . . .' P. Clément, ed., *Lettres, Instructions et Mémoires de Colbert*, ii pp. 218–19. Also, the Letter of 1 June 1674 to M. de Menars, *Intendant* at Orléans: 'you must continually read your *commission*, know it by heart, as indeed you should know all the articles which deal with the powers of the *maîtres des requêtes* in the provinces.' This last advice was occasioned by de Menars having attempted to impose his jurisdiction over the *lieutenant-général* of Gien. Disputing his competence to do this, Colbert reminds him that his 'principal application must be to know fully the extent of the power which the King has given' him. P. Clément, op. cit., iv p. 109.

135 R. Mousnier, 'L'évolution des institutions monarchiques en France et ses relations avec l'état social', in *XVIIe Siècle* (1963) p. 64.

136 J. H. M. Salmon, op. cit., p. 33.

137 Ibid., p. 32.

138 e.g. Letter of 18 May 1674 to M. de Sève, *Intendant* at Bordeaux: 'Therefore, I feel it my duty to notify you that you could do nothing more pleasing to His Majesty than to suppress this great number of *sub-délégués*.' P. Clément, op. cit., iv p. 108; also, the general circular to the *Intendants* of 15 June 1682: 'The King has noticed in various matters frequently brought to his *conseil des finances* that MM. *les intendans et commissaires départis dans les provinces* have often pronounced judgements on matters over which His Majesty has not given them any authority, and that even notwithstanding the letters which I have written to them on his instruction . . . on the conduct of permanent *sub-délégués*, the majority of the said *intendans* . . . have established them and establish them daily . . . His Majesty orders me to write to you that he wishes you to examine with care all the matters which you have power to take cognizance of . . . and in addition His Majesty desires that you do not appoint any general *sub-délégués* to undertake all sorts of business, but only for particular items of business which you cannot undertake personally.' P. Clément, op. cit., iv pp. 155–6.

139 G. Pagès, *Les Origines du XVIIIe siècle au temps de Louis XIV (1680–1715)* (Centre de Documentation universitaire, Paris, 1961) p. 23.

2 A Century of Conflict: the Economic and Social Disorders of the 'Grand Siècle'*

HUBERT MÉTHIVIER

I

Let us finally reject the legend of the French seventeenth century, which sees it as an age of royal grandeur and unquestioning conformity, the apogee of the *ancien régime*, an age between a turbulent and strife-torn sixteenth century and an eighteenth century already stagnant and in process of dissolution. We are duly impressed by the monarchical exteriors of the Louvre and Versailles, the French hegemony in Europe and the achievements of classicism in literature and the arts; but the real social drama enacted in the towns and countryside of seventeenth-century France was something altogether more tragic. Foreign and civil wars, with their constant passage of troops, left ruin on the land. Gaston Roupnel[1] documented well enough the almost thirty years of pillage and atrocity which made of Burgundy in the mid-seventeenth century an accurate enough reflection of the art of Jacques Callot. The 'Grand Siècle' was a harsh and insensitive age, when even the kindly Mme de Sévigné could recite with equanimity the atrocities committed in the suppression of the Breton uprising of 1675. It was an age when everything was in conflict, and nothing suggests an age of resolution, serenity and classical order.

There is always a great temptation to schematise the seventeenth century into a simplifying model; with a first period seen largely as a continuation of the turmoil of the sixteenth century, the age of Henry IV, Louis XIII and Mazarin, the age of the 'Baroque', of mysticism and ultramontanism, of gallicanism and Jansenism, of preciosity and *libertinage*, culminating in the multiplicity of the Frondes; followed by a middle period of seventeenth-century classicism, from about 1660 to 1685, with Louis XIV at his zenith, surrounded and served by the minds of constructive statesmen, establishing order in all spheres of the

* Translated from H. Méthivier, 'Les fièvres économiques et sociales du "Grand Siècle"', *L'Ancien Régime*, 6th ed., revised (Presses Universitaires, Paris, 1974) pp. 63–78.

national life, the age of Colbert, Louvois, Vauban, Bossuet, Boileau and Le Brun, radiating serenity over a submissive and bemused Europe. And then, at length, the 'end of the reign', bringing decline, with everything checkmated and everywhere distress and a sense of failure.

In fact, current research suggests a more complex and disconcerting reality: Roland Mousnier envisages a seventeenth century in crisis in every aspect, whether spiritual, intellectual, economic, social or political. The word 'crisis' indeed recurs in his general study of the age like a *leitmotiv*.[2] Robert Mandrou talks of the period 1660–80 as the 'temps difficiles',[3] and Pierre Leon discerns the elements of a final crisis through to 1715.[4] Pierre Goubert, however, suggests a more varied image;[5] and Carrière,[6] Delumeau[7] and Morineau[8] contrast the continuing prosperity of the maritime fringes of France with the general stagnation of the interior.

II

The background of the period is one of an increasing shortage of specie, resulting for the most part from war and a fall in mining production, combined with a major movement in prices.[9] The sixteenth-century price-rise continued until about 1630 and was then followed by a period of stagnating prices from 1630 to 1650, although we must of course take into account variations in the general pattern, according to product and region. Prices remained more or less depressed until about 1730, although the curve was broken by violent short-term movements upward in the years 1693–4, 1709–10, 1720 and 1725.

The *seigneurie*†, which regulated the legal relationships between the inhabitants of the landed estates, weighed heavily upon the rural population. It was rare for a whole *terroir*† or administrative village to belong to a single *seigneur*, since the *seigneuries*, large or small, were often divided into quite small units. The *seigneur* levied the rents, the *métayages*† or *champarts*† on the *domaine proche*†; and the *cens*†, *banalités*† and *lods et ventes*† on the tenants of his *mouvance*†. Although the political influence of the *seigneurie* had been eroded by the action of royal *officiers*†, it nevertheless remained an economic force through the customary dues it raised on agricultural labour. A seigneurial fortune, however, could only be made out of a host of small revenues, whose levying, and also use in the case of rents in kind, required efficient administration. Hence the negligence of numerous *seigneurs* and the falling into disuse of various seigneurial rights. *Seigneuries* indeed tended only to prosper in the hands of families who possessed other sources of income, such as trade, and who could direct into their estates the surplus from their other activities and their business experience. The *domaine eminent*† brought in little to the *seigneur* except from his rights over land transfers, the *lods et ventes*, and the proceeds from exercising justice. It was, however, the most tangible survival of 'feudalism' and it was this which maintained the social primacy of the nobility. The *domaine utile*†, on the other hand, was profitable. Hence the attempts by both old and new families to resume control over so many *métairies*† and the reconsolidation of the *domaines proches* previously let out on lease. Families whose fortunes were solely 'seigneurial', in the sense that they possessed nothing beyond the power of their *directe*† over a *mouvance*, were often reduced to fertilising their estates by marriage into the Robe or finance. Although the old nobility benefited from the fall in prices under Louis XIV, through less heavy expenditure on consumption (except at Court), it remained nevertheless extremely vulnerable to agricultural crises, which caused its rents virtually to dry up; and it found itself powerless in face of the periodic and catastrophic rises in the price of agrarian products which characterised the end of Louis XIV's reign.

Throughout the century, both during the period of rising prices, which favoured the large-scale producer, and during the period of falling prices under Louis XIV, the regrouping of estates slowly pursued its course. This was as much for legal possession as for economic exploitation, since the *seigneur* could in spite of everything bide his time in selling his grain and wine and thus profit from the movement of prices, which the tenant or *métayer* could not do. We must without doubt follow Marc Bloch and distinguish between two types of *seigneurs*: those who brought to the land capital acquired elsewhere, in the way Colbert did, from those who drew their incomes solely from their estates, in the way Mme de Sévigné did. These latter managed to make do from the produce of their estates, but being unable to buy back alienated tenures, often sought to enclose lands through their rights of *triage*, which affected a third of these.

In economic terms, the *seigneurie* lived from agriculture; directly in the case of those who cultivated the soil, and indirectly for those deriving rent from it, namely the *seigneurs* and those who exacted tithe. Agricultural techniques did not permit production beyond a level scarcely affording subsistence, nor the avoidance of the harsh effects of crop failure. Except for local specialisation, which was very common and included the production of such crops as hemp, flax, madder-wort and woad, the major cultivation was of the vine and corn, which included all bread-producing grain, wheat being a luxury of the rich. Second-class cereals indeed predominated, and a great deal of *méteil*† – a mixture of wheat, rye, barley and oats – was grown. Millet and buckwheat were grown in the west and centre; maize in the south-west. Peasant food consisted largely of black bread, rough pastries, porridges, soups, milk products and cheese, together with beans, chestnuts, peas and lentils; on feast-days this was supplemented with coarse bacon and poultry.

The Problems of the Peasantry

The primary need was for the peasant to crop as much of the land as possible, since bread was the staple of all existence, symbolised by the ritual cross marked with a knife on bread about to be cut. From this elemental need also derived the periodic uprooting of vines by official order. Pasture was poor and cattle accordingly lean; usually two-thirds to a half the weight of twentieth-century beasts. Pasture was restricted to the fallow, the waste, the heath and the common forests, and to the fields after harvest, through use of the right of *'parcours'*† and *'vaine pâture'*†. The problem of manure was a vicious circle. Poor beasts and few in number, reared on poor feed because of lack of manure, created in turn only poor manure themselves. The soil was incapable of enriching the cattle and the cattle could not enrich the soil. Restoration and nourishment of the soil was achieved by the system of the fallow; one year in two in the Midi, one in three in the north. Often, and to some extent almost everywhere, there were pockets of land in cultivation only three or four years in ten. Labour was unproductive. Cows and poor-quality horses were harnessed to the plough. Yoke-oxen represented affluence. Swing-ploughs scratched the surface of the soil without actually working it. The plough itself is a tool of the fertile plain. Work in the main was done by hand, with spade, hoe, sickle and flail. Seed was often forced to make good the lack of manure, but often withered in the stem. As a result came the poor feed and the poor yields.

The depressed and undernourished rural population, victim of incessant epidemics, with a low life expectancy for men, who were old at forty, constantly tended to overtake the capacity for subsistence and existed on the verge of famine. And this was not only at times of agricultural crisis. The peasant was incessantly required to make monetary payments, either for royal taxes, for tithe or for payment of seigneurial dues or rent. To meet these multiple demands the peasant was constrained to sell his produce. Prices fell after 1640, but his payments did not. Moreover, he was always the victim of the seasonal fall in prices which followed the harvest, since he was compelled to put his grain on the market, whereas the large-scale producer or *rentier* could bide his time. He was, moreover, the victim of spasmodic price-rises, since if his own production fell below his family requirements, he was forced onto the markets to satisfy his need for grain or bread. Even if, initially, he produced enough for subsistence, he often had to sell a large part of his harvest in haste. Then he found himself forced to borrow and involve himself in debt, or sell off his land, or finally join the great army of seventeenth-century vagrants.

To a society so vulnerable to the slightest movement in prices, to seasonal variation and bad weather, changes in any of these areas brought immense social and demographic consequences. Among these we are beginning to discern movements of both short- and long-term duration:

(a) *Movements of short duration*. Periodic crises occurred, interrupting long periods of either rising or falling prices. These arose from accidental circumstances which were either meteorological, agricultural, financial or demographic in origin. All these crises of the *ancien régime* arose in the first place from the land and the actual conditions of agrarian production. The virtual monoculture of cereal crops was enough after two bad years in succession to create famine conditions and widespread *mortalité*. Not a year passed without one province or another being affected. Sometimes the whole realm was hit. Excessive drought or its reverse, hail, floods or late frost, could bring social disaster.[10] Late frosts, indeed, could paralyse the water mills and stop the transport of grain. The great '*mortalités*' of the century were those in 1629–30, 1636–7, 1648–51 (had this indeed no influence on the Fronde?), 1660–2, 1693–4, 1698, 1709–10. These all brought disastrous increases in the price of grain, which, for example, reached some 300 per cent in Beauvais in 1693. Social remedies for this situation were both difficult to implement and ineffective. Works of public and private charity, the 'King's bread' given out free in Paris in the crisis of 1693–4, corn imports brought in from Poland or North Africa, were all merely palliatives and entirely inadequate to the problem.

Famine always brought epidemics. Smallpox, typhus, cholera and child-birth fever could increase the death-rate four or five times and sometimes cut down twenty-five to thirty-five per cent of the population, multiplying at the same time the number of vagrants, already high in normal times. The countryside always suffered more than the towns, since these held stocks of grain in reserve. In times of dearth, villagers were reduced to eating the roots and grasses which contemporary sources constantly speak of. In these periods, the poor lost two or three times more than the rich, who were always better provided for. Contiguous areas were often hit differently. The plateau of Picardy, a highly populated corn-producing region, suffered far greater '*mortalités*' than the region of Bray, where there was crop-diversification and cattle-rearing, which confirms the vulnerability of the old peasantry dependent on the production of a single crop. In the same way, the parish registers show that children paid most dearly, and that these '*mortalités*' brought in their train a fall in the number of marriages and births (often by more than fifty per cent), which in due course brought a decrease in the number of marriages and births some sixteen to thirty years later. The evidence suggests that as soon as good harvests returned, the number of children rose once more and the population took another step forward.

Dearth also brought economic crisis. It created a shortage of labour, lowered agricultural and manufacturing production and depressed commercial demand. It brought unemployment and distress to artisans, a lowering of monetary capacity all round and the denuding of the royal treasury. An undernourished proletariat existed in both countryside and town, candidates for death in the next ensuing famine.

It has been suggested that the normal growth of the population was alone sufficient to increase demand beyond the inflexible limits of subsistence; and that from this arose the periods of high food prices, which were followed inexorably by a tide of death from the ensuing distress, which in itself brought about, as an inevitable consequence, a lowering of prices through the falling away in demand. This may well have been so. Roland Mousnier and Pierre Goubert both insist on directing research through the parish registers, grain prices, notarial records and family inventories, in order to determine whether, leaving aside the question of climatic disaster, demographic growth precedes and then accompanies the rise in prices, and, inversely, whether a fall in population precedes a fall in prices. One thing is certain: growth in a population renders it more vulnerable to dearth and the causes of high mortality.[11]

(b) *Movements of long duration.* The absence of adequate censuses makes it exceedingly difficult to determine the demographic curves of the century. It seems likely that there was a general rise in population until about 1648, bringing the population to about twenty millions. From 1649 and the period of the Fronde a reversal ensued, followed by a semi-catastrophic fall. In general terms, the period 1650–1720 saw a decline in population, which was a common European phenomenon. The research of Pierre Goubert into the region of the Beauvaisis reveals a decline amounting to twenty and sometimes to as much as fifty per cent;[12] and this decline was accompanied by an impoverishment of all social groups. The rural nobility becomes indebted, marries its daughters to wealthy peasant owners or larger farmers and compels its sons into careers involving *dérogeance*†, in order to save the family estates. The lowering of land values and of all rents from land lowered the purchasing power of the rural classes as a whole, both of *seigneur* and peasant alike. It is to be noted that to some extent almost everywhere the situation of the provincial *gentilhommerie* continued to worsen until about 1730.

In 1700 Vauban estimated the French population at nineteen millions. This was certainly an underestimation, because he relied on counting '*feux*'†, or the registers compiled for purposes of the new Capitation tax; and, in addition, he failed to take into account the whole mass of vagrants. After the disastrous winter of 1709, Forbonnais estimated that the population had fallen to sixteen or seventeen millions. It is impossible in fact to estimate the fall with any precision; but whatever its scale, the importance is that it was accompanied by monetary and economic difficulty, and, except for spasmodic thrusts of prices upward, by a general lowering of prices.

There are two general observations to be made. First, the *'mortalités'* of 1649–51, 1660–2, 1693–4 and 1709–10, followed as they were in due course by troughs in the population figures, seem to have occurred more frequently and to have been more serious than in the first half of the century. Second, the period of rising prices (Phase A) continued until about 1640 (the 'long sixteenth century') and then turned down into a period of falling prices which reached its lowest point toward 1690. This was followed by what may be termed a 'saw-edge' of price fluctuations, caused by monetary inflation and seasonal dearths, which did not however mask the real situation, which was one of stagnating prices. From 1650, France entered a Phase B, of depression, stagnation and restriction. These were the 'difficult times' of Colbert, who strove to stimulate the economy while at the same time heralding an age of *gloire et magnificence* and asserting that France was not in 'un règne de petites choses'. Everything contracted: the quantity of specie, the level of demand, production, commercial profits and population. The recession was aggravated by monetary manipulations on the part of an impoverished government, especially during the period of Pontchartrain as *contrôleur-général*, from 1689 to 1699, which provoked a cascade of inflation and deflation, severe in its consequences for both producers and consumers, paralysing business contracts, creating bankruptcies and unemployment, with all their social consequences. Boisguilbert noted that in thirty years the price of lands and rents had fallen by half.[13]

It is certain, as Mousnier has observed, that the movement of prices cannot explain everything. During both 'Phase A' and 'Phase B', separated as they were by the plateau of 1640–50, violent fluctuations occurred. For example, the *'mortalité'* of 1630 brought a fall in prices through falling demand after a short-term rise. It was indeed this fall which made the financial demands of the state all the more oppressive and served to bring about the explosion of popular uprisings which culminated in the years 1636–9. The general transition from rising to falling prices, which represented a major reversal in the economic *'conjoncture'*, must have played an essential role in producing these uprisings, which convulsed province after province during the period 1623–75, over and beyond the role played by climatic crises and disease. The undernourished mass of the population, already depressed by the heavy taxation and high prices of Louis XIII's reign, suffered in turn the harsh consequences of prices which were too low to enable them to assemble enough money to pay their seigneurial dues, their rents and the king's taxes. A great deal of research is needed to provide the detail of regional variations, especially in regard to the 'geography of prices', and to establish the relationships between fluctuations in prices and demographic movements.[14]

III

Town and Countryside: some Examples and Soundings

A progressive appropriation of the land by bourgeois elements was in process everywhere, a slow regrouping of rural property by the urban bourgeoisie. The *seigneurie* of Les Rochers near Vitré only escaped the fate of appropriation with great difficulty. Mme de Sévigné declared that her rents and dues only came in very slowly and the Sévigné family, like so many others, hesitated between farming the estate themselves and leasing out the *domaine proche*, and for the *directe*, between introducing the system of the *domaine congéable* and alienation in perpetuity. In Haut-Quercy, the estate of Belcastel, already reduced by alienation, only just escaped falling into the grasping hands of a creditor, who, naturally enough, was a local merchant. Everywhere, Robe families, financiers and merchants were buying up deserted or indebted land of both *seigneur* and peasant alike, just as, for example, in the wake of the ravages of the Thirty Years War and the extreme rainfall of the whole period from 1646 to 1666, the leading citizens of Dijon restored the land of the whole province; in the depopulated villages, widows, beggars and landless workers predominated.

In Burgundy, the new seigneurs preferred leases and *métayages* to the old system of 'rent' in the form of dues in kind, and the proportion of *métayers* and day-labourers accordingly increased incessantly over the tenant-farmers and the traditional form of *'rentiers'*.[15]

In Bas-Languedoc, the regrouping of land into large scale estates was achieved through the purchase of entire *seigneuries*, mostly to the profit of judicial and financial *officiers* in Montpellier, accompanied by an increased amount of land devoted to the production of corn. The eviction of the small freeholders resulted in the ruin and depopulation of many villages.[16]

In Brie, the land was basically owned by three main elements: the Court nobility, Parisian bourgeois and the chapters of well-endowed canonries. The elimination of small tenures was widespread, to the profit of large-scale farms leased out in turn to *laboureurs*, the wealthy peasant élite numbering some 4000–5000 who dominated the wine-dressers, numbering some 15 000, the day-labourers, who numbered some 17 000, and the farmhands, small-scale artisans and tradesmen, who numbered about 25 000. This agrarian capitalism very clearly drained off landed revenues toward Paris, and the rural prosperity coincided with a decline in manufacturing and commercial enterprise. The bourgeois landowners preferred office in the state because of the social advancement it provided.[17]

On the corn-growing plateau of the Paris region, the same consolidation of estates occurred, to the profit of certain individual *seigneurs* and above all of members of the Parisian bourgeoisie, who saw in the land a means of deploying their capital, with the added pleasure of acquiring a house in the country. To exploit his estates, the *bourgeois-seigneur* leased his land to *laboureurs*, the wealthy peasants, whose affluence depended above all on their livestock and their improved farm implements. They aimed to capitalise to the maximum the production demanded by the Paris market. A newer social hierarchy established itself in the life of the parishes, descending from the *bourgeois-seigneurs* through the *laboureurs* to the landless farmhands. On the other hand, in the valleys and on their hillsides, a rural 'democracy' sustained itself, of wine-dressers and small-scale market-gardeners.[18]

In the region of Beauvais and Picardy, agricultural techniques remained primitive. Cereal yields were less than nine quintals† per hectare.† Inadequate ploughing and poor cattle prevailed. A hierarchy of livestock existed. Horses were the preserve of the rich *laboureur*; cattle were rare and ill-nourished; the sheep was indeed the typical beast of the region. In the *Election* of Beauvais, the peasants held less than half the land, and it was the worst of the land at that. In spite of supplementing their farming with textile work, they were grossly in debt. A family needed from fifteen to twenty-five hectares to maintain itself.[19] We can distinguish three periods: a first phase of great expectations, from 1600 to 1647. This was followed by a reversal of trends, accentuated by the bad harvests of 1649 and 1651. The third phase was one of stagnation and widespread mortality, between 1691 and 1710. The victims of this social development were the nobility and the small peasants. It was the *laboureurs*, who had been able to speculate on the grain market, and the bourgeois who expropriated the nobility who were the victors. The 'rural bourgeoisie' established itself triumphantly.

Industry in Picardy was above all in the countryside and 'revolved' with an agricultural rhythm. Each year saw a long period of industrial vacation, from 15 July to 15 October, for the purposes of the corn and wine harvests. In an over-populated Picardy, where three-quarters of the peasants did not hold a tenth of the land, the only possible recourse was to linen and woollen manufacture. By 1708, out of a total work-force of 8000, only 3000 were inside the towns in organised gilds. Dozens of thousands of rural workers in general belonged to capitalist '*manufactures*', entirely outside the urban corporations. The great merchants of Amiens and Beauvais controlled these '*manufactures*' and their family dynasties dominated the whole life of the region.

The general curve of the manufacturing graph is not surprising, given the economic '*conjoncture*': a thousand workers in Beauvais before 1640; some six hundred under Louis XIV, and approximately nine hundred after 1715. The same curve developed at Amiens, at that time the leading textile city of France, coming before Reims, Rouen and Beauvais.[20] The coarsest and cheapest cloths sold best during the reign of Louis XIV; but production of these also experienced recession, with small independent manufacturers failing and becoming owners of small workshops only, often in debt and serving as jobbers for the large-scale traders. The likelihood is that in this area, as in the ports,[21] there was a reinforcement of commercial capitalism arising from the general impoverishment and proletarianisation of the small craftsman.[22]

IV

French Seventeenth-Century Society according to Porshnev and Mousnier

The Soviet historian Porshnev has used the important papers of Chancellor Séguier in the Leningrad archive to draw up an inventory of the popular uprisings in France from 1623 to 1648, and to attempt to draw from them an interpretation of the politico-social structure of seventeenth-century France.[23] The reports of the *intendants* speak in unison of an endemic insurrectional situation, with peasants and workers confronting the agents of the king, the '*gabeleurs*', the tax-officials and the tax-farmers. Sporadic explosions occurred in a chain reaction, sometimes anti-feudal, always anti-fiscal. The deep-rooted cause was the excessive tension of the masses, undernourished and existing precariously on the frontier of famine and social despair, after years of enduring dearth and inflation, followed as we have seen by deflation. The occasion of the revolts was the flood-tide of royal taxation. It was an attempt to introduce *élus* into Quercy in 1624 which occasioned revolt. It was the same in Burgundy in 1630 and in Provence and Languedoc in the same year and again in 1631. Who can determine whether these attempts on the part of the government were part of a systematic design to create a unified and reformed financial structure, aimed at transforming the *pays d'états*† into *pays d'élections*†? And, if this were indeed so, whether its author was Marillac or Richelieu? We do know that in the event the latter compromised everywhere. One knows too the years of confusion and chaos in France. From 1630 to 1632, Dijon, Aix and Lyons rose in revolt. In 1636 the *Croquants* convulsed Périgord, Limousin and Saintonge, and likewise in 1639 the *Nu-Pieds* convulsed Normandy. In 1643, the west, centre and south-west of France were everywhere in insurrection.

According to Porshnev, a 'class-front' existed; a bloc, consisting of the monarchy, the nobility and the bourgeoisie, united in defence of the

'feudal-absolutist order' against the mass of the people. The revolts and
the peasant *jacqueries* were at one and the same time anti-feudal and
anti-fiscal, from the very fact that an alliance existed between the pro-
perty-owning and ruling classes, whether they were noble or bourgeois,
and that both were sustained in their social primacy by the framework of
the monarchy. The social structure remained entirely feudal. Capitalism,
restricted as it was by privilege and the monarchy, only affected the
towns. The bourgeoisie was only able to enter the ruling class by raising
itself and by merging little by little with the nobility, by sliding, so to
say, into the aristocratic state. 'Venality has not led to an *"embourgeoisement"* of the state but to a *"feudalisation"* of a section of the bourgeoisie', according to Porshnev. For him 'venality of office was a means of
separating the bourgeoisie from the revolutionary struggle with feudalism.' The *officier* of bourgeois origin, living *'noblement'*, in his *'dignité'*
and with his *'qualité d'honneur'*, to use the expression of Loyseau, was
the instrument of the *noblesse d'Etat*, of whom Richelieu himself was
representative.

In reply to Porshnev, Roland Mousnier has reasserted the classic
schema of Pagès. For him, the monarchy had despoiled the feudal class
of its public power through the use of bourgeois *officiers*, and then, in
the seventeenth century, it had had to destroy the power of the *officiers*
by means of *commissaires*, recruited indeed from the same elements in
society. But, says Mousnier, the *officiers* sought to defend themselves;
hence the Fronde. He accepts that the social escalator ascended constantly and that a part of the bourgeoisie became integrated gradually
into the nobility, through acquisition of estates, through marriage and
through office in the state, and that the Robe rivalled and ultimately allied
itself with the Sword. But, for Mousnier, Porshnev omits to take into
account or confuses several points:

(a) Porshnev defines as 'feudal' what is in essence 'seigneurial', which is
to perpetrate a confusion of terms. In the French seventeenth century
there were no longer medieval feudal domains, surviving as closed economies, based on servile labour. There was instead a peasantry which
was legally free and often owning land, even though it was under the
economic domination of the *seigneurs*. Capitalism had already determined
that an economy based on exchange should exist everywhere, even in the
rural areas, where the peasant-artisans, working for large-scale merchant-
manufacturers, were legion. Far from acting as a brake on capitalist
development, the privileges and monopolies granted to the large-scale
merchants stimulated such development during this primary stage, since
competitive prices would have been too low to be profitable.

(b) Mousnier accepts that an *officier* of some importance was legally
'noble'. There is no doubt of it. But he was never at that time regarded
as a *gentilhomme*. He was the object of irony on the part of the true

nobility, who considered him a '*gentilhomme of the pen and inkhorn*'. Loyseau complained bitterly that *officiers* were not considered truly noble, even though they were marquises and barons.[25] And, in regard to the authority of the state, the monarchy is most certainly a very different thing, Mousnier maintains, when the *Conseil* is formed from a majority of the *noblesse d'épée* from when, in the seventeenth century, it is formed from a majority of *robins*.

(c) Mousnier has also noted that Porshnev saw in these rebellions a conflict between classes formed on a horizontal basis, superimposed one on the other. Now, although there was no longer anything either economically or politically which could rightly be termed 'feudal', there were nevertheless many residual traces of feudalism in the psychological, moral and social structure of the period. The existence of '*clientèles*' and family dynasties surrounding a great nobleman in the provinces bears witness to this; as do the vendettas for the sake of honour and '*gloire*' pursued by the heroes of Corneille against the 'tyranny' of the state. Many of the nobles justified their sedition by an appeal to 'fidelity'. They belonged, they would say, to M. de Rohan or to M. Montmorency. We should therefore, according to Mousnier, speak rather of a 'vertical society'. All the reports of the *intendants* are indeed explicit about this; that even though the rural and urban poor constituted the shock-troops of revolt, there were always those ready to organise and encourage them, whom we should call the 'middle-class', sometimes members of the clergy, and there were always *gentilshommes* to lead them. If it is true that peasant *jacqueries* occurred, there was also involvement and general collusion between *seigneurs* and peasants, to advance their common interest against royal taxation and the agents of the royal fisc. Even in normal times, increased taxation limited the proportion of rents and dues the peasant could render his *seigneur*. In a bad year, or in the event of a fall in prices, royal taxation actually prevented the peasant altogether from paying his feudal rent, the *champarts* and other dues.

The *seigneur* accordingly encouraged the peasant in his refusal to pay taxes. The *seigneur* was after all close at hand, powerful in the locality, surrounded by friends, family and his *protégés*, armed withal with the power of local justice. The peasant had therefore more interest in following his *seigneur* than in remaining loyal to a remote king. The revolts always began by acts of violence against the tax-collectors or the agents of the tax-farmers. Taxes could no longer indeed be raised except by force. Rebellion frequently enjoyed the complicity, tacit or active, of certain of the royal *officiers* themselves. This was so in Aix in 1630 and again of members of the Rouen *Parlement* in 1639. It is true, and Mousnier accepts Porshnev's point, that many *officiers* 'feudalised themselves' in order to integrate themselves into the nobility; and, further, that these ennobled *officiers* of the high Robe, the *parlementaires*, social hybrids as they were, half-bourgeois and half-seigneur, then defended the interests of privilege, even to the extent of defending what may be termed a 'feudal order' of society, when they pleaded for a 'limited' monarchy against the harsh fiscalism of Richelieu and Mazarin.

But, far from perceiving an alliance between monarchy and nobility against the common people, Mousnier sees an *entente* between people and *seigneurs* against the king, who was 'guilty of levying the taxes' for the national defence against Spain. The king found himself compelled to reinforce the absolutist state through the use of *commissaires*, the *intendants*, sent out from his *Conseil*; in order to enforce the obedience of the *'populace'* as well as that of members of the nobility who were 'feudal' in spirit and of *officiers* who were anxious for noble status, by dispossessing them of part of their function and power. This was the great point of incidence between politics and society in seventeenth-century France.

NOTES

1 G. Roupnel, *Les Populations de la ville et de la campagne dijonnaise au XVIIe siècle* (Paris, 2nd ed., revised, 1955).

2 R. Mousnier, *Les XVIe et XVIIe siècles* (Paris, 1954).
   [Editor's note:] It is this work which has been the subject of extended adverse criticism by A. D. Lublinskaya in *French Absolutism: the crucial phase, 1620–1629*, trans. B. Pearce (Cambridge, 1968) pp. 6–38.

3 [Editor's note:] The phrase *'Les temps difficiles'* is also used by J. Meuvret as the title of his chapter on the French economy under Louis XIV in *La France au temps de Louis XIV* (Paris, 1965) pp. 57–83.

4 [Editor's note:] P. Léon, 'La crise de l'économie française à la fin du règne de Louis XIV (1685–1715)', in *Information historique*, Vol. xviii (1956) pp. 127–37.

5 [Editor's note:] P. Goubert, *Louis XIV et Vingt Millions de Français* (Paris, 1966; translated *Louis XIV and Twenty Million Frenchmen*, London, 1970). See also supra, Chapter 1, pp. 28–9.

6 [Editor's note:] C. Carrière, *Les négociants marseillais au XVIIIe siècle*, 2 vols (Marseille, 1973). Also, C. Carrière (with P. Léon), 'L'appel des marchés', in *Histoire économique et sociale de la France, 1660–1789*, Vol. ii pp. 161–215.

7 [Editor's note:] J. Delumeau, *Le mouvement du port de Saint-Malo à la fin du XVIIe siècle, 1681–1720* (Institut de recherches historiques de Rennes, 1966); also, 'Le commerce extérieur français au XVIIe siècle', in *XVIIe Siècle*, Nos. 70–171 (1966) pp. 81–105.

8 [Editor's note:] M. Morineau, 'Flottes de commerce et trafics français en Méditerranée au XVIIe siècle, in *XVIIe Siècle*, Nos. 86–87 (1970) pp. 135–71.

9 [Editor's note:] For the expansion of the economic material of this chapter, see, initially, *Histoire économique et sociale de la France*, Vol. ii, 1660–1789, and in particular P. Goubert, 'Le "tragique" XVIIe siècle', in *Troisième partie*, 'D'une économie en contraction à une économie en expansion'. Also, R. Mandrou, *Les XVIIe et XVIIIe siècles*. (Nouvelle Clio), (Paris, 1967)—and the excellent bibliographies of both these works.

10 [Editor's note:] E. Le Roy-Ladurie, 'History and Climate', in *Economy and Society in Early Modern Europe: Essays from Annales*, ed. P. Burke, pp. 134–69.

11 [Editor's note:] See Chapter i, notes 60 and 61.

12 [Editor's note:] P. Goubert, 'En Beauvaisis: problèmes démographiques du XVIIe siècle', in *Annales, ESC* (1952) pp. 453–68; also, *Beauvais et le Beauvaisis de 1600 à 1730* (Paris, 1960).

13 [Editor's note:] It is interesting that Boisguilbert's figure of 1695 was given by Locke in his Journal on 1 May 1676: 'The rents of Lands in France fallen above ½ in these few years . . .'. *Locke's Travels in France, 1675–9*, ed. J. Lough (Cambridge, 1953) p. 89.

14 The works of François Simiand, Marc Bloch, Lucien Febvre and Jean Meuvret deal with the economic aspects of the French seventeenth century and the problem of subsistence. The works of Charles Carrière, Jean Delumeau and M. Morineau oppose the activity and prosperity of the 'maritime fringes' of the realm at the end of Louis XIV's reign to the economic 'Phase B' which affected the interior. The volume of trade could be more indicative than price-movements.

15 P. de Saint-Jacob, *Documents sur la Communauté villageoise en Bourgogne* (1962).

16 E. Le Roy-Ladurie, 'Montpellier et sa campagne', in *Annales, E.S.C.* (1957); also *Les Paysans de Languedoc* (Paris, 1966; published in an abridged form by Flammarion, Paris, 1969, under the same title).

17 E. Mireaux, *Une province française au temps du Grand Roi: La Brie* (Paris, 1952).

18 J. Meuvret, 'Le Commerce des grains et farines à Paris', in *Revue d'histoire moderne et contemporaine* (1956); also, M. Venard, *Bourgeois et paysans au XVIIe siècle: le rôle des bourgeois parisiens au sud de Paris* (S.E.V.P.E.N., 1957); also, M. Philipponneau, *L'évolution historique de la vie rurale dans le banlieue parisienne* (unpublished thesis, 1955).

19 [Editor's note:] See P. Goubert, 'The French Peasantry of the Seventeenth Century: a Regional Example', in *Past and Present*, No. 10 (1956; reprinted in *Crisis in Europe. 1560–1660*, ed. T. Aston, 1965, pp. 154–6), where Goubert estimates 'a minimum of 12 hectares . . . in years of plenty, and 27 hectares in years of shortage'.

20 P. Deyon, *Amiens, capitale provinciale au XVIIe siècle* (Paris, 1967).

21 See the work of Jeulin and Martin on Nantes; of Trocmé and Delafosse on La Rochelle; Vignols on Saint-Malo and Carrière on Marseilles.

22 P. Goubert, *Beauvais et le Beauvaisis*; also, 'Les techniques agricoles dans les pays picards aux XVIIe et XVIIIe siècles', in *Revue d'histoire économique et sociale* (1957); also, 'Aspects sociaux des manufactures picards et beauvaisiennes au temps de Louis XIV', in *Bulletin de la Société d'histoire moderne et contemporaine* (1953); P. Deyon, 'La production manufacturière en France au XVII siècle et ses problèmes', in *XVIIe Siècle*, Nos. 70–71 (1966).

23 See supra, Chapter 1, pp. 22–6, also infra, Chapters 3 and 4.

24 G. Pagès, 'La Vénalité des offices dans l'ancienne France', in *Revue Historique*, CLXIX (1932) pp. 477–95; 'Autour du "Grand Orage": Richelieu et Marillac, deux politiques', in *Revue Historique*, CLXXIX (1937) pp. 63–97; also infra, Chapter 5.

25 F. Bluche, in an interesting article, takes the opposite point of view to Saint-Simon and proposes that 'Louis XIV governed without recourse to the collaboration of a single bourgeois'. Legally this was so; but socially it was not. Colbert may have been noble to the second generation, but he was never a *gentilhomme* in the eyes of his time. The ministers of Louis XIV, all noble and rich in their *seigneuries*, were seen merely as *parvenus*. It was deplored that the *true* nobility was without employment in the state, except in the army. [Editor's note:] See supra, Chapter 1, pp. 45–6.

3 Popular Uprisings in France before the Fronde, 1623–1648[*]

BORIS PORSHNEV

Three motives prompted the author to undertake this present study.
First, there was the enigma of the Fronde. The common interpretation
of the Fronde of the period 1648–53, which sees it as the last attempt
of the French feudal nobility to halt the progressive development of the
absolutist monarchy, cannot satisfy anyone who has investigated the real
sources of its history. These direct one indeed toward an entirely opposite interpretation; namely, that the Fronde was a French variant of the
English bourgeois revolution which was in process of unleashing itself on
the opposite side of the Channel at that time, and a distant prologue of
the French Revolution of the eighteenth century. This is not a widely
accepted interpretation, however, because of many deeply entrenched
attitudes to French history. For Marxist historians, the bourgeois revolution existed within French society from the moment when capitalist
relationships make their appearance, that is to say in the sixteenth
century. This means that the roots, in depth, of the Revolution of 1789
extended through three centuries of the *ancien régime*. Against this
position, over the last century bourgeois historians have advanced proofs
that the Revolution of 1789 was the unique product of the eighteenth
century, even indeed of its second half. A concept of evolution underlies
their thinking. For them the Revolution did not, in fact, really change
anything; nor indeed could it have changed the gradual orientation of
French social development. On the contrary, it is seen as having returned
that development to the general line of its evolution, from which it had
been temporarily and partially deflected during the course of the eighteenth century; in the sense that the French bourgeoisie was already enjoying a considerable share of political power at the time of Colbert, but

[*] This is a translation of the author's preface to his *Narodnie Vosstaniya vo
Frantsii pered Frondoi, 1623–1648* (Moscow, 1948), made from the French edition of
the work, *Les Soulèvements Populaires en France de 1623 à 1648*, published in Paris
in 1963 under the direction of Fernand Braudel and Robert Mandrou. This translation is for the most part the preface intact. I have indicated in brackets any short
sections I have omitted, giving a summary of them for purposes of continuity.

had been expelled from it by the eighteenth-century nobility. The effect of the Revolution was therefore to restore the bourgeoisie to a position it had lost and to continue to confirm it. In the same way, according to the terms of this bourgeois explanation of French historical development, feudalism disappeared almost totally from the French countryside at an early stage, yielding place to small-scale peasant ownership; but the 'feudal reaction' of the eighteenth century revived feudalism and provoked a movement of opposition among the peasantry. Revolutionary legislation destroyed feudalism and then re-created the system of small-scale peasant ownership of the land. In face of such theories, any effort to see the Fronde as a seventeenth-century manifestation of a development entirely similar to the class-struggle which, on a much greater scale, broke out in the form of the Revolution of 1789 comes into conflict with an enormous mass of traditional opinion and academic prejudice on the part of French historiography. To the extent that this is so, however, the more interesting it becomes to undertake the effort.

The author has, however, devoted his work not to the history of the Fronde itself, but to its pre-history; in pursuance of the rule that if we wish to understand anything we must look for its origins. In order to break free from the narrow circle of arguments, so many times put forward and as many times contested by historians of the Fronde who have approached it from so many different standpoints, the author has broken away from the chronological limits of the Fronde itself. His subject of study has been those social movements which were born and multiplied in France during the course of the twenty-five years or so preceding the Fronde, namely the uprisings of the peasants and the urban poor. These formed the real base and sole possibility of all other forms of opposition to the absolutist regime, including – strange as it may seem – the opposition of the feudal aristocracy itself. It is proper to begin, therefore, by studying this base. Let us reconstruct the history of these popular uprisings, which occurred over the space of twenty-five years, and the enigma of the Fronde will be readily resolved.

The second motive for this study is the author's conviction of the elemental importance of these great popular movements, and in particular those of the peasants, if we seek to explain in a scientific manner the political, economic and cultural history of past ages. The past cannot be scientifically explained if the historian loses sight of the thrust of this subterranean and gigantic force for a single moment. Political regimes and religions, and moral, legal and ideological systems have been created to suppress and tame it.

Bourgeois historiography does not accept this. It sees popular uprisings as the result of social changes, and only minimally as their cause. To put it otherwise, it sees in these movements only transitory and temporary symptoms of disorder in the State, and in no way a force responsible for all the political and social changes in the established order. To adopt a different position would of course be to recognise in every State, including the bourgeois State, and in every religion, its class nature. We must recognise that all these agents of class domination not only suppressed but above all prevented and deflected the revolutionary action of the masses. Bourgeois historiography, however, prefers to be totally blind when it is simply a question of revolutionary threats, hidden as they are perhaps but nevertheless always there; and half-blind still when such threats break through to the surface in the form of actual uprisings. To acknowledge the existence or threat of such uprisings would be for bourgeois historiography to create its own critique of itself.

The history of the popular uprisings to which the author had decided to devote a study in depth represents in this sense a fairly typical case. French historians have of course noticed a great number of popular uprisings in seventeenth-century France. But, as a general rule, they attribute to each of them, by virtue one might say of a tacit agreement, only a local significance; as if simultaneous and analogous events elsewhere were totally unknown. In this way the revolts are prevented from influencing the traditional image of the 'Grand Siècle', taking it as a whole. No book or article exists where these localised facts are, even in some measure, dealt with as a whole and generalised on in the total perspective of French history. As a result, it is not possible to decide on their historical reality and their intrinsic value in relation to the life of this period of French history. In works of general synthesis, the popular uprisings are either not drawn attention to or are rapidly and superficially mentioned as happening by chance.

It is true that, at the end of the nineteenth century, a great French historian, Boissonnade, at the outset of his career, had the intention of making a general study of the popular uprisings in France under Richelieu. But this would no doubt have caused such a scandal in the eyes of academic circles that he preferred to abstain from this enterprise, sacrificing the time and work he had already devoted to it. He only published a short article, in 1902, which was localised in character;[1] and then, at the end of his life, in a work devoted to another subject, he gave a list of certain archives he had gone through, showing what a vast and unexplored terrain still waited to be uncovered in the French archives.[2] In other words, the theme of French seventeenth-century uprisings, taken as a whole, has not had its historian; and, in this sense, it is now being studied for the first time. The essential aim of this present study is to establish the given fact, namely the saturation of French social life during this period by these popular uprisings.

[A short section follows at this point, giving details of the increasing accessibility of local archive material necessary for such a study.]

The author's third motive for undertaking the present study is precisely the existence of a most valuable manuscript source in one of the archives of the U.S.S.R., which casts a new light on the history of the popular uprisings in France before the Fronde, in the years 1630–40; namely, part of the archive of Chancellor Séguier, preserved in the Department of Manuscripts of the Saltykov-Shchedrin State Public Library in Leningrad, which in turn is part of the Dubrovsky collection of autographs and manuscripts. It was in 1933, during research into the history of the Fronde, that the author came quite by chance upon this unedited source for the history of the popular uprisings, and this led him, as a result, into a detailed study of them.

We must pause a moment to discuss the origin and history of this archival source and to give its characteristics. Pierre Séguier (1558–1672) was one of the most important men of state of the French seventeenth century. By birth, he came from the high *parlementaire* bureaucracy. In the governmental hierarchy of absolutist France, initially under Richelieu and then under Mazarin, Séguier occupied the second position immediately after the first minister. He held within his hands the two highest functions of government. In 1633 he became Keeper of the Seals, and, in 1635, Chancellor of France.[3] For forty years Séguier enjoyed the entire confidence of those in power: Richelieu, Louis XIII, Anne of Austria, Mazarin, Louis XIV and Colbert.[4] The nature of his office placed him throughout this period at the very centre of political life. The Chancellor was to some extent head of the foreign policy of the state. The Séguier papers clearly contain a rich collection of documents relevant to the international relations of seventeenth-century France. Affairs of war did not of course escape him. A historian of the Thirty Years War could extract a mass of documents from the Séguier papers relating to the organisation and equipment of the French army, regarding both isolated engagements and whole campaigns. But Séguier's attention was concentrated primarily on internal affairs. This was wholly natural. His office as Chancellor made him the 'supreme chief of justice'. In this capacity he was head of both the central and local organs of justice, as well as of provincial administrators in their capacity as *intendants de justice*, and of all the organs, both governmental and municipal, in so far as they had responsibility for the maintenance of public order. That is to say, police and justice were, *par excellence*, his essential province.

Pierre Séguier was past master in his domain and enjoyed the performance of his office. His whole life was a relentless struggle to safeguard the existing regime. He suppressed uprisings and seditions without mercy, to such an extent that his name became surrounded with a sinister fame; especially after the visit he made to Normandy to punish the '*Va-nu-pieds*'. It would not be enough to say that the Chancellor was unpopular; he was execrated by the people as a hangman. This is why, when the Fronde broke out in 1648, as soon as the crowd felt itself master of Paris it tried, before everything else, to mete out justice to Séguier by lynching him. Only chance saved his life.[5]

But Pierre Séguier's historical reputation is not solely that of executioner. By a strange psychological contrast, he was at the same time passionately concerned with learning and an admirer and collector of ancient works and manuscripts. Even during his expedition to Normandy, in the midst of the terror and executions, he found time to go to booksellers and search out rare manuscripts, as the journal of his expedition kept by an official named Verthamont bears witness. Séguier was without doubt one of the most learned men of his age, philologue, palaeographer, lover of antiquities; founder with Richelieu of the *Académie française* and its official protector, he was one of its original members.

All his life he concerned himself with the composition of his own library; or, more precisely, his collection of rare books and manuscripts, which were richly and scrupulously bound and for which he had a splendid and special gallery constructed. According to the inventory compiled a month after his death in 1672, and published in the form of a special sale catalogue[6] fourteen years later, his manuscript collection comprised several series; contemporary manuscripts as well as manuscripts in Latin, Greek and Oriental languages. The series which interests us is actually the first, under the title 'modern manuscripts', which includes state papers, original contemporary correspondence, diplomatic documents and collections of various pieces, copied specially for the Chancellor. This first series is, in essence, the personal archive of the Chancellor.

His widow preserved her husband's library for several years. Even so, the books were gradually dispersed. It was envisaged that the whole collection might be sold intact to the *Bibliothèque Royale*, but the price of forty million *livres* was too high for the *Roi Soleil*. The collection fell at length by inheritance to one of Pierre Séguier's grandsons, Henri-Charles du Cambout de Coislin, Bishop of Metz from 1697 to 1732.

Before his death, the bishop bequeathed this valuable source to those who were then perhaps the most worthy to receive it; namely, the *Congrégation* of the Benedictines of St. Maur, who devoted themselves to the research, study and publication of historical documents. One need scarcely recall the considerable role played by the Maurists, especially in the seventeenth century, in the exact study of manuscripts, which did so much for the whole progress of historical science. The major part of their inestimable collection, dating from every period of history, patiently assembled by the Maurist monks, was housed in the Benedictine monastery of St. Germain-des-Prés in Paris. It was there that the Séguier collection was transported in 1735 – with the exception of the small number of manuscripts which had been dispersed beforehand. It remained safely there until the great Revolution. In the period 1795–6 the whole library of the Abbey was transferred to the *Bibliothèque Nationale*. But it was then discovered that, during the preceding years, enormous gaps had been made in the Maurist collection, and in particular in the manuscripts of Pierre Séguier.[7]

Even to this day, the history of the disappearance of the Abbey's manuscripts has not been cleared up. It is only established that it took place during the third year of the Revolution in 1791.[8] Whatever happened, the majority of the lost manuscripts were found, we do not know how, in the possession of Peter Dubrovsky, the secretary of the Russian ambassador, a passionate collector and amateur of ancient manuscripts, who knew equally well how to appropriate a part of the archives of the Bastille, thrown on the streets by the Revolution, together with other valuable objects of the same kind. In 1800 he returned to St. Petersburg, and in 1805 he sold his priceless collection of manuscripts to the Russian government, following his nomination for life as Keeper of the Public Library, with a considerable pension. The 'Collection Dubrovsky' has been preserved with care until today, in the Saltykov-Shchedrin Public Library in Leningrad.

In this work, we have used solely the fraction of the collection which at one time belonged to the actual archive of Pierre Séguier. This seems to have been divided arbitrarily into two parts; the section which left France has been separated without chronological or any other reason from the section in the *Bibliothèque Nationale* in Paris. The total number of documents stemming from the Séguier archives in the Public Library in Leningrad amounts to several thousands; among these the single category of papers dealing with internal policy numbers not less than 2500 to 3000 documents. [A short section deals at this point with the preliminary investigations of the Séguier archive by Count Hector de la Ferrière and Hovyn de Tranchère, who visited Leningrad in the nineteenth century. Porshnev compiles a list of the documents he has used from the archive, which may be referred to on pp. 24–5 of the complete French edition of his work.]

The documents [I have used] emanate from various provincial officials, especially *intendants*, and various provincial institutions. The provinces are very unevenly represented in this correspondence. Some fairly completely, others very poorly. From the chronological point of view, there is the same unevenness as between years. For the years 1636–7 the correspondence is most abundant; for the years 1638–42 it is thin and fragmentary. For the years 1643–9 it is abundant again; but the years 1660–7 are only represented by disconnected letters.

It should be noted that the regrettable gaps for the years 1638–42, which are important years for the history of the popular uprisings, are compensated for to some extent by the fact that in 1842 a Norman historian, A. Floquet, extracted the section devoted to the uprising of the

Va-nu-pieds (1639–40) from the Séguier papers in the *Bibliothèque Nationale* and published it.[9] Even so, the *Bibliothèque Nationale* must contain without doubt other collections on this period which would provide most valuable information on the popular uprisings.

These letters to Chancellor Séguier do not of course treat solely of uprisings in the provinces. Reading this correspondence to the Chancellor, the historian feels himself plunged into the daily labour undertaken over the years by the administrative machine of the absolutist monarchy, shielded from the gaze of the curious. Hovyn de Tranchère justly calls it the 'underneath of history'. Here, among these papers, thrown together by chance, lies a whole mass of private and public business; the reports, requests, anxieties of the officials, all in that primitive chaos in which archives relating to government activity are usually found, while awaiting the authoritative hand of the historian to extract from confusion the material necessary to study a particular problem. The multiple governmental functions of the Chancellor reinforce the syncretic nature of this mass of archive material. There is something indeed of everything here: the quarrels and squabbles of the *parlementaires*; the inside history of the provincial Estates; the struggle of the corporations of the provincial judicial *officiers*† against the establishment of new organs of justice in competition with the old; the corruption and indiscipline of the military; the rivalry of the *intendants* and the provincial *gouverneurs*; the aims and frustrations of municipal and other local authorities; the struggle of the Huguenots for their political rights under the limitations of the 'Edict of *Grâce*'; and many other things besides, without taking into account the multitude of isolated judicial and administrative cases, individual claims, letters of introduction, etc. It is precisely this syncretic nature of the archive, however, which serves to throw light on the weight to be attached to the problem of the popular uprisings and on their role, in the context of the other administrative concerns which the French absolutist government had to face.

On page after page of the Séguier papers, we meet either an account of some uprising or a report on the distress of the common people, which was enough indeed to provoke rebellion among them; or, finally, accounts of the severe repression which followed the uprisings. Sometimes whole letters are devoted to them; at other times simply passages in letters relating to other things. This habitual and relentless struggle on the part of the government apparatus, in particular that of the local administration, in face of this characteristic phenomenon of French social life in the period, reveals itself in very concrete terms here. It will suffice for us to note that about ten per cent of the whole collection of documents has been selected and used; a very high percentage if one takes into account all that has been said about the character of this mass of documents. But the tone of the letters when they refer to the uprisings is also characteristic. The usual embellishments, the rhetorical periods, the flattering digressions disappear. Matters are directly and seriously recounted. The tone indeed discloses to some degree the way in which the French hierarchy looked on facts of this nature.

We must not believe however that the local authorities wrote the whole truth to the Chancellor about these uprisings. The provincial administration was responsible for public order; the uprisings were imputed to them as proof of their negligence. Therefore they tried, as far as possible, to suppress the disorders without referring them to the central government. This may explain the absence of mention in the Séguier papers of a fairly large number of rebellions known to historical science through provincial archives and other local sources – although, on the other hand, we do find in the Séguier papers information about certain uprisings entirely unknown to us from other sources. For the same reason, letters or reports had a tendency to minimise rather than exaggerate the importance of the uprisings. Most often such and such a rebellion only came to the knowledge of the Chancellor through the rivalry of local interests disputing among themselves the right to suppress it, or trying mutually to avoid responsibility for the uprising or for badly handling its suppression. In any case, to the extent that they kept the central authority current of the facts, not solely for information, but when a governmental decision was needed – such as the sending in of troops or the withdrawal of a particular tax – the authors of the letters would not wish to be suspected of exaggerating the danger or of playing up their own merits, since events in the end would only unmask them. The abundance and verisimilitude of the information when it occurs can also serve as a criterion of their veracity. It must be remembered that not only do we not have the complete Séguier archive at our disposal, but that even in the complete archive we would not find all the letters informing of popular uprisings. There is evidence that in the case of certain reports of this kind, and more especially perhaps those which required important political decisions, Séguier showed them and transmitted them to Richelieu. It was unlikely that documents of this nature always found their way back to the Chancellor. Some might also have been referred to the secretaries of state, who were each responsible for such and such an area of the provincial administration.

It was a rule that only a general summary of information was sent from the province to the Chancellor. Detailed information – matters of procedure, judicial verdicts, lists of arrested rebels, etc., – was sent direct to the secretaries of state. In the letters to Séguier there is frequent reference to more detailed information that has been sent to the Secretary of State, La Vrillière. It is fairly rare that a copy to the Chancellor is attached. As a result, the La Vrillière archive could well be used to complement that of Séguier. They have been preserved, it seems,

and indeed constituted one of the numerous sources on the popular uprisings discovered by the historian Boissonnade.

In spite of all their gaps, however, the Séguier papers are of the first
importance for studying the popular uprisings of the thirties and forties
of the seventeenth century. Since the Chancellor did not normally en-
cumber himself with detail, but always tried to keep before himself a
general picture of the kingdom at any given moment, and especially
during the period of the popular uprisings and the struggle constantly
sustained against them, the archive gives the historian a valuable opportunity to grasp this general picture and to establish a fairly complete
schema of the main centres of unrest, while adding additional sources for
the study of each particular uprising.

[After some further general comments on the nature of the Séguier
archive, Porshnev turns to his main theme.]

We have said above that the subject of the popular uprisings in seventeenth-century France has not as yet found it historiographer. Therefore instead of devoting space in this introduction to a survey of previous historiography, to a discussion of his predecessors, the author had
rather to give reasons for their absence. What precisely were the ideas, the
traditions of French historiography which prevented the study of these
uprisings until now? Unless we answer this question, we cannot evaluate
these uprisings with any precision.

French historians have given the French seventeenth century – the
century of Richelieu, Mazarin, Colbert and Louis XIV – the title of the
'*Grand Siècle*'. Veneration for the *Grand Siècle* has been for a very long
time in France a tradition in schools and an aspect of French patriotism.
It is natural therefore that whole libraries of historical works should
have been devoted to the seventeenth century. One might well feel that
it has been studied so much that historians might now only add to what
is already there and be able to affect its history only in respect to secondary detail, without there being any possibility of touching the essential
outlines of the general picture. But in fact the *Grand Siècle* has been
studied with formidable partiality. It represents indeed a blank page in
the economic and social history of France. Works devoted to its agrarian
system, industrial structure and internal trade are almost entirely lacking for the seventeenth century, except for rare exceptions.[10] Its surrounding centuries, the sixteenth and eighteenth, are far better served. French
historians themselves have sometimes noted this anomaly. 'We know
French medieval society and the societies of Rome and Ancient Egypt
better', said Lavisse in 1905, 'than we know the society of seventeenth-
century France, which remains hidden in obscurity behind the décor of
Versailles.'[11] There has been little change in the fifty or so years since
this statement.

But how do we explain the interest of historians in the economic and social problems of the French eighteenth century? Because those problems demanded recognition as soon as the social developments of the period 1789–94 came to be studied. The interest, likewise, which attaches to the analogous problems of the sixteenth century derives from the time when the profound social conflict of the period of the Wars of Religion came to be studied. Or, to put it in a different way, the great social movements in history, in particular the uprisings of the popular masses, play in historiography the role of bridge between the 'history of events' and the 'history of social conditions', thanks to which historians are able to penetrate the political nature of an age as readily as its profound economic and social problems. The seventeenth century was also, however, full of an intense class-struggle, although this does not figure in any way in the traditional account of the *Grand Siècle*. If, therefore, we begin the study of popular uprisings with those of the seventeenth century, overthrowing to some extent the traditional account as we go along, then questions concerning the economic situation itself will quite naturally arise, and future generations of historians will have to resolve them.

In other words, nineteenth- and twentieth-century French historiography is above all spoiled, in its study of the seventeenth century, by the very idea of that century's '*grandeur*'. French bourgeois historians fear lest the study of popular uprisings should diminish the *Grand Siècle* in some way, and deprive it of its customary brilliance, dispelling the legends and illusions which surround it. They pass over these uprisings in silence, and in this way remain ignorant of its social and economic history.

What then are the reasons for this exaltation of the seventeenth century? The first, and least well-founded, lies in the important role which it played in the development of French culture. It was indeed the *Grand Siècle* of literature, theatre, architecture and painting; the age of the formation of the modern literary language, of French classicism, of Corneille, Racine, Molière, La Fontaine and Boileau. The brilliance of Pushkin however scarcely illumines the sombre reign of Nicholas I, any more than the great figures of Raphael, Michelangelo and Leonardo conceal the economic and political realities of early sixteenth-century Italy. Even so, to the extent that French seventeenth-century culture was attached to the Court and the Court was identified with the France of that particular age, an involuntary error has taken shape; the brilliance of the culture has been extended to the Court, playing the role of Maecenas as it did, and, by extension, to the whole of France. The picture of popular seditions, famine and epidemic disease might, it seems, undermine the image of the Court, tarnish its beauty, and tarnish the classical culture itself of the French seventeenth century. We need not pause for long over this error, since it has been sufficiently exposed: the Court, surely enough, was not France; and as to its role of Maecenas, it is still open to debate

D

how far it really developed or, on the other hand, destroyed the germs of a new culture.

A second reason for the glorification of the seventeenth century in bourgeois historiography lies deeper. It lies in the military and diplomatic success of the French seventeenth century, in French European hegemony. France could then indisputably defeat Germany. The French bourgeoisie turned increasingly toward this period as capitalist Germany strengthened itself and the Franco-German struggle intensified in the nineteenth and twentieth centuries. It found its political ideal in the seventeenth century, with a strong government capable at one and the same time of forcing Germany to her knees and stifling all threat of internal revolution. Anything which hindered French absolutism in its conflict with the Habsburgs, which in any way weakened it, was considered as historically retrograde. This is why, in the view of French historians, the social uprisings against seventeenth-century absolutism were to be entirely condemned, or, best of all, were not worthy of study. It is indeed only in periods when Franco-German hostility relaxes that French historiography adopts a more tolerant position regarding the social history of the seventeenth century. During the period of peace from 1830 to 1850, the history of the seventeenth century was indeed made the object of a liberal, even a democratic interpretation, in the works of Michelet, Feillet, Capefigue and others. The approach of the Franco-Prussian war and the Paris Commune, however, caused the veneration for absolutism to revive and intensify. In the same way, Ernest Lavisse, an active champion of *rapprochement* between France and Germany at the end of the nineteenth and beginning of the twentieth century, devoted particular chapters of the volumes on Louis XIII and Louis XIV of his *Histoire de France* to the popular uprisings of the seventeenth century. Boissonnade's essay, which we have already cited, was approximately of this period. During this same period, Charles Normand devoted attention to the popular uprisings in his work on the French seventeenth-century bourgeoisie. But the first great war was already in gestation, and these new stirrings were not in the end to have very much effect on the study of seventeenth-century France.

An objective historian of France in the seventeenth century cannot in any way consider her external policy as unreservedly progressive, and subordinate all judgment to that. The policy of the French kings was progressive in the sense that it contributed to the establishment of the national State. This task was achieved in its main outlines at the end of the fifteenth century. In the sixteenth and seventeenth centuries, national defence and aristocratic aggression seem inextricably intermingled in the external policy of French absolutism. For this reason alone, it is already not possible to determine scientifically the credit or blame attaching to those who frustrated the external successes of France. In other words, if we free ourselves from the introverted national class-attitudes which

animate bourgeois historiography in France, we see that French absolutism pursued a dual campaign, externally and internally. Both aspects were
serious and demanded a maximum concentration of effort. It is the
internal struggle however which must be given primacy. It is in studying
that that we shall discover the fundamental criteria which will enable
us to comprehend the absolutism of the French seventeenth century.

Finally, the third reason for the glorification and, at the same time, the
falsification of the French seventeenth century lies deeper still. It lies in
the false concepts created by the bourgeoisie about its own past. In
this, it is necessary to go back fairly far. The initial source of falsification
in historical matters derives from the 'enlightened *philosophes*' of the
eighteenth century, in particular from Voltaire and the historians of his
school. Voltaire, as the ideologue of the bourgeoisie with revolutionary
tendencies, not only did not want revolution involving the participation
of the masses, but brought to bear all his political science in order to
discover the means to prevent it. 'Enlightened despotism' seemed to him
the most effective form of government; a bourgeois utopia, which would
maintain the existing order without imposing any constraint whatever on
the bourgeoisie, above all on its intelligentsia. It was necessary to establish the credibility of such a utopia, and Voltaire the historian did it.

In *La Henriade*, in his *Siècle de Louis XIV* and *Histoire de Pierre le
Grand* and even, in negative fashion, in his *Histoire de Charles XII*, he tried
in varying degrees, to clothe this utopia with concrete historical reality.
He wished to persuade his reader that his ideal had been realised, to all
intents and purposes, not in some far-off age of gold, but quite recently,
in the seventeenth and eighteenth centuries. Without these historical
works, Voltaire's critique would have resounded, willy nilly, like a revolutionary appeal for the destruction of the existing order. As a result of
these works, it appeared like a claim for the re-establishment of a recent
past; it made an appeal for conservative reforms. Against the 'bad absolutism' of Louis XV, Voltaire opposed, if not the ideal, at least the 'good
absolutism' of Henry IV, Louis XIII and Louis XIV. In this way, a specious
eulogy of the *Grand Siècle* was created as a contrast with the eighteenth
century. Everything in it was embellished and set out under an enchant-
ing exterior. But the ensemble effect of the bewitching image had to
expose only those characteristics which were needed to prove that
seventeenth-century absolutism satisfied the political ideals of the principal *philosophes*. The Edict of Nantes became in the eyes of Voltaire's
disciples a kind of incarnate symbol of all the liberties of conscience,
thought and expression; in other words, all the liberties of which bourgeois intellectuals dreamed. Somewhat later, a silhouette came to stand
out in the foreground, surrounded by the radiant halo of the 'simple
bourgeois' who had access to power and who undertook the protection
of the interests of the bourgeoisie – namely Colbert, who symbolised the

political and economic power of which the bourgeoisie dreamed. The 'fall' of French absolutism, its tranformation from 'good' absolutism into 'bad', was equally naïvely dated from the death of Colbert in 1683, or from the Revocation of the Edict of Nantes in 1685. Without any really valid reason, the reign of Louis XIV was divided into two parts: a 'rise' and a 'decline'. Historical truth was sacrificed to the political ideas of the moderate eighteenth-century bourgeoisie. The *Grand Siècle* became populated with illusion, dressed up in haphazard fashion in historical costume and mask.

Historical science in the nineteenth century inherited a somewhat falsified image therefore of the seventeenth century. But, in this respect, the critical mind of the nineteenth century not only abstained from correcting the error, but in itself reinforced the legend of the *Grand Siècle*[12] and endowed it with a second source of false historical identity.

After achieving dominance in fact, the bourgeoisie, and especially the French bourgeoisie after the upheavals of the close of the eighteenth century, attempted to establish its dominance historically. To this end, its intellectuals had to provide two diametrically opposed explanations: firstly, that the bourgeoisie had been dominant all the time, that is to say that it was designed for domination by nature: and, secondly, that it had always been revolutionary in its struggle against feudalism; that the revolution was due to its action alone and the fruits of the revolution therefore belonged to it alone. In consequence, neither of these two assertions corresponded to historical truth. It is, moreover, difficult to demonstrate both the one and the other at the same time, since the legend of the victorious march of the revolutionary bourgeoisie in conflict with the *ancien régime* is contradicted by the other legend, whereby it held authority before the revolution, and vice versa. It was at this point that the heritage of eighteenth-century historiography intervened, with its already deeply rooted metaphysical concept regarding French historical development; namely, that the bourgeoisie had been principally dominant in the *Grand Siècle*, whereas in the eighteenth century it had been involved in conflict. If, indeed, it had been in conflict with the *ancien régime* during the *Grand Siècle*, this was because it was not yet entirely dominant. If, on the other hand, it was not involved in continuous conflict in the eighteenth century, this was because in some sense it continued to be dominant.

In order to achieve this double task, which was necessary to the idealisation of both the past and future of the bourgeoisie, French historians discovered something new during the first decades of the nineteenth century. They came to base their interpretation of French history (in which the *Grand Siècle* crowned, so to say, the successful if interrupted rise of the bourgeoisie, which for a time the eighteenth century was indeed to interrupt) on an idea which was properly scientific; namely, that of the class-struggle. This fertile idea, was, however, in great measure evacuated of content by their limiting the terrain of the struggle to the relationships between the exploiting classes themselves – the nobility and the bourgeoisie. The really fundamental antagonism between classes, the antagonism which opposes those who work to those who exploit, was not taken into consideration. The fundamental motive force of history, that of the popular masses, was forced to efface itself, to withdraw into the shadows, yielding place on the main stage to the progressive and victorious advance of the bourgeoisie.

The true founder, the father of this concept, was Augustin Thierry, and it is fitting to pause here to consider his case. He was not the first to embody the effort of the French bourgeoisie to transfigure and embellish its past, following its victory. But it was he who first discovered the historical category, the concept which was to become in time the principal working tool in this particular respect, the concept of the 'Third Estate'. Until the publication of Thierry's *A History of the Formation and Progress of the Third Estate*, even the term 'Third Estate' was only rarely to be found in the pages of French history, and then essentially in relation to the history of the Estates General. It is true that the quarrel between Boulainvilliers and Dubos had already drawn attention to the historical destiny of the Third Estate. But from the publication of Abbé Siéyès's famous pamphlet *Qu'est-ce que le Tiers Etat?* on the eve of the Revolution until the publication of Thierry's work, it occurred to no one that a major historical category was involved in the term 'Third Estate'. Thierry, it goes without saying, placed it in a primary position and transformed it into a prism through which he examined the whole history of France. To this term, essentially narrow in its specialist meaning, he gave a wide significance in terms of class, and in this way brought about progress in the recognition of the existence of classes and the struggle between them in history.

But, essentially strange as it may be, Thierry developed the idea of the class-struggle, which he borrowed from the *Saint-Simoniens*, only to establish the idea of a peace between the classes. The class-struggle, according to Thierry, was already the property of the past at the time when he was composing his work. One of the two classes, the privileged class composed of nobility and clergy, which had struggled for centuries to survive, had been defeated and overthrown for ever. The second class remained, the Third Estate, which in fact no longer had anyone to fight, and whose existence merged with that of the nation. In its internal organisation, the Third Estate presented itself to Thierry as the incarnation of the idea of peace between the classes. He did not take into account the isolated revolutionary explosions and conspiracies which seemed to him merely unfortunate and accidental phenomena in the history of the Third Estate.

In spite of his affirmations, Thierry's concept was not so much the result of study based on 'original texts' as a weapon of combat directed against the contemporary workers' movement which was proving itself destructive of public order. Thierry wished to demonstrate that the antagonism between proletariat and bourgeoisie was the creation of only yesterday, and came solely from the influence of 'prejudice' and 'systems' which tended to divide a basically united nation into enemy classes.[18] In other words, Thierry's work was a polemic directed against the ideas of revolutionary socialism which were widely disseminated in France. Marx, in a letter to Engels of 27 July 1854, made an ironic criticism of this attempt on the part of Thierry, while at the same time recognising certain scientific qualities in his work. He wrote: 'I have been livelily interested in the work of Thierry, in his *History of the Formation and Progress of the Third Estate*, 1853. It is surprising to see that this gentleman, the Father of the Class-Struggle in French historiography, fulminates in his preface against the "moderns", those people who assert that there is an antagonism between the bourgeoisie and the proletariat and who seek the traces of this contradiction in the history of the Third Estate from before 1789.'[14]

Parallel to the idea of a peace between the classes, the idea emerges *chez* Thierry of a government above class, and in particular that of the monarchy since its appearance in France. Thierry sees nothing 'feudal' in the monarchy, nothing '*nobiliaire*'. The monarchy for him is quite simply a national tradition, whose representative was precisely the Third Estate. 'For six centuries', he writes, 'from the twelfth to the seventeenth, the history of the Third Estate and the history of the royal power were indissolubly bound together; so that in the eyes of a man who indeed knows how to understand them, the one seems like, so to say, the reverse of the other.'[15] All this construct of ideas had above all else the July Monarchy in view, of which Thierry was a passionate protagonist. He tried to represent it precisely as the ideal realisation of the national historical tradition: 'In my eyes, it is like the fulfilment of centuries-old efforts, which started in the twelfth century' – a tradition interrupted solely by the unfortunate developments of the eighteenth century, which was punished for it by the Revolution. And to prove that the French monarchy occupied a position above class (in other words, to prove its bourgeois character), throughout its long historical past, it was enough to interpret its history in the widest terms and highlight its conflicts with certain elements of the feudal class.

What did Thierry therefore do? He concealed the true nature of the bourgeoisie under the *ancien régime*. Its true nature was to oppose two forces, simultaneously, which were themselves in turn in opposition to each other – a position involving a profound contradiction therefore. Thierry concealed the opposition between bourgeoisie and people behind the concept of the Third Estate; and he concealed the opposition between the bourgeoisie and the ruling class (the feudal nobility) by using the concept of a monarchy above class; whereas, in reality, the supremacy of the feudal nobility expressed itself precisely in the monarchy. Nevertheless, to some extent, Thierry sustained his position with realities. The opposition between the bourgeoisie and the feudal nobility in effect compelled the former into constant, if cautious, attempts at alliance with the people, which culminated indeed in the bourgeois revolution at the close of the eighteenth century. The opposition between the bourgeoisie and the people however led, in reality, to a stable and lasting alliance between the bourgeoisie and the '*monarchie nobiliaire*', which then assumed the appearance of an absolutism above class. The factor, however, which created the internal contradiction of the bourgeoisie in its historical development, Thierry describes as an idyll, stranger to all impediment in its progressive march.

Thierry was to witness the total foundering of his historical construct in 1848. Even so, his theory had a considerable influence on French historiography in the nineteenth century. In particular, it became a serious obstacle to the study of popular revolutionary movements in the seventeenth century. If the right wing of French conservative historians avoided this subject for obvious reasons, the current liberal majority adopted Thierry's concept of the Third Estate and the absolute monarchy, and saw popular uprisings against the monarchy (and especially when the bourgeoisie did not support them) solely as regrettable events without significance, to use Thierry's expression. As for the democratic wing of nineteenth-century historians, such as Sismondi, Michelet and some others, they showed more sympathy toward the people than a capacity for creating scientific ideas capable of establishing the true role of the popular masses in history and of opposing the liberal school with ideas based on different principles. In the nineteenth century, for the great majority the idea of evolution remained synonymous with the idea of the 'scientific spirit' in historical research. That is why almost all the various schools of bourgeois historiography are unanimous in asserting that the Revolution of 1789 could not have upset the direction of the evolutionary march of French history, and that it came about solely as the result of a temporary and partial deviation in the long-term evolution of French society. The heritage of the Voltaire school, as well as the ideas of Thierry (and Guizot), led to the following concrete judgment: the Revolution of 1789 redressed the entirely regrettable deviation of the eighteenth century. The French bourgeoisie, growing in strength from century to century, had almost attained political supremacy in the seventeenth century; but, from the close of that century, the nobility had striven, not without success, to oust the bourgeoisie from power; then, at the close of the eighteenth century, the latter took it back by means of Revolution. It is certain that, according to this schema, the seventeenth century remains the *Grand Siècle*, in spite of all its weaknesses; and the popular uprisings of the century, directed against a government that was 'almost bourgeois', appear to historians as of only secondary importance and entirely regrettable.

We cannot of course retrace here the whole development of the historiography of the *ancien régime*. It suffices to indicate that even if it has been subject to numerous modifications this schema, based on the concept of evolutionary development, has not served any the less as the basis for the most divergent models and theories of French historians in the nineteenth and twentieth centuries. In the twentieth century, however, it is clearly undergoing a very tangible crisis. The progress of modern research has swept aside the traditional theory which made the first half of the reign of Louis XIV the 'reign of the bourgeoisie', and which proposed the revocation of the Edict of Nantes and the death of Colbert as the point of departure for the '*réaction nobiliaire*'. In particular, modern research devoted to Colbertism has destroyed a number of legends attaching to the idea. Facts of the greatest importance have been established as evidence in support of the case that French absolutism in the seventeenth century was an aristocratic state and French society in the seventeenth century was a feudal society, or at least more feudal and more aristocratic than in the eighteenth century.

In 1932, a great specialist in the *ancien régime*, G. Pagès, justly recalled in one of his articles, using certain examples, the multiplicity of popular uprisings under Richelieu. He drew from this new proof of the evolutionary theory of French historical development and of the contrast traditionally made between the seventeenth and eighteenth centuries. In a quite unexpected way, his ideas placed the question of venality of office at the centre of the problem. It is generally thought, Pagès says, that the sixteenth- and seventeenth-century monarchy in France could not suppress the system of venality, simply because it did not possess the resources to repurchase the offices already sold. 'Not sufficient account is taken', he asserts, 'of the fact that by the seventeenth century venality had become an essential element in the political and social structure of the realm; in suppressing it, the whole edifice would have been overturned.'[16] The sale of offices, according to Pagès, gave the absolute monarchy 'a wide and solid base in the nation'; or, in other words, it carried the bourgeoisie to power:

> As a result of venality, the French realm was administered for nearly two centuries, the sixteenth and the greater part of the seventeenth, by those who acquired office. At the top there were the magistrates who formed what has been called the '*grande robe*'. But beneath them, there were an infinite number of regional and local corporations:

bureaux de finances†, in the chief towns of the *généralités†*, *conseils de bailliage†*, municipal corporations, etc. Almost all these *officiers†* originate from the region where they exercise their offices; and it is venality which has brought them forth from the people. They are controlled from afar by the *Conseil du Roi* . . . with them the whole of the bourgeoisie, down to its lowest members, is associated in the exercise and profits of public power. This is indeed why the bourgeoisie had an interest in sustaining the absolute monarchy, which it has come to the aid of with its money and which has in return gradually relinquished to it the honour and benefit of administering the realm in its name.[17]

According to Pagès, Richelieu understood the political and social consequences of the abolition of venality, but at the same time he tried to supplant the purchasers of office by functionaries of another kind (essentially the *intendants*) appointed by the government. The Fronde was, in its beginning, the defensive reaction of the proprietors of office against the *intendants*. During the reign of Louis XIV, the authority of these functionaries was gradually reinforced. Colbert, at the outset of his ministry, had the intention of confiscating all offices, even though he understood that with this reform '40000 families would be brought to nothing'. But he quickly realised the possible repercussions of this undertaking, a rupture between the monarchy and the bourgeoisie – and he therefore abstained from taking action. Even so, the eviction of the proprietors of office continued to increase, in spite of the creation of a great number of new offices during this period for fiscal reasons. An abrupt step toward the abolition of venality takes place at the time of John Law. From that moment, the monarchy rapidly loses 'its base in the nation' and proceeds toward the Revolution.[18] Thus, according to Pagès, the seventeenth century saw the apogee of venality of office; the eighteenth century saw its liquidation, with all the social and political consequences which flowed from it.

Pagès's article, brilliant in its scholarship and its unexpected conclusion, produced a strong impression in France. It provided an entirely new foundation, and as it seemed a more solid one, for the current but largely collapsing theory according to which the French bourgeoisie had been in power in the seventeenth century, had lost power in the eighteenth century and had regained it in a new form after 1789. Historians have of course set themselves to develop to the full this seam opened up by Pagès. In 1945, R. Mousnier published his major study of venality of office in France during the main period of its development under Henry IV and Louis XIII, that is during the first decades of the seventeenth century. Mousnier's study rests on an enormous documentary base and a vast historiography; it contains indeed whole mountains of fact, analysed in the most scrupulous and most systematic fashion. Among other things,

Mousnier is capable of referring quickly and several times to the popular uprisings, and considers them rightly as an essential element in Richelieu's policies. Taken as a whole, many of his observations and conclusions have great scientific value. Mousnier uses the concept of class, sees and analyses, sometimes with subtlety, the relationships and conflicts between the classes. But, taking it as a whole, that same schema, based on the evolutionary development of French history, weighs heavily on his work.

In a long preface, he seeks to show that venality of office is far from being the unique property of the sixteenth and seventeenth centuries. This French phenomenon is 'perhaps' more characteristic still of the French Middle Ages, although little is known about it. Thus Mousnier, like Thierry, opposes the eighteenth century, pregnant with revolution, to the whole history of the French monarchy and not only to its neighbouring century, the seventeenth. For him, the latter was the culminating point of previous development. Already, at the close of the Middle Ages, in the fifteenth century, according to Mousnier, the political consequences of venality of office were considerable. Rich families, having bought office in the state, assume a role in the direction of public affairs and 'share the administration of the realm with the king . . . the royal authority is substantially limited by the ownership, recognised in actual fact, of the public authority by these individuals . . . the realm is under the dominance of rich families and a new form of feudality takes shape.'[19]

Let us take note of these last words. In this and later passages, Mousnier, in distinction from Pagès, is several times on the point of accepting that venality of office was nothing other than a way of furnishing the feudal class with new recruits issuing from the bourgeoisie.

The idea prevails constantly, with Mousnier as with Pagès, that venality represented a form of political supremacy on the part of the bourgeoisie, since it held in its hands, in all spheres, the administration of the state: all justice, all local, regional and central administration, and even, through the right of remonstrance on the part of the *Parlements*, a share in the legislative power itself, which in theory belonged to the king alone. 'Ever since the king himself sold offices, he shared the public power with the well-to-do and the rich, who had bought part of it from him, in fact, if not by right. The monarchy, with a king in theory absolute, was in fact limited, *"une monarchie tempérée"*, through the process of venality, in the sixteenth and first half of the seventeenth century.' The system of sale of office attained its full maturity at the beginning of the seventeenth century with the legalisation of the right of hereditary succession to office. But, already under Richelieu, Mousnier says, the government made a first step toward the liquidation of the system: it confided a part of the judicial and administrative function to *intendants*. 'A great step was made in this, the reduction of the power of the *officiers*, the last obstacle to absolutism, had begun. From a monarchy limited by venality of office to the absolute monarchy, this was the beginning of a revolution.'

Those who had acquired office saw their power reduced; they were burdened with taxes which took from the bourgeoisie the desire to buy office. These measures continued under Louis XIV, whom Mousnier calls for this reason 'the Great Revolutionary of France'; and the same movement continues throughout the eighteenth century. This Revolution, Mousnier declares at the end of his book, separated the King from the rich; the latter, having lost their access to power, then turned away from the King and rose against his 'theory of absolutism'. Some of them became bogged down in a fruitless *parlementaire* opposition. They appealed to the liberties of times past. Others conceived of 'political organisations which would return to the well-to-do and rich the public power which they had almost lost and all the social advantages which flow from its possession, under a new form, adapted to the ideas of the time. They took advantage of the financial embarrassments of the King and the popular movements to impose on him one of these new organisations, namely, the Constituent Assembly.'[20]

This is the way in which the modern historical concept of the bourgeoisie in France explains the genesis of the Revolution of 1789. It was not so much a revolution, the theory maintains, as a counter-revolution against the 'absolutist revolution' which had expelled the bourgeoisie from power; a counter-revolution already projected by Richelieu and Colbert, but which for various reasons could not be executed by them, and was only fully accomplished in the eighteenth century.

We shall return to the question of venality of office at the end of this work. But, at this stage, in face of this concept of Pagès and Mousnier, which simply refurbishes the old legend of the *Grand Siècle*, we wish to assert a radically opposed point of view, which is centred on the question of the development of capitalism, within feudal and absolutist France. To raise this question is to remove any possibility of seeing the Revolution of 1789 as a return (even on a new basis) to the situation of the seventeenth century, which had been temporarily disturbed in the eighteenth. The Revolution of 1789 put power for the first time in the hands of the French bourgeoisie; that is to say that, as a result of that revolution, political power came into relationship with the more or less developed state of the bourgeois economy. In the seventeenth century, the bourgeois economy was palpably less developed than in the eighteenth. The bourgeoisie, as the representative of capitalist relationships of production, had in no sense been close to obtaining power in the seventeenth century.

These are some of the aspects then of the legend of the *Grand Siècle* which have prevented a scientific study of the popular uprisings of the French seventeenth century.

Let us state again the questions raised in this present study, in order to explain its plan and essential principles.

The history of the Fronde, as we have indicated, is enveloped by such a density of myth, it has been so falsely interpreted by contemporary mémoire-writers and researchers, that the historian who wishes to arrive at an objective view of the Fronde finds himself confronted from the outset by very great difficulties indeed. It is enough, however, if we survey the decades preceding and those following the Fronde, with their almost uninterrupted series of civil wars at the heart of the feudal-absolutist regime itself, to see that the Fronde is situated at the hinge of two great cycles of popular uprisings, both rural and urban, each of which occupies about twenty-five years, approximately 1623–48 and 1653–76. The Fronde was in some way the culmination of these uprisings, and played the role of 'turntable' when this latent civil war almost transformed itself into a general crisis in the feudal-absolutist regime, when it moved from being a social crisis in depth to the surface of politics. However, the forces in French society which should have acted politically partly feared a victory over the king and partly could not even wish for it. It is clear that, after the failure of the Fronde, the civil war once more became imprisoned within continuing popular uprisings, but with certain minor differences. The history of the two cycles of peasant and popular urban uprisings provides a mass of material which enables us to determine the characteristics of the Fronde and shows in particular that it was not the '*frondeurs*' who incited and led an obedient crowd of followers in their wake, but that it was a matter of freely spontaneous uprisings creating the various types of *frondeurs* and the situations of the Fronde, rather like an electric charge, with both positive and negative aspects. In this work, the author does not deal in any way whatever with the second cycle of uprisings. Those uprisings and their influence on the development of French social thought constitute the theme of another work in preparation.[21]

[A brief section follows in which the author once again refers to the sources available and why he was led to construct his work in the way he has, by first giving a general account of the uprisings for the period 1623–48, followed by a detailed study of one example of them, the *Va-nu-pieds* uprising in Normandy in 1639, with a concluding section on the issues posed by the Fronde.]

An examination of the popular uprisings raises problems which go far beyond the limits of the given theme. It ultimately raises the whole question of the political, economic and social structure of seventeenth-century France, and it would be an error to disregard these problems. Even so, the author has made it a rule for himself to approach them only from evidence drawn from the history of the uprisings themselves.

These problems divide into two principal groups. In the first place, any researcher into the popular uprisings must familiarise himself with the organs of political repression, that is to say the apparatus of the state, and, more widely, the political regime of absolutist France in the seventeenth century. The necessity therefore emerged of characterising the military and police aspects of justice and the provincial administration, together with the functions and roles of their different agents, such as the *intendants*, the provincial *gouverneurs*, the *parlements*, etc. The question is also raised of the importance which the repression of popular uprisings assumed among the other functions of the absolutist government and, by extension, the whole question of the regime's major political and social aims. Declarations of men of state and governmental measures taken in regard to the suppression of the revolts, together with the whole structure of authority within the provinces, furnish material for a reply to this question. The general conclusion (and at the same time the premises of this study) resides in this: French seventeenth-century absolutism was above all an organ for the suppression of the labouring classes. According to Marxist theory it was so under the regime of serfdom and feudalism, and it was to remain so under capitalism. The essential function of any government during these periods was to effect control over an exploited majority.

It is true that the *'monarchie nobiliaire'* of the French seventeenth century itself provoked a great amount of popular discontent by its own fiscal policy, but this was the result of an unusual increase in the exploiting function of the state, which was not normal governmental action. These taxes were the last straw, breaking the patience of the people already exhausted by other forms of exploitation. The first and principal aim of French absolutism in the seventeenth century was therefore to prevent and suppress the popular rebellions. Its relationship with the bourgeoisie cannot be understood except on this basis.

In the second place, study of the uprisings is impossible without approaching them from underlying economic and social premises. The chapters devoted to a summary description of the popular uprisings can only contain summary conclusions as to their pretexts and causes. But the chapters devoted to the detailed study of a single uprising can and must penetrate to the economic roots. Thus even with local documents from a single province (Normandy), certain elemental problems of the economic and social organisation of seventeenth-century France reveal themselves. One must take one's departure from the history of the uprisings as such in order to penetrate, at successive levels of consideration, to the base of the economic problems involved. In relation to the history of the *Va-nu-pieds* in Normandy in 1639, the author has taken their spontaneous demands as the point of departure and has analysed in detail the weight of taxes, which was the most direct cause of this uprising. But, through the prism of these fiscal problems, he ultimately attempts to throw light on the more complex characteristics of the agrarian, commercial and industrial structures of the province.

The general conclusion drawn from these investigations into the economic and social regime of seventeenth-century France is clear. It was, in its main outlines, a society which was still feudal, characterised by predominantly feudal modes of production and by feudal economic forms. Capitalist relationships, in terms of structure, were only sparsely distributed among the feudal mass. They were concentrated principally in the towns, but not, as yet, in all of them. Taking French agriculture as a whole, the most authentic medieval feudalism still reigned, and only the Revolution of 1789 was to deal it a mortal blow. As Marx has said: under Louis XIV and Louis XV 'the social, industrial and financial superstructure, or more exactly the façade of the social edifice' seems an irony in face of the generally retarded state of the principal area of production, namely agriculture, and in face of the distress of the producers.[22]

In the French countryside, said Engels, 'small-scale agricultural exploitation was still in 1680 the normal means of production, and large-scale exploitation was the exception'; the level of productive forces was so low, in this essentially feudal agriculture, that 'as soon as one or two harvests were bad, confusion, alarm and discontent spread throughout the whole country', which we find corroborated indeed in the descriptions of Boisguilbert and Vauban. Industrial manufactures which reposed on this base could not yet signify the triumph of capitalism. The essential condition for the development of capitalism was lacking, namely the internal market. The important manufactures, benefiting from governmental protection, were themselves semi-feudal organisms. They were created to the detriment of the peasantry and indirectly encouraged feudal reaction in the countryside and regression toward a natural economy: 'a national manufacturing industry, in the conditions then existing, could not be created except to the detriment of the peasantry. The peasant natural economy was destroyed and replaced by a monetary system; an internal market was created, but it was nearly destroyed, at least for a time, by the very process itself, by the nameless violence with which the new system imposed itself. To which must be added the increase in fiscal pressure.'[23] As we shall see later, royal taxation itself was in essence nothing other than a transferred form of feudal exploitation.

It was within this context of a still dominant economic feudalism, within which a capitalist regime was developing, that the popular uprisings of the seventeenth century took place. For this reason, the author has no intention of separating the history of these popular uprisings from the other problems raised by the political, economic and social structure of seventeenth-century France. On the contrary, in placing the rebellions under the microscope, so to say, we illumine with very great clarity the whole anatomy of French seventeenth-century society.

NOTES

1 P. Boissonnade, 'L'administration royale et les soulèvements populaires en Angoumois, en Saintonge et en Poitou pendant le ministère de Richelieu (1624–1642)', in *Bulletin et Mémoires de la Société des Antiquaires de l'Ouest*, 2e série, xxvi (1902).

2 P. Boissonnade, *Le socialisme d'Etat: l'industrie et les classes industrielles en France pendant les deux premiers siècles de l'ère moderne (1453–1661)* (Paris, 1927).

3 After Séguier's death in 1672, Louis XIV allotted the two offices to two persons.

4 [Editor's note:] Séguier does not seem to have retained quite the degree of confidence suggested here, after 1661. Louis XIV speaks coldly of him in his *Mémoires*, in surveying the personnel from among whom he could have chosen his ministers: 'But to know whether I could have done better, one would need to know the other subjects to whom I could have given the same positions. The Chancellor was truly very skilful, but more in the sphere of justice . . . than in affairs of state. I knew he was very loyal in my service, but he had the reputation of not possessing all the firmness necessary for great affairs; his age and the continual business of his office might have rendered him less assiduous and less suitable for following me in the places where the needs of the state and foreign wars might lead me.' Louis XIV, *Mémoires*, ed. J. Longnon (1927) p. 29.

5 [Editor's note:] See infra. Chapter 6, p. 175.

6 *Catalogue des manuscrits de la bibliothèque du défunct Mgr le Chancelier Séguier* (Paris, 1686).

7 The complete history of the Séguier manuscripts is given in the work of L. D. Delisle, *Le Cabinet des Manuscrits de la Bibliothèque Nationale*, ii (Paris, 1874) pp. 40, 52, 78 and 100.

8 The fact that a number of manuscripts which had belonged to the archives of the Abbey bear traces of fire may doubtless clarify the circumstances of their disappearance.

9 [Editor's note:] The Séguier papers in the Bibliothèque Nationale have now been researched by Roland Mousnier: *Lettres et Mémoires adressés au Chancelier Séguier (1633–1649)*, 2 vols (Paris, 1964).

10 [Editor's note:] Although this is of course no longer so, there was perhaps an element of justification in this assertion when it was made in 1948.

11 E. Lavisse, *Histoire de France depuis les origines jusqu'à la Révolution*, vii, i (Paris, 1905) p. 323.

12 The publication, in the nineteenth century, of the *Mémoires* of the Duc de Saint-Simon contributed a great deal to disseminating the idea that the reign of Louis XIV was a 'reign of low-born bourgeois'.

13 A. Thierry, *Selected Works* (Moscow, 1937) pp. 1–14.

14 K. Marx and F. Engels, *Works* (Russian edition) xxii p. 48.

15 A. Thierry, op. cit., pp. 4–5.

16 G. Pagès, 'La vénalité des offices dans l'ancienne France', in *Revue Historique*, Vol. clxix (1932) p. 493.

17 G. Pagès, ibid.

18 G. Pagès, ibid.

19 R. Mousnier, *La vénalité des offices sous Henri IV et Louis XIII* (Paris, 1945) p. 19.

20 R. Mousnier, ibid., pp. 523–4.

21 The following extracts from this work have been published: (*a*) 'Les soulève-

ments populaires en France sous Colbert', in *Moyen Age*, ɪɪ (1946); (*b*) *The Aims and Demands of the Peasants during the Breton Uprising of 1675* (Moscow, 1940); (*c*) 'The Bordeaux Uprising of 1675', in *Reports and Communicati ̣ns of the Faculty of History of Moscow University*, ɪɪ (1945).

22 K. Marx and F. Engels, *Works* (Russian edition) xxvɪɪ p. 34.
23 *Letters of Marx and Engels to Nicolas (Daniels)* (Russian edition, 1908) p. 65.
24 See p. 124; also note 70, p. 135.

4 The Bourgeoisie and Feudal-Absolutism in Seventeenth-Century France[*]

BORIS PORSHNEV

I

A comparison enforces itself spontaneously between the Fronde and another failed attempt at bourgeois revolution, the German Reformation of the sixteenth century. In both instances, the bourgeoisie was afraid of the leap forward made by the popular revolution and betrayed its own cause accordingly. In both instances, representatives of the feudal nobility, acting in their own interest, adopted certain slogans and revolutionary demands. Equally, in both instances, the peasantry paid the cost of bourgeois betrayal. It would be unwise, however, to push this comparison too far. Although analogies may be drawn between them, we must not ignore the deep divergence between the historical situations of sixteenth-century Germany and seventeenth-century France.

We must therefore attempt a definition of the essential characteristics of the French seventeenth-century bourgeoisie which determined its conduct in the history of the Fronde. As a point of departure, we may use the commentary made on the Third Estate and the place which the bourgeoisie occupied in the French monarchical state by the eminent jurist, Charles Loyseau, who died in 1627 and whose works were the favourite reading of all privileged members of the French bourgeoisie, because they expressed and established its claims and aspirations with great clarity. His works were reissued many times, and especially in the seventeenth century. Loyseau had great ability in conveying the state of mind of the bourgeoisie, since he himself was part of it, as a lawyer in the *Parlement de Paris* – about which Cardinal de Retz made some very relevant remarks in his *Mémoires*: 'If we as *frondeurs* seek to occupy the place of the *Parlement* we shall attract the hatred and jealousy of a third of

* This is a translation of sections 1 and 3 of Chapter II of the Third Part of Boris Porshnev's work on popular uprisings in France before the Fronde, made from the French edition of the work, *Les soulèvements populaires en France de 1623 à 1648* (Paris, 1963) pp. 539–61 and 574–82.

the population of Paris, and of the most important bourgeois who are bound to this assembly by I know not how many different ties.'[1]

The three fundamental works of Loyseau are his *Traité des seigneuries*, the *Traité du droit des offices* and the *Traité des ordres et simples dignitez*.[2] In these works, Loyseau formulates a well co-ordinated system whose goal is essentially to establish proof of the political and social equality of the bourgeoisie with the nobility, and to raise the bourgeoisie in theory to the same level in the state as the nobility, on the grounds that the bourgeoisie occupy the offices of the public administration.

Loyseau therefore divides men in the first place into two categories, those who command and those who obey: 'Since we may not all live together on the footing of equality, it is very necessary that some should command and that others should obey.'[3] In other words, the bourgeoisie is anxious to affirm through its spokesman Loyseau that it belongs to the dominant classes. Loyseau's arguments are entirely rational: just as in Nature everything is based on hierarchical relationships between the different parts, so, in the State, the division between those who command and those who obey serves to transform the multiple divisions and relationships of men into a wise and viable whole. Those who command are in turn themselves divided into two essential groups: the *seigneurs* and the *officiers*†. A common characteristic of these two groups is that both are representatives of authority, but their authority is different. The two first treatises are devoted to these representatives of authority, the *seigneurs* and the *officiers*. The third, the *Traité des ordres*, has the task of clearly establishing the frontier between the two categories, between those who command and those who obey, and of classifying the latter.

Loyseau does not in any way oppose the bourgeoisie to the absolute monarchy. He cannot conceive of the bourgeoisie except within the framework of the monarchy, even if this means giving the latter a rather unusual image. Whereas the feudal ideology saw God as the highest suzerain of the feudal hierarchy, the king being his first vassal, the lawyer Loyseau proposes a characteristic amendment. For him the king is not only God's vassal on earth, but also an *officier* established by God in that position. From this dual bond of the king to God, Loyseau deduces a comparable duality for all power on earth:

The king [he writes] is the perfect *officier*, having the full exercise of all public power, as well as perfect *seigneur*, having the full ownership of all public power. But I declare him to be an *officier* and feudatory at once, both in regard to God and to the people. In the first place, he is God's *officier* . . . And the truth is that just as the power of the *officiers* is but a ray of the princely power, so the power of the prince is merely the ray and brilliance of the omnipotence of God . . . In like manner, they [the princes] are vassals and feudatories of God.[4]

It is to be noted that the king as *officier* takes precedence over the king as feudatory. But the essential thing for Loyseau is not to establish the primacy between them, but to establish the dual nature of power. Just as the duality of the kingly power derives from God, so in the same way the dual power of *officiers* and *seigneurs* flows from the king. The right to create *officiers* belongs to the sovereign alone;[5] and the sovereign alone can create *seigneuries*†.[6]

What then is the difference between these two powers? The power of the *seigneurs* is only a 'simple property' and may be exercised through intermediaries, whereas *officiers* hold their power within themselves and by reason of their functions.[7] The following is the definition which Loyseau gives to *seigneuries*, to distinguish them from offices: 'in general, the *seigneurie* is "power in property." ' A brief enough definition, which comprehends at one and the same time the characteristic common to both *seigneuries* and offices – the 'power' – and the factor which differentiates them, namely 'property'. This it is which separates *seigneuries* from offices; the 'power' of the latter consists in their function and the exercise of that function, but not in terms of 'property', as with the *seigneurs*.[8]

Despite the differences between the two kinds of power, Loyseau is not concerned to oppose them to each other. He tends on the contrary to reconcile them with each other, by on the one hand (in his *Traité du droit des offices*) raising the significance of offices to the point where the differences between nobles and *officiers* become insignificant, and, on the other (in his *Traité des seigneuries*), by diminishing the seigneurial power, by presenting the *seigneur* as a sort of *officier*. According to Loyseau, in the beginning *seigneurs* were only *officiers*, but their power was transformed progressively into property, into hereditary property. Loyseau says that the resemblance between the power of the *officier* and that of the *seigneur* is so great that neither the Greeks nor the Romans knew how to define them under different names.[9] And even now, he says, it is easy to rediscover this similarity. Loyseau distinguishes a private *seigneurie* from the public *seigneurie*. A private *seigneurie* in France, where there is no longer either slavery or serfdom, no longer represents a power exercised over men, but almost exclusively a power over land, a form of landed property. But the public *seigneurie*, or suzerainty, is uniquely the property of the king. If this were not so, we should find ourselves faced with a usurpation of power and a logical absurdity. Now an aspect of this suzerainty, namely sovereignty, may be transferred by the state to the *seigneurs* in the form of rights and legal and political functions. Thus, in legal terms, the *seigneurie* resembles an office to a considerable degree, since an office was nothing more than the transfer of the sovereignty of the State to a private individual. One can see now that in these terms the difference between an *officier* and a *seigneur* becomes insignificant; it lies solely in the title of nobility. This difference can easily become blurred however. Loyseau indicates that just as, according to ancient custom, the possession of a *terre noble* for three generations confers the title of nobility upon a commoner family, so, in exactly the same way, the ownership of an office through three generations confers hereditary nobility upon a family. Thus, says Loyseau, the essential point is not the automatic ennoblement, but the fact that the two aspects of power, the *seigneurie* and the office, are equal and similar, since both derive from the power of the king. The nobility is therefore not a caste by birth, since the king can confer the title and privileges of nobility upon a commoner.[10]

The first part of his programme seems therefore achieved; namely, to represent the bourgeoisie as a dominant class in an '*Etat nobiliaire*', which means presenting it as some kind of double of the nobility. The second part of the programme remains to be done; that is, to separate the bourgeoisie from the ordinary people, by demonstrating that the right to hold office represents the inherent characteristic of each bourgeois, and that it is this which distinguishes him from the people. Loyseau does not immediately invoke the power of money in support of his argument, but introduces the concept of '*dignité*' or '*qualité d'honneur*'. And it is with this idea in support of his case that he finally succeeds in reconciling the idea of the 'bourgeoisie' with that of the '*officier*', in the same way as he identifies the idea of 'landed proprietor' with that of '*seigneur*'.

In his *Traité des ordres et simples dignitez*, Loyseau gives himself the task of defining not the characteristics of those who command, but the different estates and ranks of those who obey.[11] Now, each person who possesses the power of command, whether as an *officier* or as a *seigneur*, must himself in turn submit himself to another. Does the frontier therefore disappear between those who command and those who obey? In no way, since there exists a sign by which we can know whether an individual is capable of commanding or only of obeying. This sign is '*la dignité*'. With this word, Loyseau defines the characteristic of the dominant classes. All those who obey are divided into those who possess *dignités* and are also capable of command, and those who do not possess *dignités*, and are incapable of command. The former can also be divided into groups according to their *dignités*. In this way, the *dignité* of ecclesiastics raises them to a special ecclesiastical order, and the *dignité* of the *seigneurs* places them also in a special order of nobility.

But what was there to be done with the *tiers etat*? Loyseau resolutely cuts short the question. He categorically refuses to accept the existence of such an estate: the Third Estate is not an estate in the true sense,[12] but simply a form of expression. Since an order is a form of *dignité*, the Third Estate is not really an estate at all, since it includes the totality of the French population, with the exception of the clergy and the nobility. If it were an 'order', the whole of the population would therefore possess a kind of *dignité*,[13] meaning that everyone commanded, which would be an absurdity. We realise that it is not a matter of creating a fourth order, which could, in Loyseau's scheme of things, save the situation. Loyseau avoids all the obstacles in his path. He does not divide this Third Estate into two, but affirms rather that there are many degrees or levels at the heart of the single Third Estate,[14] which is the same as to say that the idea of a Third Estate is in itself an imprecise one. What variety of degrees had Loyseau in mind? There were, he declared, men of letters, financiers, professional men of all kinds, merchants, land-owners, bureaucrats, artisans and manual workers, who had all to be spoken of separately[15] and who were not therefore to be merged into a single order.

This was on his part merely a tactical manœuvre, however, since, on examining these groups more closely, Loyseau does indeed find a frontier dividing them into two: namely, those who possess the '*dignité de bourgeois*' and, with it, access to office, and those who do not. His scale in fact stops short at merchants. In this way, *dignité* becomes a matter of etiquette, a title which enables us to classify all the various social functions, from the king down to the bourgeois. These are all given the title '*honorables hommes*', and '*honnestes personnes*'.[16] Those who come below the bourgeois have no right to any title whatever: 'merchants are the last group to bear the *qualité d'honneur*, being ranked as *honorables hommes* or *honnestes personnes* and *bourgeois des villes*. These are the *qualités* which are not attributable to *laboureurs* or to constables or artisans, and less still to manual workers, who are all to be considered *viles personnes*.'[17]

We see therefore that for Loyseau the word 'bourgeois' has the sense of a feudal title. It confers on the individual all the privileges and all the prerogatives of medieval cities.[18] According to him, the lowest people have no right to the title of bourgeois, nor do they have the right to the honours of the town, nor to any voice in its assemblies, which indeed form the very privileges of the bourgeoisie.[19] Or, to put it differently, to be bourgeois means to have the right to take part in urban administration and to hold municipal office, or, better still, office in the state. Merchants, according to Loyseau, classify themselves as bourgeois, to the extent that they enjoy privileges and are capable of holding urban office, which must never be confided to '*gens mécaniques*'.[20] Thus to be bourgeois and to be capable of exercising office are one and the same thing — which was, in the first place, the thing to be proved.

Besides the argument from feudal and legal premises, we notice here something more concrete in the words Loyseau uses, in that the sign which separates '*viles personnes*' from the bourgeois is in fact formulated. '*Viles personnes*' are those who pursue work which is '*mécanique*'. To belong to the ranks of the '*gens de qualité*', it is clearly necessary either to practise an intellectual profession or to possess a fortune large enough to enable one not to work. Loyseau defines these distinctions in this way: 'artisans and *gens de mestier* are those who exercise the mechanical arts, called thus to distinguish them from the liberal arts, since the mechanical arts were previously exercised by serfs and slaves. Indeed, we commonly term '*mécanique*' that which is low and mean.'[21]

In Loyseau's mind, the distinctive features of the liberal professions take second place to a more important feature, that of wealth. What is it that enables merchants to become bourgeois and to exercise office? Loyseau replies simply enough: 'their habitual wealth, as much as their utility and the public need for trade, brings them trust and deference.'[22] In effect, in order to be placed on the register of the bourgeoisie of the towns, it was enough to satisfy certain material conditions; to own a town house, to furnish a certain sum of money, etc.[23]

Here we reach the very foundations of Loyseau's theory. French seventeenth-century society was already deeply affected by the new division of men, based on an opposition between labour and capitalist property, which broke through the traditional feudal and corporate barriers. It is just this sense of opposition which informs the mind of Loyseau. All those who gain their living by mechanical work, that is to say all the direct producers, and especially those among them who sell their work, the 'mercenaries', are for Loyseau '*viles personnes*', and exist only to obey. All the rest are called to command, and, in one way or another, to rule.

It is in Loyseau's attitude toward the manual workers that this opposition really shows itself, as the basis of all his theories. We have seen that he declares the artisan class a '*métier mécanique*'. But the new social and economic division has already destroyed the unity of this idea of the 'artisan'. Whereas the majority of the artisans were becoming ruined and stranded among the plebeian mass, the richest among them were becoming capitalists, belonging to the class of the well-to-do and therefore to the bourgeois class. This is how Loyseau extricates himself from this difficult situation:

No matter how much artisans are properly mechanics and reputed to be *viles personnes*, there are nevertheless certain crafts which are crafts and trade together, which in so far as they are crafts are treated in the same way as simple crafts, but in so far as they participate in trade are *honorables* and those who exercise them are in no way considered among the *viles personnes* . . . in this way they are able to qualify as *honorables hommes* and bourgeois, like other merchants; such as the Apothecaries, Goldsmiths, Jewellers, Mercers, Wholesalers, Drapers, Hosiers and other such like, as is to be seen in the Ordinances.

On the contrary there are crafts, in which bodily discomfort is more important than trading in merchandise and which involve no subtlety of mind; these are the lowest in rank . . .

And with even stronger reason, those who pursue no craft, nor trade, and who gain their living with the work of their arms, whom we call '*gens de bras*', or 'mercenaries', such as common carriers, building labourers, carters and other day-labourers, are all of them the lowest of the lower classes. For there is no worse vocation than to have no vocation.[24]

We know already that not only does Loyseau in no way deplore the existence of a class of *viles personnes*, but, on the contrary, considers the existence of this class as one of the laws of nature, of reason and divine wisdom. He sees no necessity to modify the condition of those who, according to God's law, gain their living with the sweat of their body. What disquiets him is the beggary, the vagabondage which is developing in French society, principally from financial pressure. He considers that this unproductive burden could seriously threaten the equilibrium of public life:

In a few words, if one does not give order to this [problem], two disadvantages will arise from the enormous increase which occurs daily in the number of this rabble; in that, first, the needs of agriculture will not be met, from the lack of men wishing to gain employment in it; and, second, travellers will no longer have security on the roads, nor rural people in their houses.[25]

Evidently, Loyseau was not conscious that he was describing the characteristics of a process of 'primary accumulation', which, on a large scale, brought capital and labour, that is bourgeois property and the impoverished workers, into opposition. On the other side of the Channel too, where this process was also developing in classic fashion, the ideologues of the bourgeoisie saw pauperism as a social calamity, while at the same time, as they bewailed it, pleading for the most sanguinary legislation against it, as indispensable to capitalism, for use against the expropriated.

The legal treatises of Loyseau, in spite of their typically bourgeois limitations, contain not only the ideal of the French seventeenth-century bourgeoisie, but also, so to say, the anatomy of the feudal-absolutist regime. That is indeed their value. These treatises reveal clearly enough that the bourgeoisie could not define its frontiers on both its sides; and that, since it had the choice, it preferred for a long time to define its frontier on the side where its exploitative nature revealed itself most; that is to say on the side of the people. This definition of frontier, expressed so well by Loyseau, corresponds perfectly to the economic opposition which had arisen between labour and capital in the formation of capitalism. But to the extent that the bourgeoisie discovered its own characteristics in the sub-soil of society, it had at the same time to lose them on the surface of it, at the point where its *rapprochement* with the nobility was effected; since the nobility was also opposed to the people, and even more radically so than the bourgeoisie. This *rapprochement* between the bourgeoisie and the nobility manifested itself in political terms in the form of absolutism.

If we consider the history of the western European bourgeoisie during the whole medieval period, we can assert that it did not participate in the political power of the state, except to the extent that it ceased to be a capitalist class. This thesis does not require special explanation until the end of the fifteenth century, since before then we find ourselves confronted almost exclusively by a 'feudal bourgeoisie' (to use the term of F. Engels), that is the artisans of the *faubourgs*, in short the urban population of the Middle Ages. To this 'feudal bourgeoisie', we must add the medieval representatives of capital, which was not dependent on production, namely the merchants and moneylenders. Their existence was not in any way in opposition to feudalism. To understand the validity of our theory for the period from the sixteenth to the eighteenth century, a complex dialectic must be taken into account, an internal contradiction which was characteristic of the bourgeoisie in this transitional period.

A celebrated Marxist thesis asserts that the bourgeois revolution habitually begins when more or less achieved forms of the capitalist system exist, which have established themselves and have matured well before the revolution declares itself within feudal society.

This concept contains the whole destiny of the bourgeoisie during these centuries, in all aspects of its internal contradiction, when capitalism was already in existence but the political revolution of the bourgeoisie had not yet taken place. The bourgeoisie would not have been bourgeoisie, if, to a certain extent, social and political power did not belong to it. But in contrast to the earlier period, when the capitalist system did not yet exist, it had constantly to transform itself now through artifice into a 'feudal bourgeoisie', which involved renouncing its class, renouncing itself even, in order to obtain a share only of social and political power.

This necessity expressed itself in the first place in the claims the bourgeoisie made about its position in the feudal and absolutist regime.

Loyseau's work shows clearly that the French bourgeoisie was unable to consider itself a dominant class, and could only oppose itself to the people in so far as it could accommodate itself to the nobility or identify itself with it. It was unable to consider itself simply as bourgeoisie, since to oppose the king and the nobility would have involved uniting with the people, in the Third Estate, and thus to decide on revolution, in order to discover on the other side of the revolution its true class identity. But this moment was not yet come. We have already seen how the French bourgeoisie of the seventeenth century was daily obliged to avoid this question and finally avoided it each time, in the same way.

The problem was not however limited to the mind of the bourgeoisie. In denying itself, in renouncing the revolution from its very depth, it infallibly lost many of its class-characteristics. *Rapprochement* with the royal power and the nobility brought in its train an effect which ran counter to its very social identity and changed its economic activity. In this way the evolution of capitalism itself took two steps forward and one step back. This is why we speak of the internal contradiction at the heart of the bourgeoisie in this period.

This *rapprochement* of the seventeenth-century bourgeoisie with the feudal-absolutist regime (and its consequent loss of certain of its class-characteristics) may be considered under three aspects:
1 the political *rapprochement*, arising from large-scale creation of offices.
2 the social *rapprochement*, arising from the bourgeoisie adopting the way of life of the nobility.
3 the economic *rapprochement*, arising from the transformation of industrial and commercial capital into capital in the form of credit.

We cannot give here a detailed description of the French seventeenth-century bourgeoisie. French historians have accumulated a considerable amount of documentation on this subject.[26] We must however give certain explanations and clarifications in this area.

1   *The Political Rapprochement*

In the eyes of Marx, the essential characteristic of French history is that from the time of the rise of the towns the French bourgeoisie was influenced to a too great extent by establishing itself in the *Parlement* and the royal bureaucracy, at a time when the English bourgeoisie was solely preoccupied with commerce and industry.[27]

In fact, in seventeenth-century Dijon, for example, two-fifths of the population, in their role as *officiers*, had the privilege of fiscal exemption.[28] Loyseau, in identifying the bourgeois with the *officier*, is not speaking of an ideal but of the real situation of things: in the towns every *honnête homme* had his office, just as every monk had in his monastery.[29]

Since to become an *officier* it was enough to possess the means for buying an office, and, for some at least, to have some facility with Latin, every Frenchman in comfortable circumstances sought to acquire an office in town or state, or at least to reserve one for his children. Judicial and financial offices and many others were already put on the market in the sixteenth century. Office was a kind of private property; and, from 1604, it was transformed into hereditary property on condition that the owner paid an annual idemnity to the Treasury, called the *'paulette'*. It is at this moment that a very great rise in the price of offices begins which is to last throughout the seventeenth century; while at the same time the government never ceases to multiply the creation of them. Offices were at various prices and degrees of importance. They were to be found to suit all purses; from village bailiffs and notaries up to the *conseillers*† and *présidents*† of the *parlements*†. New offices found immediate buyers. The demand was inexhaustible.

We cannot give a detailed description here of this very interesting phenomenon of the social and political history of seventeenth-century France. We would refer the reader to the work of Roland Mousnier which we have already cited, *Venality of Office under Henry IV and Louis XIII* (1945). R. Mousnier's study is a very considerable achievement in defining the precise origins of the system of venality of office and its different characteristics at the time of its zenith in the first half of the seventeenth century. Today, no serious study of the bourgeoisie and of the French bourgeoisie in particular could be undertaken without using Mousnier's work. The work is notable for showing the detailed mechanism of the creation of an office, and of installation in office through the royal trade in offices. Mousnier establishes the number of offices which were for sale, the different categories and prices, the rights concerning transfer, resale and inheritance, the importance of the trade for the royal finances, the significance of their purchase as capital investment by the bourgeoisie and the proportion of such purchases in the fortunes of the wealthy at that time. These problems largely transcend the study of the administrative apparatus of the French state. Offices were created, not because they were needed, but because the state simply had a need for money. Frequently they were entirely useless, even harmful; frequently they were bought not for the purpose of exercising the function concerned, but of selling it again to another purchaser. Mousnier shows that between 1600 and 1643 the revenues from the *Parties Casuelles*† represented from twenty-five to fifty per cent of the royal revenues, and that the major part of these came simply from the creation and sale of new offices.[30]

After studying a number of biographies, Mousnier concludes that almost all the *officiers* were bourgeois in origin. The richer the bourgeois was, the more important was the office he acquired.[31]

What profit was there in all this to the purchasers? Contemporaries, speaking of the 'folly of office', suggest two motives: vanity and avarice. An office brought its purchaser not only revenues and privileges (total or partial exemption from taxes), but also the prestige of power and authority, honour and consideration, and, in the end, even the smallest office was a first step toward nobility: at a certain rank in the profession the title of personal nobility was automatically conferred, and inheritance of office through three generations conferred the title to hereditary nobility. A large number of *officiers* thus became noble. In Brittany, for example, the *officiers* and judges in the *parlement* all sat with the noble order in the provincial Estates, since their offices conferred these rights. Every rich man could purchase an office, don the robe, and thus draw near to the nobility. Loyseau's ideas were therefore only an idealisation of what the bourgeoisie actually put into practice.

The motive of 'vanity' was therefore inseparable from that of 'avarice'. But the first derived many of its origins from the social order. Many contemporaries considered venality of office as no more than a sale of honours, a tax on vanity. Richelieu explains the introduction of venality under Francis I from the fact that there had been no surer or swifter means to acquire the wealth of his subjects than to confer on them honours in return for money.[32] Montesquieu said that although the king of France did not possess gold mines like the king of Spain, he was however rich, since the vanity of his subjects was more inexhaustible than any mine.[33] Loyseau criticises severely the simplification of the system of selling offices, in which no account was taken of the merit of the *officier*. This new system, he says, profanes the idea of authority itself, in transforming office into a simple form of property, like the *seigneurie*. And he mocks the purchasers of office:

This is why, having discovered in the time of our fathers, this fine financial secret for raising by means of offices an immense but nevertheless imperceptible source of taxation, voluntarily contributed to and desired through the ambition and folly of the wealthy of our realm, it is used daily, both at need and indeed without it. It is a form of mania, without any restraint; a bottomless fund, a source which although drawn on daily can never be exhausted. It is entirely idle to create new offices, since on the rumour of new creations, they are bought up before the edict is registered. The king can create as many as he likes, he will always be sure of getting rid of them, for, as Le Sage says, the number of madmen is infinite and it is now a common saying among us that "there are always more fools than the number of offices on offer". If there is ever a king of France with the ambition to appropriate the wealth of his subjects, as the king of Egypt did in the year of his dearth, he would only need to create offices. Everyone would vie in bearing his purse to him. He who had no money would sell his land; he who hadn't enough land to sell would sell himself if he were allowed to do so, and would willingly agree to become a slave in order to become an *officier*.[34]

In part, Loyseau is certainly motivated here by zeal for his own caste against interlopers, and by his attachment to municipal and paternal nomination to office. But he is also disturbed by a situation which in his eyes was a serious one. The massive movement of the bourgeoisie into office threatened to ruin the foundations of bourgeois wealth. 'Half the inhabitants of our towns are now *officiers*', he wrote, 'commerce is deserted, agriculture is abandoned to the peasants.'[35]

In effect, the ever-increasing number of *gens de robe* had a direct repercussion on the economy of the realm. Describing the situation of France at the beginning of the seventeenth century, an Englishman notes that the profession of merchant was much less highly regarded there than anywhere else, but that nowhere else was there such haste to acquire office as in France.[36]

According to an *intendant* at the time of Colbert, as soon as a merchant had some substance, he thought only of one thing, how to become a member of a municipal corporation, and no longer wished to concern himself with trade.[37] The author of *Le parfait négociant*, J. Savary, writes at the end of the seventeenth century: 'As soon as a merchant in France has acquired great riches from trade, far from it that his children should pursue the same profession. On the contrary, they enter public office; whereas in Holland the children of merchants ordinarily pursue the profession and trade of their father.'[38]

We see therefore how the bourgeoisie lost its class-characteristics through this large-scale transformation of merchants and *manufacturiers* into *officiers*. Moreover the establishment of the bourgeoisie within the feudal-absolutist regime placed a brake on its economic development, diminished capital accumulation in trade and industry and deprived the nascent capitalist class of its most active elements. When Henry IV created his *commission de commerce* to consider measures necessary for the development of industry and trade, he found himself unable to appoint a single merchant or entrepreneur to it who was either experienced or active enough. He was accordingly obliged to constitute his *commission* entirely of *officiers*.[39] Throughout the seventeenth century the situation deteriorated. At the time of Colbert, the Dutch ambassador wrote that France was totally incapable of undertaking overseas trade, since the character of the nation was opposed to it, being too much devoted to pleasure and vanity. 'Here there is no merchant who, having acquired a hundred thousand *écus* and sometimes less, does not seek to buy some landed estate or some office, and, as a consequence, withdraws all his money from trade.'[40] It was evidently not simply a matter, however, of 'national character', and the 'vanity' which is in question here contained, beyond its social and political elements, a factor of self-interest. The race for office was not in fact in any way meaningless from a monetary point of view. The *Mercure françois* wrote in 1624: 'the over-population of our colleges proves that many abandon commerce, and cease to occupy themselves in agriculture and other *métiers* useful for life and the general good, in order to devote themselves to law-school, in the hope of increasing their fortune when they wear the longer robe.'[41]

2 *The Social Rapprochement*

In France, the different orders were not so much separated by their status as by their mode of existence, their conduct in life and their general appearance, extending from their sources of income to their clothes and manners, which unmistakably defined their membership of a particular order. Thus a noble must wear coloured clothes in order to distinguish himself from the black and grey of the Third Estate.

The noble must have a 'seigneurial' and 'noble' life-style, in comparison with the household of an ordinary citizen or peasant. Under no circumstances had he to engage in commerce, industry or manual work, which were occupations reserved to the Third Estate. Loyseau explains why a noble following a trade or any other work unworthy of his rank had to pay *taille* and thus enter the ranks of the *taillables*: 'it is not enough to be noble if one does not live in the style of a noble.'[42] The inverse reasoning imposes itself: it was enough to live in the style of a noble in order to be noble *de facto*. Quite evidently the idea of living *'noblement'* played an important role in the aspirations of the French seventeenth-century bourgeoisie. It was the goal that the well-to-do strove to attain, and according to the degree with which he could attain it, this life-style established the desired frontier between himself and the ordinary people. There was no detail of dress, no detail of etiquette which the bourgeoisie would not employ to enter the ranks of the nobility. We find in Loyseau a truly curious reasoning in this respect: the wives of the bourgeoisie appropriated the title of 'madame', which previously had belonged only to women of the nobility, in order to distinguish themselves from the wives of the artisan class.[43] The author of a pamphlet of 1619 wrote with every satisfaction: 'What is a merchant today? And what is there more *honorable* today? One can recognise him now by his fortune. He is clad in silk and a coat of plush.'[44] On the other hand, the couplets of a certain Collete, which were inspired by noble circles in Paris, published in 1665 under the title of 'The Vanity and Pomp of the Simple Bourgeoisie', vibrate with indignation; the author complains, among other things, that one can no longer distinguish gentlewomen from ordinary women because the latter wear clothes 'inappropriate to their rank'.[45]

But the principal sign of the noble's life-style was the source of his income. In this regard, the social mimicry of the bourgeoisie, the progressive disappearance of its class-characteristics, had a decisive repercussion on its economic activity. French seventeenth-century architecture is justly notable for a fairly curious detail: the street-level shop disappears from houses belonging to well-to-do bourgeoisie; it is now separated from their dwelling, for the simple reason that one cannot live *noblement* and at the same time take part in trade. These are two things which cannot go together. As soon as he became rich a merchant blushed to be a trader; and if he did not actually withdraw from his business, he entrusted it most often to assistants or agents. An *intendant* writes at the time of Louis XIV that merchants could have become rich to an unheard-of degree if only they had been more enterprising than usual; their greatest defect in his eyes being that they lacked enthusiasm for what they were doing.[46] But how could it have been otherwise when they saw in their activity only a dishonourable and low-born means of attaining higher rank? Richelieu himself expressed this paradoxical idea: if honours and in particular offices could be obtained without money, commerce would find itself abandoned.[47] This is how Savary sought to persuade merchants to remain in commerce: every day, he writes, we see merchants and traders who amass great fortunes and present their children with the highest offices in the magistracy.[48]

Mousnier offers us rich source material to illustrate everything we have just said:

> In this society of the first half of the seventeenth century, so modern in so many of its aspects [he writes], the Middle Ages lived on. This nobility, so frequently the subject of criticism, is always highly regarded, highly envied and closely imitated, on account of its titles, its rank, its privileges . . . All members of the inferior classes have their eyes fixed on the nobility, usurp their dress, their insignia, their mode of life and speech . . . But all that was only a question of appearances. The constant thought, the dream of all men of ambition was to become, in fact, a *gentilhomme*.
> It was entirely possible [that they could become so]. This society was not composed of castes, where men were imprisoned by their birth; but a society of classes. They could pass from one to another, providing they fulfilled certain conditions . . .
> Thus between the merchant class and that of the *gentilshommes* there was a great gap, entirely filled by *officiers*. On the other hand, a section of the *officiers* finds itself on a level with the different categories of the *bourgeois des villes*. Since venality provides access to the highest

offices, it is thus possible to reach up to the superior classes of society . . . The *officiers*, especially those of the *Parlements*, frequently obtain letters of nobility for their services with the title of *écuyer*; the *Présidents* of the *Parlements* are *chevaliers* even, and some members of the sovereign courts are *barons*.[49]

The well-to-do bourgeois did not invest his capital in office alone. When a merchant or trader had succeeded in accumulating a considerable amount of capital, he often sought to purchase landed estates and thus assimilate himself into the class of *seigneurs*, although this form of capital investment might not be entirely profitable. It is precisely in the seventeenth century that massive purchases of estates were made by well-to-do citizens who at the same time acquired offices in the magistracy, the municipality and other offices. They then added with pride the words '*sieur de*' to their names; that is to say, owner of such and such a landed property.[50] After the purchase of an estate, they could benefit from feudal rents. It was in this way that capital accumulated in trade and industry passed into landed property and lost its capitalist character. In the methods of exploitation of these new landed properties (whether it was a question of smallholdings in the *faubourgs* of towns or only medium-sized *seigneuries*, or on the contrary a question of usurping enormous feudal properties together with the titles they conferred), we do not perceive any attempts to reform the traditional seigneurial regime, no capitalist effort tending toward the investment of funds in agriculture.

Let us once more refer to Mousnier. He has studied the fortunes of a large number of *officiers*. As a general rule, these were composed of three main elements: real estate (land and houses), rents and offices. The proportion of these three elements varies in individual cases a great deal; but generally the real-estate element – land and houses – amounted to more than offices, in spite of the advantages these conferred – such as privileges, sources of revenue (which were more important), exemption from numerous taxes, together with an advantageous position in the social hierarchy and local influence. The reason for this was that offices seemed to contemporaries a less secure business than land. Every *officier* was attracted to landed property, which assured him of a solid domestic regime, and permitted him to maintain a distinguished mode of life and to own a fief. To own a fief signified proximity to the nobility and permitted him to hope that his grandson would become effectively and indisputably noble:

Such sentiments [Mousnier thinks] deflected capital from industry and trade much more effectively than foreign competition. Agriculture itself scarcely benefited, because the development of the land was most often left to farmers without the means. The taste for offices and land thus contributed – in addition to the incessant appeals of the king for the resources of the thrifty under various guises – to the reduction of capital available to new enterprises. It is this which in large part explains . . . why France remained essentially an agricultural country, in which industry only made slow progress and maintained its traditional character, at a time when in fact a primary industrial revolution was taking place in England. It is this which enables us to understand better why, in spite of the successes of the mercantilists in the king's entourage and the interventionism of the state, the serious efforts of Henry IV to develop manufactures and the immense efforts of Richelieu to make France a victorious rival of the Dutch and English, to give her indeed economic hegemony through the growth of industry and the creation of great trading companies, should have in the end failed. The country did not fall into line.[51]

The bourgeoisie did not utilise its wealth to pursue capitalist activity, but to take its place instead among the ranks of the nobility. This was the second way in which the bourgeoisie lost its class-characteristics; the first being the almost universal infatuation of the bourgeoisie with offices in the state, whose role indeed was, very precisely, to prevent the bourgeois revolution in France.

Malesherbes described in a celebrated formula in the eighteenth century the strange situation of French society: every nobleman is not rich, but every rich man is noble. We can read in a comedy of 1635 that a 'man is already noble if he possesses money'.[52] La Bruyère expresses the same idea, though with more subtlety and more profundity:

Rehabilitation, a word in use in the courts, has made the term *lettres de noblesse*, once so French and so much in use, old-fashioned and barbarous; to rehabilitate oneself implies that a man who has become rich was originally noble and that it is necessary, rather than a matter of moral right, that he should be so. His father may in truth have lost his noble status through either using the plough or hoe, or through being a pedlar or wearing someone's livery; but it is only a matter for him to enter once again into the original rights of his ancestors and to continue using the arms of his house, which however he has invented for himself and are in truth entirely different from those on his pewter vessels. In brief, *lettres de noblesse* are no longer suitable for him; for they merely honour a commoner, that is to say a man who still seeks the secret of becoming rich.[53]

In the pamphlet of 1619 cited above, the author asks 'What can be said about the Parisian bourgeoisie?' and replies:

When the Scripture speaks of the excellence of Man, it says that he was created a little lower than the angels; as for me, I say of a bourgeois that he is only a little lower than the nobility; and if I said they were equal, I do not know that I would be wrong, in view of the fact that the nobility joins itself and annexes itself to him by marriage, in such a way that they form only one body, one family, one purse, one union, one consanguinity, which makes this *qualité* of bourgeois lose itself in exchange for nobility.[54]

It would be quite erroneous of course to assimilate the seventeenth-century bourgeoisie into the nobility. That remained a dream for the majority, which went no further than external parody. But it has nevertheless to be said that intermarriage between bourgeoisie and nobility did not merely satisfy the self-esteem of the bourgeoisie, it also had important social consequences. By becoming the relation of a *seigneur* of a certain rank, a bourgeois obtained his protection, entered into a kind of vassalage with him. This often applied to his whole family, sometimes even to a whole corporation of *officiers*. In acquiring a noble fief, a bourgeois came to imitate the noble life-style; but above all he arranged matters so that he lived from seigneurial rents and abandoned the office which had served him as a step in his social ascent, while his sons and grandsons merged entirely with the other country nobility. This explains why the actual percentage of *officiers* among the landed proprietors did not increase in the seventeenth century, although the purchase of estates by *officiers* never ceased to increase.[55] A large number of them, on becoming landed proprietors, renounced their offices, and thus finally broke with their bourgeois past. To prove one's nobility in seventeenth-century France, it was enough to certify that one had owned a *seigneurie* exempted from taxes for three generations, and presumably bribes and frauds often cut short those requisite periods of delay. We already know that other bourgeois families received titles of nobility in cognizance of the exercise of certain high offices for three generations. Many bourgeois also obtained titles of nobility for service in the army and at Court. In sum, the social *rapprochement* of the bourgeoisie with the nobility expressed itself in the complete ennoblement of a section of the bourgeoisie, without, we may note, any comparable *embourgeoisement* of the nobility, as was the case of course in England.

3   The Economic Rapprochement

The motivations within the social and political system which induced the bourgeoisie to withdraw its capital from commercial and industrial activity were finally inseparable from purely economic motivations. It was fiscal pressure which forced the bourgeoisie along its path. As part of the Third Estate, it belonged to the taxable population, the commoners. The distinction between the three estates in France was traditionally formulated in the statement that ecclesiastics served the king with prayer, the *seigneurs* with the sword, and the Third Estate with its possessions. In fact, royal absolutism considered the possessions of its unprivileged subjects as its own. This was not only a matter of social theory; the more absolutism reinforced itself, the more it laid claim to the possessions of the Third Estate through taxation.

The reactionary Saint-Simon wrote with great vexation at the beginning of the eighteenth century that it was simply property which created the strength and *raison d'être* of the Third Estate; contrary to the two first orders, which placed little emphasis on material goods, the Third Estate held on to its property as its only happiness. It was this which determined its exalted rank and the stability of its position in society.[56] How could these same possessions however, which absolutism coveted and appropriated without scruple, even to the point where they had to be concealed and lied about, represent the reason both for the exalted rank of the Third Estate and for the stability of its social position?

For this reason: in the same way that the Third Estate did not constitute a unity, so its fortune presented very varied aspects. The fiscal burden weighed differently on the property of those who acquired it by work than it did on the bourgeoisie.

The former were oppressed very considerably by the fiscal pressure of the state. Already, Loyseau speaks of the crowd of sturdy beggars with which France was gorged as a result of excessive *taille*, which forced workers to leave everything and become beggars and vagabonds, living in idleness without resource, at the expense of others, rather than continue working for nothing beyond what was needed to pay their *taille*.[57] At the beginning of the eighteenth century, Vauban also exposed the effect of fiscal pressure on the condition of the mass of the people:

> Things are reduced to such a state that the man who might use his talents to learn an art or trade, which would place him and his family in a position to live a little more at their ease, prefers idleness instead; and he who might more or less have had one or two cows and some ewes and lambs, together with what he needs to improve his farm or his land, is obliged to do without it, so as not to be ruined by the *taille* of the following year, as he would certainly be, if he made any surplus for himself, and his harvest was seen to be a little more plentiful than usual. This is why he lives very poorly, both he and his family, and at a very low level of consumption. Even more important, however, he allows the little land he has to deteriorate, by only working it by half, for fear that if it yielded all that it could, with good manure and good cultivation, the opportunity would merely be taken to double his *taille*.[58]

This characterises very well the condition of wealth acquired by labour. But it only corresponds to a half of the reality, since a section of the

Third Estate had another source of wealth which was bourgeois and capitalist. What was the source of that?

It can be seen notably in Normandy. Although the absolutist administration maintained strict surveillance over the property of the Third Estate and constantly expropriated it, capital accumulation nevertheless occurred, within the heart of society itself, through the pores and cracks of the feudal edifice, by the most diverse means and with a remarkable tenacity. As a result, capitalism renewed itself constantly. We recall the celebrated story of Rousseau, about the poor peasant who refused him refreshment on the pretext of his own misery, right up to the moment when he could be finally persuaded that his visitor had nothing to do with the royal fisc. Only then did he bring forth from its hiding place everything needed to make a good meal.

In one way or another, wealth accumulated in embryonic form in the hands of peasants, artisans, small shopkeepers, money-lenders, merchants, entrepreneurs. But it was only short-term and small-scale accumulation As soon as wealth began to show itself, care was needed to protect it from expropriation. To save it involved straightaway changing its use, even if that meant lending it out to avoid taxation. A peasant who had become wealthy would immediately lend his money to his *seigneur*, against his obligation to pay *banalités*† for the use of his mill, and in this way continued to enrich himself undisturbed. The line dividing the wealth of the Third Estate into two kinds was in reality only a distinction as to quantity. Wealth turned toward credit whenever it presented itself in the form of money and in sufficient quantity.

In this situation, all those possessing such wealth sought not only to protect it from fiscal pressure, as with all possessions we fear to lose, but even more to preserve it as working capital, which naturally they sought to increase. There was no other solution therefore than to lend this accumulated wealth to members of the ruling class, who were free from all taxes; or otherwise lend it to the state itself, which imposed the taxes.

The bourgeoisie was therefore very much distinguished economically from the ordinary people. Apparently inseparable from them, it was nonetheless very different. What did this difference consist of? Wealth gained from personal labour does not contain work taken from others. It does not arise from exploitation like the wealth of the bourgeoisie. The expropriation which is contained within bourgeois wealth requires solid security and legal sanction. Since feudal domination by the nobility was perpetuated in both society and state, that security and sanction were obliged to have a feudal character. This is why Engels said that bourgeois property in the Middle Ages was still solidly restricted by feudal limitations and consisted essentially of privileges.[59] In pursuing the course of its historical development, it was to free itself in time from these characteristics, which it held in common with feudal property, just as it was to free itself from all resemblance to personal property acquired by labour. But at the time of which we speak, the acquisition of privileges, especially by loans made to *seigneurs* and the state, represented a necessary condition for differentiating bourgeois wealth from the wealth of the people acquired by labour.

It was first of all a matter of acquiring fiscal privileges. The two first estates of the realm paid no taxes.[60] Their property was preserved by custom and feudal law from expropriation by the state. This is why payment of taxes carried within itself something dishonourable, while tax-exemption 'sounded well' in the feudal society of the French seventeenth century. For a long time, the exercise of various honorary public functions carried with it exemption from taxation, which raised, so to say, the owner of the wealth in question to the level of the privileged seigneurial class. It was, according to contemporary opinion, precisely this flight from taxation which induced the bourgeoisie to acquire office. All the members of the highest courts of justice, all the *officiers des finances*, together with a great number of other *officiers*, were exempt from taxation; so much so that the expenses involved in purchasing an office were paid in advance, because the office concerned rendered the remaining fortune untouchable, that is to say protected it from all royal taxation by a privilege which was seigneurial in origin.

What was more important still, however, was that the wealth acquired by the bourgeoisie was conveyed in the form of credit into the hands of those who were not threatened by expropriation, those who possessed or distributed privilege, namely the nobles and the king himself.

We cannot here research into the reasons why, for centuries, the nobility and the feudal State in Europe constantly lacked credit. We will indicate solely that this situation derived from the contradiction between the monetary system and the natural basis of the feudal economy. In seventeenth-century French society, everything, or almost everything, was bought and sold. Everything however maintained a feudal character. The dominant class and the State had continual need of credit. The bourgeoisie provided this, to the extent that it was able to raise itself above the people. Saint-Simon characterised this state of affairs in a brief formulation: 'In fact, for every creditor from the second order [nobleman], there were a thousand from the Third Estate; and, inversely, for every debtor from the Third Estate there were a thousand from the second.'[61] La Bruyère expressed the same thing more simply: 'The need for money reconciles the nobility with the commoner and abolishes privileges founded on four generations.'[62] The feudal State was indebted to the Third Estate in the same proportions.

We can divide all the credit operations of the bourgeoisie into two groups: namely, credit granted to the nobility and credit made available to the feudal State. Different forms of credit are distinguishable within each group. In the first place, credit was advanced to *seigneurs* in return for the right to farm, either entirely or partially, the seigneurial dues of the landed proprietors concerned. The creditor advanced the amount to be collected from the peasants and then extracted from them something in addition. In this way he profited from feudal relationships, in that the feudal dues became a form of interest on the capital advanced. Loutchiski says that it was rare in the eighteenth century for large or medium-sized properties not to be in the hands of such creditors,[63] and we might say as much for the seventeenth century. The extension of credit to *seigneurs* was also effected by the purchasing of various offices from them, the exercise of which soon brought in the sum invested. Similarly, loans were made direct, either on the security of the landed property of the *seigneur*, or simply with ordinary payment of interest, without security.

The extension of credit to the feudal State was effected in virtually the same forms. The largest accumulations of capital, made from previous credit transactions, were made available to the royal tax-farms, for both the direct or indirect taxes. An agreed sum was paid to the Treasury for a certain tax, usually after an auction. The tax-farmer then had the absolute right, without any form of control whatever, to exact the whole amount from the population, with the addition of his 'interest'. Some of the important tax-farmers redistributed their tax-farms in several lots to less important tax-farmers. These in turn often distributed theirs to lesser men still. This crowd of investors in the tax system consisted of *officiers des finances*, called at this time *les gens de finances*. Also, the bourgeoisie acquired various offices in the State, which we have already referred to, by which they gained a position of advantage in the affairs of the State. The purchase of offices in the judiciary and the State administration did not offer as large returns as the operations of the tax-farmers, but nevertheless guaranteed a secure income for life far in excess of the capital sum invested;[64] partly in the form of a salary, representing in most cases a return of from one to three per cent on capital, with payments however made fairly irregularly, or mainly in the form of legal exactions made on the general population.[65] 'He who buys justice wholesale can sell it retail.'[66] The gifts, the '*épices*', which litigants made to the judges of French courts in the seventeenth century were made quite openly and were a custom accepted by law. The *gens de finances* and the *officiers* were competing groups of royal creditors, and frequently came into conflict. It would, however, be difficult to establish a frontier between them, all the more so since the possessors of financial offices represented an intermediate group between them.

Loyseau wrote that 'because little power and little honour' was accorded those who possessed financial offices 'high salaries had been granted them in compensation', and that it was reasonable that it should be so, in that 'just as a man who handles pitch keeps some of it on his fingers, so those who manage the royal finances should keep their share of them in their hands; a thing which in fact these *officiers* scarcely ever forget.'[67]

Finally, credit was advanced directly to the state, either on the security of the royal domain or without security, by capitalists possessing municipal *'rentes'*, that is to say bonds at interest issued by the state in the name of certain urban corporations.

All these various forms of credit had the same effect. The bourgeoisie was able to free its capital by these means, both directly and indirectly, from all fiscal exactions, which meant that the latter were borne exclusively by the people. In this way, the bourgeoisie preserved its wealth from threat of expropriation, and it remained in the form of capital bringing in an assured and permanent revenue. The bourgeoisie did not however achieve this except in so far as it withdrew its money from trade, industry and agriculture. Fagniez rightly says that the valuable returns assured to capital from investment in office and in the tax-farms removed it from use in agriculture and commerce.[68] Capital created in the heart of society by productive labour was transferred immediately into credit circulation. Industrial and commercial capital was transformed into credit-capital, removed from capitalist sources and indifferent to modes of production.[69] The tax-farmers, the *officiers* and all State creditors in general gave not the slightest character of capitalism to the seigneurial economy or to the economy of the State. This is why they themselves became members of the system of feudal exploitation, appropriating to themselves feudal rent, in the form of seigneurial rent itself or in the form of centralised taxation.[70] It was in this way that the bourgeoisie lost its principal class-characteristics – its economic characteristics.

We cannot of course conclude from this that in seventeenth-century France there was no significant amount of capital engaged in production. If that had been so, we should have had to speak of the actual disappearance of the capitalist bourgeoisie rather than of its internal contradictions. The example of Normandy shows us clearly enough that the development of capitalism pursued its course, albeit slowly. The emergence of important industrial enterprises and the successes achieved in external trade, especially in colonial trade, in the seventeenth century, principally at the time of Colbert, are too well known for it to be necessary to give detailed information here. The bourgeoisie contained within its ranks a group of important manufacturing entrepreneurs, large-scale merchants and members of French colonial society. Even so, they all possessed specific traits which cannot be comprehended except in terms of what has just been said above. The enormous expansion of money-lending set its imprint on non-credit capital. Great capitalists who kept their capital voluntarily in commerce and industry (frequently, certain of them were forced to do so) demanded and received their reward for not engaging in money-lending. This reward was often a local matter. Thus at St. Malo a group of some thirty merchant ship-owners, who were related to the local nobility, and in part themselves 'ennobled', held the whole town and its trade in their hands and received enormous privileges. Ordinarily, however, the State granted these rewards in the form of royal privileges, subventions and monopolies, and, as a final bait, by generously distributing titles of nobility to merchants for their zeal. Thus, the reward for commercial activity was translated into terms of privileges, which always involved the *rapprochement* of the bourgeoisie with the nobility. Around these 'favoured ones', who profited fully from these rewards, many others gathered, awaiting the conferring of privilege. We must emphasise that capitalist production evolved particularly in this contradictory and scarcely natural fashion. In seventeenth-century France, the number of privileged royal manufactures increased rapidly and reached almost three hundred in number, while the number of non-privileged enterprises (for the most part domestic capitalist *manufactures*) diminished. Moreover, the only capitalist production which could prosper was that providing luxury articles for the nobility or products necessary to the State.

We may thus agree with Hanotaux that the ambition and activity of the French seventeenth-century bourgeoisie was nothing more than an energetic thrust for privilege. We have been able to set out the three ways in which the bourgeoisie lost its class-characteristics. It was solely to the extent that it renounced its identity as a capitalist class that its alliance with the dominant feudal and seigneurial class could operate, which was indeed the foundation itself of absolutism.

II

The Behaviour of the Bourgeoisie during the Fronde

At the beginning of his period of government, Richelieu, supported by Vancan and other theorists, wished to put an end fundamentally to venality and hereditary office. In 1625 he presented a memorandum to the king and a programme for the regulation of the affairs of the whole realm, where he developed in detail the need for their immediate abolition.[71] But at the Assembly of Notables in 1626, not only did he not present this programme, but he actually inspired the publication of (or wrote himself) a pamphlet inviting the Notables not to arouse the discontent of the *officiers* without at the same time relieving the distress of the people and gaining their support, otherwise everything would founder in disorder. In fact, neither the international nor the internal situation of France permitted any thought of relieving popular distress. New taxes were always being levied; popular uprisings became more and more frequent. However, at the end of 1628 and at the beginning of 1629 Richelieu prudently tried to return to his programme of reform, and at the same time to legalise the activities of the *intendants*, who were provoking the violent opposition of all office-holders. Now, Mousnier says, the *ordonnance* of 1629 provoked the fury of the *Parlements* and 'succeeded in creating a revolutionary situation in the realm'.[72] He continues:

> Already in 1627 and 1628, the increase in levies and taxes of all kinds, on the people, the artisans and the *officiers*, had caused 'popular riots', uprisings and revolts. The *Parlements*, the *officiers* of the *présidiaux*,† mayors and municipal *officiers* had shown no haste to maintain public order and to punish the ring-leaders.[73] Even the *Parlements* were sometimes opposed to the measures taken against the rebels and the government had no recourse other than to use the *intendants* even more widely. But in 1629 and 1630 the revolts increase in number. They become more serious still and the *Cours souveraines* are no longer content to leave things to take their course or to incite situations covertly . . . A general revolt could perhaps have broken out to limit the power of the king, to impose on him respect for the 'fundamental laws' of the realm, and to oppose the development of royal absolutism.[74]

In these conditions, Richelieu had to choose. If he wanted to pursue a policy of reform to the extent of abolishing venality and hereditary office, taxes had to be reduced, and an end put in that way to the popular uprisings. In that event, opposition from the *officiers* would have posed no threat to the government. But to diminish taxes would inevitably have meant renouncing the new orientation of France's foreign policy which had only recently been formulated, that is her renunciation of intervention in the Thirty Years War and her resistance to Habsburg aggression. That would have meant her pursuing a Catholic rather than a unilateralist foreign policy. Chancellor Marillac, the predecessor of Séguier, was the protagonist of peace and internal reform. Richelieu chose war and renounced the possibility of reform.[75] It was just after this that he came to write his *Testament Politique*.[76]

But this does not mean that the 'revolutionary situation', to use Mousnier's not entirely precise expression, disappeared in 1630. At the base of it were the popular uprisings; and we know the situation in this respect over two decades, during the whole period when France was participating either secretly or openly in the Thirty Years War. Popular uprisings continued right up to the Fronde, and even after the Fronde the revolts started again. Through rejecting a policy of reform, Richelieu was able to maintain the bourgeoisie on the side of the '*monarchie nobiliaire*', and prevent its forming an alliance with the revolutionary struggle of the people. Accordingly, the *parlements* and all the organs of public administration, functioning under the direction of a whole army of bourgeois *officiers*, with the bourgeoisie organised into a police militia in the towns, remained in general loyal to the social order. Even so, their 'loyalty' was, at this time, exceedingly frail; since, although the *officiers* had not been deprived of their rights in their offices, they had many reasons nonetheless for discontent and protest:

> Seditious proposals were put abroad; scandalous acts committed and the suppression of the popular uprisings lacked severity. Several times, the government perceived the limit beyond which the royal fisc could not go. Nevertheless, in spite of all that, even though certain *officiers* failed in their duty, as happened in every period of trouble, in a realm filled with unrest, even during 1636 and 1639, when the truly popular insurrections of the *Croquants* and *Va-nu-pieds* occurred, when almost all the conditions for revolution were present, the majority of the *officiers* remained loyal, and the *Cours souveraines*, upon whom everything ultimately depended, did not revolt. The energy of the king and Richelieu, the support given them by their *clientèles*, the presence of the royal armies, the fear of the people in the minds of the rich, all these things certainly contributed a great deal; but venality and the *droit annuel* must also be taken into account.[77]

Richelieu's ideas on the bourgeoisie and its role in maintaining order in the State accorded well with the reality of things. And when Richelieu's successor, Mazarin, violated Richelieu's precepts, this sanction from reality enforced itself even more strikingly. At the moment of difficulty which marked the end of the Thirty Years War, Mazarin had need of additional extraordinary revenues. The people were already so overburdened with taxes that the uprisings had reached their greatest pitch of violence and it was impossible to extract more from them. In the period from 1646 to 1647 Mazarin therefore tried to fleece the bourgeois *gens de finances*, the tax-farmers and agents of the royal fisc, who were wealthier and less inclined to incite rebellion, as Mousnier has forcefully shown.[78] Their reaction, however, thrust the royal finances into terrible confusion, and the war was not yet over. In 1647, Mazarin tried an attack on the *droit annuel* and other inviolable privileges of the *gens de robe*. It was at this moment that, according to Richelieu's own prediction, everything was thrust into disorder, because he had indeed done nothing to relieve the distress of the people. The bourgeoisie of office in Paris and throughout almost the whole of France became spontaneously aware of the sad fate of their lesser confrères and dealt such a blow to the absolutist regime that catastrophe seemed imminent. But, fearful of the vista of popular revolution it perceived, the bourgeoisie laid down its arms.

Let us try to analyse with more precision the position of the bourgeoisie during the Fronde. In our preface, we have set out the theory of the contemporary French historians, Pagès and Mousnier. They affirm that the institution of venality and hereditary office had brought the bourgeoisie to power, and thus royal authority was limited by the will of the bourgeoisie. According to Pagès, the Fronde was in its beginning an act of self-defence on the part of the bourgeois proprietors of office against the *intendants*, who could simply be nominated and as easily dismissed by the king, and who were the stay and support of rising absolutism. As we have shown earlier,[79] our disagreement with this new theory consists in the fact that, without contesting their argument, we draw an exactly opposite conclusion from theirs. We conclude indeed that venality did not bring about the *'embourgeoisement'* of power, but rather the 'feudalisation' of a part of the bourgeoisie, on the grounds that we cannot determine the class-spirit of a state according to the social origins of its officials. The agents of the *'Etat nobiliaire'* of seventeenth-century France defended objectively the intangible character of feudalism against the forces of revolution. A large number of bourgeois became *officiers*, but not the bourgeoisie in the sense of a class occupying a definite place in capitalist production. On the contrary, each bourgeois, from the moment when he became an *officier*, ceased to represent capitalist modes of production. He passed into the ranks of another class, living on feudal rent (transformed into taxes and royal salaries). Does a peasant employed in a factory remain a peasant? Is he not transformed into a worker? Could we say that an industry becomes 'peasant' from the single fact that it recruits its labour-force from among the peasantry? Clearly, if workers maintain a close link with their villages, that must have a certain influence on their psychological state and their behaviour. In the same way, the *officiers* of seventeenth-century France carried into the exercise of their offices the ideas and sentiments of the class among which they had grown up, namely the bourgeoisie. They maintained close links with that class. But influence was reciprocal. The influence which came so to say from 'above', from the *monarchie nobiliaire* through members of the bourgeoisie who had attained a high point in the social scale, on the mass of the ordinary bourgeois who remained below and who did not belong to the Robe, was certainly the more powerful influence. The authority and influence of these 'elder brothers' to some extent drew the whole of the French seventeenth-century bourgeoisie into the flow of the aristocratic State, which had been created to defend feudalism. Influences the other way were essentially feeble. Venality of office was not therefore the means whereby the monarchy submitted to the bourgeoisie, but, on the contrary, the means whereby the bourgeoisie temporarily submitted to the *monarchie nobiliaire*. Venality of office was one of the means whereby the bourgeoisie was deflected from the revolutionary struggle against feudalism.

In the course of the eighteenth century, the rapid evolution of capitalism in France so strengthened and developed the non-privileged section of the bourgeoisie that it disengaged itself from the influence of its 'elder brothers'. From that moment, the institution of venality of office no longer corresponded to its initial object. Politically useless, economically damaging, this institution was gradually liquidated by the *monarchie nobiliaire*. The process of the revolutionary development of the French eighteenth-century bourgeoisie does not enter the framework of this study. Nevertheless it is certain that its origins derive from the seventeenth and even from the sixteenth century. What triumphed in the history of the French bourgeoisie in the eighteenth century was most assuredly one of the two opposed tendencies in the behaviour of this class during the earlier stage of capitalist development. We can fully appreciate how this victorious tendency revealed in the eighteenth century should have been less visible in the seventeenth, even indeed hidden at that time, since it was a youthful tendency which had to affirm itself in the future. In the seventeenth century the other opposed tendency was still uppermost, entirely different in essence, since it embodied the feudal past and not the capitalist future of the bourgeoisie. The historian of the seventeenth century has no right however to ignore this other less apparent aspect of the bourgeoisie at that time, since it was a prior announcement of what was to come in the eighteenth century.

At the moment when a worker who has maintained connections with his village loses his employment in a factory, he reverts to being a peasant again. In the same way, when Mazarin attempted to retrieve their property rights in their offices and their privileges from the *officiers*, which included depriving them of their privileged status as nobility, they virtually fell back automatically into their original character as bourgeois. Already, the nature of the bourgeoisie itself could no longer permit a solely peaceful transition, but demanded a decisive struggle against the yoke of feudal-absolutism, as was indeed to be the case in the eighteenth century. Under the injuries inflicted by Mazarin, the *officiers* felt themselves bourgeois again; and at the beginning of the Fronde their attitude was that of the whole bourgeois class. They placed themselves accordingly at the head of the revolution.

No less characteristic of this privileged bourgeoisie, tied as it was to the interests of the *monarchie nobiliaire*, was its division into two opposing groups, the judicial *officiers* and the *officiers de finances*. This division at the heart of the privileged bourgeoisie reflected the contradictions of the situation which it occupied in noble society as a whole. The judicial *officiers* detested and denounced the *gens de finances*. The latter played a more direct role in the exploitation of the French economy, in levying with very great rigour and in appropriating to themselves part of the centralised feudal rent in the form of royal taxation, which ruined and stifled the growth of the capitalist economy. The judicial *officiers* did as much from the economic point of view, but in other more oblique ways, and moreover with less advantage to themselves. Hence their jealousy toward the *gens de finances* and their conviction that the exactions of these *traitants*†, *partisans* and extortioners were the reason for all the 'disorders' of the realm, and prevented them, the *officiers*, from defending law and maintaining order. On all counts, they accused the *gens de finances*, and sometimes even went so far as to accuse the State of complicity with them. In both instances, they were the mouthpiece of vast numbers of discontented, who for their part accused either those who were closest at hand, namely the *collecteurs*† and tax-farmers, of being responsible for their distress, or those who were equally responsible, but at a distance, namely the government itself. This meant that, although they were called upon to defend the feudal-absolutist regime, the judicial *officiers* played the role of opposition to the regime in the eyes of public opinion and partially even in the eyes of the government, as a result of their animosity to the *gens de finances*. This is why every time the revolutionary dynamic formed in the seventeenth century, directed as it inevitably was against taxation, and therefore against the financiers, the judicial *officiers* were carried to the head of the movement. Thus it was that at the beginning of the Fronde there was a ruthless struggle between the 'magistrates' and the *gens de finances*.

The French seventeenth-century bourgeoisie was not therefore entirely withdrawn from revolutionary impulses, even at its own privileged levels. During the Fronde, those impulses were indeed on the point of becoming transformed into a revolutionary struggle. However, although the Fronde represented a crisis in the feudal-absolutist order, a powerful uprising in itself for bourgeois democracy, it was unable to transform itself into a bourgeois revolution because the leading groups of the bourgeoisie surrendered at the decisive moment and betrayed their own cause. The bourgeoisie took refuge under the wing of a protecting absolutism. It was unable to bring itself to break with the *Etat nobiliaire* and the feudal society it defended. Why was this so?

We have already examined the *rapprochement* which on the one side was affected between the bourgeoisie, the nobility and the feudal State, and on the other between the feudal State and the bourgeoisie. In spite of the complexity of motives which induced each to keep ahead of the other, in the final count the fundamental motive for both parties was the same – namely the fear of a popular anti-feudal revolution.

It is not necessary to explain in logical terms why the threat of revolution was the *ultima ratio* for an absolutist aristocratic monarchy, since it had been founded to resist such a threat. It remains however for us to show why this threat was also the *ultima ratio* for the French seventeenth-century bourgeoisie.

French historians frequently say that the seventeenth-century bourgeoisie simply feared for their possessions during popular disturbances and therefore felt an aversion toward all insurmountable uprisings of the people, for fear of pillage. But when it is a question of the attitude of a whole class, and not only of individuals, this explanation ceases to be adequate, and more profound reasons are to be looked for.

Political experience, both everyday and at moments of great crisis, had shown the French bourgeoisie, clearly and indisputably, that once it was projected into revolution together with the people it might never be able to halt the people again at will.

In fact, by reason of the conditions of French historical development, a revolution such as that in the Low Countries in the sixteenth century or that of the English in the seventeenth was impossible for France: that is to say, a revolution halted in mid-stream, before it has defeated feudalism, a revolution whose pendulum has swung logically a little beyond the realisable claims of the bourgeoisie, but which has stopped still far short of the critical point. This type of bourgeois revolution was possible in England and in the Low Countries because a part of the nobility had become '*embourgeoisée*'. The high bourgeoisie in those instances found in this '*noblesse embourgeoisée*' an ally to the right, and in the peasant and plebeian mass an ally to the left. In this situation, the bourgeoisie could easily assure itself of preponderance in the movement, and be able to prevent a democratic revolution from escaping from its control, to prevent, that is, a kind of Jacobin dictatorship. But in France, feudalism possessed both a perfection and a vitality which was classical and which prohibited any *embourgeoisement* of the nobility. Feudalism was solidly entrenched in the countryside, and with the exception of certain maritime regions, such as the Bordelais, the nobility was not touched by the new economic currents. In the revolutionary struggle, the French bourgeoisie could not have an ally on the right. It had to struggle against feudalism with only one ally, the peasant and plebeian masses. From the beginning, such a revolution had inevitably to assume a well-defined democratic character, formulating a Jacobin programme to express the desire of the masses for freedom. The bourgeoisie clearly risked losing control over such a movement, allowing the dynamic of an anti-feudal revolution to escape from its control. In a word, it had to ally with the people on a badly defined route to revolution, which gave it little reassurance and aroused its fears.

In every bourgeois-democratic revolution, we may discern deep contradictions between the motive force (at the head of which Lenin placed the peasantry) and its objective result, which is the simple substitution of another form of exploitation, namely capitalist domination, for the earlier feudal domination of the labouring masses. In every bourgeois-democratic revolution, the bourgeoisie has always to resolve a difficult problem: how to appropriate to itself the fruits of a victory which it has not won with its own efforts. It has accordingly to reserve for itself the dominant role in the movement. The interests of the bourgeoisie are not those of the popular masses who make the revolution, since the latter struggle against all forms of exploitation, and not for the substitution of a new form of exploitation.

In the twentieth century, when the new revolutionary proletariat matures, this contradiction within every bourgeois-democratic revolution will enable it to cast aside the aid of the bourgeoisie and to become itself the dominant force in the revolution. From that time, the transformation of the bourgeois-democratic revolution into a socialist revolution can begin. But in the seventeenth and eighteenth centuries, when the proletariat did not exist, there was only one recourse. The bourgeoisie could engage itself in a revolution, in those precise historical conditions, only when it could be certain of controlling the vessel according to its own will.

We see that the French bourgeoisie did not behave as the English bourgeoisie did. It was not that the French bourgeoisie was more retarded. Far from it, since England in the first half of the seventeenth century did not represent anything very remarkable in the way of industrial development, or in the development of its capitalist system. But the particular characteristics of the French economy rendered a grouping of classes, which would have permitted a semi-democratic revolution on the English model, impossible. In France a bourgeois revolution was possible only after a further development of the contradictions between feudalism and capitalism than England experienced, following an increased maturation of the French bourgeoisie. This is why a hundred and fifty years separate the French and English bourgeois revolutions. It is also why the French eighteenth-century bourgeoisie had to develop and express a bold anti-feudal ideology. Although capitalist development was always directing it toward revolution, it would not resolve on such a course before it could feel itself master over the minds of the masses.

This is why, in the sixteenth and seventeenth centuries, the French bourgeoisie retreated rather than went on the attack, laid down its arms rather than seized them. This recoil from the struggle expressed the 'feudalisation' of the French bourgeoisie – the indirect consequence in France of the 'non-*embourgeoisement*' of the nobility. It was not in any way a question of a conscious prevision or reasoned generalisation on the part of bourgeois leadership. The situation was such that during the period of the popular uprisings each member of the bourgeoisie had, more than once in his life, to resolve, on his own personal level, the general problem which posed itself to the bourgeoisie as a class: either to follow the lead given by the people in their revolutionary struggle against the existing aristocratic absolutist regime, or, conversely, to associate itself with that regime against the revolution of the people. It made attempts to act in both ways, but these attempts always revealed, in concrete situations in the localities, that the bourgeoisie was not sure of maintaining its control as the uprising developed.

In the course of its evolution, the French bourgeoisie therefore traversed a long road, staked out with goals which were full of contradictions. Toward the end of the eighteenth century, when it was confronted with a historical situation that was without egress, it was compelled to decide for a revolution which held within itself Jacobin tendencies, together with others which were perhaps even more radical than those of the Jacobins. But in the sixteenth and seventeenth centuries, the French bourgeoisie occupied a very ambiguous position in the feudal-absolutist regime. The contradiction between feudal production and nascent capitalism already led the bourgeoisie to struggle against feudal and aristocratic domination. But, at the same time, for the reasons we have given above, it was forced into a *rapprochement* with that dominant class. As in Germany at the time of the Reformation, the French bourgeoisie of the sixteenth and seventeenth centuries feared the anti-feudal uprisings of the peasants and plebeian masses. For the French bourgeoisie, the disappearance of feudalism was an objective necessity, but, to attain that goal, it could not resolve on forming an alliance with the masses. More than once it sought the protection of absolutism against the dangers of the revolution toward which the course of its own development inexorably led it. It is precisely to the French bourgeoisie of the sixteenth and seventeenth centuries that the Marxist formulae apply. According to these, the bourgeoisie, in aiding the development of capitalist industry, could not accommodate itself to the inevitable regrouping of social forces which had ineluctably to find their fulfilment in revolution both against the royal authority whose favour it so highly appreciated and against the nobility whose ranks a number of its members dreamed so often of swelling.

The formulae of Karl Marx give the key to the history of the French bourgeoisie in the sixteenth and seventeenth centuries: 'Nothing could any longer prevent the victory of the French bourgeoisie when it decided in 1789 to make common cause with the peasants.'[80] Our researches fully confirm this thought.

NOTES

1 Retz., *Oeuvres, Coll. des Grands Ecrivains de France*, II pp. 278–9.
2 C. Loyseau, *Traité des seigneuries*, Paris, 1620; *Traité du droit des offices*.
3 C. Loyseau, *Traité des ordres*, p. 1.
4 C. Loyseau, *Traité du droit des offices*, II, Chapter II p. 621. Cited from E. Lacour-Gayet, *L'Education politique de Louis XIV* (Paris, 1898) p. 337.

5   C. Loyseau, *Traité des seigneuries*, p. 37.
6   Ibid., p. 58.
7   C. Loyseau, *Traité des ordres*, p. 3.
8   C. Loyseau, *Traité des seigneuries*, p. 9.
9   Ibid.
10   Ibid., p. 106.
11   C. Loyseau, *Traité des ordres*, p. 3.
12   Ibid., p. 129.
13   Ibid.
14   Ibid., p. 130.
15   Ibid.
16   Ibid., p. 180.
17   Ibid., p. 137.
18   Ibid., p. 130.
19   Ibid.
20   Ibid., p. 139.
21   Ibid., p. 138.
22   Ibid., p. 137.
23   A. Babeau, *La ville sous l'ancien régime* (Paris, 1884) ı pp. 22–3.
24   C. Loyseau, *Traité des ordres*, pp. 139–40.
25   Ibid., p. 140.
26   See especially C. Normand, *La Bourgeoisie française au XVIIe siècle* (Paris, 1908); A. Babeau, *Les Bourgeois d'autrefois* (Paris, 1886); A. Bardoux, *La Bourgeoisie française* (Paris, 1886).
     J. Aynard, *La Bourgeoisie française; essai de psychologie* (Paris, 1934).
27   K. Marx and F. Engels, *Works* (Russian edition) xxıı p. 49.
28   G. Roupnel, *La ville et la campagne au XVIIe siècle* (1922) p. 130.
29   C. Loyseau, *Traité du droit des offices*. Cited from Hanotaux, *Histoire du Cardinal de Richelieu* (Paris, 1896) ı p. 459.
30   R. Mousnier, *La Vénalité des offices sous Henri IV et Louis XIII* (Paris, 1945) pp. 391–4.
31   Ibid., pp. 518–24.
32   Richelieu, *Testament Politique* (Russian edition) ı p. 158
33   Cited from W. Golzew, *L'économie nationale en France au XVIIe siècle* (1878) p. 86 (in Russian).
34   C. Loyseau, *Traité du droit des offices*. Cited from C. Normand, *La Bourgeoisie française au XVIIe siècle*, pp. 44–5.
35   C. Loyseau, *Traité du droit des offices*. Cited from Hanotaux, op. cit., p. 459.
36   From F. Filatow, 'The Economy of the Ancien Régime', in *Modern History*, ıı p. 222 (in Russian).
37   From G. Depping, *Correspondance administrative sous le règne de Louis XIV* (Paris, 1852) ııı p. 765.
38   J. Savary, *Le parfait négociant ou instruction générale pour ce qui regarde le commerce des marchandises de France et des pays étrangers* (Lyon, 1697) ıı p. 183.
39   E. Fagniez, *L'économie sociale de la France sous Henri IV*, p. 346.
40   P. de Groot, *Lettres de Pierre de Groot, Ambassadeur des Provinces-Unies à Abraham de Wicquefort, 1668–1674* (The Hague, 1894) p. 94.
41   'Les universités de France au Roi', in *Mercure françois*, x p. 432.
42   C. Loyseau, *Traité des ordres*, p. 83.
43   Ibid.
44   *Archives curieuses de l'histoire de France*, ed. F. Dangou and L. Cimber, 'La chasse au vieil grognart de l'antiquité', *2e série*, ıı p. 371.

45 J. Aynard, op. cit., p. 285.
46 *Etat de la France: Extrait des Mémoires dressés par les intendants du royaume par ordre du roi Louis XIV*. Par M. le Comte de Boulainvilliers (London, 1737) IV p. 155.
47 Richelieu, op. cit., I p. 160.
48 J. Savary, op. cit., I p. 1.
49 R. Mousnier, op. cit., pp. 501–3, 515 and 559.
50 G. Roupnel, op. cit., *3e partie*.
51 R. Mousnier, op. cit., pp. 458–62.
52 P. du Ryer, *Les Vendanges de Suresnes*, from E. Fournier, *Théâtre français du XVIIe siècle*.
53 La Bruyère, *Les Caractères* (Paris, 1905) pp. 308–9.
54 *Archives curieuses de l'histoire de France*, II pp. 371–2.
55 R. Mousnier, op. cit., pp. 493–4.
56 Saint-Simon, *Mémoires* (Russian edition 1936) II pp. 256–7.
57 C. Loyseau, *Traité des ordres*, p. 140.
58 Vauban, *Projet d'une dîme royale*, ed. Coornaert, p. 28. The adverse influence of taxation on economic activity was well described by Boisguilbert at the end of the seventeenth century.
59 K. Marx and F. Engels, *Works* (Russian edition) XVI, I p. 446.
60 [Editor's note:] This general statement requires of course much refinement, if only in regard to the *don gratuit* paid by the Church and the payment of *taille réelle* by the nobility in the Midi on their 'non-noble' land.
61 Saint-Simon, op. cit., p. 250.
62 La Bruyère, op. cit., p. 317.
63 Loutchiski, *The Situation of the Peasant Classes in France on the Eve of the Revolution* (Russian edition, 1912) p. 31.
64 [Editor's note:] It was of course the insecurity of the investment in the period of Mazarin, through non-payment of salaries, the proliferation of office and the intervention of *commissaires*, which made for so much resentment among the *officiers*.
65 R. Mousnier, op. cit., pp. 425–38.
66 Richelieu, op. cit., I p. 157.
67 From J. Aynard, op. cit., p. 246.
68 E. Fagniez, op. cit., p. 74.
69 K. Marx, *Capital*, II p. 36.
70 [Editor's note:] It is Porshnev's thesis that royal taxation was a form of 'centralised feudal rent', in the sense that, through tax-immunity, ennobled *officiers* benefited from the 'dues' of taxation without in any way contributing to them; i.e. taxation represented 'dues' drawn from the '*seigneurie*' of the whole realm.
71 Richelieu, *Lettres*, II pp. 159–62 and 177.
72 R. Mousnier, op. cit., p. 609.
73 It is to be remembered that these authorities had the bourgeois militia in the towns under their control.
74 R. Mousnier, op. cit., p. 610.
75 [Editor's note:] See G. Pagès, 'Autour du "Grand Orage": Richelieu et Marillac, deux politiques', in *Revue Historique*, CLXXIX (1937) pp. 63–97.
76 The *Testament* was begun in 1633 and completed in 1639.
77 R. Mousnier, op. cit., p. 619.
78 Ibid., p. 614.
79 Supra, Chapter 3, pp. 94–7.
80 K. Marx and F. Engels, *Works* (Russian edition) XXII p. 49.

5 Research into the Popular Uprisings in France before the Fronde[*]

ROLAND MOUSNIER

I

For about twenty-five years, during the ministries of Richelieu and Mazarin, the Fronde was preceded by a period of almost uninterrupted popular revolts, both by peasants in the countryside and by artisans and beggars in the towns. There was no year when revolts did not occur, at least in one province or in some of the towns. Sometimes almost a third of the realm was affected. These revolts have been the subject of numerous and detailed studies by French historians[1] and they have been referred to in general works.[2] But no synthesis has been attempted, and this has been a gap in our historiography. B. Porshnev has tried to fill it. He has produced a study in depth[3] of works on the popular revolts of this period by French historians, and it seems that none of these has escaped his notice; which is very creditable, since there are more than one hundred. He has obtained printed texts of the period and documents published since which contain information about the uprisings, together with various contemporary accounts, the *Mercure françois*, the correspondence of Richelieu and Mazarin, and various journals and *mémoires*. We may well believe him when he says that this was not done without difficulty. He has used many documents, and with great care. He knows many important works well, such as those of Loyseau and the *Political Testament* of Richelieu. Most importantly, he has had a quite exceptional source at his disposal. He has used the letters addressed to Chancellor Séguier between 1633 and 1648 from provincial *gouverneurs*, such as the duc d'Epernon, and from *intendants* and magistrates; in all some 2500 to 3000 documents emanating from the provinces and informing the Chancellor of the internal situation in

* This is a translation of Roland Mousnier's article, 'Recherches sur les soulève- ments populaires en France avant la Fronde', *Revue d'histoire moderne et contem- poraine* (1958) pp. 81–113.

France. Chance brought these documents to Russia. They had been bequeathed in 1732, as part of Séguier's library, to the Abbey of Saint Germain-des-Prés by Henri de Cambout, Duc de Coislin. In 1791, during the upheaval of the Revolution, a part of these letters was stolen and fell into the hands of Peter Dubrovsky, a secretary at the Russian embassy in Paris, as indeed did other manuscripts from the Abbey. In 1800 Dubrovsky took the manuscripts to Russia and in 1805 he gave them to the Russian government.[4] These papers are today in Leningrad, in the Dubrovsky collection of the Saltykov-Shchedrin Library. Porshnev, working from 1933, used ten registers of them and published seventy-nine of the letters in French translation in his *Appendix*.

On the basis of this solid documentation, Porshnev set himself three tasks. In the first part of the work he gives an account of the principal workers' and peasants' uprisings from 1623 to 1648, and then seeks to extract their common characteristics and the attitudes of the other social classes towards them, without deceiving himself as to the precarious nature of his findings, since in the case of all these uprisings the local archives have been inadequately used.

In the second part, he devotes himself in particular to the revolt of the *nu-pieds* in Normandy in 1639, because that revolt is least badly known, and also because we can perceive in it something of its economic and social elements. Finally, in the third part, he attempts, in the light of the results he has already achieved, to resolve the enigma of the Fronde, to discover whether it is a feudal reaction or an attempt at bourgeois revolution. Then, in search of the role of the bourgeoisie in French seventeenth-century society, he criticises the theories of Pagès and those I myself have formulated elsewhere,[5] and in this way arrives at a tentative explanation of the internal history of France under the absolute monarchy.

B. Porshnev makes frequent use of my work on *Venality of Office under Henry IV and Louis XIII*, declaring a great many of my observations and conclusions to have great scientific value.[6] He does not in any way contest the force of the arguments I advance in favour of theories he attacks.[7] I have no difficulty in returning my compliments to him in the same terms. Porshnev knows the French seventeenth century very well, to the extent that it can be known today, except perhaps its economic situation. Many of his observations and conclusions have real scientific value and several of the arguments he adduces to support his theories have considerable force. But I cannot adhere to the theories themselves, because it seems to me that Porshnev wants at all costs to force precise facts and relationships, which he correctly perceives and appreciates, into a framework of Marxist theory which the facts themselves explode. I have a double task to fulfil therefore: first, to set out Porshnev's theories,[8] and then to criticise them, primarily by means of the remainder of the 'Letters addressed to Chancellor Séguier' in the *Bibliothèque Nationale* in Paris.[9]

II

For Porshnev, the Fronde was at the hinge of two great cycles of peasants' and workers' uprisings which lasted respectively from 1623 to 1648 and from 1653 to 1675. For him, the Fronde is the culminating point of an attack on the social organisation of 'feudal absolutism',[10] and we cannot understand it without studying the twenty-five years preceding it to see how it was formed. We must devote attention to the peasant uprisings and to those of the urban poor. They form the true foundation and the sole condition which made all other forms of opposition to the absolutist regime possible, including that of the feudal aristocracy. They were the motive force of everything else, the State, religion and intellectual thought. For Porshnev, French bourgeois academic history has neglected them. French historians consider them as solely local episodes. They do not see them as a whole, in importance and significance. Boissonnade had started to study them, but it was a scandal in the eyes of academic circles and he renounced the idea accordingly.[11]

All these uprisings, he maintains, arise from the introduction of new taxes or new financial institutions which rendered taxation even heavier. They depend therefore on the worsening of the financial situation caused by the increasing involvement of France in the Thirty Years War. They are entirely spontaneous. Governmental circles at the time, and bourgeois historians afterward, always looked for the invisible 'conductor of the orchestra', the great nobleman, the provincial *gouverneur*, the *prince du sang*†, the magistrate, the *officier*†, at the root of these revolts. But such conjectures have no solid foundation. They are nonetheless interesting, however, because they reveal the narrowness of bourgeois historiography, as well as the position of seventeenth-century politics, which found it difficult to accept that the ordinary people were capable of resisting the king and his servants.[12] The State is an 'aristocratic-feudal organism'.[13] The popular uprisings in fact are always spontaneous. They are only subsequently utilised by the bourgeoisie and the nobles.

These uprisings were the acts of the poorest classes: in the countryside, the peasants; in the towns, the 'pre-proletariat of manufactures and workshops', together with the small masters, *compagnons* and apprentices of the lowest crafts, the vine-dressers of Dijon, the coopers of Bordeaux, the shoemakers, dyers, locksmiths, masons, street-porters, weavers, carpenters, clocksmiths, innkeepers, butchers, etc.; finally, disbanded soldiers, vagrants and beggars. The revolts are therefore the acts of a whole lower class, whose minimum standard of living was always being threatened, the 'people', the 'populace', the '*canaille*', the '*menu peuple*', the '*bas peuple*', the 'dregs' of society, the 'lowest people', no longer such and such a corporate body of people, but a whole social group which was entirely motley and heterogeneous in composition, the 'plebeians'.[14]

These uprisings, for Porshnev, were not anti-monarchical. The political thinking of the revolts goes no further than the idea expressed in the cry of 'Vive le Roi sans gabelle, vive le Roi sans impôts'.[15] But they are unequivocally anti-feudal. In the countryside, the peasant revolts begin by attacking the persons and property of those who could sublet the tax-farms established for new taxes or buy up new offices as *élus*†, which exempted them from taxation, causing the *taille*† to fall more heavily on the poor; witness the attempts to introduce *elections*† in Quercy in 1624, in Burgundy in 1630 and in Provence in 1631. The rebels begin by burning houses, destroying trees and uprooting vines. But, since in the end all the rich could become *sous-fermiers* or *officiers*, that is '*gabeleurs*'†, to use the word of the rebels, the rebels do not hesitate to attack the houses of the rich. At the same time as they protest against the burden of taxation they raise claims against feudal rights, against ecclesiastical tithe, against the legal system and government administration. They pillage and burn châteaux (in Angoumois, Saintonge and Poitou, in 1636). In the towns, where the inhabitants of the *faubourgs* can penetrate into the town itself, or where the situation is such that the lower classes have their own *quartiers* inside the town, the rebels destroy the houses of the '*gabeleurs*', of mayors and *échevins*†, *officiers de justice* and tax-farmers. Sometimes the portraits of Richelieu or Louis XIII are burned in the streets, as in Dijon in 1630, in Aix-en-Provence in 1631 and Lyon in 1632, etc. The rebels threaten all those who benefit in any way from feudal rent, either directly, as *seigneurs*, or indirectly, through receiving a state salary or through some privilege in the tax-system.

In effect, for Porshnev, French seventeenth-century society is a feudal society, characterised by the predominance of feudal economic forms and feudal modes of production. Capitalist modes of production were only just penetrating the feudal mass and were concentrated in a certain number of towns, but not in all. As a whole, the Middle Ages in their purest form reigned in the French feudal economy of the seventeenth century, and it was the Revolution of 1789 which first dealt it a mortal blow.[16] The 'yoke of taxation' is solely 'the expression of the dominance of feudalism over the town and its industry.'

Through taxation, the State levies a centralised form of feudal rent on the towns.[17] The landed feudal nobility possess the economic primacy and 'the State is above all things the power-instrument of the class possessing economic primacy, in order to maintain the exploited classes in a condition of subservience'. Moreover, the absolutist monarchical State also plays the role of exploiter when it raises on behalf of the nobles, serving either at Court or in the army, a centralised form of feudal rent in the shape of taxation. The absolute monarchy is the apparatus for keeping the exploited majority in a state of subjection.[18] The State is feudal. The king has simply taken and centralised political power and, in consequence, feudal rent. But the king maintains the 'feudal order', of which he himself is the primary beneficiary. Absolutism is a 'kind of great landed property'.[19] By maintaining the 'feudal order', the State maintains the supremacy of the feudal nobility. It is, therefore, an *'Etat de noblesse'*,[20] an *'Etat de nobles'*,[21] a 'State governed aristocratically, formed for the defence of feudalism'.[22] 'French absolutism in the seventeenth century was an *Etat de noblesse* and French seventeenth-century society was a feudal society.'[23]

Porshnev uses the words 'feudal', 'feudalism' and 'feudality' here in the Marxist sense. He includes seventeenth-century France within the 'feudal mode of production', which, according to the Marxists, existed in China for more than two thousand years and in western Europe from the fall of the Roman Empire (in the fifth century) until the bourgeois revolutions of the Netherlands in the sixteenth century, of England in the seventeenth century and of France in 1789; and which existed in Russia from the ninth century until the peasant reform of 1861. In seventeenth-century France, the basic relationship of production in feudal society remains that of the property of the *seigneur* over the land, and more rarely the limited property of the *seigneur* over the producer himself, the peasant serf. The fundamental economic law of feudal society resides in the production of a surplus product to satisfy the needs of the feudal *seigneurs* who exploit their peasants. The *seigneurs* leave the enjoyment of a small tenure to their peasants, on terms which make them servile, if they are in fact no longer serfs. In exchange for the hereditary enjoyment of his tenure, the peasant owes his *seigneur* a feudal rent: when he has produced enough for his own subsistence and that of his family, the peasant owes his *seigneur* either an amount of 'surplus-labour', in the form of *corvées*, or a 'surplus-product', either in kind or in monetary dues. 'The exploitation of dependent peasants by the *seigneur* constitutes the principal characteristic of feudalism in all societies.' Although in seventeenth-century France the feudal regime might be in process of dissolution under the influence of capitalist development, feudalism was still dominant.[24]

This situation explains, for Porshnev, the defeat of the peasants and workers. The peasant revolts cannot succeed unless they are led by the workers. But, in seventeenth-century France, the working class is too little developed, too feeble and has too few political ideas to take control of the open struggle against the 'feudal-absolutist order'. Moreover, peasants and workers are opposed by a 'class-front which constituted the basis of absolutism',[25] consisting of nobles, clergy and, in large measure, the bourgeoisie; whereas in 1789 the bourgeoisie was to form an alliance with the peasants and workers.

In fact, the nobility, the dominant class and first beneficiary of the regime, plays the role of active guardian of the 'feudal-absolutist Order'. At Bordeaux in 1635, and at Valence in 1644, the nobility contributed very considerably to the suppression of the uprisings. It is not that they were always in accord with the king. The levying of centralised feudal rent, which taxation represented, impeded the levying of feudal rent by the *seigneurs*. For this reason, the nobility sometimes supported the peasant uprisings in opposition to taxation. At other times, it sought to utilise them for its own reactionary political interest. But, at decisive moments, it abandoned the rebels, or arrayed itself against them.[26]

The clergy is opposed to the rebels. It preaches obedience to them: 'He who rises against the King, rises against God. For the King is God's anointed one, given to us by Him, to be our Lord on earth, to whom we must, after God, show all true fear, honour and obedience.'[27] The clergy seeks to screen the exactions of the nobility, as the bishop of Clermont did in 1643.[28] Sometimes they even took up arms against the rebels, as at Dijon in 1630, where the clergy, including monks, armed themselves with muskets, pikes and out-of-date halberds, and even with 'iron and other stakes'.[29]

The position of the bourgeoisie is revealed, for Porshnev, in the works of Loyseau, who not only formulated the ideal of the bourgeoisie, but also produced an anatomy of the 'feudal-absolutist Order'. According to Loyseau, there are two groups in France: those who command and those who obey. Since only a noble class can command in a State governed by the nobility, Loyseau seeks to identify the bourgeoisie as much as possible with the nobility. The king, as vassal of God, is first *seigneur* of the realm, but, as first *officier* of God, he is also first *officier* of the realm. The *officier* possesses solely a transfer onto his private person of the public *seigneurie†* or sovereignty which the king alone holds. But the *seigneur* possesses no more than the private *seigneurie*, which gives him solely power over the land. Thus, in the end, the *officier* and the noble are very close to one another. The *officier* can also raise himself into the ranks of the nobility through possession of either an office conferring nobility or a noble estate, for three generations in either instance. The bourgeoisie is therefore a kind of mirror-image or double of the nobility.

Conversely, the bourgeoisie is clearly separated from the people. For Loyseau, the Third Estate is not a true order. The bourgeoisie have '*dignité*' and a '*qualité d'honneur*', giving them a share in the privileges, prerogatives and offices of the State, as well as in the judiciary and town assemblies. But who are the bourgeois? All those who do not work with their hands, who are not '*mécaniques*'. The bourgeois men-of-letters, financiers, practitioners of the law, wholesale merchants and traders; to whom we may add apothecaries, goldsmiths, jewellers and retailers of fashion, since in all their cases trade is more important than manual work. All of them share membership of the group who command along with the nobility.[30]

The nobles who are at the head of the State and of whom Richelieu is a typical example, employ bourgeois as *officiers* and *commissaires*† in various posts within the State apparatus, in the military and administrative machine. For Richelieu, this is a necessary evil. The apparatus of the State cannot be left in the possession of nobles, since its control by one group of them merely arouses the opposition of the rest. 'Moreover, separatist and particularist tendencies were very strong in the nobility. A solution was only to be found if the apparatus of the State were placed in the hands of *officiers* who were not themselves members of the nobility. This solution was the result in itself of the development of absolutism.'[31] On the other hand, looking at it from the financial point of view, it was in the interests of the absolutist State to have at its disposal a form of wealth which was not feudal in character, which the capital of the bourgeoisie provided, in order to avoid arousing too much opposition from the nobility over the levying of 'centralised rent' in the form of taxation, in competition with rent levied by *seigneurs*. In order to avoid conflict between the aristocratic State and the interests of the nobility, the royal fisc had to demand a contribution from the bourgeoisie. Absolutism, therefore, tried to promote industry and commerce through a policy of mercantilism and the granting of privileges, monopolies and titles of nobility to capitalists. It was in this way that the State became bound to the bourgeoisie.

'The alliance of the State with the bourgeoisie ensured the failure of the Revolution of the people.' 'Any humiliation of the bourgeoisie of office would have thrust it into the arms of the people and would have created the inevitable Revolution.' 'In seventeenth-century France, the feudal order and the aristocratic monarchy which protected it depended in the last resort on the political situation of the bourgeoisie.'[32] In effect, with the nobility engaged in the army on the frontiers, the bourgeois militia is the only real force remaining in the interior. The bourgeoisie, facing the *plebs* alone, has the decision in its hands. It has the military power. It can either allow the insurrections to develop or stop them, entirely according to its own wishes.[33] In fact, it often allowed them to spread, in order to forward its own demands. But, when it was threatened in its own property by the revolts, it always ended by contributing to their suppression.

But the bourgeoisie could not become the ruling class by itself, nor could it do so as a bourgeoisie. It could not enter the ruling class except by identifying with the nobility, by becoming analogous to it, by ennoblement, by losing its class-characteristics. In political terms, it becomes a bureaucracy. It separates itself from industry and commerce; it rises socially in the 'feudal-absolutist order', seeking to live *'noblement'* and to penetrate the ranks of the nobility. It buys estates and lives on feudal rents, finally abandoning office itself. The grandsons of the *officiers* merge with the nobility. Economically, the bourgeoisie lives by money-lending, by providing credit, by making loans either to individuals or to the king. By lending to the king, it frees its capital from taxation and leaves the tax-burden to be borne by the people. A part of the bourgeoisie lives indeed from manufactures and colonial trade. But the mercantilist monarchy grants privileges, subsidies, monopolies, titles of nobility to the capitalists, and in this way brings them into the 'feudal-absolutist order'. The great *manufactures* themselves become semi-feudal organisations, living at the expense of the peasantry and indirectly provoking feudal reaction and regression toward a natural economy. The 'feudal-absolutist' State retards the rise of capitalism, since in the end the development of capitalism requires the suppression of all privilege. Capitalism takes two steps forward and one step back. The thirty major shipowners of Saint-Malo marry into the local nobility. The bourgeoisie merge with the nobility.[34]

Hence, the error of Pagès and Mousnier. For them, venality and hereditary office brought the bourgeoisie to power and limited the monarchy by the will of the bourgeoisie. This is an error on their part. Venality of office did not lead to the *'embourgeoisement'* of power, but to the 'feudalisation' of a section of the bourgeoisie. We cannot define the class-character of the State according to the social situation of its public servants. The public service of the seventeenth-century aristocratic State defended a solid feudalism against the revolutionary forces of the people. A great number of bourgeois became *officiers*, but, and it is important, this was not the bourgeoisie as a class, characterised by holding a definite position within capitalism. On the contrary, each bourgeois on becoming an *officier* ceased to represent capitalist modes of production. He entered another class, which lived from feudal rent in the form of royal taxes and royal salaries. 'Do peasants who come to work in a factory remain peasants?' Are they not transformed into workers? Would it be just to speak of a *'paysannisation'* of industry, on the basis that an industry draws its work-force from the ranks of the peasantry? When workers remain in close contact with their villages, this naturally exercises a certain influence over their psychology and conduct. Similarly, the *officiers* of the French seventeenth-century monarchy did not carry into the public service merely a matter of a few sentiments and ideas from the milieu in which they had grown up, that is the sentiments and ideas of the bourgeoisie. They maintained indeed the closest liaison with it. But the influence was two-way. The influence which came from above downward seems the stronger – that is to say, the influence of the aristocratic monarchy on the bourgeois who were in process of climbing the social ladder and on those who remained at the bottom, the mass of ordinary bourgeois who did not belong to the bourgeoisie of office. Through the example and influence of their 'more highly placed brothers', the whole mass of the French seventeenth-century bourgeoisie was drawn into the main political flow of the aristocratic State, formed for the defence of feudalism . . . In consequence, venality of office was an instrument which did not contribute to the subjection of the monarchy to the bourgeoisie, but to a progressive submission of the bourgeoisie to the aristocratic monarchy. Venality was a means of separating the bourgeoisie from the revolutionary struggle against feudalism.[35] Thus, Porshnev's thought develops.

III

These solidly constructed ideas contain a great many partial truths. But they cannot be accepted as a whole, because as a whole they seem to force reality into frameworks which distort it; and they do not seem to give an account of the whole reality.

First of all, let us be clear that study of the popular revolts has never constituted a scandal in French academic eyes. Ernest Lavisse, professor at the Sorbonne and a member of the *Académie française*, in his *Histoire de France*, Vol. vii, Part i, published in 1911, gave a résumé of what was then known of the uprisings from 1662 to 1675, and arrived at one of Porshnev's most important conclusions: 'Almost everywhere two camps formed; on the one side, the nobles, the *officiers* of the king, "those who have the honour of conducting the business of His Majesty", the "*bons bourgeois*"; and, on the other, the people, the "*canaille*." '[36] His collaborator, Mariéjol, in Part ii of Vol. vi of the same work, examined the popular uprisings under Richelieu and made use of Boissonnade. That French historians have not studied these revolts more leaves a gap, as it does that they have not had the means of executing a number of studies and partial syntheses which are lacking on several important subjects, but there is most certainly no desire among them to run away from the popular uprisings just because they themselves are bourgeois.

Porshnev is right to insist on the universal nature of the uprisings, in terms of both time and space. He has given an account of the most important, those which struck contemporaries as important events. But minor rebellions involving assault and the taking of the law into one's own hands were endemic, a matter of daily occurrence in the France of this period. The multitude of lesser revolts indeed prepared the way for the major uprisings. Now, on this question of the spontaneity of the peasant and urban uprisings, both great and small, I feel some doubt. There is certainly no question of disputing that there were riots and even spontaneous revolts on the part of the lower classes. The problem is to know whether the majority of such uprisings and the most serious outbreaks have this spontaneous character. We must not take too lightly the accounts of the disquiet and suspicions of the government concerning the role of nobles and magistrates in these uprisings. Let us remember the number of plots and aristocratic rebellions under Richelieu and Mazarin. Let us remember the bonds of fidelity which united these nobles to all the social classes and to the peasants themselves, and the bonds which in general bound peasants to *seigneurs*, even when the latter were *officiers* or bourgeois. The peasant often had feelings of 'fidelity' and devotion toward his *seigneur*. Some *seigneurs* most certainly treated their peasants with cruelty and rapacity; but a *seigneur* had to be very bad for his peasants to feel hatred and a spirit of violence toward him. The *seigneur*, through his judicial and administrative officials, could render life either quite insupportable or fairly reasonable for his peasants. Moreover, *seigneur* and peasant had common interests against the king. Royal taxation entailed a decrease in rent. In bad years it threatened payment of dues and rents. The majority of *seigneurs* therefore protected their men against the fisc or against the effects of soldiers passing through or being billeted. They intervened against royal *officiers*, had their peasants' *taille*† reduced,[37] and obtained dispensation for them from tolls and *corvées*†. In times of trouble, they armed their tenants and farmers, formed leagues for mutual assistance and enforced respect for the cattle and crops of their men.[38] They organised resistance against taxation, stirred up peasant discontent against the royal fisc and provoked revolts. There are examples of their chasing off the agents of the fisc from their lands by main force and of their inciting their peasants to do the same. They aided them in it, sowing false reports of the reduction or the annulling of taxes, gave rebels cover, even when they were guilty of murder, and, moreover, did this with the assistance of bourgeois magistrates. There are many examples of this in the correspondence of Chancellor Séguier. The *intendant*, du Boulay Fabvier, sends a 'report' to Séguier from Mortagne sur Perche on 6 November 1643 'of the procedures I have taken against the rebels, one of whom fell into our hands and was condemned and executed. I hope to have another hanged, since this will provide the best example possible. It has been a very important matter and extremely necessary to stop this notorious rebellion in its tracks, since it was just about to spread very rapidly, there being six other adjoining parishes all on the point of doing the same thing . . .' He shows subsequently how he cannot apportion the *tailles* among the parishes and make them pay, except by moving about accompanied by soldiers; and how in one village they were met with arquebus fire and had to lay siege to a tower and arrest eight rebels: 'I can well advise you that if I had not proceeded to hang these, the whole province would have risen . . . The greatest part of the nobility foment these rebellions and openly prevent the bailiffs from entering their parishes; to such an extent that the king's taxes remain uncollected . . .'[39] Du Boulay Fabvier writes again from Normandy on 10 January 1645:

> Whole *élections* could very well pay what has been apportioned to them, if the protection of the *gentilshommes* did not stir them to open rebellion in order to prevent their tenants, who provide their own funds, from paying or to see that they pay very little of their *tailles* . . . The *Election* of Domfront continues [in this manner] . . . the visit that M. de Matignan and I have made has not succeeded in inducing them to pay any the more . . . The inhabitants of Mantilly . . . have moreover killed a constable some time ago . . . on account of *tailles*; and although one could take action, it is virtually impossible to discover anything about the murderers. It is the judges and the *gentilshommes* who ruin everything.[40]

Normandy was in no way an exception in this. Things were the same in Limousin. The *intendant*, de Vautorte, reminded Séguier on 10 September 1643: 'I have already informed you that everything is in a state of confusion in this province on account of the *tailles*. This is not just a recent matter, since the people in these parts are not docile to authority nor are they prompt to pay their taxes, and the *gentilshommes* encourage their vassals in this attitude and profit thereby . . . The king has recently written to the principal *gentilshommes* about this matter . . .'[41] De Corberon, *intendant* of the Limousin and Angoumois, indicates very clearly the mechanism of these revolts, in a letter from Limoges dated 26 August 1644:

> Monsieur and Madame de Pompadour, under the influence of their servants and agents, among whom there is a certain *procureur-fiscal*† of the estate of Treignac, in which one of the principal *bureaux* for the receipt of taxes in the *élection* of Tulles is situated, rather than from any feelings of hostility toward the king's business, have treated those presenting themselves for the levying of *taille* on the numerous estates belonging to them in such a manner and have spoken so forcefully of their own power and so contemptuously of those in authority in the province that it was not in any way a difficult matter to make the people believe that given their protection no one would dare touch them. Under this assurance, the inhabitants of the said estates have paid their taxes so badly that in truth they have scarcely discharged, since the year 1641, a third of the amounts for which they have been assessed . . . If these parishes are not the most prosperous, they are at least a great deal less distressed and have had more relief than others . . . since fifty or sixty of the parishes involved are being

charged two-thirds and less of the sums they bore last year . . . I would have thought that this reduction, agreed with the aforesaid *dame*, both for the good of His Majesty's business and from the feelings of respect and deference which I have and shall always have for *Monseigneur* the Chancellor, would have expedited the drawing up of the tax-rolls for the future and brought in all arrears. On the contrary, however, it has been set abroad in the parishes that if soldiers set about their duty and come in, and they have indeed let this be understood by their commanders, one would not be answerable for their persons or their lives, since M. de Pompadour's protection extends even to estates not personally belonging to him, he having written letters to the officers commanding the *fuzeliers*[42] to have them withdrawn from houses not coming within, except remotely, the competence of his own judges and *procureurs-fiscaux* . . . M. de Saint-Germain, at present the son-in-law of M. *le Surintendant*, who owns considerable property in the province . . . has told me to say that having the honour of now belonging to M. *le Surintendant*, he would hope to be treated no less favourably than the aforesaid *sieur et dame* de Pompadour. You may judge whether in this business one does not need courage and strength of mind.[43]

In due course, the estates of Parvez and Budgeat, belonging to Mme de Pompadour, rise in revolt against the '*fuzeliers*'.
De Corberon writes again from Brives on 23 October 1644:

Monsieur le Comte de Bonneval has not only permitted the *archers* of the *prévosté*† to be roughly treated when they entered his estates with a single *sergent* to enforce payment of *taille*, but has also had a brigade of *fuzeliers* chased off, whom I had sent to have the writs executed with more authority to oblige his estates to satisfy payment of their *tailles*, which they have not paid for the past three years. I remit the matter to your discretion to order such punishment as you think suitable . . .[44]

Things were the same in the Auvergne. The *intendant*, de Sève, writes: 'In the matter of the *tailles*, I have as much trouble in combating the *gentilshommes* who prevent payment as in combating the ill-will or the incapacity of the tax-payers to pay. I persist in telling you that this province is more suitable for the employment of a *Chambre des Grands Jours*† than an *intendant de justice*.'[45]
Things were indeed the same in Touraine. The *intendant*, de Heere, speaks in this way at Saumur on 18 July 1643:

On my arrival in this province, I found the majority of the parishes determined not to draw up any tax-rolls whatsoever. It is true that the distress in these parts is considerable, since they have very little corn and wine. I can nevertheless say that there has been a great deal of obstinacy, because at the moment the poorest parishes have had their taxes equalised[46] and it is only the richest parishes and those belonging to persons of quality which are in a state of disobedience. Besides which several persons of quality have so imprinted on the minds of the people that their *tailles* would be remitted that they live eternally in the hope of it . . .

And again, on 19 October 1643, from Tours: '. . . the most rebellious parishes are now in a state of complete disobedience. The exemplary punishment I have had imposed on the leaders of the rebels of Vernay has surprised everyone. They could not imagine that one would dare enter this parish, because it was under the protection of several *gentils-hommes* . . .'[47]

And again, it was the same situation in Périgord. On 13 December 1644 de Lauson writes to Séguier from Périgueux, to the effect that he is '. . . in Périgord, where the protection which the *gentilshommes* afford their *métayers*†, their parishes and their friends, causes great delay in the levying of the royal taxes. They form assemblies, they attempt to spread fear, they threaten, they foment rebellions. But as I have not allowed my company of soldiers to become split up,[48] and it marches as a body, affording good protection, no one dares attack it . . .'[49]

In these years, 1643 and 1644, the peasant uprisings are constant throughout the west, the centre and south of France. The northern and eastern limits of the uprisings pass through Normandy, Berry, the Auvergne and Dauphiné. Peasants refuse to pay their taxes, chase away the agents of the royal fisc, murder tax-officials, seize châteaux and threaten towns. Regarding affairs in Angoumois, Poitou, Aunis and Saintonge, Porshnev writes: 'the particular mark of the uprisings in these provinces was the universal attempt on the part of the local nobility to support them and utilise them for their own profit.'[50] We may go further, however. In the various parishes involved, the nobility did not so much support the uprisings as provoke them. These peasant uprisings were not spontaneous. In these instances, the peasants were the agents of the nobility.

So far, we have had clear cases: direct rebellions of nobles chasing off the agents of the king and their troops by force of arms, the use of the nobles' own men in pursuing their aims, incitement of peasants to do the same, promise of protection to rebels in face of the apparatus of the state, the spreading of false reports and the hiding of rebel murderers. There are less clear-cut cases, where the peasant uprisings seem spontaneous. But often, without doubt, it is in appearance only. A letter from the *intendant* Villemontée, from Les Sables d'Olonne, of 1 November

1643, reveals the following situation. He has had several rebels imprisoned and executed for refusing to pay their *tailles*:

> . . . but that cannot prevent greater trouble which threatens us as a result of the revolt of the nobility and certain clergy, because of the inventory which we wish to make of their cellars in regard to the new tax of twenty *sols* per hogshead of wine which is called the tax of the *escu pour tonneau* . . . I received news yesterday that the whole nobility of Xaintonge and Angoumois is assembled over this and that dangerous speeches are being made, prejudicial to His Majesty's interest, for if some *gentilhomme* should begin to have officials killed in regard to this new tax, the next thing will be the *tailles* . . .[51]

What strikes us is that the *intendant* is speaking of the eventuality of the murder of tax officials by men in the service of a nobleman, which could unleash revolt against all the taxes, and he seems to envisage it as nothing extraordinary, as something quite natural, an everyday event, in the normal run of things. These popular uprisings which seem spontaneous and which usually begin with the murder of agents of the royal fisc, how many times indeed do they arise from the initiative of the nobility?

This induces us to reflect on other popular uprisings which were apparently spontaneous, such as those of the *Croquants* from 1636 to 1637. This was a peasant war which was, for Porshnev, even more serious than the *jacqueries* of the fourteenth century. Contemporaries saw the hand of the *gentilshommes* and the *Grands* in it. Porshnev calls such opinions baseless 'conjectures'. However there are texts whose authors do not conjecture but categorically affirm. Here, for example, is a '*Mémoire* touching the disturbances which occurred from 1629 to 1643', drawn up at the end of December 1643 for the *Surintendant des Finances*, which discusses the problem of the measures to be taken in face of the agitation of the nobles of Aunis, Saintonge, Poitou and Angoumois. Speaking of the insurrection of the *Croquants* in 1636, the author says this: 'These *Croquants* formed political assemblies at that time in which the clergy and *gentilshommes* connived . . .' In 1637, '. . . Villemontée has had the principal authors of and those responsible for this uprising punished; but although it was clear enough that a great many[52] clergy and *gentilshommes* had taken part in it, nevertheless because their conviction for it presented difficulties and because it was important for His Majesty's interest to establish order in these provinces, the said *sieur de Villemontée* discontinued the pursuit . . .'[53] The author affirms categorically that the facts were known, but that it was difficult to bring viable proof against the guilty according to the normal processes of justice. Now, let us recall that the *Croquants* of Périgord had at that time a *gentilhomme*, La Mothe La Forêt, openly serving as their general, and other *gentils-*

hommes as officers, and their conviction would not have been difficult. They may have been simply *déclassés*. But there is something more intriguing in the situation. La Mothe La Forêt had among his principal lieutenants a certain *gentilhomme*, named Madaillan, who escaped after the defeat of the uprising. Some years later, however, in 1641, the rebel leader Pierre Greletti, an old peasant, who still held the countryside between Périgueux and Bergerac with two hundred men, and who was widely popular, received a visit from this same Madaillan, who came to him to make overtures on behalf of a *prince du sang†*, the Comte de Soissons, concerning participation in an uprising against Richelieu. Historians know this detail because Greletti, anxious to obtain his pardon, revealed everything to the government. But, if Madaillan was acting as an agent of the princes in raising the peasants to rebellion in 1641, we are perhaps justified in wondering under what title did he, as a *gentilhomme*, command a troop of the *Croquants* in 1637?

Royal *officiers*, who were considered bourgeois, but who were fairly frequently *seigneurs*, also 'connived' at the peasant revolts. In the first place, these *officiers*, in the same way as the *gentilshommes*, resist the royal fisc and provoke rebellion among the peasants. The *intendant*, de la Potherye, writes from Caen on 8 June 1643: 'The *officiers* of Bayeux . . . have each been fined a hundred *livres* and suspended from office for a month, and those who have incited this disorder have been fined one hundred *livres* each and have been suspended for a year . . . The poor have paid their taxes everywhere. It is only the rich and the *officiers* who create these difficulties.'[54] In other instances, without it seems directly provoking revolt, the *officiers* at least contributed to the creation of a situation leading to explosion and continuing trouble, through general opposition to taxation and absolutism; through efforts to favour rebels in the courts and to give them the assurance that they could proceed with impunity. A report to Séguier of 1643 speaks of:

> . . . a judgment of the *Parlement†* of Toulouse . . . which troublesome spirits have used as a pretext to stir up the people in several parts and incite them to refuse payment of their taxes, principally in Upper Languedoc. Those sent there to levy taxes imposed by virtue of certain special commissions, which had been annulled by this judgment, have withdrawn from the province and have brought their complaints to me, demanding safeguards and protection for their own persons. Rumour has amplified the said judgment beyond its proper terms. One does not know how to remove from people's minds the idea that by virtue of this judgment they are only obliged in future to pay the original royal *taille* and that extraordinary commissions, even those of *intendants*, have been thereby revoked, and that from henceforth they need recognise no orders other than those of the *Parlement*

... I have seen the beginning of sedition in Guyenne ... It is most certain that if the two sovereign courts[55] in the province are not kept in order and if the bishops are not exhorted to see to it that the orders of the *Conseil* are put into execution, we shall see the people in a state of rebellion in a very short time, not of their own initiative, because, in this province, they are incapable of it, but through the bad example which will have been set them.[56]

Judicial *officiers* did their utmost to assure the rebels of immunity in the courts. We have already seen du Boulay Fabvier complaining of not being able to arrest certain peasant rebels, who were guilty of murder, because of the judges.[57] De la Potherye sat with the *présidial*† in Caen to judge the affair in Baycux. The *Parlement* of Rouen however reversed the judgment, although in this instance the *intendant* acting in the *présidial* should in fact have been sovereign. De la Potherye is forced to request the Chancellor to protect the *officiers* of the *présidial* of Caen against retaliation by the *Parlement* of Rouen for having assisted the *intendant*, since otherwise it will be impossible for the *intendant* to find any more judges in the *généralité*†. The *Parlement* of Rouen had forbidden the *lieutenants criminels* to issue writs and it was quite impossible to arrest any of the guilty.[58]

I do not therefore see any class-front against the peasants. It seems to me no less impossible to declare the existence of a peasant bloc against the *seigneurs*.

We are especially badly informed about the different peasant groups and their effective participation in the revolts. We may however perceive that the peasant revolts were very complex phenomena and that sometimes they were the acts of various groups which were in fact comparatively fairly limited in size. We know that if the *taille* was apportioned between the *élections* by the *Conseil du Roi* and between the parishes by the *élus* under the authority of the *Trésoriers-généraux de France*†, it was apportioned between the actual tax payers by certain inhabitants of a village elected by the others, who also had the task of collecting it. Are these the subject of this letter from the *intendant* de Sève to Séguier, dated 18 October 1643, from Calvinet near Aurillac:

A number of *collecteurs*† who assume responsibility for levying taxes for the *consuls* have contributed to the ruin [of certain villages] by their exactions. It is this kind of people who secretly make themselves the principal instruments of sedition in order to prevent themselves being proceeded against by the *receveurs*† and to help themselves to the moneys they collect. I have instituted proceedings against the principal one of them. He is one of the most seditious men in Aurillac and has perpetrated various malversations of funds in the village of which he has the right of exercising the office of *collecteur*.

F

I hope in this way to satisfy the people by making an example of one of those who exploit them and that by punishing one of these seditious spirits I shall cause his fellows to be apprehensive of pursuing a like course . . .[59]

Is it a question here of 'assessor-collectors' who abused their functions in order to exact more than they should from the taxpayers, and who kept what they collected without turning it in to the *officiers de finances*, inducing peasants to revolt in order to avoid proceedings against themselves? If so, these would be influential peasants, capable of exerting pressure, well-to-do peasants, the '*coqs de paroisses*'. And yet we know the latter avoided the office of *collecteur*. Is it perhaps a question of another kind of *collecteur*? For another sort of tax, since the chief one of those operating in the villages lives in the town of Aurillac? And since they act for the *consuls*, are they officials levying, for example, a tax on the well-to-do? Whatever they were, given their exactions and exploitations, could they be supposed to have led more than very limited numbers of people?

In certain uprisings, texts exist which show us tenants of *gentilshommes* actually mounting guard to defend their owners' châteaux. The question of attacks on châteaux by rebels calls, however, for certain observations. Even during the uprisings of 1643, which were indubitably provoked as we have seen by the nobility, the peasants of Angoumois, Poitou, Aunis and Saintonge seized certain châteaux. Their reasons were tactical. It was in their own interest to hold certain strong points in open country. It was not a question of attacking the *seigneurs* or the seigneurial order of things. On 14 September 1643 the *intendant* Charreton wrote to Bullion, the *surintendant des finances*, about the uprisings in Rouergue:

Four days ago, peasants from the parishes of Saint-André and Saint Salvadour, belonging to the said *sieur* Raynaldi and La Fouliade, near Villefranche, assembled together in the night, to the number of about 400, of whom only 111 carried fire-arms, among whom there were ten good *fuzeliers* from Nagac and some soldiers from around the said Nagac and Salvaterre, all of whom slept under arms. On the following day, in the morning, they seized the château of Salvadour, where they placed about twenty soldiers as a garrison, to be maintained at the expense of the said parishes. The said rebels also tried to surprise the château of Roumergon, belonging to the Marquis de Malente, but his tenants preserve it from harm until the present time.[60]

There are cases where certain nobles placed their châteaux at the disposal of the peasants. In 1643, peasant revolts had lasted since 1640 in the marsh area of Rie and de Monts, seven leagues from Nantes, and government circles deplored 'the boldness of the peasants which becomes extreme as a result of the permission which they say Mademoiselle de Rohan has given them to arm themselves against the attempted invasion of the Spaniards. They mount guard in two châteaux belonging to the said Mademoiselle, who sanctioned this rebellion, concerning which measures need to be taken.'[61]

Even on the occasions when there was plunder and destruction of châteaux, we would need to be able to distinguish between cases, to know whether the châteaux concerned did not belong to *financiers* or to *officiers de finance*, or to *seigneurs* who were not in sympathy with the peasants but were supporters of the king, or to *seigneurs* who were brutal and rapacious, as indeed some were. We would need to know who the assailants were. Once the uprisings were unleashed, all kinds of men joined in the general uproar and many vagabonds became involved who had nothing in common with the peasants, nor any object other than plunder.

It is by no means certain therefore that the rebels were in most cases attacking the seigneurial system. Certainly, they sometimes drew up articles of grievance about taxes, about payment of feudal dues and the payment of tithes to the Church, and about justice and government administration. This was the case in 1636 in Angoumois, Poitou and Saintonge. They demanded the suppression of all indirect taxes, complained about the burden of 'feudal' dues, and exposed the injustice of the nobility's exemption from payment of *tailles*. It is a long way from that, however, to revolution. The real fact of the situation was that in a period of dearth and rising prices the peasants cried out against everything which exacted money from them. Their revolts, even those which were not organised by *seigneurs*, were without doubt no more directed against the seigneurial order than the uprisings of their descendants between 1815 and 1848, during similar periods of dearth, when the seigneurial order and 'feudal' rights no longer existed.[62] Perhaps it was the growth of communications and the progress of agricultural techniques, no less than the disappearance of seigneurial leadership, which made the peasant uprisings of the nineteenth century progressively rarer, rather than the suppression of 'feudal' rights.

We can be no more certain that, when the *'communes'* of Périgord assembled prior to the capture of Bergerac and declared that none of them would attack persons or private property except with the permission of their general, this was a deviation from what they would normally have done, simply because they had a leader who was not of their own class but a 'feudal' landed *seigneur*, the *gentilhomme* La Mothe La Forêt. There was indeed probably a majority of property-owners among the rebel peasants who had a personal interest in the protection of property, even when this amounted to no more than a house and a garden. In general, these rebels were far from being paupers. They had to provision themselves at their own expense, and arm themselves likewise. The *intendant* Charreton notes in 1643 that in Rouergue: 'the peasants from a great number of parishes have for some time purchased guns and prepared themselves for campaign . . .'[63] Moreover, these rural uprisings were not unified. In 1637, five thousand 'peasants' in Périgord revolt against the majority of peasants led by La Mothe La Forêt, and they have to be beaten before the majority can confront the royal army. But just who were they, these rebels against those in revolt?

It is for certain that the study of all these uprisings must continue before we can seek to place them within the framework of a general theory.

In the towns, it was frequently royal *officiers*, municipal magistrates and rich bourgeois who fomented revolts, taking the lead in them and openly directing them, at times when provincial or municipal privileges were under threat or simply when taxation seemed excessive. At Aix-en-Provence in 1630, and again in 1631, when the government sought to transform the province, a *pays d'états*†, into a *pays d'élections*†, it was Coriolis, the *président*† of the *Parlement*, together with other *officiers* and bourgeois, who directed the revolt. Their followers, the *Cascaveoux*, number among them men in rags swearing that they will cut their own throats rather than suffer the appointment of *élus*, men who burn the houses of *financiers*, while the bourgeois militia refuses to march against them.

At Lyons, in 1633, the presence of the *maître des requêtes*† Moric, sent as *intendant de justice*, alone prevents the renewal of the uprising of 1632, since, he says, 'the *présidial*, or at least the greatest part of it, was implicated, together with the principal citizens of the town', in the preparation of a new uprising.[64]

During the troubles in Montauban in 1633, de Villeneuve, *avocat du Roi*, in the *présidial*, informs Séguier that 'the *Consuls* were to be found consorting with those who wear livery . . . and we have seen a sedition equal to the last rebellion against the *officiers* of the king who exercise justice . . .'[65] At Angers in 1641 the *intendant*, de Heere, writes: 'I have just received a letter from Issoire, from the Maréchal de Boisse, which informs me that Angers never obeys except by the use of soldiery. The population there goes about armed and he advises me to present myself to you . . . then return with troops . . . It is several merchants who are fomenting rebellion there . . . The people[66] have reached such a degree of insolence that they threaten those they can [?] to burn down their houses; and they care nothing whatsoever for the town magistrates . . .'[67]

At Sablé in 1646 it is the *bailli*† himself who takes the initiative:

The farmer for the tax of thirty *sols* per pipe of wine and twenty *sols* per hogshead in the *Election* of La Flèche has brought me a report of rebellion and the violence done to him by the *bailli* of Cellé, which is fully attested to by the *huissiers*† and *archers*, whom I have confirmed it with, the which report I now send to you . . . The said farmer, *Monseigneur*, has wanted to go to the *Conseil* to declare his abandonment of the tax-farm and yourselves and complain to you of all the acts of violence perpetrated against him by the said *bailli*. I have dissuaded him from this course and have made him understand that he must never complain direct to you over matters such as these and that I shall bring to bear the necessary orders in regard to them . . .[68]

In other instances, when the bourgeois do not seem to have actually organised and unleashed revolts – that is until we have further information – they at least created conditions for revolt, by denouncing taxation as excessive and useless, by criticising royal government, by their example and the hope they instilled of rebellion going unpunished. And then, when the popular uprising is unleashed, the bourgeois militia refuses to suppress it and it is allowed to spread. This is what happened in Dijon in 1630, where, during the initial stages of the uprising, the *Parlement* of Burgundy and the *Chambre des Comptes* bore a heavy responsibility; and at Bordeaux, in 1635, after incitement from the *Parlement*, the bourgeois militia simply let things continue and the majority of the bourgeois refused to support the Duc d'Epernon until the very end, since they saw in the rebels their own liberators. This was also the case at Rouen in 1639, where the attitude of the *Parlement* was such that the king suspended it from its functions. It was the case again at Moulins, in 1640, where the *gouverneur*, Saint-Géran, was obliged to have an *échevin*, Tridon, imprisoned.[69] The *gouverneur* positively accuses the *lieutenant-général*, who was mayor at the time, of having abandoned him at the start of the revolt. He expresses his distrust of the judges, who were favourable toward the rebels. He asks for *commissaires*† to be sent, 'because I am entirely fearful for the state of justice in Moulins'.[70] As to the punishment of the guilty, he does not believe that the '*Présidial* would be capable of doing this, because the majority were influenced either by self-interest or fear . . .'[71] The *intendant* de Chaponay, sent to Moulins to undertake the punishment of the rebels, begs Séguier to 'allow him to hold the trial arising from the sedition outside the town . . .', because of

the favours and assurances of protection which all these murderers and thieves receive from the principal *officiers* and magistrates of the town, who openly favour their crimes against the known wishes of the king . . . During the three months I have been in this town I have asked the said *lieutenant-général* for the reports he has compiled as mayor, giving the names and surnames of the *officiers*, the military captains of the various *quartiers*, the bourgeois and inhabitants of the town and *faubourgs* who have not been prepared to take up arms . . . and have refused to support him in opposing the violence of murderers and thieves . . .

But the *lieutenant-général* does not produce the reports for him. Warrants have been issued against several of these 'notorious murderers and thieves', but they 'cannot be executed, because of the knowledge and connivance of the *officiers* and inhabitants of the said town . . .'[72]

When it is not bourgeois, it is the *gentilshommes* who provoke the outbreak of popular revolts in the towns by their example, and who assure the continuation of revolt by their own inaction. According to the *intendant*, de Chaulnes, at Issoire in 1643:

> Following the example of the nobility, who have scandalously and illegally taken up arms in their own interest and on behalf of individual grievances, the *menu peuple* think that they are also permitted to dispense themselves from their duty. I am not speaking of what they have done to the *commis* who are responsible for the said tax of a *sol pour livre* in the town of Issoire, which belongs to *Monsieur* the bishop of Clermont and where the *Messieurs de Canillac* are all-powerful, where they threw one of the *commis* into a cauldron of quicklime used by curers to depilate cattle hides, from which the wretched *commis* came out half-boiled. I am not speaking either of a rebellion in the same town in which an officer of the watch of *Monsieur le Grand Prévôt*, named la Noue, received more than twenty wounds from swords, stones and pistols, from which he was in great danger of his life, in executing decrees of the *Conseil*. But I will tell you that the trouble increases . . . It is openly proclaimed in the mountain parishes of the *élection* of Clermont, Brionde, Aurillac and others, that the king has announced a remission of the *subsistance*†[73] and of a part of the *tailles* . . . Rebellions occur everywhere . . . There are even priests who have put it about publicly and in their sermons that one no longer has to pay *subsistances* nor arrears of *tailles*, one of whom is in the hands of the authorities of the *Cour des Aides*†, but there is a chance that he will be treated too leniently, since *Monsieur* the bishop of Clermont has declared himself his protector, having canvassed on his behalf . . . In the situation in which I find myself, to which I have been reduced by M. de Canillac and M. d'Estaing, I have no other desire than to return to Paris . . . I dare not leave the walls of this town, where I have been the prisoner of these *Messieurs* for more than two months, during which time they have taken advantage of the fact that I have had no communication with the *Conseil*, not even a letter which I could set against their false reports and rumours.[74]

In the same year, after several meetings, the nobles of Angoumois, Aunis and Saintonge propose a joint assembly with those of Poitou for 15 December:

> Methods for the relief of the provinces were put forward, among others was included the getting rid of the office of the *intendant* and obtaining reduction of the *tailles* and other taxes. Finally, these *Messieurs* miss no opportunity for demanding the relief of the people, assuring them that the whole of France takes an interest in their case . . . The rumour is widespread in Poitiers and apparently elsewhere of the usefulness of these proceedings of the nobility, and this may attract the rest of the people, if they are not promptly dealt with . . .[75]

The spontaneity of the urban uprisings seems as dubious as that of the peasant uprisings. In the same way, the 'class-fronts' seem very doubtful propositions. I do not see a 'class-front' of the nobles and bourgeois against the urban lower classes, no more than a 'front' of these last against the bourgeois and nobles. At Moulins, there are 'very few persons of quality' participating openly in the revolt on the side of the rebels. But there are indeed some. As for the *plebs*, in the *faubourgs*, they did not revolt as a body. A part indeed helped in the arrest of the principal rebels, and we may wonder whether the rebels themselves were anything other than a strong minority, even in the *faubourgs*.

But, we are told, nobility and bourgeoisie both ended by arraying themselves against the people and contributed to the suppression of the revolts. We must however distinguish things a little. Noble intervention against the rebels, whether peasant or urban lower class, seems to have been rare. When the nobility take up arms, as in Bordeaux in 1635 or in Valence in 1644, it is because an important nobleman leads them, someone in the king's service, a nobleman with prestige and influence towards whom other nobles have obligations of 'fidelity'. In Bordeaux, it is the Duc d'Epernon; in Valence, it is the Duc de Lesdiguières. At Angoulême in 1636, Villemontée awaits impatiently for M. de la Rochefoucauld to arrive, since 'he enjoys such a high reputation in all the provinces in this region . . . that he will be able to muster a large number of volunteers among the *gentilshommes*.'[76] But, in the event, de la Rochefoucauld found the greatest difficulty in obtaining the voluntary support of certain *gentilshommes*. Likewise, in the course of the trouble at Moulins, the nobility abandon the *gouverneur*.

> I do not think there are six *gentilshommes* who have come forward to offer their services to M. de Saint-Géran on this occasion; and if what has been reported to me is true, all the *gentilshommes* of this *généralité* give evidence of their satisfaction at the death of Monsieur Puesche and his followers,[77] because of the great extortions which are said to

have come to light in the examinations made into taxes paid by the wealthy involving the off-loading of *aides*† onto the less well-to-do, by dint of the power which he claimed to have . . .

With the nobility refusing to come to the aid of Saint-Géran, he had to be allowed to use the first regiment which came to hand.[78] In general, the *gentilshommes* did not take up arms against the rebels. Porshnev thinks that the absence of reaction on the part of the nobility stems from the fact that the majority of them were away with the army on campaign. But there were most certainly an even larger number still remaining, who could have taken up arms against the rebels in the provinces. D'Epernon and Lesdiguières found some. When the Prince de Condé approached Moulins to put an end to the revolt there, he blamed Saint-Géran greatly for not having mustered the nobility.[79] Saint-Géran had not indeed issued a summons because the nobles would most probably not have responded to it. But it is clear that Condé considered there were enough nobility in the province to serve effectively; and this was also the opinion of the mayor of Moulins. If the nobility were, as Porshnev thinks, the active guardians of the 'feudal-absolutist order', it has to be accepted that they played their role very badly.

The bourgeoisie intervened less rarely. On several occasions, when rioters began attacking houses belonging to the bourgeoisie, the bourgeois militia fired on them, and from that moment the bourgeoisie assisted in the suppression of the uprising. In general, the bourgeoisie closed the gates of towns against the *faubourgs*, preventing their people from entering the towns, and they did this if necessary by use of force. Sometimes and there is no doubt of it, a true class-conflict existed. But we must nevertheless ask against whom did the bourgeoisie most frequently direct its fire. Against the people, as people, as a class, as a lower stratum of society? Or was it against groups from within the people, mingled with renegade soldiers, beggars and vagabonds, forming themselves into armed bands? It is notable that the bourgeoisie manifested the same hostility toward royal troops. To attempt to introduce troops into a closed town, even if it were merely mooted, was in fact to risk revolt, as was the case in Paris in 1588, or to risk its renewal, as happened yet again in Paris in 1648.[80] We find this at Montpellier in 1645, where, on the orders of Marshal Schomberg, both *officiers* and bourgeois combine in putting down the rebels.

M. *le maréchal* fought both with his intelligence and the arms at his command against the fiercest and most determined sedition I have ever witnessed . . . The people were discontented over taxes and the tax-farmers, but he did everything he could to induce them to return to their proper duty. The orders he gave have been so effective that the town now has an altogether different countenance. All the judicial *officiers* in the town have taken up arms in company with the principal bourgeois of both religions and have rendered themselves masters of the town. M. *le maréchal* has been obliged to issue an *ordonnance* severely attacking the taxes and the tax-farmers, in order to restore order . . .

This was all very well; but when the *intendant* proposed bringing a regiment into the town, one of the magistrates immediately warned Séguier that the troops would merely bring about an alliance of the whole town against them. M. Baltazar, the *intendant*, 'colours the mind of M. *le maréchal* with the most violent advice, and if his counsels had been adopted there would have been a worse situation created than ever, because he wanted to bring in the Normandy regiment, against which all the inhabitants of the town, of both high and low estate, were resolved upon arming themselves . . .'[81] The presence of troops in the town carried with it the prospect of plunder and rape. All armed assemblies, however, of whatever kind, inspired this same fear by their very nature, since in the end all revolts unleashed the pent-up feelings of beggars and vaga-bonds. We would need to know more about the uprisings to interpret the meaning of the part played by the bourgeoisie, when it took action.

The clergy were very far from being uniformly hostile to the rebels. We have the evidence of the events at Issoire.[82] During the revolts of 1636, on 6 June of that year, the inhabitants of the *châtellenie* of Blanzac set out on the march, 'numbering 4000 men, armed with arquebuses and pikes, in some twelve or fifteen companies, led by their priests.' It will be said, however, that these were members of the lower clergy.[83] But, in the following, we have the bishops themselves. In Languedoc, 'under the pretext of the public good, the bishops of certain dioceses, over which they have absolute mastery, do not exert themselves to the extent that they could to confirm the people in their duty . . . If the prelates are not exhorted to see to the execution of the orders of the *Conseil*' their bad example will induce the people to revolt.[84]

What then becomes of the 'class-front' against the people, of which Porshnev speaks? It disappears. Examination of the relationships between nobles and peasants in these troubled years suggests rather the existence of social groups, composed of cultivators of the soil, lawyers, *officiers*, priests and *seigneurs*, united by mutual ties of protection and service, in a society divided vertically and in which these vertical divisions were more important than horizontal stratifications. Porshnev tells us that *seigneurs*, priests, lawyers and *officiers* exploit the cultivator, on the grounds that the latter does not retain all he produces and yields part of it to other members of the group, either directly in the form of dues, rents, tithes and fees, or indirectly in the form of salaries distributed by the *seigneurs*. This is true, if we accept that these men had only to satisfy their need for food, clothing and lodging, and that, whatever the circumstances, the cultivator could have continued his cultivation in peace. If however we accept that, on the contrary, man has not only need for bread, but that he has, for example, religious needs – which do not seem to have been negligible for these peasants, if we are to judge by the number of mystics who were to be found in their ranks; if one also accepts that a social group must be protected from aggression, that disputes between its members must be judged, that relationships between them must be regulated and that, division of labour being advantageous, these operations are better confided to specialists, who are then in return granted dispensation from the labour of the producer but without whom production itself would be impossible, what then becomes of the notion of exploitation? Naturally, a man may neglect his duties or abuse the powers deriving from his function, and examples of such abuse on the part of the nobles are indeed not lacking.

All these facts contribute in their different ways to dissuading us from seeing the absolute monarchy as '*un Etat de noblesse*', defender of a 'feudal' regime, and from seeing the 'Order' of seventeenth-century France as a 'feudal-absolutist Order', since in fact we see the State continually in conflict with the nobles and with social groups united by bonds of fidelity. There were of course other motivations involved. It is not without out reason that Porshnev employs such terms, since the nobility was the primary order of the State and the dream of every French commoner was to become noble. There were still fiefs and a hierarchy of landed estates bound by relationships involving service. Homage was still rendered in this society, and we find accounts of it in the archives. Nevertheless I have to declare my extreme repugnance to considering the seventeenth century as a 'feudal' epoch, and, even if we do take into account the relationships of production, to accepting that 'as a whole, the feudal Middle Ages in their purest form reigned in the French economy of the seventeenth century'. If one uses these expressions accurately and as our author does, without distinguishing between seigneurial regimes and feudal systems, 'the Middle Ages in their purest form' materialised from the eighth to the eleventh century between the Loire and the Meuse, in the regime of great landed domains cultivated by tenant-serfs, who were compelled to fulfil unlimited seigneurial dues above all in the form of work, domains which lived in a virtually closed economy, with workshops of artisan-serfs. All these serfs submitted themselves to the *seigneur*, whose 'men' they were and who exercised over them most of the powers of the State. This regime is most certainly not that of seventeenth-century France, where the majority of the peasants are free and considered as proprietors of their tenures; where the *seigneurs* have lost their most important powers, which have been resumed by the State; and where not only does a barter economy predominate, with simple merchant-production on the part of small-owners and master-craftsmen, but where a commercial capitalism has profoundly penetrated the country. Commercial capitalism is not segregated in the towns, as Porshnev thinks. In vast areas of France, it profoundly influences the countryside and modifies productive relationships. Numerous peasants devote a part of their time to working for the large-scale merchant-manufacturers who sell their products in foreign markets – in the Spanish Low Countries until 1635, in Holland, England, the Baltic countries, Muscovy, Portugal, Spain and Spanish America. Alongside this concentration of a commercially motivated industry, an industrial capitalism has made its appearance in the towns. It is not only a matter of large-scale *manufactures*. In textiles, for example, the type of manufacturer has become widespread who can bring together some twenty crafts on a local basis which he owns and which no longer give work to '*compagnons*'† but to 'workers'. The term indeed appears in the texts. Although this type of manufacturer depends economically on the large-scale merchant and although his methods are often crude, ownership of the means of production, which he does not work himself but which he confides to workers, makes him a capitalist. In the countryside, as in the towns, *seigneurs*, lawyers, *officiers* and spinsters invest money in the enterprises of these merchants, under forms which play the role of our own debenture stock, and thus participate in the profits of commercial capitalism. The French were certainly more interested in the possession of land than in anything else. The characteristic of an ancient, consolidated fortune of either an *officier* or bourgeois living '*noblement*' is that the greatest part of it consists of landed estates. But, even if this is so, these are more frequently estates let out to tenants, or even to *métayers*, under a contract of association; and if the proprietor still charges a rent for his land, it is no longer a 'feudal' land rent. The monopolies and privileges granted to large-scale merchant-manufacturers do not retard the rise of capitalism. They were indeed a condition of its development at this stage, without which prices would have been too low to be profitable.[85] It seems to me difficult even in terms of the economic aspect of things to contain the France of the seventeenth century under the same heading as that of the eleventh. What is to be said if we seek to include in the same global category, by making an abstraction of the immense total of reality in terms of the same productive relationships and the same fundamental economic law, countries as different as France and the England of the Stuarts, where peasant possession remained essentially precarious, or as France and Russia, where the great seigneurial domain develops and devours, or 'bleeds', the peasant tenures. It seems to me that we must not fail to recognise the profound differences in this respect between Europe west of the Elbe and Europe east of that river.[86] Moreover, we may ask whether Porshnev is not projecting onto seventeenth-century France ideas especially relevant to Russia. Does it not involve us

in a world of difficulties to consider China a 'feudal' country for two
thousand years. If it were true, for example, that Chinese seventeenth-
century society was still founded on the extended family which was
analogous to the Roman *gens*, then we should have a mode of 'feudal'
production, the infra-structure of a society tied, according to the Marxists,
to what they term the mode of production of the primitive community.
This however would be a misunderstanding. Equally, to extend the use
of the word 'feudal' without distinguishing feudality from the seigneurial
regime; to consider civilisations so strongly individual in character, and
also so diverse, in terms simply of 'superstructures' possessing the same
feudal mode of production; to propose that this is the same mode, without distinguishing how the same cause has produced such different
effects; to accept that civilisations such as the Chinese and French had
simply to slow down or accelerate the development of their respective
modes of production – all this seems scarcely able to satisfy the historian.

It is highly doubtful whether we can accept that the French seventeenth-century State was '*un Etat de nobles*', and that a 'feudal-absolutist
Order' existed. In reality, the State of the absolute monarchy disrupted
the seigneurial groupings of society. The State destroyed, or at least
weakened, the bonds between man and man, which were of the essence
of the seigneurial regime, by constantly insinuating its justice, its laws,
its fisc, its army between the nobles and their 'men'. What was the
objective of the great revolts of the nobility? It was not after all to
consolidate an absolute monarchy which was defending the 'feudal order'.
It was to return to the institutions of Hugh Capet – 'and better still if
that were possible'; that is to say, to ruin the whole work of the
monarchy, to return to a feudal order which in fact no longer existed.
Even the most moderate wanted to take the monarchy back to what it
had been before Louis XI. The *gentilshommes* had the firm conviction
that absolutism did not further their interests, that the absolutist State
was not their State. They lay, indeed, outside the State. It is impossible,
therefore, to subscribe to the views of Porshnev, who sees the absolutist
monarchical State as the intrument of the landed feudal nobility.

An *officier* of some importance was legally noble. A noble, but not a
gentilhomme, not a feudal lord. Porshnev never makes any distinction.
Were those great merchants, the Venetian nobility, a feudal corporation?
In France, the public itself imposed some distinctions. An *officier* ennobled by office was a bourgeois.[87] It was deplored that the nobility,
the true nobility, that of the *gentilshommes*, should be without employment in the State and that public office should be the apanage of those
who were called ironically '*gentilshommes* of the pen and ink'. Bourgeois
is what one was, if one were an *officier* or a *commissaire*, even when
seated on the *fleur de lys* and wearing purple, even when tricked out
with the title of *chevalier*, or *baron*, or even *président de Parlement*,

or when a member of the *Conseil du Roi*. Porshnev does not wish to recognise that all these *officiers* have a bourgeois identity. He claims that they have lost their class-characteristics in becoming *officiers*, because they have separated themselves from industry and commerce, and no longer carry with them the means of production. This is however what happens ordinarily, in fact, to *officiers*, *commissaires* and functionaries in most regimes. It was equally the case with the functionaries of the French nineteenth century. Their offices obliged them to separate themselves from industry and commerce. Even so, I do not think that there would be very much question of denying them their status as bourgeois. In fact, the *officiers* of the seventeenth century held values and pursued social customs which differentiated them clearly from the *gentilshommes*, even when they conducted themselves as *seigneurs*. What does the work of Loyseau signify unless the *officiers* were not considered as true nobles? Most probably, absolutism resulted in the first place from the defence needs of the realm, from wars against the foreigner. Absolutism was originally the 'construct' of a government at war. But, further than that, I see nothing to change in the theory that the development of the absolute monarchical State had been facilitated by the possibility of its opposing bourgeois to *gentilhomme*, of utilising the bourgeoisie in the apparatus of the State. The monarchy is assuredly something different when the *Conseil du Roi* is composed of a majority of *noblesse d'épée*†, from when, in the seventeenth century, it is composed of a majority of *robins*.

Neither Georges Pagès nor I have ever said that the bourgeoisie had subjected the monarchy. It is the monarchy which subjected all classes in reconstituting the State. But in this work it had the aid of the bourgeoisie, and I maintain that it allowed it to participate in the political and administrative power. Porshnev thinks that the social origins of the *officiers* are of little significance, since they passed into the service of the absolute monarchy, whose ideology they had to adopt and whose will they had to obey. This is to misconceive the character of the status of an *officier*, the role of the corporations of the *officiers*, and the consequences of venality of office and the independent strength which the *officiers* took from it. This error arises from negligence in the study of political institutions, which comes from concentrating excessively on the relationships of production, and from the unfortunate habit of considering everything as 'superstructure', as of secondary importance, whose influence and inter-action are, at the very least, misconceived. I reaffirm the conclusions of my study of *Venality of office under Henry IV and Louis XIII*.

The bourgeoisie of office participated so much in the political and administrative power that in time it was necessary to retrieve power from it. The struggle carried on by the French absolute monarchy externally, in defence of the liberty of France, against the pretensions of the Habsburgs to universal dominance, and, internally, on behalf of the general interest against particularist interest placed it in opposition to the bourgeoisie of office. Everyone knows the grievances and the opposition of the *Parlements*. This indeed gives the revolts their rhythm. It is this which frequently created the revolutionary situation.[88] We doubtless know much less about the opposition of the *officiers de finances*, the *Trésoriers* de France and the *élus*. These last complained bitterly of being pressurised unmercifully by the king. The *élus* calculated that between 1624 and 1654 they had subscribed more than two hundred million *livres* to the king for confirmation of imaginary rights or grants of fictitious supplements to their salaries, which in the event they did not receive, besides the forced loans on which they never saw their interest. To assemble these sums, they had to enter into debt by raising loans with relatives and friends. Moreover, the king undermined the value of their offices. Between 1640 and 1648 he progressively suppressed practically all their salaries and privileges; and the creation of new offices reduced the importance and profits of every *élu*. The *Trésoriers de France* voiced similar complaints.[89] To imagine that the *officiers* did not contribute to the expenses of the State because a good number of them were exempt from paying *taille* is an illusion. Also, to think that by loans to the king they freed their capital from taxation is another.[90] This assault on what the *officiers* considered their interest was a major factor in their growing opposition to the king. It induced them to use the powers which their status as *officiers*, corporate organisation and venality of office gave them for resisting the absolute monarchy. The king had constantly to have greater recourse to the use of *commissaires*, and especially to the authority of the *Conseil* and *intendants*, in order to enforce obedience and even to dispossess the *officiers* of part of their powers and functions. The struggle between, on the one side, the *Conseil* and the *intendants* and, on the other, the *officiers* clarifies the situation.[91]

To see the absolutist monarchical State as the agent of an economically dominant class, whose interests it assured through the oppression of other classes, seems to me therefore an error. Yet again, the facts seem to overflow the limits of the theory.

The Marxist synthesis of Porshnev does not seem to me to be confirmed by the facts. Porshnev only obtains his findings by disregarding a large number of characteristic facts. A theory cannot evidently be accepted by a historian, however, unless it integrates all the categories of known facts, not when it abstracts only a certain number of them. It is certain that many obscurities remain. Our knowledge of the economy, the society and the institutions of seventeenth-century France is still inadequate. To resume the study of the uprisings, which are termed popular, in seventeenth-century France is one of the principal means of progress. It would be of the utmost interest initially to publish the reports of the *intendants*, which are to be found in the 'correspondence addressed to Chancellor Séguier' in the *Bibliothèque Nationale*. I hope to find an editor for these.[92] Monographs would be needed on each uprising, using local sources. Besides local reports, letters, journals and *mémoires*, the archives of the *bailliages* and *présidiaux*, the papers of the *Trésoriers de France* and family records could all without doubt teach us a great deal, without taking into account of course the archives of the *Cours des Aides†*. The study of each uprising could not however be separated from an enquiry into the local society and economy concerned. Why did the rural revolts occur above all in the west, the centre and the south-west? Is there a possibility of classifying the towns according to the degree of development attained by capitalism within them, and of examining whether this was a constant factor in the revolts? One would have to determine the *'conjoncture'* and take into account the general move-ment of prices. Taking the problem as a whole, the uprisings, which we term popular, were particularly numerous and serious from 1623 to 1675, that is during the period when the secular movement of rising prices of the sixteenth century stops, levels out and then turns downward, the lowest point being reached toward 1675. This fall in prices was of long duration and was complicated by interspersed rising and falling of prices of the most extreme kind. Did not this movement of prices play a more important role than the structure of society itself, at a time when people were exhausted by food shortage, by inflation, by heavy taxes, or, conversely, by prices too low to enable the amassing of enough money to pay the taxes? Agricultural crises caused by climate and the *mortalités* deriving from them, together with the consequent long-term dislocation of the economy, would have to be taken into account. The *mortalité* of 1629–30 certainly contributed to the peasant and urban insurrections of those and subsequent years. But, beyond the great *mortalités*, which affected the whole kingdom, there were regional or local occurrences almost every year.[93] All this requires the collaboration of several researchers. It would be instructive to compare the French uprisings with those of other European states. It is a question of organising international cooperation. It would finally be useful to consider again the problem of the characteristics and the extent of the seigneurial and feudal regimes in this period. And would it not be necessary to pose the question of the value to be attributed to the concept of social class in the seventeenth century, and to give further reflection to, among others, the concepts of the bourgeoisie, the nobility, the people and the peasants in this period and to the different senses which are accorded to these words? It is after all our concepts which to a great extent direct the line of our historical studies.

NOTES

1 Let us recall at least the study of P. Boissonnade, 'L'administration royale et les soulèvements populaires en Angoumois, en Saintonge et en Poitou pendant le ministère de Richelieu (1624–1642)', in *Mémoires de la Société des Antiquaires de l'Ouest, 2e série*, XXVI (1902); also G. Pagès, 'Autour du 'Grand Orage': Richelieu et Marillac, deux politiques', in *Revue Historique*, CLXXIX (1937) pp. 63–97.

2 Mariéjol, *Histoire de France*, Vol. VI Part II pp. 431–5: 'The financial policies of the government provoked riots and insurrections throughout the reign.'

3 [Editor's note:] In a brief section which I have omitted, the author refers to the publication of Porshnev's work on the popular uprisings in Russia in 1948 and subsequently in German translation in 1954, which made the work widely available to historians in France.

4 L. Delisle, *Le Cabinet des Manuscrits de la Bibliothèque Nationale*, II p. 52.

5 G. Pagès, 'La vénalité des offices dans l'ancienne France', in *Revue Historique*, CLXIX (1932) pp. 477–95; also R. Mousnier, *La vénalité des offices sous Henri IV et Louis XIII* (Paris, 1945).

6 B. Porshnev, *Die Volkaufstände in Frankreich vor der Fronde, 1623–1648* (Leipzig, 1954) p. 23; et supra, Chapter 3, p. 96.
   [Editor's note:] All page references given by the author to Porshnev's work are to the German edition of 1954. I have added a second reference (as above), if the passage referred to is contained in the sections of Porshnev's work translated in this volume.

7 Ibid., p. 479; et supra, Chapter 3, p. 96 and Chapter 4, p. 112.

8 [Editor's note:] Although there is some repetition here from chapters 3 and 4 above, the whole of Mousnier's account of Porshnev's work has been included, since it is important to have his understanding of Porshnev's ideas, and his account contains references to sections of Porshnev's work not included in those chapters.

9 Manuscript references may be found on p. 83 of the original publication of this article in the *Revue d'histoire moderne et contemporaine* (1958).

10 B. Porshnev, op. cit., p. 25; et supra, Chapter 4, p. 130.

11 Ibid., pp. 8–9; et supra, Chapter 3, p. 80.

12 Ibid., p. 104.

13 Ibid., p. 125.

14 Ibid., pp. 218–21.

15 Ibid., p. 227.

16 Ibid., p. 28; et supra, Chapter 3, p. 100.

17 Ibid., p. 230.

18 Ibid., p. 240.

19 Ibid., p. 468.

20 Ibid., p. 22.

21 Ibid., p. 468.

22 Ibid., p. 479.

23 Ibid., p. 22; et supra, Chapter 3, p. 100.

24 *Manual of Political Economy*, 2nd ed., *Academy of Sciences of the U.S.S.R.* (1955); French translation, *Editions sociales* (1956) pp. 48–72.

25 B. Porshnev, op. cit., p. 239.

26 Ibid., p. 237.

27 Ibid., p. 35 (an extract from an official publication on the revolt of the *Croquants* in Quercy).

28 Ibid., *Appendix*, No. 37 pp. 513–14.
29 Ibid., p. 109.
30 Ibid., pp. 447–52.
31 Ibid., p. 468.
32 Ibid., pp. 473–5.
33 Ibid., p. 283.
34 Ibid., pp. 457–68.
35 Ibid., pp. 478–9.
36 [Editor's note:] Porshnev does of course note Lavisse's interest in the popular uprisings, but accounts for this by the fact that he was an active champion of *rapprochement* between France and Germany during a period when, because of the *détente* between the two Powers, it was easier for French historians to see the French seventeenth century in its reality. See supra, Chapter 3, p. 88.
37 [Editor's note:] This could however only mean the shifting of the burden of the *taille* onto other peasants less able to obtain protection from a powerful *seigneur*. It was indeed one of the more flagrant corruptions of the system, and was constantly referred to as such in the *instructions* issued to the *intendants* under Colbert.
38 R. Mousnier, op. cit., pp. 309–11 and 532–42; also R. Mousnier, *Les XVIe et XVIIe siècles (Histoire générale des civilisations)* 2e éd. pp. 160–3.
39 B.N. ms. fr. 17375, *fol*. 45.
40 B.N. ms. fr. 17383, *fol*. 31.
41 B.N. ms. fr. 17376, *fol*. 5.
42 Special troops recruited to enforce payment of taxes by the parishes.
43 B.N. ms. fr. 17380, *fol*. 102.
44 B.N. ms. fr. 17382, *fol*. 17.
45 De Sève to Séguier, at Calvinet near Aurillac, 18 October 1643; Porshnev, op. cit., *Appendix*, p. 515.
46 That is to say, the tax had been apportioned among the taxpayers according to their ability to pay.
47 B.N. ms. fr. 17377, *fol*. 29 and *fol*. 196.
48 Troops used to assure the collection of the *taille*.
49 B.N. ms. fr. 17382, *fol*. 80.
50 B. Porshnev, op. cit., p. 70.
51 Ibid., *Appendix*, p. 516.
52 [Editor's note:] Mousnier notes that the word '*plusieurs*' in the original French meant 'a great number'.
53 B.N. ms. fr. 15621, *fol*. 259–60.
54 B.N. ms. fr. 17378, *fol*. 108.
55 *Parlement* and *Chambre des Comptes*.
56 Bosquet to Séguier at Montpellier, 22 June 1643; Porshnev, op. cit., *Appendix*, p. 510.
57 Supra, pp. 145–6.
58 B.N. ms. fr. 17378, *fols*. 106, 120, 139.
59 B. Porshnev, op. cit., *Appendix*, p. 515.
60 B.N. ms. fr. 15621, *fol*. 247.
61 Ibid., *fol*. 260.
62 H. Sée, *Histoire économique de la France*, II (1942) pp. 142–3.
63 B.N. ms. fr. 15621, *fols*. 247–8; 14 September 1643.
64 B. Porshnev, op. cit., p. 120.
65 B.N. ms. fr. 17367, *fol*. 170; 20 April 1633.
66 Used in the seventeenth-century sense of the word, to include all those who were neither *seigneur* nor *officier*.

67 B.N. ms. fr. 17374, *fol.* 92; 25 October 1641.
68 B.N. ms. fr. 17385, *fol.* 68; de Heere to Séguier, 3 June 1646.
69 B.N. ms. fr. 17374, *fol.* 37; 29 August 1640.
70 Ibid., *fol.* 35; 11 August 1640.
71 B. Porshnev, op. cit., *Appendix,* p. 503; 21 July 1640.
72 B.N. ms. fr. 17374, *fols.* 72–3; 23 January 1641.
73 A special tax for the maintenance of troops.
74 B.N. ms. fr. 17375, *fols.* 161–2; December 1643.
75 B.N. ms. fr. 15621, *fol.* 264.
76 B.N. ms. fr. 17372, *fol.* 194; Lafosse to Séguier, 28 August 1636.
77 Their murders had started the outbreak of the revolt.
78 B.N. ms. fr. 17374, *fols.* 5 and 9; Roy, mayor of Moulins to Séguier, 30 June and 4 July 1640.
79 B. Porshnev, op. cit., *Appendix,* p. 503; 4 August 1640.
80 R. Mousnier, 'Quelques raisons de la Fronde. Les causes des journées révolutionnaires parisiennes de 1648', in *Bulletin de la Société d'Etude du XVIIe Siècle* (1949) p. 71. See infra, Chapter 6, pp. 169–200.
81 B.N. ms. fr. 17384, *fols.* 146 and 148; 3 and 4 July 1645.
82 Supra, p. 156.
83 B. Porshnev, op. cit., *Appendix,* p. 494; Lafosse to Séguier, at Angoulême, 9 June 1636.
84 Ibid., *Appendix,* p. 510; 22 June 1643.
85 Just as the great monopoly companies were necessary in the maritime trade of England and the United Provinces because of low prices caused by the competition of too many free merchants.
86 F. Hartung and R. Mousnier, 'Quelques problèmes conçernant la monarchie absolue', in *10th Congress of Historical Sciences* (Rome, 1955), *Relazioni,* IV, *Modern History,* pp. 46–7.
87 R. Mousnier, *La Vénalité des offices,* p. 505; also, supra, Chapter 1, pp. 16–20.
88 R. Mousnier, 'Quelques raisons de la Fronde' in *XVIIe Siècle* (1949); also, 'Comment les Français voyaient la France au XVIIe siècle', in *Bulletin de la Société d'Etude du XVIIe siècle* (1955) pp. 9–36; also, *La Vénalité des offices,* p. 609.
89 B.N. *imprimés,* L 9, 17, 31; also, R. Mousnier, 'Recherches sur les syndicats d'officiers pendant la Fronde', article announced for publication in the *Bulletin de la Société d'Etude du XVIIe Siècle.* [Editor's note:] The article actually appeared in Nos. 42–3 of the *Bulletin;* translated infra, Chapter 7, pp. 201–30.
90 The State returned to circulation all the money it received in taxes by way of payments, wages, salaries and purchases; and thereby stimulated an active monetary system which in turn stimulated production generally. See R. Mousnier, *Les XVIe et XVIIe Siècles,* pp. 249–56.
91 R. Mousnier, 'Recherches sur la création des intendants de 1635 à 1648', article announced for publication in *Forschungen zu Staat und Verfassung, Festgabe für Fritz Hartung.* [Editor's note:] This article was actually published in Berlin in 1958. Also, R. Mousnier, *La Vénalité des offices* pp. 604–22; and 'Le Conseil du Roi de la mort de Henri IV au gouvernement personnel de Louis XIV', in *Etudes, Société d'histoire moderne* (1947) I pp. 60–7.
92 [Editor's note:] The Séguier correspondence in the *Bibliothèque Nationale* was in fact edited by Mousnier himself in *Lettres et Mémoires adressés au Chancelier Séguier,* 2 vols (Paris, 1964).
93 R. Mousnier, 'Etudes sur la population de la France au XVIIe siècle', in *Bulletin de la Société d'Etude du XVIIe Siècle,* No. 16 (1952) pp. 527–42; also, *Les XVIe et XVIIe siècles,* pp. 145–9.

6 Some Reasons for the Fronde: the Revolutionary Days in Paris in 1648*

ROLAND MOUSNIER

I

The Days of the Barricades in Paris of 26, 27, and 28 August 1648 transformed a latent civil war into a situation of acute crisis. Fairly well known as a sequence of events, these *journées révolutionnaires* are only poorly understood as to their causes. Historians have been concerned above all with narrative accounts, which describe events without attempting to explain them.[1] They have extracted a fairly accurate account of these colourful events from confused and often contradictory sources. But they never approach them in a real spirit of historical enquiry. They summarise texts with care, but without seeking to present the realities which the words themselves should evoke. They neglect to study the words which were actually used, which in themselves are so revealing and which warrant very careful examination. Political and administrative institutions, economic evidence, social and religious developments and changes in the general sensibility have been neglected, although these alone enable us to understand the words and actions of the period and to relate them to the total situation of the realm and the structure and life of French society at that time. Historians have moreover tended to see in the texts factors which seemed to them to correspond with their own political predilections, as citizens enamoured of liberal parliamentary regimes of the nineteenth and twentieth centuries, ignoring what was important to men of the seventeenth century, through a failure to envisage the society of the age and the mind of its contemporaries. It is certainly time to resume the study of these events of August 1648.

Numerous original sources enable us to distinguish the role and motives of the courtiers, the *Conseil*, the *Parlement*† and the municipal *officiers*

* This is a translation of Roland Mousnier's article 'Quelques raisons de la Fronde: les causes des journées révolutionnaires parisiennes de 1648', in *XVIIe Siècle* (1949) pp. 33–78.

better than those of other groups, such as merchants, artisans, labourers, beggars and those who came in from outside the city. These are principally narrative sources, which were either contemporary with the events or in the form of *mémoires*. They divide into several categories. First, there are three texts emanating from persons who were at Court, but who had no part in the government. These must be placed above the others, because they are the most extended and the most detailed.[2] Then, there are four texts from persons who entered the *Conseils* or were close to those who did.[3] There are also three sources emanating from the *Parlement de Paris*, written with partiality and needing to be controlled very closely, but nevertheless rich in evidence of important discussions, remonstrances, decrees, *déclarations* and *lettres de cachet*†; and in accounts of interviews with the queen and ministers and of sessions of the *Parlement*.[4] Only four sources emanate from persons who were involved very closely in the life of the city during these three days, but one of them is of primary importance: namely the Registers of the *Hôtel de Ville* of Paris, to which the municipality consigned the reports which it received from the municipal officers at different times and from the various *quartiers*, the opinions expressed by certain of the bourgeois, and the steps taken throughout the city and the orders which it issued.[5]

Sources on economic and social life are few. The Registers giving 'the values of grain sold in the markets of this city of Paris' are in the *Archives nationales*.[6] A statistical record of the population of Paris by profession and of its food supply in 1637 has been published.[7] But we must regret the lack of information on price movements, on commercial and industrial activity, on the food supply of the capital and its relationship with the surrounding countryside and on the material standards of the people, and also the absence of precise studies on taxation. It is easier therefore to discern the political, administrative and psychological causes than to discern those stemming from financial, economic and social factors. To arrive at the truth on certain points and to pose numerous questions regarding others is all we may really aim to do.

II

It is necessary to retrace the principal events of these days in order to insist on certain points which have been neglected until now and which are important for research into causes: namely, the categories of people who are seen to take action, the way in which they acted and the *quartiers* where the various episodes took place.[8]

On Tuesday, 25 August, the *Conseil d'en haut* (consisting of the Regent, the Duc d'Orléans, the king's uncle and *lieutenant-général* of the realm, Cardinal Mazarin, the Maréchal de la Meilleraye, *surintendant des finances*, Chancellor Séguier, Bouthillier de Chavigny (?)) decides on the arrest of the members of the *Parlement de Paris*† who were most violent in their opposition to the Court; namely, Broussel, *Conseiller* in the *Grand 'Chambre*, Blancmesnil, the *président aux Enquêtes*†, and the *président*††, Charton. The *conseillers*† Laine, La Nauve and Loisel are to be exiled. The operation is decided on for the following day, Wednesday, 26 August. The circumstances will then be favourable; a *Te Deum* was to be sung in Notre Dame in celebration of the victory at Lens.[9] The regiments of the *Gardes-françaises* and the *Gardes-suisses* will be deployed from the Palais-Royal to Notre Dame and will be able to contain the people, if this should become necessary. Comminges, *lieutenant* of the *Gardes de la Reine*, is charged with the execution of the orders. He reserves himself for the most difficult arrest, that of Broussel.

Wednesday, 26 August, is the day of unexpected developments and confused reactions. It is market day in the city. After the *Te Deum*, toward one o'clock it seems, the queen confirms Comminges' instructions. But he waits for some moments in Notre Dame, to carry out certain orders that had been given. Normally, of course, officers of the royal bodyguard never leave the side of those they have the duty to protect. Some of the members of the *Parlement* still inside the church notice the anomaly, take fright and flee in such haste that the doors of the church are no longer wide enough to take them. The crowd in the square outside hear the murmur, see the disquiet. Alarm is aroused and groups begin to form.

Comminges goes to Broussel's lodgings in the Rue Saint-Landry on the Ile de la Cité, near the gate of Saint-Landry, and arrests Broussel. The cries of an old servant and a young lackey of the *conseiller* resound in the narrow street. In a moment, the street is full of people crying out that 'they want to take our liberator from us'.[10] Some seek to cut the horses' reins and smash the coach; others begin to draw the chains across the street. Pursued by a howling and threatening mob, all the time growing in size, Comminges has to zigzag his way across the city, changing coaches twice, once on the Quai and then in the Rue Saint-Honoré. At length, he manages to leave Paris by the Tuileries and so reach Saint-Germain. However, during his journey across Paris everything was in a state of uproar and noise of the arrest spread like lightning.

It is the *petit peuple* of Parisian society who try to resist the arrest, and who, therefore, start the insurrection – the boatmen of the Cité and La Grève, the artisans of the Palais, the Pont Saint-Michel and the Halles, who are joined, most probably at once, by beggars and vagabonds. The bourgeois traders are less prompt. Broussel's arrest disturbs them and when, toward two o'clock, news of it spreads, they begin to close shop, to form groups in the streets to discuss the situation. But they do not seem disposed to do more. Fear of the lower orders and the soldiery causes them, one by one, to take up arms. A great band of rioters (with swords and hunting spears, pistols and torn-up paving stones) goes on the rampage as far as the Rue Saint-Honoré, smashing windows and breaking down doors, crying nevertheless 'Vive le Roi – free the prisoner!' The *canaille*, bearing various kinds of weapons, mass at the Croix-du-Tiroir (at the corner of the Rue Saint-Honoré and the Rue de l'Arbre-sec) and 'forced the bourgeois in that area to come out into their doorways with weapons in their hands, having broken down the doors and windows of those who refused to do so.'[11] Advised of the disturbance at two o'clock by the *quartenier*† of the Cité, the *Bureau de Ville*[12] dispatches several persons to inspect the various *quartiers*. They report, toward four o'clock, that they have seen a 'quantity of vagabonds who only sought plunder and who were causing apprehension and terror in the minds of the bourgeois, telling them that there were soldiers, as many on horse as on foot, who would come and bear down on them if they were not in a state to defend themselves.'

Toward five o'clock, the disorder has spread to various *quartiers*, 'there being people crying "aux armes", with the idea of intimidating the bourgeois and finding occasion for pillage'. All this happens as if the *bas peuple* and the beggars, taking refuge in Paris because of the war, want to force the '*bons bourgeois*', the masters of the various crafts, to take up arms. With the *bas peuple* intent on releasing Broussel, with vagabonds taking advantage of the disorder, with the hostility of the population toward the soldiers and the cutting off of certain streets by chains and barricades, there is clearly considerable likelihood of trouble.

To preserve themselves from attack, the bourgeois begin to draw the chains across the streets. Some of them go to the *Hôtel de Ville* and obtain a mandate from the *Bureau de Ville* to all the *quarteniers* to have the chains drawn across in all *quartiers*. This was an unhappy decision, since although the chains must have certainly hindered the exploits of the vagabonds in the city, they must have hindered no less the movement of troops. The *Bureau de Ville* sends an order to the *colonel* of the Cité to have the captains hold themselves in readiness, but he is ill and cannot take action; and since the disturbance is beginning to take hold of the streets, the *Bureau* sends an order to all *colonels* to advise the captains to hold themselves in readiness. It goes however no further than that. The *Bureau* doubtless hopes that peace will restore itself of its own accord.

The Court is evidently taken by surprise by the violence of the reaction. The *Gardes*, the *Gardes de la Reine* and members of the Court with a number of their '*domestiques*'[13] are summoned to the Palais-Royal. An extraordinary meeting of the *Conseil* is held. The Maréchal de la Meilleraye leaves with a company of light horse (fifty men or more), some *gendarmes* and some of the *Gardes de la Reine*. Several times he runs up against chains, notably in the vicinity of Saint-Eustache, at the Pont Saint-

Michel and the Rue Neuve Saint-Louis. Stones are hurled at him. There then follows a sequence of very obscure and very confused events, where all attempts to reconcile the texts seem in vain. The only facts which seem well established are, first of all, the arrival at the Palais-Royal of the *coadjuteur*† of the Archbishop of Paris, Paul de Gondi, the future Cardinal de Retz, who, *en route*, attempts to calm the people, and tries to represent to the queen the true seriousness of the situation. But he is only turned away with ridicule. Then, reinforcements arrive at the Palais-Royal, in particular all *Garde-françaises* from the *faubourgs*. The queen orders these troops to draw themselves up in battle formation in front of the Palais-Royal, as well as on the Pont-Neuf, the hub of communications, and on the Quai du Louvre, where the boatmen were showing very great violence. Finally, a second sortie of La Meilleraye takes place, this time with a 'quantity of *gens d'armes* and light horse' and a 'company of *gardes*'. In the *quartier* of La Friperie, these are greeted with a hail of stones hurled down from windows, which the musketeers reply to with a round of fire, but they do not pursue the attack.[14] It seems that the Court too anticipates a rapid return to normal and contents itself with precautionary measures and with making a show of the forces at the king's command.

The end of the afternoon and evening seem to prove the optimists right. Negotiations take place. Certain bourgeois seek out the *premier président*† of the *Parlement*, Mathieu Molé, and call on him to demand the release of Broussel. Toward evening, he goes to the Palais-Royal, but is turned away without a reply. Under the constraint, perhaps, of the people, he returns, but with no more success. The *coadjuteur*, also perhaps under threat from the people, goes himself for a second time to the Palais-Royal. He is met with mockery, he says, and leaves 'in a rage'.

The *Parlement* is at a loss. Thoroughly taken by surprise, they wish to assemble in the period after dinner, but the day is now well advanced and they defer their meeting until the morrow.[15]

But even if the 'people' do force the natural representatives of the city to intervene, in the persons of the *Premier Président* and the Archbishop (through his *coadjuteur*), without perhaps respecting the usual forms, they do not however dream of carrying things to extremes. *There is at this time not a single barricade in Paris.* Moreover, the Court, in order to allay disquiet, gives the order for the *gardes* to withdraw. They abandon the Pont-Neuf and regroup in front of the Palais-Royal. The 'people' then seem to become a little more calm. Toward six in the evening everyone returns home.[16]

The bourgeois, at least the masters of the principal *métiers*, the *bons bourgeois*, continue to respect authority and are more concerned to protect themselves from dangerous elements and the troops than to attack the Court. The *Bureau de Ville* has sent Fournier, a *Président*, to the

Palais-Royal to report on the situation, without going itself as a body, since in the general confusion it cannot find the twenty or so constables it needs to ensure its safety in the streets. Fournier returns to say that the Court is well satisfied with the *Messieurs de la Ville*, but they are 'nevertheless requested to have the chains removed from across the streets'. At the same time, Fournier declares that the *bons bourgeois* do not dare arm themselves without the express command from the *prévôt des marchands*† and the *échevins*† of the city. Toward evening, at the instigation of the Court, the *Bureau* sends an order to all *quarteniers* to have the chains removed and to open the shops on the following morning; this is accompanied by a further order, on its own initiative,[17] to each of the sixteen *colonels*, to hold everyone under arms, 'so that no general assembly of the people would be possible throughout the whole extent of the city' – a mistake indeed, since it in fact sanctioned the taking up of arms by the rebels, as well as by those responsible for the maintenance of order.

The Court hoped that the night would soften spirits. It took dispositions however to ensure its own victory. The *Conseil d'en haut* decided to send the Chancellor to the *Parlement* itself on the following morning, 'to forbid them to assemble and in the event of their disobeying to impose a total prohibition upon them.'[18]

In appearance, the night of 26 to 27 August seems calm. In fact, however, everyone is taking action. The soldiers who had spent the night under arms in front of the Palais-Royal seize the Porte Saint-Honoré and the roads about the Louvre. This assures them of communication with the outside, either to bring in reinforcements or to facilitate the withdrawal of the government at need.

According to Guy Joly and Retz, the relatives and friends of Broussel and the other exiles, together with those who were dissatisfied with the Court, send messages 'all through the night to the *officiers* and bourgeois of their acquaintance, exhorting them to behave properly in a situation of this importance.' Retz seeks the support of his friends through his relative the *Chevalier* de Sévigné, and through M. d'Argenteuil and M. de Laigues. He comes to an agreement with one of his friends, Miron, a *Maître des Comptes*, *colonel* of the *quartier* of St. Germain l'Auxerrois and also with Martineau, a *conseiller aux Requêtes*†, captain of the Rue Saint-Jacques. During the night, indeed, spirits are becoming heated. Barricades are raised.

The 27 August is the day of the barricades. At five o'clock in the morning the *Bureau de Ville* learns through messengers that everything is in a state of mutiny. Already there are chains and barricades 'at various places' in the heart of Paris: in the Ile de la Cité; on the left bank in the Faubourg Saint-Germain and in the University; on the right bank at La Grève, at the Halles and in that area;[19] either because these were the *quartiers* of the insurgents, or because the insurgents wanted to seize the principal lines of communication across Paris. Whether by chance or not, the Palais, where the *Parlement* sat, was like the geographical centre of the insurrection. The members of the *Bureau de Ville* would affirm to the *Parlement* on 28 August that they had dispersed themselves throughout the city to achieve the laying down of arms, and that artisans were already beginning in some places to open shop, when the intemperate gesture of the Chancellor threw everything back into confusion.

Indeed, toward five or six in the morning, the Chancellor carries into effect the orders he has received and goes by carriage to the *Parlement*. He cannot get through the Quai des Orfèvres because of barricades. He takes the Quai des Augustins, proceeds to attempt to cross the Pont Saint-Michel, comes up against barricades again, gets down, and attempts to pass on foot and to remonstrate with the 'people'. The 'people' become enraged, pursue him and try to lynch him in the Hôtel de Luynes, where he goes into hiding. The court is advised of the situation. La Meilleraye arrives and occupies the Pont-Neuf with a company of *garde-françaises* and the Quai des Augustins with the *Suisses*, and rescues the Chancellor. During his withdrawal, stones are hurled at him on the Pont-Neuf and he comes under musket-fire from the direction of the Rue Dauphine; some of the *Suisses* and one light cavalryman are killed. It is the *petit peuple* who act, the *canaille*, the street-porters.

The movement of troops and the firing increase the general sense of disorder. The deployment of soldiers frightens the inhabitants of the Rue Saint-Honoré, who draw the chains across the street and take up arms. The 'people' on the Quai de la Mégisserie run at the sound of musket-fire to the other end of the Pont-Neuf, but cannot prevent the Chancellor from escaping. Then five or six hundred hoist a piece of linen on the end of a pole, take a drum and begin to march towards the Grand-Châtelet. It is now nine or ten in the morning. The captain of the *quartier*, fearing looting, has the chains drawn across the streets and the drum beaten to summon the bourgeois to arms. This example is followed throughout the city and barricades become general. 'In less than half an hour' all the chains are drawn across; a double row of barrels, filled with earth, stones and dung, is raised in many places; behind them the bourgeois are under arms 'in such great numbers that it is almost impossible to imagine the situation'.[20] Up to 1260 barricades were counted throughout Paris. From the Palais to the Palais-Royal, by way of the Quai, the Pont-Neuf, the Rue de l'Abre-sec and the Rue Saint-Honoré, eight are raised, made up of chains, cross-beams and casks filled with paving, earth and rubble.[21]

The *Parlement* assembles towards eight o'clock. Feelings have by now become 'infinitely heated'. A little before nine o'clock, the *Parlement* is informed that 'all the shops are evidently closed and the bourgeois are up in arms.' It learns of the Chancellor's escapade. The *Conseillers* decide not to concern themselves with that. They decide rather to go as a body to the Palais-Royal to ask the queen for the prisoners and the exiles. 'And in regard to the insurrection, they in no way wished to speak of it, saying that the true way to end it was by rendering up M. de Broussel; and I was told by *messieurs les présidents* that they were equally in no way resolved to re-establish order, since they believed that the public sedition would serve to have their colleagues restored to them.'[22]

The *Parlement de Paris* decides to go fully robed to the Palais-Royal. On its way there, the people call frantically for Broussel's release. The bourgeois declare more calmly, but to the same effect, that they will not lay down their arms until Broussel is returned to them. At the Palais-Royal, the queen at first refuses to concede anything, and, accusing the *Parlement* of having provoked the insurrection, calls upon it to restore the situation, and threatens it with the anger of her son when he reaches his majority. Then, on the advice of Mazarin, de Molé, the *président* de Mesmes and her Chancellor, Bailleul,[23] she agrees to yield the prisoners, but only on certain conditions. *Parlementaire* sources assert that she asked solely for the suspension of the sessions of the *Parlement* until Saint Martin's Day.[24] Court sources however assert that she granted the request to release the prisoners only on condition that they renounce their union (with the other sovereign courts), that they do not touch the King's Declaration (of 31 July 1648), that they do not interfere in future in the affairs of the *Conseil* and that they grant the king an annulment of all their proceedings since the assemblies (with the other sovereign courts) began.[25]

The *Parlement* expresses its wish to return jointly to the Palais to deliberate on the position. It leaves the Palais-Royal. It will be said by certain sources that some of the Court officials said to it 'Hold firm and you will have your prisoners returned to you', and that the *garde-françaises* declared that they would not fight the bourgeois.[26] But, at the Croix-du-Tiroir, the *Parlement* is halted by a barricade. Certain bourgeois (a cook and an iron-merchant who was captain of his *quartier*, with twelve or fifteen bourgeois in a company, are cited as responsible)[27] demand the release of Broussel. The *premier-président*, Molé, is howled down, threatened and roughly treated. The rebels try to kill him or retain him as a hostage. The *président* de Mesmes extricates him successfully by indicating that, since he is head of the *Parlement*, he is indispensable and should remain to act as its spokesman. Many of the *conseillers* and *présidents* have taken flight, somewhat disturbed now to see the Parisians turning on them. The others, still numbering one hundred and twenty-four, are forced to return to the Palais-Royal. They meet to discuss the situation in the *grande galerie* of the king. But no one is any longer in control of the population, who believe that a treason has been committed, through the collusion of Court and *Parlement*, and as a result Court and *Parlement* are equally threatened. The question is which of them will know best how to resist to the end the demands of the other, right up to the last moment when the attack of the Parisians could be expected to unleash itself, sweeping both of them away. The *Parlement* held its ground better. By seventy-four votes to fifty, it decides to discontinue its sessions and to defer discussion of public affairs until Saint Martin's Day, 'without however making a formal declaration' to that effect, in order to maintain face. It will nevertheless continue to discuss the question of the proposed tariff on merchandise entering the city, together with the *rentes* issued on the *Hôtel de Ville*. The queen and her circle realise the gravity of the situation. They fear that the people of Paris may go to extremes. The *gendarmes* and the light cavalry hold themselves at the ready. Horses were kept, under sealed orders, until midday on the 28 August to take the king, queen and minister to safety, if it became necessary.[28] Under pressure, the queen, hastily and doubtless without knowledge of the latest feelings of the rebels toward the *Parlementaires*, finally decides that she must content herself with the inadequate concessions offered by the *Parlement*. She has *lettres de cachet* issued for the release of Broussel and Blancmesnil. Certain gentlemen leave, with two carriages, one belonging to the king, the other to the queen, to fetch the prisoners. They show their *lettres de cachet* to the rebels and promise that Broussel will be in Paris at eight o'clock on the following morning. People and bourgeois then allow them to pass, but with execrations and renewed vows to remain under arms, together with threats to sack everything if the Court and *Parlement* are in collusion to deceive them.

During this period, the *Bureau de Ville* remained in an almost complete state of inertia. In the morning, it convenes the *Conseillers* and the *colonels* for one hour. Only fourteen *Conseillers* out of twenty-four, and eight *colonels* or their *lieutenants* out of sixteen come. But the only decision taken is to await the result from the Palais-Royal, and everyone leaves. At five in the evening, the *Messieurs* of the *Bureau de Ville* tour the city with twenty constables and four *sergents*, and try in vain to dispel the fears in the minds of the bourgeois. At eight o'clock they arrive at the Palais-Royal, learn of the order for the release and return of the prisoners, and are requested to have the barricades pulled down, the chains removed and the shops opened on the following day. They immediately send the necessary orders to the *colonels* and the *quarteniers*.

During the night of Thursday, 27 August, to Friday, 28 August, the insurrection spreads however. New barricades are raised 'in the University'. Houses are armed with stones torn from the paving in the streets. Sentinels are posted as far out as the country to the south of Paris. 'The bourgeois fired incessantly.'[29] The bourgeois had been brought to believe that there was an intention to trick them, notwithstanding all the promises that

had been made to them, and that it was only a question of 'gaining time
to bring in troops to force their surrender' or to remove the king to
Compiègne or Tours. In fact, the Court had ordered in some 350 to 1200
horse from the cavalry of the regiment of La Meilleraye stationed at
Etampes. On arrival at Bourg-la-Reine, they had received orders to go to
Saint-Cloud to fetch the king, the queen and the Duc d'Anjou.[30] But the
Court had in fact renounced policies of either force or flight, unless it
was compelled to leave Paris by the violence of the Parisians themselves,
which it very much feared. Great alarm continued throughout the night
at the Palais-Royal. In spite of her courage, the queen herself was disturbed. Soldiers remained under arms. Some of the cavalry, perhaps that
of La Meilleraye, were stationed in the Bois de Boulogne to facilitate
eventual flight. The Cardinal was fearful, more than all the rest, and not
without reason. He remained clothed, ready to mount his horse.

Friday, 28 August, the day when in fact arms were laid down, was
punctuated by outbursts of extreme fury, arising for the most part from
fear, which in fact placed the Court on several occasions in a more dangerous position than on the previous day. Toward five o'clock in the
morning, the bourgeois, still under arms and adopting a threatening
posture, refuse the orders issued to them by the messengers of the *Bureau
de Ville* to lower the chains and pull down the barricades. They fear a
trick on the part of the Court, and when, toward eight o'clock, they
ascertained that in fact Broussel was still absent and that there was
delay, 'there was such a redoubling of cries and such terrible threats that,
at this point, Paris took on a truly frightening appearance.'[31]

Learning of the presence of cavalry in the Bois de Boulogne, the people
fear reprisals. They imagine that there are ten thousand men ready to
punish them for their insurrection, and fear of this keeps them under
arms.[32] They are alarmed by various disturbing elements in the city. The
bons bourgeois are equally disturbed by the danger that the *petit peuple*
will turn on them. When the *Bureau de Ville* sets out on its tour of
inspection between seven and eight o'clock, the bourgeois excuse themselves for being under arms, because of the presence of 'certain vagabonds
and strangers roaming everywhere and attacking anyone they find without arms, with very great boldness, robbing and plundering them.'[33] In
addition, the *Bureau de Ville* finds a barricade at the Pont-Marie manned
by beggars who will allow no one to pass unless they are given the
wherewithal to drink, and who declare themselves there to defend their
lives and their livelihood. In spite of the protection of its company of
archers, the *Bureau de Ville* do not dare to force them, 'for fear of the
consequences'. Another barricade of the same kind is found in front of
the convent of the Béguines de l'Ave Maria. But besides these criminal
elements, the *Bureau de Ville*, representative of the *grande-bourgeoisie*,
finds in the neighbourhood of the Palais, still in the Cité, a 'quantity of

servants under arms who spoke with very great insolence', and the captains of the *quartier*, who were *bons bourgeois* indeed, declared that they were not in control of them.[34] The *Bureau de Ville* reports to the *Parlement* and sends an order to the *quarteniers* to give the lie to the rumour as to the presence of troops around Paris.

Meanwhile Broussel arrives at ten in the morning in the king's coach. He crosses Paris by way of the Porte Saint-Denis, the Rue de la Ferronnerie, the Croix-du-Tiroir, the Pont-Neuf, the Quai des Augustins, the Pont Saint-Michel, the Marché-Neuf and the Rue Saint-Landry.[35] Along the route, there is very great acclaim for Broussel, cries of extreme joy at the sight of him, with shots fired in his honour: everyone indeed discharging his arms as Broussel goes by. One might well think that the revolt would now die out.

But the musket-fire provokes a redoubling of the crisis in the Faubourg Saint-Antoine, from the Porte Baudoyer as far as the Bastille. At the sound of firing, certain people cry out that the cavalry has arrived, and that throats are being cut in the Quartier Saint Honoré, at the Pont-Neuf and toward the Palais. There is one clamour only – the call to arms. The inhabitants rush to take up arms in a state of great tension. In an hour there are fifty new barricades. The *Bureau de Ville* goes to the area. 'They find the people so angry and with such a determination to defend themselves that they had very great difficulty in convincing them.' The *Bureau* succeeds at the Porte Saint-Antoine and in the Rue Petit-Musc.

Meanwhile Broussel goes to the *Parlement*, which, 'on his advice', decides to issue a decree toward midday for the removal of the barricades, the lowering of the chains and the opening of the shops, 'and forbidding all vagabonds and vagrants to carry arms on pain of punishment . . .'[36] The decree is published with the sounding of a trumpet. Everyone obeys. Toward two o'clock, all is quiet. The barricades are either opened up or pulled down. Traffic is freed. A little before six o'clock in the evening, Gaignières finds no one under arms at the Pont-Neuf and all the barricades destroyed. A little after five o'clock the *Bureau de Ville*, on learning that the bourgeois had laid down their arms everywhere, go to the barricade at the Pont-Marie with a company of *archers*, and this time those on the barricade take flight. It was however at this very moment that news came that everything was in uproar again around the Porte Saint-Antoine.

Between five and six in the evening, three carts filled with gunpowder leave the Arsenal for the Palais-Royal. A barrel bursts and powder spills out. The people of the *faubourg* see it, hurl themselves on the carts and loot them. They immediately declare that the powder is for the troops filling the Bois de Boulogne, who wish to carry off the king and then lay siege to Paris or starve her out. They cry out against the treachery. 'This idea struck their imaginations with a thousand fears, making them believe, like criminals fearing punishment, that the queen's design was to punish them.' In half an hour, everything was just the same as it had been in the morning.[37] In fact, after the barricades were thrown up again in the Faubourg Saint-Antoine, the Parisians re-erected them everywhere, but especially in the Rue Saint-Honoré, where they place lights in the windows, since 'people said' the cavalry from Saint-Cloud was at the Porte Saint-Honoré.[38]

The *Bureau de Ville* goes to the Faubourg Saint-Antoine, but is unsuccessful in persuading the inhabitants to lay down their arms. It returns to the *Hôtel de Ville*, where 'news came in from various parts that there was a considerable army around Paris and that these supplies of gunpowder and cannon balls brought from the Bastille,[39] and plundered, had been intended for them and that the king was to be carried off that night and the whole city put to plunder.'

The *Bureau de Ville* decides to go to the Palais-Royal to report on the situation and receive further orders. La Meilleraye tells its members that the departure of the gunpowder carriages was merely in pursuance of an order given on the Wednesday, which it had been impossible to countermand. He himself, the queen and Villeroy assure them that there is nothing to fear, and give as proof the sending back of the regiment of *gardes* to their quarters. The *Bureau* return to the *Hôtel de Ville*, but:

> They were astonished to find two thousand souls, both men and women, there, who begin to cry out against them, that they had taken their arms from them, when they still had need of them; that they were in league with the Court to ruin them; that they should be allowed to take their arms again, as much to stand up for themselves as to save their lives and those of their wives and children. This was said with so much vehemence that all the *Messieurs de Ville* could say to them was of no avail. So much so that in the end, in order to satisfy them, they had to promise to send and have the gates of the city closed, and the keys deposited with the *quarteniers*.[40]

The *Bureau* thereupon sends its orders to the *colonels* and the *quarteniers*. It denies all the alarming rumours that are circulating, and gives orders for the gates to be closed, making it clear all the time that there was no need to take this action, and that it was being done solely to satisfy the people. Toward eight o'clock, the noise seems to subside. Suddenly, however, uproar breaks out again in the Rue Saint-Honoré:

> Certain men had been ill-intentioned enough to throw handbills onto the streets and public squares, advising the bourgeois to take up arms, and carefully warning them that there were troops in the outskirts of Paris and that there was definite information that the queen intended to carry off the king and then use the troops to sack the city as

punishment for the revolt . . . There were *bourgeois groups mingled with the 'canaille'*, who said right out that they wanted the king and were determined to have him in their own hands to guard him themselves at the *Hôtel de Ville*; that they wanted the keys to the city-gates for fear he might be carried off; and that once he was outside the Palais-Royal, they scarcely cared about the rest and would willingly set fire to it.

At the Palais-Royal indeed, where there was no moat and no guard, there was very real fear of invasion and the rape and massacre which would inevitably follow. Mazarin prepared for flight. The queen, almost alone among them, kept her head. She issues orders for the keys of the city to be carried to the bourgeois. The *colonels* and the *quarteniers* patrol the streets all that night, reassuring everyone that there is no cause for alarm.

After midnight, calm begins to spread among the bourgeois and they gradually disperse to their homes, most toward two or three o'clock; the more militant at about four.[41]

On Saturday, 29 August, at seven o'clock in the morning, all is quiet. The shops are opening, the Halles and street markets are well supplied. Olivier Lefèvre d'Ormesson, returning that morning from the country, finds no more than a few street corners with their paving torn up and barrels filled with stones.[42]

III

Broussel's arrest had clearly been the immediate cause of the Parisian revolt. Broussel was one of the leaders of the *Parlement de Paris*. To imprison him together with some of his more turbulent colleagues and to exile others was to deprive the sovereign Court of its agitators and to restrain the rest by threat of similar treatment. What was at stake, however, made the risk worth taking, since the opposition of the *Parlement* brought the whole structure of the monarchy into question.

In matters both of policy and legislation, the *Parlement*, a court of justice, had pretensions to erect itself as a power independent of the king, acting on its own initiative, deliberating on its own, able to impose its decisions. It wished to take cognizance of the affairs of state, that is to say of all foreign and internal policy, on its own behalf, whereas by virtue of long-standing tradition, confirmed by edict on 21 February 1641, it could not do so unless the king gave orders for it to do so. It claimed that for this purpose it had the powers to convene at will the vassals of the king, the *Princes du sang*†, both lay and ecclesiastical peers, the great officers of the Crown and the *Conseillers d'Etat*, and to unite them in one vast assembly, which reconstituted the *Curia Regis*†, representing the Orders of the Realm; whereas in fact the king alone had the power to convene his vassals to require the service of counsel from them, when he deemed it good to do so. It also wished to assemble together the other *officiers* of the king to take cognizance of the affairs of state, as it had on 13 May 1648 through the *arrêt d'union*, which brought together the deputies of the other *Cours souveraines* of Paris in the *Chambre Saint-Louis* for joint discussions on the reform of the state. It strove to examine afresh, and alone, without the presence of the king, edicts which had been registered in the presence of the sovereign attending in his *lit de justice*, which reconstituted the old *Cour-le-Roi*. The edict of 21 February 1641 permitted this, on condition that, if the king persisted in his wishes, the *Parlement* should accept his wishes upon his first remonstrance. But the *Parlement*, in spite of the warnings of the Court, in spite of the decrees of the *Conseil d'en haut*, had modified or revoked edicts or separate articles of edicts after they had been registered in a *lit de justice*, by its own decrees. It went further. The *Parlementaires* only accepted the *lit de justice* as a form of visit from the king, coming to take their advice on a matter of general policy. When it was a matter of their legislating, they declared the presence of the king to be a violation of their freedom of suffrage, and they claimed the right to deliberate and vote on edicts and *ordonnances* without the presence of the king. Right of assembly at will of the realm's representatives; the right to take cognizance of all affairs; laws voted without the sovereign's presence – this was to create an assembly separate from the king, with legislative power and control over the executive – this was a sketch of an imperfect system of the separation of powers. The *Parlement* proclaimed the absolute power of the king, limiting it solely by care for convention and Christian moderation.[43] But, in fact, the *Parlement* was advancing toward a limited monarchy, *une monarchie tempérée*, and even opening the way to a republic. Its action was contrary to the fundamental laws of the realm, to the very essence of the monarchy itself. King and realm formed a whole. The presence of the king did not violate the liberty of opinion of members of the *Curia Regis*, because the *Curia*, the epitome of the realm, did not exist without the king. The king took advice through the Chancellor, but then he himself extracted a sense of the fundamental will of the *Curia* and adapted it for himself. Legally, this fundamental will could differ from the individual wills as they were expressed in the *Curia*, and the king could decide against majority opinion. The position of the *Parlement* was therefore revolutionary; it was an overturning, a separation of elements by conceiving them as two when in reality they were one, inseparable and indispensable to each other: King and Realm, Sovereign and Nation, a single entity. The *parlementaire* position was a negation of the monarchy.

But this revolution was in other respects profoundly conservative.

Alone, or with the other *officiers*†, the *Parlement* represented nothing. As a fragment detached from the *Curia Regis*, it possessed solely its own functions and the authority which the king wished to give it. It was in no way qualified to represent the realm. It aimed solely at protecting the positions acquired by possessors of office and fiefs, those with provincial and local power, against another entirely different kind of revolution, the centralising and, to some extent, egalitarian revolution of the absolute monarchy.

Also at stake, in fact, in the conflict between Crown and *Parlement*, was the authority of the *Conseils* over the *Cours souveraines*, and, in more general terms, of the royal *commissaires*† over the *officiers*.⁴⁴ The proposals of the deputies of the *Cours souveraines* of Paris were very clear on this point when they assembled in the *Chambre Saint-Louis*. These were at first imposed on the *Conseil* but were in part rejected by it in the royal *Déclarations* of 18 and 31 July. The courts fought the tendency of royal government to substitute *commissaire* for *officier*, and, in particular, the *Conseil* for the *Cours souveraines* and the *intendant* for the various judicial and financial *officiers*.

The *Parlement* and the assembly of the *Chambre Saint-Louis* asserted in the first place that the *Conseil* was only a simple regulator of justice and was not superior to the *Cours souveraines*, which were in fact the true 'sovereign Court'. They denied the *Conseil* the right to reverse their judgments at will or on a simple plea. They recognised merely its power to apply *ordonnances*, and in particular Article 92 of the *Ordonnance de Blois* of May 1579, which stated that on a plaintiff's plea regarding errors of fact, or on a civil plea based on a proposition of wilful misrepresentation and surprise of one of the parties concerned, a *maître des requêtes*† should be charged with the brief and report concerning the same to the assembled *maîtres des requêtes*. In the event of their finding the plea sustained, the *maître des requêtes* concerned should report the fact to the *Conseil*, which would, if it accepted the report of the *maître des requêtes*, return the case to the respective court, which would then be obliged to initiate a new trial. In reality, however, the *Conseil* did not consider itself in any way bound by these procedures and reversed at will all kinds of judgments of the *Cours souveraines*, on the basis of the public good.

The *Parlement* protested against the tendency of the *Conseil* to dispossess the *Cours souveraines* and the ordinary judges of their functions. As the organ of the 'retained justice', that is the judicial power retained by the king as sovereign '*justicier*'†, who indeed drew all his judicial powers from his role as *justicier*, the *Conseil* regularly 'evoked' cases from the jurisdiction of other courts on behalf of tax-farmers, courtiers, and certain towns and individuals, and used the same procedure in cases affecting noble or Protestant rebels, so that all these cases could

always be judged 'sovereignly' by the *Conseil*. The *Conseil* also reserved
to itself cases which had given rise to appeal, and instead of returning
them to the relevant court, judged them itself. The *Conseil privé†* acted
in the same way when a litigant denounced the presence of relatives
or friends of his opponents in the court which was initially exercising
justice. Also, when there was uncertainty as to which sovereign court
was competent to deal with a particular case, the *Conseil privé* judged
the case afresh from the beginning. instead of deciding the matter
according to regulations concerning the relationship between the various
jurisdictions. Special *commissions*, emanating from the *Conseil d'Etat*,
judged numerous cases of political importance as sovereign tribunals in
place of the ordinary courts. Finally, since appeals from the judgments
of the *intendants* in the provinces came direct to the *Conseil*, the *Cours
souveraines* found themselves deprived of a whole host of cases which
would normally have come to them on appeal, if they had been dealt
with in the ordinary way by the ordinary judges.

Therefore the courts demanded the suppression of the *intendants*,
who instead of simply examining pleas, prior to referring them to the
ordinary courts, exercised justice themselves, through the powers conferred on them by their *commissions* from the *Conseil*. In this way, the
présidiaux†, the *conseils de bailliages†* and *sénéchaussées†*, among other
courts, were deprived of their proper functions. In the same way the
intendants also performed the function of the financial *officiers*, the
Trésoriers de France†, the *élus†* and others. In this conflict, the *Parlement*
sustained the interest of all *officiers*. It demanded that all *officiers* should
be re-established in the exercise of their offices and in the enjoyment of
their salaries; that they should no longer be deprived of their functions
by simple *lettres de cachet*, but only by due process in pursuance of the
ordonnances of the realm. The *Parlement de Paris* thus created a union
of all *officiers* in opposition to the royal government. And in so doing,
it raised not only the question of justice itself but of the whole administration of the State, since justice and administration were so closely
interfused. It was the judge who administered, through regulating
judgments and through judgments between parties. It was a question
therefore of deciding who was actually to administer the realm. Was it
to be done by royal functionaries, nominated by the king and revocable
at his will, acting in the king's interest, which it was claimed was identical
with the general interest of the realm, acting in the name of the public
good and the interest of the State, that is by *commissaires*; or was it to
be done by the corporations of *officiers*, with their responsibility limited
by their collegial character, proprietors in legal terms of the value of
their office, but, in fact, proprietors of their offices themselves, in the
same way as possessors of fiefs and enjoying the full powers of *seigneurs*,
allied with or related to *nobles d'épée†*, exercising power in the provinces

and in the localities, and therefore, for the most part, particularist in their interest. Without doubt, the war imposed the need for absolute, even dictatorial government; and the royal government of the sixteenth and seventeenth centuries was essentially a war government, which in practice went far beyond what the king himself would have wanted in theory. Without doubt, the monarchy had a natural tendency, as has all authority, to develop its power, provided resistance was not too strong. But venality of office and the characteristics of the landed *seigneur*, which the *officiers* thereby acquired, compelled the sovereign to use the *commissaires* to reassert control over the public authority and achieve the triumph of the public interest over the particular.

The *Conseil*, under the inspiration of Mazarin, and not judging what resistance was possible, revoked all extraordinary *commissions*, and in particular those of the *intendants*, by the edict of 18 July 1648. By the edict of 31 July, it accepted the claims of the *Cours souveraines* as regards justice and administration. For the *Conseil*, these were however entirely unacceptable concessions. They made the continuation of the war impossible. They also meant the end of the monarchy, through a temporary decision, taken in despair, which was therefore to be reversed as quickly as possible, as soon as the power of the *Parlement* could be destroyed.

The *Parlement* was paralysing the conduct of the war through its financial opposition – a good means indeed of making itself popular and of placing the government at its mercy. It claimed to be able to forbid the *Conseil* to create taxes by simple decree, and on 3 July it demanded that only taxes created by properly registered edicts should be levied. On 1 July, it had already demanded the recall of all the leases of the tax-farms, at a time when the government had had to farm out even the *tailles*† and remit a quarter of them, which was the share taken by the tax-farmers. On 2 July, the *Parlement* had forced a kind of bankruptcy on the state and a transformation of short-term into long-term debt; all loans and advances to the state were declared null and void; only those subsequently recognised as valid after enquiry would be repaid in due time with interest. The *Déclaration* of 18 July remitted the *tailles* by twelve per cent. The *Parlement* registered the *Déclaration*, but insisted on a remission of twenty-five per cent for 1647, 1648 and 1649. The result was a frightening shortage of public funds. No one paid his taxes any longer. The peasants were persuaded that the king was about to abolish all taxes. The tax-farmers made scarcely any further advances to the state. Badly paid, the armies began to fall into disorder.

If the *Parlement* was prepared to push matters thus far, it was in part because of the interest its members had in the situation as owners of capital invested in office. This indeed determined them upon a course of violent opposition, which was to be one of the principal causes of the

Parisian revolt. It was a question of their preventing the creation of further offices, since by increasing the supply this diminished the market value of the merchandise.[45] It was a question above all of obtaining the renewal of the *paulette*, or *droit annuel*, the insurance premium which permitted the *officiers* to keep their office or its value in their family. Granted for nine years, permission to pay the tax had expired on 31 December 1647. Its renewal had given rise to the usual bargaining. The government delayed the concession for as long as possible, in order to force the *Parlement* to register certain contentious edicts. The *Parlement* however assumed a posture of vigorous opposition, both to obtain the *annuel* and to obtain it on the best possible terms. The government then decided to offer the *annuel* on very strict terms indeed. The *officiers* accordingly continued their protest and increased their opposition. The government replied by suppressing the *annuel* altogether, declaring it a favour, an act of grace on the part of the monarchy which it was not obliged to extend, and, if the *officiers* did not want it on the conditions offered, then it would not grant it to them at all.

Howsoever, after all the negotiation, after all the threats and pretences, government and *officiers* ended by reaching agreement. This time, indeed, events had at first proceeded in the usual way. When the *Parlement* seemed to be weakening, the *Conseil* conceded the *annuel* by a *Déclaration* of 30 April 1648, but only on condition that the *Parlement* accepted the cancellation of four years' salaries. Only the *Parlement de Paris* was to obtain the *annuel* for nothing. The *Parlement*, however, remembered how in 1621 and again in 1630 the king had remained master by dividing the *officiers*, by offering different conditions for the renewal of the *annuel*.[46] The *Parlement* this time decided to make common cause with the other *officiers*, and the outcome of the *Déclaration* of 30 April was the decree of the *Parlement* of 13 May, the *arrêt d'union*, which created the joint assembly of the *Chambre Saint-Louis*. On the 18 May, the *Conseil* abolished the *annuel*. In order to regain it, however, the *Parlement* took no notice of the verbal prohibitions of the Chancellor and the queen, or of the decrees of the *Conseil d'en haut* of 7 and 10 June which annulled the *arrêt d'union*. It began to make more and more serious demands, and adopted an increasingly extreme position, with a view to constraining the government. At the same time as she issued the *Déclaration* of 31 July, prohibiting the *Parlement* from holding further sessions, the queen granted it the *droit annuel* on the most advantageous terms, namely those of 1604. The *Parlement* however found that it had gone too far. It was now afraid of losing its entire popularity and all the authority it had gained with the people of Paris, if it disclosed by a retreat that it had only been working in its own interests. It had within it, moreover, members who envied the *conseillers d'Etat* and the tax-farmers. The successive capitulations of the Court had revealed its weakness. The *Parlement* therefore continued in its policies. Given the extremely serious nature of the situation, however, the *Parlement* almost ruined, by its action, the monarchy and the realm.

The example set by the *Parlement de Paris* brought about a general revolt. The provincial *Parlements* rebelled, as did the towns. Each had its own particular grievance against the government and took its opportunity in the situation. The realm sank into anarchy and disintegration. If the battle of Lens had been lost, it is not entirely sure what might have happened.[47] Then on 22 August the *Parlement*, in great heat against corruption, and on Broussel's advice, decided on taking proceedings against the principal tax-farmers, Catelan, Tabouret and Le Fèvre, who had for some time been raising with the *Surintendant* the question of measures to reduce the power of the *Parlement*. The tax-farmers, acting on their own accord, but with the support of certain important persons who had invested their money in loans and advances to the state, pressed for the arrest of the leaders of the *Parlement de Paris*, together with its suspension, in order to re-establish the absolute authority of the king. When news came through, on 21 August, of the victory at Lens on the previous day, the *Conseil* thought that the triumph would give it the necessary prestige and no longer hesitated to act.

It was then the lesser people of Paris, the watermen, porters, small artisans, who first rose in support of Broussel. At first sight their reasons seem simple enough. They were in a state of distress, crushed by taxes, the victims of rising corn prices, and they therefore came to the defence of those who defended them against financial edicts. The revolt, that is, was one of dear bread. On examination, however, the situation appears a great deal more complicated. In the first place, the people were not apparently in great distress. The highest prices of grain and flour had been reached in 1644.[48] Then, prices had collapsed in 1645, rising again slowly from one year to another until 19 August 1648, which was the last trading day before the insurrection. In comparison with the corresponding month of August 1645, the prices on 19 August 1648 were up 19·8% for best quality wheat, 14% for the lowest quality *méteil†*, 9% for rye, 24% for best quality flour and 15% for the lowest. The prices for the poorest wheat and the best *méteil* were the same as in 1645. Barley was lower by 16%. In total, the rise was not very great, nothing comparable to what had preceded other *journées révolutionnaires*. In comparison with the corresponding period of 1644, there was in fact a fall in prices. The best quality flour was 8% cheaper than in August 1644, the less good 9% cheaper; the best wheat was cheaper by 18%, the worst by 24·5%; the best *méteil* was cheaper by 24%, the least good by 40%; rye by 22·5%; barley by 21%. But, above all, prices had actually fallen in Paris generally since the beginning of the year. Prices had fallen from 4 January. The fall was slow until 16 May, and then accelerated to a rapid fall from 18 July. From 4 January to 19 August, the best flour had fallen by 15%, the lowest quality by 10%; the best quality wheat by 18%, the lowest by 29%; the best *méteil* by 30%, the least good by 21%; rye by 28%; barley by 21%.

The relationship of wages to prices, however, escapes me completely. Were wages stable or falling? Was there unemployment or was there not? On 17 July, the *Cours souveraines*, assembled in the *Chambre Saint-Louis*, proposed protectionist measures: a prohibition on importing English or Dutch woollen and silk manufactures, Flemish *passements* and Spanish, Roman and Venetian lace, on the grounds that imports 'reduced an infinity of the *menu peuple* to unemployment'. One would need to know precisely to what extent Paris itself was affected.

It is scarcely possible moreover to tell whether the taxes were, in fact, insupportable. Paris was exempt from the *taille, taillons* and *crues†*, and thus escaped the heaviest of the direct taxes.[49] It remained however subject to various taxes for the maintenance of troops, forced loans and indirect taxes. The great increases in these last, however, seem to have been well prior to these events. To take wine, for example: a cask of wine costing 272 *livres* paid 6 *livres* 7 *sols* 6 *deniers* in 1640. By 1643, the tax had risen to 9 *livres* 7 *sols* 10 *deniers*. Since then the tax had not been appreciably increased.[50] In general the indirect taxes do not seem to have been very heavy. But the *Conseil* wanted to increase them, and the *Parlement* appeared to be taking the side of the popular interest. A new tariff on goods entering Paris had been established in October 1646. The edict establishing it had been registered by the *Cour des Aides*. The *Parlement*, in jealousy, took cognizance of it and thereby discovered a fine field in which to court popularity, since the government had created the tariff as a substitute for the 730,000 *livres* which the merchants of the *Six Corps*, the *grands bourgeois*, had been assessed for. The *Parlement* protested that it was unjust to make the weak carry the burdens of the rich. Threatened however with the creation of police offices which it considered even more onerous, the *Parlement* registered the edict on 7 September 1647, but exempted grain, coal, wine, firewood and all produce coming in from estates owned by bourgeois.[51] From the beginning of 1648, Court and *Parlement* continued to discuss the tariff. On 20 July, the *Parlement* decreed that the schedule posted on the gates of Paris announcing the rates to be paid on merchandise should be drawn up by two of its own *conseillers*. The royal *Déclaration* of 31 July suppressed the duty on wine, but ordered the levying of all the remaining tariffs and that the schedule be drawn up by the *Conseil du Roi*. On 18 August the *Parlement* decided on the execution of its own decree of 20 July, and then accepted that the schedule of tariffs should be drawn up by the Duc d'Orléans in his *hôtel*, in conjunction with *commissaires* appointed by the *Parlement*. Broussel and Ferrand were appointed *commissaires*, and from 20 August Broussel, as the active partner, was examining not only the schedule of tariffs, but the rates of tax on salt and the different tax-farms.

The *Parlement* acted in this way to court popularity. In order to assure itself of popular support in its struggle with the government in pursuit of its own interests, it persuaded the people of Paris, and, more widely, of France, that they were taxed too heavily and entirely unjustly and to no effect, solely for the greater glory of the king and the luxury of the Court;[52] this, at a time when in fact the war against Habsburg ambitions for universal domination endangered the existence of the realm, and when an impoverished Court could not even provide for its own subsistence.[53] Jealousy of the tax-farmers caused the *Parlement* to strive to force them to disgorge their profits rather than allow new taxes to be levied. It stirred up popular resistance to taxation as such and aroused fury against the *financiers* and the government, without taking into account that the king could not survive without the credit of the tax-farmers.[54] Without incitement from the *Parlement*, the people of Paris would doubtlessly have borne taxes which there is no evidence to suggest were particularly excessive. It was the inculcated sense of the pointlessness and the imaginary injustice of the fiscal burden, much more than the burden itself, which seems to have been insupportable.

It is also possible that the *menu peuple* were affected by government measures regarding *rentes*†. The government had suppressed a year's interest and had created new *rentes*, and this naturally aroused fears as to the payment of arrears of interest owing on existing annuities. There was also the edict of 31 July providing for a regulation which seemed to threaten suppression of interest payments for an unspecified period. It is possible that the *menu peuple* were affected by all this, since there were certainly holders of small-scale *rentes* in every social category.

It was important that the people of Paris experienced a kind of emotional attachment to the *Parlement* and held it in great respect. They felt for Broussel however a widespread and real sense of devotion.[55] In the first place, there was the contrast in the popular mind between his great age and apparent frailty and the courage with which he always sustained issues that were most opposed to the interests of the government. His appearance was one of very limited means. It was said that he had only four thousand *livres* in rent and had reared five grown-up children. He possessed no carriage and went on foot to the Palais through the streets of his *quartier*. He was kind to the poor and, during the sessions of the *Chambre Saint-Louis* and those of the *Parlement* and the discussions on the tariffs at the *Hôtel d'Orléans*, he came to be considered the 'party leader', always formulating proposals which were the most advantageous to the interests of the people. The fact that he had a poor intellect, and that his policy was of such a kind as to cause a military disaster and the entire ruin of the people, meant nothing. Even so, all this does not seem to explain the violence of feeling with which the people of Paris regarded Broussel. It seems as if the *menu peuple* and a considerable section of the bourgeois needed to see their desires incarnated in one man, as if the phenomenon of 'crystallisation' was attaching to Broussel. He had become a supernatural being, a sort of fetish. The Parisians were thrust into despair at having lost him, as if in some way they felt they had lost protection from above. The *Parlement* itself retreated into the background. Only Broussel existed before everyone's eyes and in their minds and hearts. The *Parlement* itself was in fact ill-treated when it left the Palais-Royal without Broussel. Blancmesnil returned to Paris before him, and was shown to the Parisians in an effort to calm them, but to no avail. They lived only for Broussel; and when he arrived there was an explosion of joy, as if the Messiah himself had descended, that all mankind should be saved. Many bourgeois shared these feelings about Broussel. There seems no doubt that this phenomenon of group psychology played the principal role at the critical moment.[56]

The Parisians who had their fetish in Broussel had their scapegoat in Mazarin. Fetish and scapegoat were together the objects of two related feelings or the complementary objects of the same feeling. The execration and contempt of the people for Mazarin grew at the same time as their adoration for Broussel. Mazarin was held responsible for all that was wrong. Everything he did was unsound and was inspired by the most malicious of intentions. It was as if the people and a good many bourgeois needed to see everything which seemed to them wrong incarnated in one man; as if they imposed on the image they made for themselves of Mazarin everything they detested. They placed Mazarin among the ranks of the lowest beasts. His name itself became an insult. Hatred and scorn extended to everything touching Mazarin, which he sullied by his presence, such as the queen, the *Conseil*, the Court. He was reproached for not being French, for speaking the French language with an appalling accent and making a farrago of it. They were repelled by his cleverness. They wished he had not been responsible for making the peace. In this, Mazarin was moreover partly his own victim, since for immediate effect he had several times boasted of having peace within his grasp. The result was that his enemies had been able to make the French people believe that the war had continued solely through the will of Mazarin and the government, that it had been unnecessary and that the Habsburgs themselves had not wanted it. Therefore the victory at Lens produced no effect. The Parisians thought and acted as if the Habsburgs had never existed, almost as if France had been alone in the world. With the Spaniards and Austrians so far away and the government and the consequences of its actions so near at hand and of such daily significance to them, Parisians had even come to hate their own government more than the enemy, to distrust their own leaders, more than the enemy. They even despised the government because of its concessions to the *Parlement*, for its capitulations. They despised the queen, the ministers and the *Conseil* for their weakness and for their granting them what they demanded. Efforts at conciliation merely increased hatred, disgust and opposition. The nature and depth of such sentiments seem to bear no logical relationship and to be out of all proportion to the economic and financial causes for discontent.

IV

The action and emotions of the bourgeois seem somewhat complex. To be able to obtain a clear picture would mean distinguishing between the different social classes which this term 'bourgeois' covers; to see whether the privileged *Six-Corps* (drapers, grocers, mercers, skinners, hosiers, goldsmiths), who spoke in the name of Parisian trade, reacted like the others; whether the master merchant-manufacturers had the same attitude as the small masters, who were sometimes close to the proletariat itself. But this is still almost impossible to distinguish.

The bourgeois did not start the insurrection. On the first day, a few took up arms under duress. Their material situation was of course relatively good. The *grands bourgeois* had been allowed a dispensation from the special tax of August 1647. All seem in fact to have escaped the tax on house-owners, since their riot of January 1648. Besides, as house-owners, they had something to lose in the event of civil disorder. In general, they show themselves respectful of public order. Many of them show no readiness to arm themselves, unless with the permission of the responsible authorities, the *Bureau de Ville* and the *Parlement*.

However, on the second and third days there were bourgeois in action. They were to be seen among the rebels who forced the *Parlement* to return a second time to seek Broussel's release. They were among those indeed who declared themselves ready to set fire to the Palais-Royal. There do not seem to have been any of the *Six-Corps* among these, and perhaps the *Six-Corps* were already separating themselves as a group from the rest, as they were indeed to do later.[57] But, even so, they did not reveal themselves, since the bourgeois militia were not to be seen anywhere intervening against the rebels.

The fact is that at least a substantial number of the bourgeois were affected in exactly the same way as the people. Their pride was affected when the government attempted to impose taxation on Paris, although it was a privileged city. Their self-interest was involved not only in taxation, but in forced loans and various other impositions of the government, in commercial monopolies which they wanted suppressed and in the import of foreign manufactures which they wanted prohibited.[58] They were affected in their moral sense and their security, through the arrest of Broussel, their fetish, by their scapegoat, Mazarin. A good many of them may have been won over to the insurrection in this way, during the nights of 26 and 27 August, by the agents of Retz and Broussel's friends in the *Parlement*.

It seems however that it was fear which played the greatest role in leading them to arm themselves. Panic and terror created their militancy. They feared attack by vagabonds and the *menu peuple*, against their own persons and their property.[59] But they feared, even more, as indeed they did throughout the history of the *ancien régime*, and it had been especially so at the time of the Barricades in 1588, the soldiery, the mercenaries whose very presence in a town was a threat of looting, atrocity, rape and destruction. The popular uprising in support of Broussel meant for many of them the arrival of royal troops in the city and therefore a risk to their lives, their wives and daughters and their property, even if the troops did not actually march against them themselves. And this is why they built barricades to defend themselves against the army. There was also the possibility that the arrest of Broussel signified a government intention to suppress all opposition and revenge itself on all its opponents. The bourgeois had indeed taken up arms in January, and had frequently been involved in demonstrations since. They might very well have feared for themselves. And that is doubtless why a good number of them apparently cried out for the release of Broussel, since that in itself would symbolise the abandonment of any idea of repression on the part of the government. This fundamental fear, this general crisis of nerve, which increased stage by stage with the general uproar, the sound of firing, the spread of alarming reports, the very alternation of calm and disturbance, was enough to transform some of the bourgeois who were calm enough on the first day into the veritable '*enragés*' of the third. Fear also had the greatest influence on the populace at large. There is indeed a whole psychological study to be done on the role played by fear in these *journées révolutionnaires*.

The royal troops did not succeed in suppressing the revolt, nor indeed did they even seriously try. The narrow and frequently tortuous streets put the regular troops at a disadvantage, as was always to be the case until the work of Haussmann. It was easy and quick to raise barricades and to haul stones to upper storeys where they could be used to fell soldiers with great accuracy. The arms of the bourgeois militia were virtually the same as those available to the royal troops. Most of the time the army was unable to deploy either its cavalry or its artillery.

The troops were also few in number compared with the Parisians themselves. The latter numbered more than 400,000, of whom some 13,000 to 14,000 were masters and about 45,000 were workers and apprentices. The number of watermen, porters and other labourers is unknown. Numerous beggars must certainly be added who were not included in the population statistics. From 27 August there were perhaps also peasants from the vicinity, since Wednesday was a market day. The hinterland of Paris could have been very quickly alerted. Bourgeois who held *seigneuries*† about Paris may also have made their men come in. In 1649, there were peasants in the city from Saint-Ouen, who came in in answer to a summons from their Parisian *seigneurs* and who fought in the ranks of the bourgeois.[60] For 1648, however, the documents are silent in this respect.

Facing them, the royal troops numbered no more than 11,000 to 12,000 men.[61] There were four companies of the *gardes du corps*, numbering 100 men each; but since these served on a quarterly basis, there were in fact only 100 of them at the Palais-Royal. The *Cent-Suisses* numbered 119 men; the *Gardes de la Porte* were 55 in number; the 109 constables of the *Grand Prévôt*†, again, serving on a quarterly basis, provided only 27 men; the *Gendarmes* of some 200 men, serving quarterly, amounted to 50; the *Cent-Gentilshommes au bec de Corbin* numbered 200; the musketeers 300; the regiment of the *Gardes-françaises* 6000 men and the regiment of the *Gardes-suisses* 4000. However, there is nothing to suggest that the actual number equalled the nominal. Moreover a good many of these soldiers could have been away with the army. Certain of them, such as the *Gardes de la Porte* and the constables of the *Grand Prévôt*, who were a kind of keepers of the peace, were of only mediocre calibre. Finally, the soldiers of the *Gardes-françaises* were not of entirely certain loyalty. Omer Talon affirms that when the *Parlement* left the Palais-Royal on 27 August, the first time, the *Gardes-françaises* declared openly that they would only fire on bourgeois.[62]

No leader emerged during the revolt. The change, however, which occurred between the evening of 26 August and the morning of 27 August, together with the common feeling exciting the Parisians to arm themselves from 26 August for fear of the army, and the pamphlets distributed on the evening of 28 August with the open intention of renewing the violence, justify the question whether there was an invisible 'conductor of the orchestra'.

The *Parlement*, as a corporate body, did not organise or direct the rebellion. On 26 August, it was obviously caught by surprise. Nevertheless it was important that, as the primary agent for the maintenance of public order in Paris, it decided on 27 August to use the revolt, which was clearly paralysing the government, for its own ends by allowing it to develop, through refraining from issuing orders to the bourgeois militia to suppress it. It was however quickly overtaken by events, and was considerably surprised when it found itself as much under threat as the king when it left the Palais-Royal for the first time. Its most determined members then indulged in a veritable game of poker, in which they were always able to make themselves appear as intermediaries between the people and the government, which in fact they no longer were, and to extort from the queen, at the same time as the release of Broussel, recognition of the essential contribution of their own role, when in fact the two things were no longer connected. The *Parlement* knew how to take advantage of a situation which unfolded alongside it, but essentially without it.[63]

The attitude of the municipality of Paris was uncertain. It was responsible for the issuing of the order to take up arms on the evening of 26 August, but without perhaps foreseeing all the possible consequences. On 27 August, it did nothing. It awaited the results of the negotiations between Court and *Parlement*. Its attitude tended toward favouring the rebels. On 28 August, it was overwhelmed by the general contagion of fear. In the worst interpretation of its actions, however, it merely pursued a policy of letting things develop. The *Prévôt des Marchands*† was always the king's candidate, since the reign of Henry IV. But among the *conseillers* of the *Bureau de Ville* there were thirteen *officiers* who came from the *Parlement*, the *Chambre des Comptes* and the *Châtelet*. The municipality only possessed limited means for taking action. We do not know what state of mind its meagre force was in. The *quartiniers* who commanded the bourgeois militia bought their offices and escaped the authority of the *Prévôt des Marchands*, who, after these events, however, expelled them from their command. The *colonels* were almost always members of the *Cours souveraines*.[64]

The *Compagnie du Saint-Sacrement* was strongly opposed to Mazarin.[65] It could not accept his ecclesiastical nominations, inspired as they were by political rather than religious considerations. The queen was greatly devoted to the *Saint-Sacrement*, and it sought during the Fronde to obtain her consent to Mazarin's dismissal. It had been certain of its own members and their friends, however, who had been the most anxious for Mazarin to adopt a policy of severity before the revolt, but who were the most insistent now on a policy of capitulation. On 9 July, Particelli d'Emery was replaced in the *surintendance des finances* by La Meilleraye, who was to be assisted by two *directeurs*, d'Aligre and Morangis. La Meilleraye and Morangis were both members of the *Compagnie*. Chavigny, as 'outside friend' of the *Compagnie*, was thought to have induced the queen and Mazarin to take violent measures against the *Parlement* and to imprison Broussel, and 'to have done so with design, in the knowledge that it might well have certain adverse effects'. He was accused of having secret talks with the Abbé Pierre Longueil, *conseiller-clerc* in the *Grand'Chambre* of the *Parlement*, who had ideas of establishing his own brother in the *surintendance des finances*, and who indeed achieved it, and who, it was said, urged Broussel on in order to make himself more important in the eyes of the ministers.[66] Chavigny was in daily, often secret, contact with Pierre Voile, a *Président aux Enquetes*, who was exceedingly hostile to the Cardinal.[67]

The Maréchal de la Meilleraye, another member of the *Compagnie*, played a suspect role. We shall never know whether he was right not to persist on 26 August. His reaction was always lenient, and he was accused of not having dared to suppress the revolt. Could it have been, however, that he did not particularly wish to suppress it, when there was still enough time to do so?

During the whole period of the revolt, the *Président* de Longueil, brother of the Abbé, gave no word to Mazarin, except 'to retreat, which advice, it was claimed, had been suggested to him by the said M. de Chavigny'.[68]

On 27 August, during the poker game at the Palais-Royal, the queen (the only 'man' in the Court at this time, and whose firmness filled even Mme de Motteville with admiration) played her hand well. It is the *Président* de Mesmes, of the *Compagnie du Saint-Sacrement*, already accused by Mazarin of working for the *Parlement* while appearing to work for the king, who pushes the *Premier-Président* into her study after her when she retires and who accompanies him there, together with the Duc d'Orléans, another 'outside friend' of the *Compagnie* favourable to its designs, the Chancellor, another member of the *Compagnie*, the Duc de Longueville, Mazarin and, perhaps, de Bailleul, the queen's Chancellor, who was yet another 'outside friend' of the *Compagnie*. It was either he, de Mesmes or de Bailleul, who finally dragged the capitulation from the queen.[69]

It is simply not possible to reach conclusion on all this. One can only hope for the discovery of fresh evidence. Some think there were many at Court who awaited the disorder for their own ends. Some hoped to make themselves the more necessary if it happened, and thus attract rewards for themselves. Some of those in the principal offices of state hoped to oust Mazarin. The Cardinal had certainly been very ill-advised. Pushed to concessions when a little firmness would have silenced the *Parlement*, he was brought to violence when it had become dangerous to use it. Although the Duc d'Orléans does not seem to have been too put out by the troubles,[70] it does not seem however that anyone belonging to the Court had organised the revolt, nor that anyone had taken direction of it as a whole. There are suggestions of certain inclinations in that direction and details of certain actions that were taken. Gondi certainly exaggerated his own role; but even so it is probable that during the night of 26 and 27 August he came to an understanding with the *Maître des Comptes* Miron, *colonel* of the militia, and the *Conseiller aux Requêtes* Martineau, *capitaine* of the Rue Saint-Jacques, to have the first barricades raised.[71] Also, between six and nine o'clock on the evening of 27 August, Gondi entered into negotiations with the Duc de Longueville,

who came to see him at the Archbishop's palace. Discussions took place
with several friends of Gondi. They envisaged the possibility of seizing
the person of Mazarin. But, in the event, the sole decision taken was to
'follow the movements of the *Parlement* and the people, and to endeavour
to involve persons of quality in the public interest, especially M. le
Prince.'[72] Mme de Motteville seems to have seen the position clearly
enough: 'Out of so many ill-intentioned men, none wished to declare
himself chief of the rebel *canaille* . . . for great ills are not made
suddenly. Men only accustom themselves to crime little by little; but . . .
one has to avow that they accustom themselves to it very readily.'[73]

Finally, there are grounds for examining whether there was intervention
on the part of foreign courts. It seems that among the beggars in Paris
who participated actively in the troubles were men from Franche Comté,
Artois and Lorraine. Agents of the king of Spain or of other powers
could have been introduced into the realm among them.[74] Perhaps
a happy find in the archives at Simancas, or in Brussels, Turin, Venice
or Vienna will provide information on this point.

It was the absence of general direction, together with the divisions of
interest among the rebels and the capitulation of the Court, which
explain why the *journées révolutionnaires* came to an end. Nevertheless,
the *Parlement* remained in control of the situation afterwards and was
able to obtain the *Déclaration* of 22–4 October 1648, which settled the
conflict with the *Conseil* in its favour. The government could not however accept this assault on the 'best part of the royal authority'.[75] The
queen appealed to Condé, and the entry of the army into the political
situation, to oppose the ambitions of the princes, prolonged and
increased the troubles.

Some progress has been achieved toward an understanding of this
subject of the *journées révolutionnaires* of 1648, mainly through the study
of institutions too often neglected in the past. There remains a great deal
to be done. We should above all like to know whether the economic and
financial factors were the determining cause of everything else, whether
they determined the feelings, the mentality and the actions of men. In
the present state of knowledge, we cannot say. The opposition of the
Parlement seems to have been the fundamental cause of these revolutionary days. Its basic attitude and its propaganda seem to have instilled
into everyone the idea that injustice, negligence, corruption and governmental tyranny held sway. The general opposition to financial policy was
therefore above all ideological and psychological. The idea of a corrupt
government rendered its financial policy insupportable, rather than the
financial policy itself being in fact insupportable and giving rise to the
idea of a corrupt government. The *Parlement* started its opposition before
the question of the renewal of the *paulette* was raised, and for reasons
which went beyond the *paulette*, reasons of prestige, influence and a

'desire for power'. Material interests, such as the *paulette*, only amplified the impact of ideas and feelings which were already formed. Until now, historical materialism does not seem to have taken into account the facts regarding these *journées révolutionnaires*. We must therefore pursue the study of the economic and social situation in Paris during this period, and also compare these *journées* of August 1648 with other similar Parisian *journées*, if we wish to distinguish their causes completely. Finally, it is necessary to go further. The Fronde was part of a whole series of revolts occurring during periods of royal minority. These revolts stemmed from certain factors in the structure of the State and French seventeenth-century society. It would be necessary to examine whether this structure had a certain economic structure as its basis.

NOTES

1 [Editor's note:] See pp. 33–4 of the original article for the author's footnote commentary on the general inadequacy of earlier narrative accounts.

2 (i) Mme de Motteville, *Mémoires* (Paris, 1891) II. Mme de Motteville was a *femme de chambre* of Anne of Austria who remained inside the Palais-Royal and who therefore saw a great many of the principal persons involved. She compiled her *Mémoires* from notes made from day to day. They are generally unemotional in tone, except for a tendency to denigrate the queen.

(ii) *Relation anonyme*, B.N. ms. fr. 20290. This account emanates from a military person involved in the actual street fighting.

(iii) Marie Dubois (a *valet de chambre* of the king), *Relation*, ed. Feillet, in *Revue des sociétés savantes*, II (1865) pp. 324–37.

(iv) Other texts, such as the *Journal* of Jean Vallier, were compiled long after the events, and are of considerably less value.

3 (i) A *Note* of 18 September made by André d'Ormesson, included in the *Mémoires* of Lefèvre d'Ormesson, ed. Chéruel.

(ii) de Goulas, *Mémoires*, ed. *Société de l'Histoire de France*.

(iii) Dubuisson-Aubenay, *Journal des guerres civiles*, ed. *Société de l'Histoire de France*.

(iv) Lefèvre d'Ormesson, *Mémoires*, ed. Chéruel.

4 (i) Omer Talon (*premier avocat-général* in the *Parlement de Paris*), *Mémoires*.

(ii) P. Lallemant, *Journal inédit*, *Bibliothèque de l'Univ. de Paris*, Ms. 64.

(iii) M. Molé (*Premier-Président* of the *Parlement de Paris*), *Mémoires*.

5 (i) *Registres de l'Hôtel de Ville de Paris pendant la Fronde*, ed. Le Roux de Lincy and Douet d'Arcq, 3 vols (Paris, 1846) pp. 1–41.

(ii) de Retz, *Mémoires*, ed. *Grands Ecrivains de la France*.

(iii) Guy Joly, *Mémoires*, ed. Michaud-Poujoulat.

(iv) Aimé de Gaignières, 'Gaignières, ses correspondents, etc.', ed. C. de Grand-maison, in *Bibliothèque de l'Ecole de Chartes*, Vol. LI (1890); letter of 28 August, pp. 577–80.

6 KK 992 (1644–1648), 993 (1648–1652).

7 R. Fages, *Comité des travaux historiques et scientifiques, Section hist. et philol.* (1907) pp. 104–13.

8 It is not always easy, because of the imprecision of the various authors. E.g. Motteville, op. cit., II p. 177: on 28 August, Mazarin himself goes to visit the *'corps de garde'* of the *bourgeois* to hear what the *people* have to say.

9 [Editor's note:] Condé's victory over the Habsburgs at Lens had been on 20 August 1648.

10 Motteville, op. cit., II p. 153.

11 Dubois, op. cit., pp. 327–9; also Dubuisson-Aubenay, op. cit., p. 51.

12 [Editor's note:] One of the several authorities responsible for the local government of Paris. Headed by the *prévôt des marchands* and four *échevins*, it was represented by a *quartinier* in each *quartier* of the *ville*, part of whose function was the maintenance of law and order. The appointment of La Reynie as *Lieutenant-général* for Paris in 1667 was an attempt to rationalise the late-medieval structure of the local government of the city. Orest Ranum, *Paris in the Age of Absolutism*, is a useful initial reference in English for seventeenth-century Paris.

13 *'Gentilshommes'* and *'hommes d'épée'* protected by members of the Court in return for fidelity.

14 Compare Dubois, op. cit., pp. 328–9; also *Relation anonyme*, ms. fr. 20290, *fol.* 333.

15 *Relation anonyme*, ibid.

16 According to Dubois, Guy Joly and Gaignières.

17 *Registres de l'Hôtel de Ville*, op. cit., p. 19, against the evidence of Guy Joly, op. cit., p. 10.

18 According to Lefèvre d'Ormesson, Goulas, Dubois and the author of the *Relation anonyme*, against Motteville, who was not herself privy to the decisions of the *Conseil d'en haut*.

19 [Editor's note:] The Registers of the *Hôtel de Ville*, Dubois, Motteville, Talon and the *Relation anonyme* give the sites of the barricades; see original article, p. 44, note 2. Not all the streets listed, Mousnier suggests, were barricaded from early morning (see infra, p. 175). Guy Joly claims that barricades were only raised in response to the sortie of the Chancellor Séguier from the Palais-Royal.

20 G. Joly, op. cit., p. 11.

21 Talon, op. cit., p. 265.

22 Ibid.

23 Dubois, op. cit., p. 331; also *Relation anonyme, fol.* 334.

24 *Journal contenant tout ce qui s'est passé, etc.*, p. 67; Lallemant, op. cit., p. 107; Goulas, op. cit., II p. 353.

25 *Relation anonyme, fol.* 334; Dubois, op. cit., p. 331; also Motteville, op. cit., II p. 165.

26 Talon, op. cit., p. 266.

27 Goulas, op. cit., II p. 355; Guy Joly, op. cit., p. 12.

28 Dubois, op. cit., p. 334.

29 Motteville, op. cit., II, p. 171.

30 Dubuisson-Aubenay, op. cit., p. 55.

31 Motteville, op. cit., II p. 171.

32 Ibid., p. 172.

33 *Registres de l'Hôtel de Ville*, I pp. 26–7.

34 Ibid.

35 Dubois, op. cit., p. 335.

36 *Registres de l'Hôtel de Ville*, I p. 37.

37 Motteville, op. cit., II p. 173.

38 Dubois, op. cit., p. 387.

39 A corruption of the truth which ran through the city.

40 *Registres de l'Hôtel de Ville*, op. cit., I p. 33.

41 Ibid., pp. 34–5; Motteville, op. cit., II p. 177.

42 Le Fèvre d'Ormesson, *Mémoires*, I p. 555; *Registres de l'Hôtel de Ville*, I p. 35.

43 Talon, op. cit., pp. 209–12, for *lit de justice* of 15 January 1648, and p. 259 for *lit de justice* of 31 July 1648.

44 R. Mousnier, 'Le Conseil du Roi de la Mort de Henri IV au gouvernement personnel de Louis XIV', in *Etudes d'Histoire moderne et contemporaine*, I (1947) pp. 29–67; also, *La Vénalité des offices sous Henri IV et Louis XIII* (Paris, 1945) *Livre* III, Chapter IV.

45 *Propositions de la Chambre Saint-Louis*, 14 July 1648 – offices should be created solely by 'edicts registered by the *cours souveraines*, with entire freedom of suffrage', i.e. without the use of a *lit de justice*; offices created without such registration and freedom of suffrage to be suppressed – such as the creation of *maîtres des requêtes* imposed by *lit de justice* on 15 January 1648.

46 R. Mousnier, op. cit., *Livre* II, Chapter IV and *Livre* III, Chapter IV.

47 Goulas, op. cit., II p. 326; Mazarin, *Lettres*, III p. 127; Motteville, op. cit., II p. 150.

48 KK 992 and 993, for the price of wheat, *méteil*, rye, barley, oats and flour of various grades on Wednesdays and Saturdays.

49 Parisians may have felt a sense of unity with the peasants from the region, who came into the Paris markets and had frequent contacts with artisans in the city and sometimes even family ties. Members of the Parisian bourgeoisie had estates and fiefs around Paris, and, according to the custom of the period, bonds involving protection and service established themselves between owners and cultivators. Paris, with its population of 415,000, had easy and frequent contact with its hinterland. The peasants themselves were discontented: 'On this day, Monday, 20 [August], a crowd of 606 peasants surround the Duc d'Orléans on his way to the *Parlement* and cry out that he should not impede the good intention of the *Parlement* to relieve their distress.' Dubuisson-Aubenay, op. cit., pp. 40–9. In reality, they were not over-taxed. Omer Talon, who proclaimed the general distress of the realm, claimed that the villages around Paris were comfortably off and capable of paying their taxes (op. cit., p. 206). The returns from the *tailles* diminish constantly from 1643; but, from 1651, in a country ruined by civil wars and in a state of distress surpassing anything previously experienced, the returns increase; and they exceed those of 1647 and 1648 during the period 1651–4. Was there more ill will than real incapacity to pay involved in the situation? Was the fiscal crisis more psychological than actually financial?

50 A. de Saint-Julien and G. Bienaymé, *Les droits d'entrée et d'octroi à Paris depuis le douzième siècle* (Paris, 1886).

51 Talon, op. cit., p. 198 et seq; A. Clamageran, *Histoire de l'impôt en France*, II pp. 548–9.

52 Talon, op. cit., p. 210.

53 Motteville, op. cit., II p. 98: 'the king's kitchen is quite ruined; the queen has to borrow money from certain private individuals; the princess and Mme d'Aiguillon have to pawn the crown jewels. Mazarin is forced to pawn diamonds to pay the Swiss guards and has to borrow from his friends.'

54 Talon, op. cit., p. 260.

55 Goulas, op. cit., II p. 321: on about 15 July 1648 'certain coachmen and lacqueys were quarrelling in the street . . . and their masters having got down to stop the brawl (these were two *gentilshommes* and a *maître des requêtes*) the one with the long robe had all the people on his side, and the rabble cried

out that one had to support the *maître des requêtes* because it was the *Parlement* that took care of their interests and prevented their being oppressed.'

56 Motteville, op. cit., II p. 155: 26 August, 'when the Parisians lost sight of their Broussel, there they were, all become madmen, crying out in the streets that they were lost . . . and that they were prepared to die with a good heart for him.' When La Meilleraye goes out for the first time to remonstrate with them, they reply 'with boldness and frenzy . . . demanding their protector all the while, protesting they will never be pacified until he is restored to them'. Motteville, op. cit., p. 171: 'never was a king's or Roman Emperor's triumph greater than that of this poor little man. He is led to Notre Dame, the people declaring that they will have a *Te Deum* sung for him.'

57 According to Dubuisson-Aubenay, cited by Chéruel in his *Histoire de France pendant la minorité de Louis XIV* (Paris, 1879–80) III p. 79, the guards of the *Six-Corps* of the *métiers de Paris* assembled secretly on 2 October 1648 with the principal merchants, 'determined to go and find the king and assure him that they would not involve themselves in anything that was happening, nor had they so involved themselves in anything that had happened contrary to his service.'

58 *Propositions de la Chambre Saint-Louis,* 17 July 1648; Talon, op. cit., p. 243 et seq.

59 *Registres de l'Hôtel de Ville,* I pp. 15, 26–7; Dubois, op. cit., pp. 328–9; Motteville, op. cit., II p. 169 and 182; Vallier, op. cit., pp. 88 and 98; and Talon, op. cit., p. 268.

60 'Portrait de Janin', in *L'Agréable conférence de deux paysans de Saint-Ouen et de Montmorency sur les affaires du temps* (Paris, 1649).

61 According to the figures for the *Maison du Roi* in the *Etat de France* for 1663. There cannot have been great changes in these figures.

62 Talon, op. cit., p. 266.

63 One does not exclude the action of certain members of the *Parlement* as individuals, or that of certain friends or relatives of Broussel and the other *conseillers,* especially since a number of them were *colonels* and captains in the militia.

64 *Registres de l'Hôtel de Ville,* pp. 1–10; P. Robiquet, *Organisation municipale de Paris*; G. Picot, 'Recherches sur les quartiniers', in *Soc. d'hist. de Paris et de l'Ile de France* (1875) p. 132 and p. 145; C. Normand, *La Bourgeoisie française au XVIIe siècle* (Paris, 1908) p. 327.

65 R. Allier, *La Cabale des Dévôts* (Paris, 1902).

66 It is possible that these discussions only began after the *journées révolutionnaires.*

67 Talon, op. cit., pp. 274–5.

68 Ibid.

69 Ibid., p. 266.

70 Motteville, op. cit., II pp. 74–5; Guy Joly, op. cit., p. 13.

71 de Retz, *Mémoires,* II p. 32 et seq. This is confirmed in essentials by Guy Joly, op. cit., pp. 9–10, who was in fact writing at the time of his breach with Retz.

72 Guy Joly, op. cit., p. 12.

73 Motteville, op. cit., II p. 179.

74 Talon, op. cit., p. 269.

75 Cited by Chéruel, op. cit., III p. 91, from the notebooks of Mazarin.

7 The Financial *Officiers* during the Fronde[*]

ROLAND MOUSNIER

I

The Fronde began by what we are all agreed to call the '*Fronde parlementaire*', and the role of the *Parlements*[†] in this great attempted
revolution is known, although less thoroughly perhaps than we commonly think. In contrast, the part played by other royal *officiers*,[†]
important as it was, remains even now virtually unknown. The Fronde
was, in one sense, a revolt on the part of what we may perhaps term the
'public service' of France; although, of course, the *ancien régime* used
only the *officier* and the *commissaire*[†] and only came to know the civil
servant as such toward the middle of the eighteenth century. Two of
the corporations of royal *officiers* in fact played a considerable role, the
Trésoriers généraux de France[†], who were the principal financial *officiers*
in the provinces, and the *élus*[†]. They were both grouped into syndicates
and the papers emanating from these constitute valuable documentary
sources. One of these sources, although its existence has been known for
a long time, has been curiously neglected until now; namely, the correspondence of one of the two syndicates, consisting of 239 letters sent
by the *Trésoriers de France* from the various *généralités*[†] to the office of
their syndicate in Paris, between 22 May 1648 and 5 September 1653.
These letters are the surviving element of a more extended correspondence
kept by the secretary-general of the syndicate, Simon Fournival. They
are now among the French manuscripts in the *Bibliothèque Nationale*.[1]
The life and activity of the *Trésoriers généraux de France* and their
syndicate materialises for us in these documents, on almost a day-to-day
basis; but for the *élus*, on the other hand, we have only, up to the present
time, certain printed manifestos and circulars.[2]

There is, finally, additional material in the reports of the *intendants*
in the provinces addressed to Chancellor Séguier, but these end however
in 1649, a little before Séguier's disgrace.

[*] This is a translation of Roland Mousnier's article, 'Recherches sur les Syndicats
d'Officiers pendant la Fronde: Trésoriers de France et Elus dans la Révolution', in
XVIIe Siècle (1959) pp. 76–117.

At the beginning of 1648, the *Trésoriers de France* and the *élus* were among the most discontented of all the *officiers*. Since 1637 a revolution had been in process, authorised by the royal *Déclaration* of 16 April 1643, as a result of which their principal functions had been transferred to *commissaires†*, the provincial *intendants*. The function of the latter changed. Instead of remaining inspectors concerned with reforming abuses, the *intendants* became administrators themselves, and carried out all the principal financial operations. They undertook the apportionment of taxes between the towns, villages and parishes liable to pay taxes within an *élection†*, and even between individuals when parishes refused to elect tax collectors. They actually levied the taxes directly, and since the bailiffs and constables were powerless in face of the frequent tax revolts, the *intendants* called on the assistance of regular troops and special companies of *fuzeliers*. They recovered tax arrears. They established and levied special taxes, sanctioned only afterwards by decree of the *Conseil*. The *intendant* would choose certain *Trésoriers de France* and *élus* to collaborate with him, as a technicality; but in reality the *compagnies* of these *officiers* were reduced to fulfilling legal formalities only, such as, in the case of the *Trésoriers*, registering the *commissions* for the levying of the *tailles* and appending their seal to them, together with the issuing of orders for the carrying into effect of such *commissions*. There were however nothing more than simple formalities, which the *intendant* forced them to carry out under his supervision. If the *Trésoriers* had refused or adopted delaying tactics, an order of the *intendant* alone would have sufficed to have the royal *commissions* executed.[3]

The needs of the Thirty Years War had forced this administrative revolution on the king. It had been necessary to create a mass of new taxes since 1635 and the entry of France into 'open war' with the Habsburgs. The *Trésoriers de France* were corporations enjoying rights of remonstrance with the Crown, and they made difficulties about their assent when tax edicts had not been registered, which was frequently the case or when taxes simply seemed beyond the capacity of their *généralités* to pay. Delays resulted which were prejudicial to military operations. The *Trésoriers de France* were also accused of neglecting their duty as regards the sending of information to the *Conseil du Roi*, and in making regular tours of inspection and supervising the *élus*. Now, in order to obtain the greatest possible return from a tax, it had to be as far as possible proportional to the capacity of individual taxpayers. Taxes had to be apportioned. It was always a question of a global sum which had to be apportioned between the parishes of an *élection* and then between the taxpayers in each parish. The *élus* were accused of deliberately reducing the tax assessments of parishes where they had relatives, friends or protectors, and of overcharging others accordingly. They were also accused of closing their eyes when *asséeurs-collecteurs†* reduced the amounts of tax charged to rich *laboureurs*†, the '*coqs de paroisses*' and tenants of *gentilshommes* and loaded the taxes onto the poorer tax-payers. The *élus* were accused of actually encouraging such activities. The result was that parishes which were without protection, whose poor were assessed beyond their capacity, did not pay their taxes, and arrears were thereby created. If indeed there had not been arrears, the taxes would have exceeded the real tax capability of the country by that very amount.

The inadequacy of the *officiers*, their delays and irregularities, were the reasons invoked by the king for using *commissaires* in their stead. This affected the *Trésoriers de France*, both in their pride and their pocket, since part of their income consisted of fees charged for what they actually did, such as the auditing of accounts and the issuing of receipts. Moreover, the *Trésoriers de France* and the *élus* also complained of the excessive charges levied on them by the king and the undermining of the importance of their offices by the increased number of offices put up for sale. At the death of Henry IV, they claimed, there were ten *Trésoriers de France* in each *Bureau des finances*, and by 1648 this number had risen to twenty-five. The ordinary value of their offices had therefore become proportionally reduced. The king had also imposed increased salaries on them against their paying him capital to the corresponding value. In this way they had paid more than 30 million *livres* into the royal coffers.[4] The *élus*, for their part, claimed that they had paid more than 200 million *livres* since 1624, of which 60 millions had been paid since 1640, 'for confirmation of imaginary privileges or for the grant of fictitious supplements to their salaries'. In fact, since 1640, the royal government, in the direst financial straits, had set about effecting retrenchments on the salaries and privileges of the *officiers*. In 1640 the *élus* had lost a quarter of their salaries. Then, as a result of progressive reductions each year, it reached the point in 1647 when the salaries of the *élus* were suppressed altogether, and in addition they were deprived of three-quarters of the privileges for which they had had to pay such large sums and for which they had had to indebt themselves to relatives and friends.[5] The *Trésoriers de France* were the victims of similar acts of plunder. Since 1643, they had lost the greater part of their salaries and privileges. Since their livelihood, they claimed, consisted solely of their offices and their salaries, five hundred families, amounting to more than ten thousand persons, counting wives and children, were apparently in the greatest poverty.

The *Trésoriers de France* and *élus* detested the *intendants*; but they detested the tax-farmers even more. In their eyes, it was the *financiers* who were responsible for the general use of *intendants* and the extension of their powers. In order to have the necessary revenues quickly available for the purposes of diplomacy and war, the *Conseil* had gradually farmed out all taxes in the form of *traites*†, even the *tailles*†. The *traitants* advanced vast sums and took responsibility for collecting the taxes through their own agents. But they insisted that the taxes should be apportioned swiftly and that their agents should have the support of summary justice and armed forces. Hence the use of *intendants*. The *Trésoriers généraux de France* fulminated on every possible occasion against the *traitants*† and 'their' *intendants*.[6] 'The tribunals of these '*juges extraordinaires*', moving about the provinces, had been the ruin of all regular justice and had overturned the ordinary forms of administration, not only financial but judicial, and this change, as much as high taxes, had truly brought about the destruction of the people.' The levying of taxes by 'an infinite number of hungry officials, without sanction of the *Trésoriers de France* and without passing through the hands of the ordinary *receveurs* has doubled the cost.' Through the use of so many *sergents*, often in whole companies, the cost of raising the taxes amounted to more than the taxes themselves. As for the *intendants*, 'their guards and companies of *fuzeliers* have ruined the parishes and desolated the provinces worse than enemy soldiers would have'. By the selling and reselling of offices, by the constant alienation of the royal domain, by exceeding the agreed amounts for the *aides*† and the other farmed taxes, by their acting without any concern for legality, which was the guarantee of the king's interest and that of his subjects, the *intendants* had brought ruin, the *Trésoriers* claimed, to both the royal domain and the king's revenues.

> Since the appointment of these *intendants*, we, the *Trésoriers de France*, have watched the royal domain perish, with our hands tied behind our backs. The domain is now entirely out of the king's control, through contracts and transfers, most of them entirely fictitious. Those who have the enjoyment of the domain constantly dismember it, in order to increase their own patrimony. They have found means of appropriating title-deeds or suppressing them as they see fit. They have had all charges made against the *tailles* omitted from the accounts.[7]

In this way, the *Trésoriers de France* returned in kind most of the criticism which the intendants levelled at them. They claimed that, when they had been able to exercise their offices, they had conducted themselves so well that at a time when the taxes raised were only half of what was being raised at the moment, the amount actually coming into the king's coffers amounted to much more. There was no *intendant*, they said, who did not on his own cost more than all the *Trésoriers de France* of a *généralité* put together.[8]

Hatred became real execration, however, when the *Trésoriers de France* and the *élus* came to consider the *traitants* and the *financiers*; since it was they, they claimed, who had proposed all the increases in the sale of offices to the *Conseil du Roi*, as well as all the fictitious increases and then all the reductions in official salaries and privileges, which, in the eyes of the *officiers*, had ruined them. Moreover, they complained that the *traitants* were seeking to confine them within the terms of edicts which related solely to *officiers de finances*, whereas they considered them- selves to be judges, and even members of the *Cours souveraines*, in their capacity as *Trésoriers généraux de France*.

The discontent of the *Trésoriers* and *élus* grew until it became a con- flict between institutions, between the *compagnies* of the *officiers* on the one hand, and the *intendants* and the *traitants* on the other. The *Tré- soriers de France* and the *élus* organised themselves in fact into syndi- cates for the protection of their corporate interests. 'This Syndicate [of *élus*] has been established with His Majesty's good pleasure by several assemblies of the deputies of the *élections* of this Realm.' These assemblies were held in Paris on 26 October 1641, 27 January 1642, 7 August 1645, 17 May and 1 and 3 July 1649. The formation of the Syndicate was confirmed by the *Conseil* in its decrees of 16 April 1644, 7 January 1645 and 27 June 1648, acceding to various of its requests. The *Chambre des Comptes*† recognised the Syndicate as such on several occasions, as its registration of the edicts of July 1643 and the *Déclaration* of 22 October 1648 bear witness. The *Cour des Aides*† sanctioned the forma- tion of the Syndicate by its decrees of 16 and 30 January 1643 and of 4 January 1644 'and finally by the decree of confirmation of the said Syndicate by the said Court on 15 October 1649'. The *Syndics* were often received in their own right by the king and queen, in the presence of the whole court and in full *Conseil*.[9] The Syndicate possessed its own statutes which it called the '*articles du Syndicat*'. The *compagnies* of the *élus* paid a subscription in March of each year to cover the costs of the '*Scindicat*' [*sic*] and to provide 'modest remuneration' for the officers of the Syndicate for their pains. In 1649 it was announced that correspon- dence should be addressed to M. Boyrot, '*Scindic* and Secretary of the *Scindicat* of the *Elections de France*, living in the Rue de la Tixeranderie, at the *Hôtel de la Moque*, near the Church of the Saint-Esprit in Paris.'[10]

Although the *Trésoriers généraux de France* avoided the term 'syndi- cate', their association for the defence of their professional interests was identical with that of the *élus*. It was in fact older, going back to 1599. In 1596, following the Assembly of Notables at Rouen, the king had decided upon the suppression of the *Bureaux des Finances*. The *Trésoriers* had sent deputies to Paris, who obtained the continuation of their rights in return for loans to the king. Following subsequent threats, the *Tré- soriers de France* ended by deciding to depute two of their number each year to reside at Court, with adequate allowances subscribed by their colleagues, 'so that by their organisation, we may all be able to march on the same foot, through sharing information for the preservation and honour of our *compagnies*'.[11] In fact, from 1599, the Syndicate was formed. In 1648, the representatives of the *Trésoriers* called themselves '*Messieurs les députés des Bureaux des Finances du Royaume* assembled in the *Chambre du Trésor* in Paris'. At the request of these permanent representatives, each *Bureau des Finances* maintained a deputy in Paris from the end of May 1648. It seems that only seventeen *généralités* were represented in 1648: Amiens, Bordeaux, Bourges, Caen, Chalons-sur-Marne, Dijon, Limoges, Lyons, Montpellier, Montauban, Orléans, Poitiers, Rouen, Riom, Soissons, Toulouse and Tours. Aix, Alençon, Grenoble, Metz, Moulins and Rennes were missing. In 1649, Alençon, Grenoble and Moulins also sent deputies and corresponded with the '*Assemblé de Paris*'. The latter had a secretary whose name, in September 1648, was M. le Clerc, *Trésorier de France* in Poitiers. The Assembly made payments from a common purse, and each *Bureau* paid an annual subscription of 100 *livres*, in the form of a bill of exchange, toward the expenses of the Assembly and for any extraordinary expenses involved. The Assembly communicated with the *Bureaux des Finances* by circular letters and despatches. Six members of the Assembly seem to have formed some kind of inner committee, since on the occasion when the *Trésoriers de France* were to be imprisoned because of a circular letter considered insolent by the government, six were actually imprisoned; and, again, when the Assembly had clothes made to enable their deputies to present themselves at Court 'in fitting dress', six outfits only were made. The representation of each *Bureau* in the Assembly in Paris presented no problems, since it was rare for a *Bureau* not to have one of its members in Paris on *Bureau* business.

These organisations rendered the *officiers* capable of active and effective defence of their interests; and when the *Parlement de Paris* took the initiative in offering resistance to the government in the decree of 13 May 1648, deciding upon the election of deputies by each of the four sovereign courts and their joint assembly in the *Chambre Saint-Louis* to consider the reform of the State, the *Trésoriers de France* and the *élus* joined in the undertaking. 'The *Présidents* and *Trésoriers de France* of the *Bureaux* now assembled in Paris' addressed a circular letter to the *Bureaux* in the various *généralités* on 23 May:

Our offices will be ruined and we shall be without resource if God does not inspire us with better counsels and give us more courage than we have shown hitherto. The financial affairs of the realm are despatched without our salaries being provided for, and they expect us to suffer all this with the same passivity as we showed when they reduced our salaries by a quarter. Our functions have not been restored to us and there is nothing left to us except our status stripped of all purpose and of everything which made it important before these deplorable times we now find ourselves in. In due time and place our Assembly will take such steps as are appropriate to achieve our common interest. Meanwhile it requests your opinion and your orders . . . After the constant representations we have already made, there seems little to hope for; nevertheless we are resolved to continue our efforts . . . We also entreat you to send us deputies to accompany us wherever we go, to render our complaints more telling from their presence. We ask you to send through them the most accurate information possible regarding the misconduct of the *intendants* in the financial administration, the extortions they perpetrate, as also those made by the *traitants* through their conspiracies and otherwise.

Seventeen of the *bureaux* responded to this appeal in June and July.

The circular letter created a great stir. 'Certain of the provincial *intendants* in company with the *traitants* and *partisans*'† denounced the *Trésoriers de France* to the *Conseil*. The *Conseil* had six of the *Trésoriers* imprisoned. The *Trésoriers* appealed to the *Parlement*. On 13 June 1648 delegates from the *Parlement* were received by the queen at the Palais-Royal. She was accompanied by the Duc d'Orléans, Mazarin, Séguier, the *Surintendant*, Chavigny, Guénégaud, and Le Tellier, the Secretary of State. The Chancellor, Séguier, declared that the circular of the *Trésoriers de France* had had a decisive influence in inducing the enemy to appear on the frontier to 'sound out the affections of the people and to discover whether the reports they had of division in the country were in fact true'. In spite of this, however, the *Cours souveraines* pursued their efforts. On 30 June their deputies assembled in the *Chambre Saint-Louis* and proposed the dismissal of all *intendants* and the annulling of all other unauthorised *commissions*. They also proposed the annulling of the schedule of the *tailles* and their lowering by a quarter, an amount which they thought was less than the profit taken by the *traitants*. Finally, they proposed the reinstatement of the regular *officiers* in the exercise of their offices, that is the *Trésoriers de France*, the *élus*, the *receveurs-généraux*† and the *receveurs-particuliers*†. These proposals were transformed into a decree of the *Parlement de Paris* on 4 July. The Court attempted to resist this. The Advocate-General, Omer Talon, represented to the *Parlement de Paris* the entire impossibility of foregoing the use of *intendants* and *traitants*; and the Chancellor did likewise to deputies from the four sovereign companies in discussions held at the Palais d'Orléans on 8 and 10 July. But the *Trésoriers de France* immediately 'offered to see that the *taille* was paid so promptly that the king would have four millions a month in his coffers, without in any way seeking the restoration of their past wages, nor even the enjoyment of them for the current year.' The *Parlement* therefore persisted. Some of its members, indeed, had certain *Trésoriers de France* in their patronage;

one such was M. Menardeau, *Conseiller* in the *Grand'Chambre* of the *Parlement*. A certain *Trésorier de France* at Moulins, by the name of Viallet, had been his 'clerk and servant' and was indebted to him 'for a considerable sum', lent to him 'to buy his office of *Trésorier de France*'. This same Viallet, together with two other *Trésoriers*, Du Buisson and De Vilaines, had been appealing to the *Parlement* since 1647 against orders issued by the *intendant* Phélypeaux, in spite of decrees of the *Conseil*.[12] At Grenoble, the *Parlement* of the Dauphiné were in open collusion with the *Trésoriers de France*: 'the *Messieurs* of the *Parlement* have admitted deputies of the *Chambre des Comptes* and the *Bureau des Finances* to confer with their own *commissaires*.'[13]

In face of this opposition, the Court was forced to yield. On 9 July, the *Surintendant des Finances*, Particelli d'Emery, was dismissed and replaced by Maréchal de la Meilleraye. A series of royal *Déclarations* on 1, 13 and 18 July 1648 were registered by the *Parlement*, transforming the requests of the *Chambre Saint-Louis* into edicts. *Intendants* were retained only in Languedoc, Burgundy, Provence, Lyonnais, Picardy and Champagne, on condition that they did not concern themselves with either the apportionment or the levying of public taxes, or indeed with anything other than military affairs. The six *Trésoriers* who had been imprisoned were released with honour. This triumph was confirmed, thanks to the Parisian Barricades of 26, 27 and 28 August, by the Resolution of 22 October 1648.[14]

The delight of the *Trésoriers de France* and the *élus* was unlimited. It was accompanied by a similar delight on the part of the ordinary people, since the *officiers* had aroused a widespread hope that with the suppression of the *intendants* the *tailles*, the 'scourge of the provinces', would no longer be raised with the aid of cavalry and that there would be peace. There was even a conviction in many places that a general remission of taxes was imminent. Du Perron, *Procureur du Roi*, in the *Présidial* at Alençon, told Séguier on 30 July 1648 that

> the excitement of the people has reached such a pitch that they assemble in the streets beating a drum and carrying effigies with seditious placards on them, which they promptly burn. Any resistance I am able to show them has not gained the support of the judges. There is even a *Trésorier de France*, named La Cointe, who has been so bold as to distribute casks of wine to the most seditious among the people and to have a great fire lit at his door and to have a May tree planted there; and the *curé* of Alençon, a person of very little sense, has had all the bells rung from morning till night, in spite of the remonstrances I have made to him to desist.[15]

The problem for the *Trésoriers* was to replace the *intendants* and the *traitants*, in order to convince the government of the inutility of the *financiers* and the *commissaires* and of the benefits of administration by means of ordinary *officiers*. The new *Surintendant*, de la Meilleraye, was well disposed toward the *Trésoriers de France*, through the influence of 'Monsieur Frotté'. The Assembly in Paris became a kind of concealed *Conseil des Finances*. Its members were received at the *Conseil de Direction des Finances*, and they formulated their own proposals there.[16] They were in daily contact with the *intendants des finances* and the *Surintendant*, and acted as intermediaries between them and the *Bureaux des Finances*. They supervised the acts of the government and the conformity of its decisions with the *Déclarations* of 22 October 1648 and of March 1649. They transmitted the orders and wishes of the *Surintendant* to the *Trésoriers de France*. They urged them to perform their duties with every diligence, since this was the sole condition on which they retained their function. They gathered information for the *Conseil*, drew up the accounts of the *tailles*, the *subsistances*† and the other taxes for the years 1647 and 1648, together with the schedules of tax arrears for the years 1644, 1645, and 1646 and abstracts of payments made into the Treasury by the various *Bureaux des Finances*.

The *Bureaux* in the provinces entered into the spirit of their *Conseil syndical*. The *Bureau* at Limoges, in September 1648, promised to act

> with every vigour in carrying out the orders you have received from the *Surintendant* (which you have already informed us of) through M. Frotté, who is a valuable ally to us in respect of the *Surintendant*. We also promise to speed up the collection of taxes and to see to it that the taxpayers pay promptly, so that His Majesty will be able to do without *traitants*, who take, through the payments made to them, what is clearly the king's money and the people's sustenance, and thereby place the state in a situation of great necessity.

On 6 September, the *Bureau* at Montauban wrote: 'we will faithfully and diligently fulfil everything relating to our duties in such a way that *intendants* will no longer be thought about. They, indeed, are no longer in fashion.' Lyons, Montpellier, Amiens and Tours expressed themselves in the same way.

Meanwhile the powers of the *Trésoriers de France* were considerably increased. The powers previously granted to the *intendants* by the regulation of 22 August 1642 and the *Déclaration* of April 1643 were transferred to the *Bureaux des Finances*, who also received some of the powers granted to the *intendants* by their *commissions* and the decrees of the *Conseil*. The *Bureaux des Finances* became therefore in a sense collective *intendants*. These collective *intendants*, in the same way as the former *intendants de provinces*, chose *Trésoriers de France* to receive *commissions* from the king for particular missions, but they elected these from among their own number. The *Bureaux des Finances* began by restoring the traditional financial administration. They 'went out' into the *élections* 'to bring the people to reason' and, in place of the agents of the *traitants*, they restored the ordinary *receveurs* who had previously been important in the financial management. They confirmed others in their functions and gave authority to nominees of the owners of offices involved in the collection of taxes, when their owners did not exercise the function of the office themselves. They forwarded all funds to Paris without delay when they became available. On the instructions of the *Surintendant*, they refused permission to anyone to draw on the tax funds for purposes of local expenditure, or to issue anything whatsoever to anyone even on presentation of receipts from the Treasury. They went out into the *élections* to audit the accounts of the *recettes particulières* and arrange for the dispatch of funds to the *recette générale* and from there to the central Treasury. They made preparations for the future collection of taxes and to that end visited the *élections* to preside over the apportionment of the *tailles* and *subsistances*. In letters from the king in 1649 and 1650, they were granted functions which had previously been delegated to the *intendants*, namely the administration and control of troops and the supply of military depots. They worked in the actual localities, to expedite the collection of the taxes. They advised the *Conseil* of the condition of their *généralité* and, like the *intendants* it seems, they provided information about everything of importance affecting the king which was happening in the province.

And they achieved results. At the end of October 1648, the *Bureau des Finances* at Montauban wrote: 'the people are beginning to pay their taxes, and . . . in four or five days, by the first coach, we shall make up a consignment for the Treasury . . .' On 26 September, the *Bureau* at Orléans wrote: 'it is with the utmost pleasure that we learn from your dispatch of the satisfaction which M. *le Maréchal* feels about the important services which the majority of this *Bureau* have rendered His Majesty.' From Champagne, on 18 January 1650, the *Trésoriers* noted: 'you will learn from the statement of accounts we send you that your *receveurs-généraux*† have these last three years, as a result of our efforts, raised the sum of 3,300,000 *livres*, without making any charge against the funds and without use of force, although two very large armies have passed through and stayed in three of the principal *élections* of this province during the course of this past year.' On 13 August 1653, Caen gloried in the fact that it had 'caused the taxes of our *généralité* to enter the king's coffers without any arrears since the *intendants* were suppressed'.

At the same time, the Assembly in Paris undertook to raise the prestige of the *Bureaux des Finances*. In August 1649 it decided to go to audiences which were accorded to it in the 'long robe', in the manner of the sovereign courts, and it urged the members of every *Bureau des Finances* to hold their sessions and attend official functions in the same dress. The *Trésoriers* acclaimed the idea. In processions and public ceremonies, they were the only ones in the 'short robe, cap and hood' and they lost prestige because of it. The *Bureau* at Chalons expressed the feelings of the *Trésoriers* very well. It was a question, they said, of

> restoring our previous habit of dress at the same time as we restore our proper function, both when we form a deputation and in our *Bureaux*. This is a convenient way of distinguishing ourselves from the common run of men and of gaining the respect of the vulgar, who have the habit of solely judging from appearances, as also of rendering our own respects to men more worthy than we are. The foremost rank we hold in the provinces and the importance of the king's affairs which we handle justify indeed our maintaining a certain degree of cere-mony . . . We must in future conform to the customs of the *Com-pagnies souveraines* to whose body we belong, and participate in all their formalities, in order to be indistinguishable from them.

In October 1649, the *Conseil syndical* approved a '*Collection*' of the 'privileges belonging to *Messieurs les Trésoriers généraux de France*' com-piled by M. le Gorlier, *Trésorier de France* at Chalons, and at the end of 1649 sent twelve printed copies of the index of it to each *Bureau* to enable them to point out any omissions. Several in fact did so, sending in a note of certain decrees of the *Conseil* and other resolutions in favour of the *Trésoriers de France*, after research into their own records and archives. At the end of 1650, the work was ready. One thousand *livres* were needed to cover the cost of its printing, and each *Bureau* was asked to contribute fifty *livres* each.

The *Conseil syndical* undertook to compile the names, ranks and coats of arms of the *Trésoriers de France*, to prove that their *compagnies* con-tained as many *gentilshommes* as the *Cours souveraines*, and even con-ceived 'the idea of displaying our escutcheons. We believe that they would confer the first degree of nobility for those who did not possess this title by birth. We believe that you would oblige a great many by addressing them by this title of honour, which is closely related to that of the members of the *Cours souveraines*, since we are deemed to be of their number.'

Finally, the Assembly of Paris looked to the maintenance of the status of the *Trésoriers* in all ceremonial. The *Trésoriers* were to conduct them-selves in every way like the members of the *Cours souveraines*. For example, they must not kneel before the king. On 3 January 1651 the *Bureau* at Tours protested that 'the shameful reproach which you have levelled against certain *Bureaux*, that they have greeted the king in an unfitting posture, not in keeping with the status of their offices, does not apply to us in any way whatsoever . . . since we have had the honour of greeting their Majesties standing up and in the same fashion as the sovereign courts.'

Thus, on every count, the *Trésoriers de France*, on the insistence of their Syndicate, made a very considerable effort to sustain their interests. Nevertheless, the monarchy never renounced the use of *intendants* and *traitants*. The period of the Fronde was only a sequence of constant attempts on the part of the Court to restore the *financiers* and *intendants*, with all their previous powers. In spite of all the efforts made by the *Trésoriers*, the government was still convinced that it had to have recourse to the good offices of the tax-farmers. Throughout the Fronde, they are to be found in operation wherever the king was master. The government practised the extremely harmful procedure, frequently resorted to in time of great financial difficulty, of assigning predetermined revenues to predetermined expenditures. In 1648 the *généralité* of Montauban had been assessed to provide taxes sufficient to cover the expenditure of the king's household. In August of that year, the *Trésoriers de l'Epargne* had negotiated terms with certain tax-farmers for the actual levying of this amount, and accordingly, on 15 August, the *Surintendant*, de la Meilleraye, ordered the *Trésoriers* at Montauban to suspend their restoration of the ordinary *receveurs* in their posts and to maintain or restore instead the agents of the *traitants*. The latter indeed continued to operate to some extent everywhere. But if they were to be really effective they needed *commissaires*, and they never ceased to work to that end in the *Conseil*, decrying the *officiers de finances* and urging the restoration of the *intendants*.

In the seventeen *généralités* where they had been suppressed, the government strove to restore the *intendants* under various designations, after the *Fronde parlementaire* ended with the Treaty of Rueil in April 1649 and the war restarted in Flanders with the siege of Cambrai ending in June. It continued to restore them during the disturbances of the *Fronde des Princes* from August 1649 to January 1650, and again following the arrest of the Princes in January 1650; and then, during 1650, when the capture of Bordeaux from the rebels in October and the victory of Rethel over the Spaniards in December showed the government holding its own over its enemies on all fronts, it continued in its policy until the coalition of the two Frondes forced Mazarin into exile in February 1651.

From June 1649, the rumour circulated that the *Conseil du Roi* was preparing to send *maîtres des requêtes*† on circuit in the provinces. The news aroused considerable concern among the *Trésoriers de France*: 'the news that *maîtres des requêtes* are to be sent out has doubtlessly alarmed all *officiers* and the people in general, since they fear that the said *maîtres des requêtes* will take it upon themselves to perform the same functions as the *intendants* previously did, whose name will for ever be hated, both to this present age and to all posterity . . . We have no power however to resist them, since the *Ordonnances* permit them to make their *chevauchées*† in the provinces.' The Syndicate advised the *Trésoriers* to refuse the *maîtres des requêtes* access to their papers, in order to reduce them to entire impotence. But what was there really to be done if 'they came armed with writs against our registrars and seized them like wildfire'. Although *lettres de cachet* in the name of the king despatched to every *Bureau des Finances*, notifying the name of the *maître des requêtes* appointed to each *généralité*, declared specifically that the *maîtres des requêtes* would under no circumstances meddle with the functions of the *officiers*, but would simply enquire into abuses, acts of violence, extortionate taxes and contraventions of the decrees of the *Conseil* and prepare reports concerning the same for forwarding to Chancellor Séguier for decision, it meant nothing, since at the same time it was made entirely clear that the *Trésoriers* would be required 'to give an account to the said *maîtres des requêtes* making the said visits of everything concerning our service and the prompt payment of our taxes'. Members of the various *Bureaux des Finances* were however by no means reassured. The *Trésoriers* at Montauban decided to have no dealings with the *maîtres des requêtes* and to take every care that they had nothing to do with matters involving either the royal domain or the taxes. The *Parlement* at Toulouse issued a decree against these agents of the *Conseil*. The *Bureau des Finances* at Poitiers promised to refuse should the *maîtres des requêtes* try to appoint one of their own number as a clerk. In face of this opposition and following representations from the Assembly of the *Trésoriers* in Paris, the government announced in November 1649 that it renounced its policy of sending out *maîtres des requêtes* into the provinces.

Even so, they were to be found in the provinces after that date. At Bourges, in December, a certain Pinon was appointed, regarding whom the *Trésoriers* protested that they owed no one an account of themselves except the king in his *Conseil* and 'principally to *Nosseigneurs des Finances*, who are our real and legitimate superiors'. Nevertheless, they knew full well that if they refused to give an account of themselves to the said Pinon, he would merely obtain a decree from the *Conseil* requiring them to obey. A *maître des requêtes* by the name of Gaulmin is to be found at Moulins in 1649 and 1650. He gives himself the title of '*Envoyé par le Roi*' in Bourbonnais, but in fact acts as an *intendant*. Other *maîtres des requêtes* act at the same time as *intendants de justice, police et finances* with the king's army stationed in the provinces, as was the case with La Margrie in Normandy. Again, on 3 May 1650, a *maître des requêtes* named Moran arrives in Montauban. The *Trésoriers* refuse to meet him, because the terms of his *lettre de cachet* signified that he was 'some kind of *intendant*'. The *Parlement* at Bordeaux and the *Cour des Aides* at Cahors were also determined upon a policy of resistance.

All the *Bureaux des Finances* discovered that the obligation to render an account of themselves to the *maîtres des requêtes* 'greatly exceeds the authority given to the *maîtres des requêtes* by the *Ordonnances*'. Even so, the government constantly sought to extend the powers of the *maîtres des requêtes* in the provinces. For example, the *Conseil* decided to address everything relating to the administration and control of troops to Gaulmin, 'whence it must be inferred that the *maîtres des requêtes* are now so many *intendants* in the *généralités*, who, although they do not take on their rank, nevertheless usurp their authority.' A regulation of 8 October 1650 attributes to the *maîtres des requêtes* important financial functions relating to army depots and garrisons, which, since the suppression of the *intendants*, had been performed by the *Trésoriers de France*.

The government also used *Conseillers d'Etat*†, or '*Intendants des Finances*', in several places during 1650 as direct superiors to the *Trésoriers de France*. In August and September 1650, we find the *Conseiller d'Etat* de Bezon in the *généralité* of Bourges. He had been despatched by Le Tellier, the Secretary of State for War (who had the reputation of being opposed to the *Trésoriers*), to deal with matters affecting the army and the victualling of troops, in place of the *Bureau des Finances*. In January 1650, Foullé, a *maître des requêtes* and *intendant des finances*, arrives in Limoges and is immediately accused of 'having this *généralité* under his direction'. Foullé attempted to work with the *Trésoriers de France*, apportioning the *tailles* with them as the *intendants* had. The response of the *Trésoriers* was immediate: 'as *intendant des finances* he claims to have the right to preside over us and do everything in association with the *Bureau*; to which we reply, *Messieurs*, that the function of *Messieurs* the *intendants des finances* is solely in the *Conseil* . . . and that in so far as he fulfils the office of *maître des requêtes* he has the right to make his tour of inspection of this *généralité*, which falls within his competence, but not in any way to carry out our function.' Foullé threatens and abuses them, and actually promulgates an *ordonnance* which he has proposed to the *Trésoriers*, but which they have in fact refused, by putting their names to it as if they had actually signed it, and thus employing a sort of procedure by *lit de justice*†. Foullé billets troops with several of the *Trésoriers* and places a garrison with the chief clerk of the *Bureau*, suspending the *Bureau* and administering the finances in its stead, investing it with a regiment of cavalry and indeed threatening to carry off several of the *Trésoriers*. Certain Treasury officials, however, are more discreet in their behaviour on being sent as *contrôleurs-généraux des finances* into the *généralités*. They establish their own clerks, and undertake the audit of the accounts and registers of the *receveurs* in place of the *Trésoriers*. Two separate decrees of the *Conseil*, of 27 September and 12 October 1650, gave power to these *commissaires* to take charge of funds in the hands of the *receveurs* and have them despatched to the Treasury. Finally, the government also used *officiers* from the *Cour des Aides* as *commissaires*. The *premier président†* of the *Cour des Aides* at Cahors undertook the examination of the accounts of the *receveurs* for the *généralité* of Montauban in July 1649: 'he undertakes our functions and introduces a kind of *intendance* here . . . This is a device on the part of the tax-farmers to restore things to their previous confusion.'

In the frontier provinces, the government tried to extend the powers of the *intendants d'armée* to the point where they too became virtually provincial *intendants*. In 1650, in Champagne, a certain Pagès fulfilled the role at one and the same time of *intendant de justice, police et finances* with the army and that of *maître des requêtes* on tour in the province, which gave him the right of surveillance over all the *officiers*. He was also general *commissaire* for the provisioning of troops, and this enabled him to deal with matters affecting army supplies in place of the *Trésoriers de France*, and in addition he reviewed troops, ordered supplies, audited expenditure and issued warrants for payment. Pagès wished to levy a special tax based proportionally on the *tailles* to defray the costs of the army depots. To this end, he asked the *Trésoriers* for their records giving details of assessments for the *tailles*, but they refused. Access to their records, they said, was the prerogative of an *intendant*, and Pagès did not possess a *commission* registered by the *Parlement*. Pagès accordingly had troops billeted on three villages of which three of the *Trésoriers* were the *seigneurs*. He obtained a decree of the *Conseil* which specifically excluded the *Trésoriers* from taking cognizance of matters relating to army depots, and a letter of support from the Secretary of State requiring the *Trésoriers* to assist him in his work as *intendant d'armée*. But, at the same time, the *Conseil* continued to send orders concerning army supplies to the *Trésoriers de France*, and they persisted in dealing with them. The conflict continued. In Picardy, *le sieur* Garin, playing the role of *intendant*, levied forage taxes by *lettre de cachet*, which was contrary to the king's *Déclaration* abolishing the *intendants*. The *Trésoriers* stopped the levying of the taxes by an *ordonnance* and lodged an appeal with the *Parlement*, in spite of the obvious displeasure of the *Conseil*. The *Conseil*, however, refused to recognise the competence of the *Parlement* in this matter, or indeed the authority of judges over the *commissaires*. It had never intended to have the *commissions* of the *intendants d'armée* registered by the *Parlement*, in the six reserved provinces. Hence the constant conflict with the *Trésoriers de France*, who in matters of finance proclaimed themselves '*intendants*', with complete powers.

Nevertheless, the government was obliged to climb down in 1651 and 1652, in face of the general war which broke out from February 1651, the exile of Mazarin and the necessity the queen found herself in of

H

negotiating with the Frondeurs and indeed confirming the dismissal of Mazarin. At the end of 1651, the *Conseil* was forced to prohibit all persons from assuming the role of *intendant* in the provinces without a *commission* registered by the *Parlements*. When, after 16 January 1652, the *Parlements* of Paris and Rouen issued decrees prohibiting *maîtres des requêtes* from assuming any aspect of the powers of an *intendant*, the *Conseil* had yet again to rein them in. For example, on 3 February 1652 the *Trésoriers* at Limoges complained of the conduct of a certain *maître des requêtes*, Baltazard, who, they claimed, had scarcely entered the *généralité* when he imprisoned the *receveur* of the *élection*, De Bellac, and set about appointing a *contrôleur* in his place. He had installed a garrison of troops in the tax office, had had the safes opened and had sought to dictate orders to the *Trésoriers de France*. The *Trésoriers* sent a deputation to the *Conseil du Roi*, which happened to be visiting Poitiers at that time, and on 4 February the *Surintendant*, de la Vieuville, sent a fine sermon to 'Monsieur Baltazard, *intendant* in the *généralité* of Poiters – remember what has been said to you; you must in no way undertake the functions of an *intendant des finances*; all you have to do is to see that the normal *officiers* carry out the decrees of the *Conseil* and the orders of the king, and live on good terms with them.' Even so, in November 1652, it seems that officials from the Treasury had once again stayed as *commissaires* in the *généralités*.

But the weariness of everyone, together with the return of the king to Paris on 21 October 1652, followed by that of Mazarin in February 1653, and the progressive ending of the troubles, which became general from the fall of Bordeaux on 3 August 1653, restored a certain liberty of action to the government. At the beginning of August 1653, the sending of *maîtres des requêtes* into the *généralités* is again spoken of. Naturally, it was said that it was simply a matter of their making their *chevauchées*, in accordance with the *Déclaration* of July 1648 and without their being provided with sealed *commissions*. The *Trésoriers de France* however were under no illusions. They knew full well that the *maîtres des requêtes* would come charged with instructions signed by the principal members of the *Conseil*, and that they would usurp all their own functions and issue financial *ordonnances* 'in pursuit of the wishes and at the instigation of the tax-farmers'. The *Trésoriers* at Moulins proposed offering the king money to avoid the sending of *maîtres des requêtes*. The *Conseil syndical* stepped up its approaches to ministers, but they in turn stressed the vital importance of the 'prompt collection and expediting of the taxes'. On 27 August it was announced that the *Conseiller d'Etat*, Miromesnil, would be coming to Rouen as a *commissaire* to deal with the apportionment of the '*subsistances*', as *intendants* had in the past. On 5 September 1653, the *Bureau des Finances* at Tours announced that Monsieur d'Hure, '*intendant* for this *généralité*' would arrive 'in a few days' time':

And that he has an order from the *Conseil* to put in the hands of our Registrar, on arrival, the decrees and *commissions* he has been given for the levying of what this *généralité* must contribute toward the 5,200,000 *livres* which the king takes in advance for the year 1654 and of the 3,800,000 *livres* to be raised during the next winter quarter; together with an order notifying us to meet in extraordinary session on the same day or at the very latest on the following day, to arrange for the registration of the same and to give our approval, concerning which he has to make a report, so that, in the event of our refusal or our causing delay, he may himself proceed to levy the taxes and apportion them among the various *élections* without our approval.

This was a return indeed to the regulation of 22 August 1642 and the *Déclaration* of 16 April 1643, which had substituted the authority of the *intendant* in financial matters for that of the *officiers*.[17] This letter is in fact the last of the collection. The *Trésoriers de France* were defeated. Little by little, the *intendants* were to be restored in all the *généralités* and to have all their previous powers re-confirmed.

II

The *Trésoriers de France* were defeated for various reasons. In the first place they were in a false situation. They created opposition and took part in the disturbances of the period. They contributed to the start of the revolt and assisted the rebels very considerably in an indirect way, by denying the government its principal means for action, the *intendants*, and by limiting the activity of other *commissaires*, notably that of the *maîtres des requêtes en chevauchée*. They thereby attracted the hostility of the government toward themselves and aroused its desire for revenge. The king and his *Conseil* could not rest easy on the humiliation which had been inflicted on the royal authority. They were almost forced to destroy the initiative of the *Trésoriers* as soon as circumstances permitted. It was regrettable for the *Trésoriers* that they associated their own movement for reform with a general movement for revolt.

Yet, in the event, it seems unlikely that they took an active part in the revolution when it came. There is some debate on this point. Their correspondence deals essentially with syndicate business and they had nothing to write to their deputies about other than professional matters. There are, however, large gaps in this correspondence. From 20 August to 26 December 1650, and from 24 April to 8 November 1652, some fifty-nine letters are missing. Was the disappearance entirely due to chance, or were these letters in some way compromising? Other texts suggest that in certain instances at least they used their dual authority as *officiers* of the king and as *seigneurs* to urge on peasants and townspeople. Even so, in the present state of our knowledge, it does not appear that they wished to create a revolution or really to participate directly in the armed revolts. The *Trésoriers de France* seek to serve the king in spite of himself. They wish to manage the provincial finances – they themselves, and no one else in their stead. In fact, to justify their opposition on the financial front they actually performed their functions with greater care. They therefore benefited from the attempted revolution, without making the revolution themselves; and they thereby aroused in the king and his followers a rancour which could not be expiated and a reaction against themselves, without it would seem really attempting to enforce their own wishes.

The *Trésoriers généraux de France* were unsuccessful in their attempts to convince the government that it could do without tax-farmers, and this enforced a return to the use of *intendants*. The *Trésoriers* had the unwisdom to attack persons who had successfully attracted the support of a good many courtiers for their financial enterprises. The tax-farmers, such as Catelan, Tabouret, Lefèbvre and de la Rallière, all had connections with Guillaume Bautru, Comte de Séran; with François Rochechouart, the Chevalier de Jars; with François Annibal, the Maréchal Duc d'Estrées; with Duc Henri de Senneterre, or with his son, the Maréchal de la Ferté-Senneterre, and with still others, who all shared an interest in advancing credit to the king. A number of members of the *Parlement de Paris* involved in the revolt were also thought to be in the same situation.[18]

Very importantly, the *Trésoriers* could not or would not, supply the needs of the state. Members of the *Conseil* levelled many accusations at them. We find among Séguier's papers a curious 'summary of the abuses and malversations committed in the *généralité* of Soissons in levying the king's taxes and other matters important to his service', drawn up in 1651.[19] It gives a good sample of these accusations. The *Bureau des Finances* at Soissons is taken as an example of what all the *Trésoriers* in the realm have perpetrated. 'They have set themselves against all the good intentions of those who have been sent into the *généralités* in the king's service to raise revenues for the supply of his armies . . .' They are accused of treating the decrees of the *Conseil du Roi* with contempt. They have levied some 300,000 *livres* for the supply of the army, when the decree of 21 January only states 220,000. They have tampered with the apportionment of the taxes, reducing the share of La Ferté Milon from 6000 to 4500 *livres* and raising that of Montmirail from 2000 to 2400. They have refused to implement the decree of 28 February, to send orders for the various *communautés* to pay what had been assessed upon them. Troops have therefore had to live freely on the peasants and have thereby brought ruin to several villages. By an *ordonnance* of 16 April, 'they have allowed the inhabitants of certain small towns and villages to assemble at the sound of the tocsin and the ringing of the bell, with the intention of attacking *le sieur* Gombauld, who supported the king's interest in the *généralité*, as also the said troops.' The *Trésoriers* and *élus* are accused of reducing the *taille* in the parishes where they themselves have farms. One such parish pays 500 *livres*, whereas it, or a comparable parish, ought to pay some 2000 to 2500 *livres*. They make abusive use of writs by the *receveurs particuliers* and of the powers of constraint exercised by the *prévôts des maréchaux*† and the constables. 'Disorder is greater than ever in the raising of the taxes, although they have had the entire control of it over these past three years.'

Shall we ever know the truth about the accusations exchanged between the *commissaires* and the *Trésoriers généraux de France*? If we took the statements of the above text at their face value, we might very well conclude that the *Trésoriers de France* showed great zeal in using writs of constraint and in changing the apportionment of the taxes imposed by the *Conseil*, from their closer knowledge of local situations. Was the *Conseil* really in good faith in attempting to saddle them with responsibility for the disorders of the tax system at a time of general civil war? On the other hand, however, it will be said that when the taxes for the supply of the troops seemed to exceed the capacity of the taxpayers, the *Trésoriers* sought to protect them, even to the extent of authorising revolt; and that they did this as landowners and sometimes as *seigneurs* who had common interests with all the inhabitants of a province, since the excessive amount of royal taxation must have reduced rents and compromised the raising of seigneurial dues. It was precisely their local interest which the king could not tolerate.

It is however by no means certain that in authorising resistance to the *commissaires* and royal troops the *Trésoriers* did not have the greater interest of the king in view. The following from the same text suggests that in fact they may have been safeguarding the royal authority in a very particular situation:

It seems that the king's protection is not enough to defend his subjects and guarantee them from oppression by troops. Certain whole villages in the Soissonais, belonging to ecclesiastics, have sought the protection of *gentilshommes* and *seigneurs* and vow themselves to their service and break their vows of service to their legitimate *seigneurs* . . . the inhabitants of these villages all submit themselves voluntarily to the payment of a *banalité* for the use of the mill of the said *gentilhomme* or *seigneur*. Others obligate themselves for their houses by means of a land rent; and by various other means they are forced to obligate themselves in perpetuity to a shameful servitude, simply to seek an unusual protection which masks the true situation in a disordered state.

This important text receives indirect confirmation from one of the articles of the regulation for the levying of the *tailles* for the year 1642, of 27 November 1641: 'and, moreover, there are still to be found certain of the said parishes under the protection or favour of certain ecclesiastics, *gentilshommes, seigneurs de paroisses, officiers* or other influential persons, whose inhabitants find refuge and retreat in their houses and châteaux, moving their possessions and cattle there and do not suffer the bailiffs and servers of writs of constraint to seek them out.'[20] To read such texts, one would think oneself back in the high Middle Ages.

In this type of society, civil war brought back the social processes of the ninth and tenth centuries, of the period of the Norman, Magyar and Muslim invasions, with 'commendations' becoming general, with the seigneurial regime extending and conditions arising which were indeed suitable for a revival of the feudal system. It was just possible to glimpse the potential ruin of the monarchy's work in restoring the State. In this situation, it might be that the *Trésoriers de France* were striving to preserve the royal authority in giving villagers the protection of the king's *officiers* against military personnel. Or was it that, as owners of their offices and possessing the means of transmitting them to their heirs, the *Trésoriers* were merely acting as *seigneurs*, prepared to use their public offices as a simple form of private property, in order to render them finally and unquestionably hereditary? Did they seek to make themselves no more than the equivalent of the counts and dukes of the later Carolingian and early Capetian periods, vassals of a king-suzerain?

Whatever the intentions of the *Trésoriers*, however, the most urgent consideration was to ensure the supplying of the army, and, in this respect, the author of the report concludes that the *officiers* were 'unnecessary to the State'. He goes on to assert that 'in face of all these disorders', the 'people begin to taste the need for *intendants* in the provinces, and that by comparing past times with the present, the wisest of them consider that a province is without a soul if it is deprived of a *gouverneur* or an *intendant*.' That at least was the opinion of those about the king.

Moreover, the *Trésoriers* and *élus* were evidently unable to undertake the role of tax-farmers and become the king's creditors, able to mobilise the very large sums that were necessary. We lack a study of their fortunes, their sources of income and the use they made of their capital. But it is certain that the *Trésoriers de France* were no longer the substantial persons they had been in the sixteenth century, before the institution of the *Bureaux des Finances* in 1577. They had become regional *officiers*, very much concerned with their own salaries, their privileges and the preservation of their offices. It was these concerns which placed them at the mercy of the government and prevented them from carrying their opposition too far. Indeed, the *Trésoriers* complain constantly of the 'retrenchments made in their salaries', that is to say stoppages in their pay. In 1652, their complaints increased in bitterness, as they constantly found themselves worse treated than members of the sovereign courts, the *Parlements*, the *Chambres des Comptes* and the *Cours des Aides*, worse even than the *Présidaux*†, in spite of the fact that the edicts recognised their status as members of the 'corporations of the *Cours souveraines*'. It was an insupportable loss of social prestige for them to find themselves reduced 'to the rank of the ordinary *officiers* of the *élections* and commonplace clerks'. In 1653, there was renewed alarm and there were renewed representations.

The dependence of the *Trésoriers de France* on the government appears again, however, in regard to the *annuel*, or *paulette*. This was the insurance premium instituted in 1604 which permitted *officiers* to be certain that in the event of sudden death their office or its value would remain in their family. The *droit annuel* was renewed every nine years. In this way, the king controlled the *officiers* through the threat of its not being renewed. Each renewal gave rise to endless discussion on the financial conditions to be imposed.[21] At the end of 1648, after many changes, the *Déclaration* of 13 March of that year renewing the *droit annuel* for nine years began to be put into effect. The *Trésoriers de France* were granted a dispensation, as in the case of the sovereign courts, from making a forced loan to the king in return for the right to pay the premium. They complained however about the increased rate of premium, which rose from 275 to 500 *livres* and was equivalent to the single quarter of their salary which the king had still left them. They protested against being obliged by the Treasurer of the *Parties casuelles*† to pay the *droit annuel* for all the past years since and including 1648, when they only wanted it for a single year. Half the *Trésoriers de France*, it was said, preferred in the circumstances not to pay the premium, but to run a calculated risk instead. Their *Conseil syndical* was subsequently successful in their request that the *Trésoriers* who wanted to have the *annuel* for 1650 should only pay it for 1649 and 1650, and not for 1648; and that those who wished to begin paying the *annuel* in future, no matter for which year, should pay only two consecutive years and not all the years that had passed since and including 1648, and after that they should only have to pay currently.

But perhaps most important in the failure of the *Trésoriers* was the fact that the *officiers*' opposition to the king was divided within itself. A serious conflict existed between the *Cours des Aides* and the *élus* on the one hand and the *Trésoriers de France* on the other, and the last were not always on very cordial terms with the *Chambres des Comptes* and the *Parlements*. The *Trésoriers* in Dijon reflected this when they wrote to their deputies in Paris that the *Parlements*, the *Chambres des Comptes*, the *Cours des Aides*, the *élus* and the *maire* and *échevins* had rendered the functions of the *Trésoriers* entirely illusory and they had therefore initiated proceedings against them all.

Scarcely had the *officiers* succeeded in bringing the government to capitulation in 1648 than they became divided among themselves in victory. The *Trésoriers* claimed that they were the heirs and successors of the small group of four *Trésoriers de France* and four *Généraux de Finances*, who, in company with the king, had administered the royal finances before the reforms of Francis I. The decision of 1552 had increased the number of *Trésoriers généraux* and had sent them to reside in the provinces, one in the principal town of each *généralité*; and that of 1577 had increased their number to five in each *Bureau* and had imposed on them the obligation to act corporately. While all this had reduced their importance to that of simple agents of the *Conseil* acting in the provinces, nevertheless, in their opinion, it had preserved to them the same honours and the same regional authority which the ancient *Trésoriers de France* and the ancient *Généraux de Finances* had enjoyed. In this, the *Trésoriers généraux de France* considered themselves entirely superior to the *élus*. The latter, they thought, owed them respect and obedience 'for their salaries and privileges and for everything relating to the business and control of the royal finances'. The *élus* were therefore required to execute the *ordonnances* of the *Trésoriers* aimed at expediting the raising of the king's taxes; they claimed that it was the function of the *Trésoriers de France* to preside over the 'establishment of the rates and apportionment of the *tailles* and *subsistances* in all the *élections* and *généralités* of the realm'.[22]

The *élus*, conversely, had never been able, for their part, to resign themselves to the establishment of the *Trésoriers de France* and the *Généraux de Finances* in the *généralités*. They saw the creation of a class of regional financial administrators between themselves and the *Conseil du Roi* as a reduction of their own importance, and they took advantage of the troubles to attempt a reversal of the policy. First, they denied that, in spite of their name, the *Trésoriers de France* could be accepted as identical with the ancient *Trésoriers de France* and the *Généraux de Finances*.

> Regarding the said *Trésoriers*, they are nothing more than provincial *officiers* and cannot lay claim to the title of *Généraux* which the former *Généraux de Finances* possessed. The latter were established as four only for the whole realm, to act as the sovereign officers for the authorisation of all payments, which is now the prerogative of *nosseigneurs les surintendants directeurs et intendants*. Now that their power is restricted to a particular province, however, and their principal function consists solely in serving as minor *commis* of our aforesaid *seigneurs*

in one province only, and now that they are increased in number to up to twenty in each *Bureau*, there is no longer any semblance of truth whatever in calling their function general. In fact, it is merely provincial and particular.

The *élus* accuse the *Trésoriers* of desiring ever since 1635 to increase their powers in order to compensate themselves for their increase in number. They also accuse them of abusing the precedent created by their having assisted in the apportionment of the *tailles* in certain of the *élections* over the past ten or twelve years. In this, they claimed, the *Trésoriers* had merely been acting as agents in the service of the *intendants*. They declared that the *Ordonnances* did not entitle the *Trésoriers* to preside over the apportionment of the *tailles*, but merely required them to investigate whether the *élus* had performed their function, and to redress errors when parishes fell into debt or when appeals were made. The *Ordonnances*, they claimed, conferred the right to determine the rates and the apportionment of *tailles* on the *élus* alone. They further accused the *Trésoriers* of seeking to perpetuate their own interest in the creation of special *commissaires*, whereas these had all been suppressed from 13 July 1648: 'the vested interest which certain of the *Trésoriers* have in the apportionment of the *tailles* . . . is one of their motives in wishing to make themselves masters of the royal taxes.'

The *élus* even went so far as to deny the *Trésoriers de France* any superiority over themselves, on the grounds that the *Trésoriers* could not properly claim to form a corporation or to have powers of jurisdiction, in the light of their being so often reduced to a situation where two of them performed their functions alternately, and that they had been deprived of their status as judges with power to promulgate judgments. The *Trésoriers* were indeed excluded from the corporations of the sovereign courts. The *élus* declared that the *Trésoriers*, deprived of sovereign status, were compelled to submit themselves to the appellate jurisdiction of the *Cours des Aides*, the *Chambres des Comptes* and the *Parlements*.

The *élus* however claimed for themselves the quality of judges and their superiority therefore to the *Trésoriers* in their public functions. Moreover, they considered themselves socially superior to the *Trésoriers*:

As for those who assert that the majority of *élus* are magistrates, barristers and attorneys, this is a monstrous calumny. We may however reproach the *Trésoriers* themselves for being the clerks of tax-farmers, sons of low-grade lawyers, commoners. They are indeed of such low birth that their relatives still have to pay *taille* assessed by *élus* who can justly claim for themselves that there are *gentilshommes* among their number, as well as sons of *officiers* from the *Cours souveraines* and from the best families in the towns where *Bureaux des*

élections are situated. There is indeed the case of an *élu* who preferred
to retain his office as *Elu de Paris* rather than become a *Trésorier de
France*, following the death of an uncle. His grandfather had, significantly, considered the office of *élu* so highly that he had conferred it
upon his eldest son and given that of *Trésorier* to the youngest . . .

The *élus* finally claimed the superiority of their general culture and
professional organisation to those of the *Trésoriers*:

> In addition to all their other injuries, the ill will of our enemies spews
> out a further gross insult as inept as all the rest, in that they call us
> ignorant and unschooled. We have to say in reply that for people who
> possess no capacity other than a confused knowledge of certain *ordon-
> nances* relating to their own offices, it becomes them well to make this
> particular reproach to us . . . There are in fact so many *élus* so
> learned, to a degree beyond anything ever attained by provincial *Tré-
> soriers*, that the latter would do well to come to school to them and
> to take lessons in their jobs. *Trésoriers* are in fact frequently so ignor-
> ant that they make themselves ridiculous when they attend the
> *Bureaux des Finances*, since they haven't the intelligence to say or
> explain why they have come.

In order to gild their pamphlets with quotations from ancient authorities,
Aristophanes, Plutarch, Cicero, the Psalms, Proverbs and Saint Paul are
all brought in by the *élus* in support of their claims to retain control over
the apportionment of the *tailles*.[23]

The two corporations indeed came into direct conflict with each other.
In 1648, the *Conseil syndical* of the *Trésoriers* gained the consent of the
Conseil du Roi to the insertion in the *commissions* sent to the *Trésoriers*
for the levying of the *tailles* for 1649 of an authorisation for them to
depute certain of their number to preside over the *Bureaux des élections*
when undertaking the apportionment of the *tailles*. A *Déclaration* of
October 1648 confirmed the *Trésoriers* in their authority in this area.
In reply, however, the *élus* were successful in obtaining the annulment of
the *Déclaration* in December 1648. Even so, certain *Trésoriers de France*
continued nonetheless to preside over the apportionment of the *tailles*,
and, in return, the Assembly of the *Trésoriers* in Paris succeeded in having
their power restored by a *Déclaration* of March 1649.

The Syndicate of the *élus* had organised their resistance to the *Trésoriers* from November 1648 by means of circular letters. They gained the
support of the *Cour des Aides* and advised the *élus* to maintain contact
with *Messieurs* Chesneau and Mauperty, who were respectively advocate
and representative of the *élus* in the *Cour des Aides*. Throughout France,
the *élus* refused the *Trésoriers de France* access to their *Bureaux*. They
resisted executing their orders and appealed against their authority to

the *Cour des Aides*. Certain of the *Bureaux des Finances* – at Soissons, Caen, Limoges and Bourges – thought it best to leave the *élus* to apportion the *tailles* alone, and in the end the *Conseil* gave orders accordingly to the *Trésoriers de France*. A projected meeting between the two Syndicates in 1649, probably toward May or June, did not materialise. The *Trésoriers* saw no solution to the problem except by means of a general regulation, in the form of a decree of the *Conseil* defining in precise terms the relationship between the *Trésoriers de France* and the *élus*. In April and May 1649, the *Conseil syndical* of the *Trésoriers* urged the *Conseil du Roi* to promulgate this regulation, to suspend the Syndicate of the *élus* and to disperse its members assembled in Paris to the provinces. They also urged the *Conseil* to prohibit the *élus* from appealing to the *Cour des Aides* and to order them to address themselves instead to the *Trésoriers de France* in regard to their salaries and privileges and in all matters relating to the financial administration, and to make any complaint they had to the *Conseil* alone. The *Conseil syndical* claimed that the *ordonnances* of the *Trésoriers* should have the power of execution by '*provision*', i.e. in spite of opposition or appeal against them, in the same way as those of the *intendants*. It also succeeded in gaining recognition from the *Conseil* of the right of the *Trésoriers* to preside over the apportionment of the *tailles* and *subsistances*† in the *Bureaux* of the *élus*. The *Trésoriers* also sought control for themselves over the administration of military personnel, and the authority to suppress rebellion or any act of disobedience among the financial *officiers*. They demanded powers to direct and administer the military depots, together with confirmation of their authority in regard to the royal domain, the maintenance of roads and the *ponts et chaussées*. As far as the *Trésoriers* were concerned, this was all the proposed regulation should contain. It would, in effect, have left very few differences between the *Bureaux des Finances* and the provincial *intendants*.[24]

Was it at that moment, or in 1653, that the proposals were drawn up which are to be found in the Séguier papers, the 'Declaration and Regulation touching the offices of the *Trésoriers de France* and their functions'; together with the 'Summary of the regulation reported by M. de la Galissonnière to M. *le président* De Bellièvre regarding the *Trésoriers de France* and the *élus*' – texts which would have given, both of them, complete satisfaction to the *Trésoriers de France?*[25] In fact, however, the *Conseil* was careful not to take obvious sides between the two parties. At one moment it would give satisfactory replies to both, although these would in fact be mutually contradictory. At another it would respond equivocally; as for example that *Bureaux des finances* who were accustomed to intervening in the *élections* might continue to do so; or indeed, as a decree of 7 April 1650 put it: 'the *Trésoriers généraux de France* should continue in the way in which they have always fulfilled the function of their offices.' The conflict between the *Trésoriers généraux de France* and the *élus* was to continue without solution until 1653.

The *Trésoriers* attributed the boldness of the *élus* to the general disturbance of the realm and the protection given them by the *Cour des Aides* in Paris. The last had not lightly forgiven the *Trésoriers* for having tried to claim for themselves the status of members of the *Cours souveraines*, when in their own eyes the *Trésoriers* were nothing more than ordinary regional *officiers*; still less for their having claimed this status when it could only in fact be conferred by the *Conseil* itself, and still less for refusing to recognise the jurisdiction of the *Cour des Aides* and for interposing themselves between that court and the *élus* as an authority in principle different but in fact in competition. When the *élus* were fined by the *Trésoriers de France*, they appealed to the *Cour des Aides* against their jurisdiction, and on many occasions the court sustained the appeals, even when the *Trésoriers* issued orders intended to 'expedite the collection of the king's taxes'. At need, the *Cour des Aides* even summoned *Trésoriers de France* in person to their bar. The *Cour des Aides* accepted royal *commissions* for their members in the *généralités*, and in registering them increased the powers granted to *commissaires*, giving them competence to preside over the apportionment of the *tailles* and the *gabelle*, at the expense of the *Trésoriers*. From May 1650, a *Conseiller* of the *Cour des Aides*, named De Bragelonne, spent several months in the *généralité* of Lyons, and usurped the function of the *Trésoriers* by attending the 'sessions when the taxes were apportioned', since he was 'invited to do so by the tax-farmers and the *élus*'. The *Conseil syndical* of the *Trésoriers* was successful in obtaining a prohibition from the *Surintendant des Finances* against such *commissaires* presiding over the apportionment of the taxes. The *Trésoriers de France* at Moulins, however, wrote in a spirit of some melancholy: '*Messieurs* of the *Conseil* will not be angry to see us in dispute with the *Cour des Aides* and to be asked to render judgment between us.'

The *Chambres des Comptes* in Paris and Rouen also strove to subject the *Trésoriers* to their own authority and to restrict their function. The *Chambre des Comptes* in Paris took it upon itself to issue the royal *Déclarations* of October 1648 and March 1649 which settled the problems concerning the *Trésoriers de France* who came within its jurisdiction, in the same way as the *Parlements* did concerning the *baillis* and *sénéchaux*. And to stress the dependence of the *Trésoriers*, it took the opportunity to call the *procureurs du Roi*, in the tribunals of the *Trésoriers*, assistants of the *procureurs du Roi* in the *Chambre des Comptes*. The *Trésoriers* however refused to allow a precedent to become established which would detract from their status as members of the *compagnies souveraines*. On the advice of their *Conseil syndical*, the *Trésoriers* refused to register the *Déclarations* transmitted by the *Chambre des*

Comptes, nor did they authorise their implementation. They waited instead to receive them direct from the *Conseil du Roi,* accompanied by letters patent addressed to them as *Trésoriers* instructing them to put them into execution. The *Chambre des Comptes* then began to encroach constantly on the functions of the *Trésoriers de France.* For example, it annulled an act for the reception of homage from a *gentilhomme* of Anjou, drawn up by the *Bureau des Finances* at Tours, and ordered that the homage in question should henceforth be received in the *sénéchaussée* of Maine by the *procureur du Roi* in the *présidial* of Le Mans, acting as sub-delegate of the *Chambre des Comptes* itself. In the eyes of the *Trésoriers,* this was a triple illegality. The *Chambre des Comptes,* in the first place, had no right to annul *ordonnances* of the *Trésoriers;* nor had it the right to appoint sub-delegates, or to receive homage outside the place where it had been established. The *Bureaux des Finances,* they declared, had the right to receive homage each in their own jurisdictions, entirely free of interference from the *Chambre des Comptes.* The *Chambre des Comptes* at Rouen allowed *receveurs* and *commis* to present their accounts to it without their being registered with the *Bureau des Finances* at Rouen, exactly as if that body had never existed. In 1650 the *Trésoriers de France* resigned themselves to the necessity of taking the dispute before the *Conseil du Roi.* As a consequence, the *Conseil* became yet again the arbiter between one corporation of *officiers* and another.

Relations were not always good even between the *Trésoriers* and the *Parlements.* In 1649 the *Trésoriers* complained bitterly of the *Parlement* at Toulouse, which they claimed treated them as subordinates and undermined their prestige in the eyes of the people. By its own decree, the *Parlement* there had ordered the *Bureau des Finances* to revise the king's *commissions* for the levying of the *tailles* for 1649 and to reduce them by 900,000 *livres,* on the grounds that the king had undertaken to raise only forty million *livres* over the whole realm, of which the *généralité* of Montauban should bear only one-seventh. The *Trésoriers* resisted; but, in opposition to them, in several *élections* the *élus* enforced the decree of the *Parlement.* In 1649 the *Parlement de Paris* rendered judgment in favour of the *lieutenant généraux*† of the *baillages*† and *séné-chaus-sées*† who undertook to receive the faith and homage of subinfeudated vassals of the king, to the detriment of the *Trésoriers généraux de France.*

The *officiers* found themselves therefore divided by deep conflicting interests. Whether their aim was to return to an ancient state of affairs, as in the case of the *élus,* or whether it was, on the contrary, to substitute themselves for newer agents of the royal authority, namely the provincial *intendants,* as with the *Trésoriers de France,* all the corporations of *officiers* had only one goal, to develop their own authority to the detriment of their neighbours. These competing ambitions forced them to address themselves to the *Conseil du Roi,* and in this way the

Conseil was able to gain recognition of the principle of its own superior authority, and by using its role as arbiter to gain time and to remain finally the master. Already by 1651, the *Bureau des Finances* at Lyons wrote sadly that it was of the utmost urgency:

> To destroy the power of a faction which has risen against us from among all the said *officiers* (i.e. the *élus*), with the encouragement and protection of the *Cour des Aides*. These take advantage of the weakness of the *Conseil*, which may well restore its authority once again and leave us defeated as a result of these disastrous attacks, because the *Conseil* may well include us within its general resentment against all the *officiers* of the realm, by whom it considers itself to have been humiliated. It is expedient for us not to await the time when *intendants* once again resume their usurpation of the function of our offices.

The *officiers* were however paralysed by their divisions, and none of their corporations was able to make its wishes prevail. The prophecy of the *Trésoriers* at Lyons was indeed confirmed by events. From the last quarter of 1653, the *intendants* were re-established in the provinces. For some years yet, however, prudence had to be exercised. The draft of the *instruction* drawn up for the *Conseiller d'Etat* Le Febvre, sent as *intendant* into the Dauphiné on 19 November 1654, is characteristic: the title of '*intendant de justice, police et finances* in the said province' which had been initially attributed to him is scored through and replaced by that of '*intendant de justice, police et finances* for the troops in the said province'. He had also been given power to make arrangements for the supply of the military depots and to audit the accounts for these, in place, that is, of the *Trésoriers de France*. These phrases are also scored through, however, and replaced by clauses giving him the right to attend the markets organised for the supply of the depots and to register the audited records of expenditure. But in the end he is sent, even so, with extended powers in regard to conspiracies, uprisings and the putting into effect of the orders of the *Conseil* for the province. It is said quite specifically that he will go 'every time and as many times as he considers it necessary, in His Majesty's interest, into the *Bureau des Finances* at Grenoble in order to proceed with and fulfil the responsibilities of his *commission* regarding the *officiers* of the said *Bureau* . . . and, in general, *le sieur* Le Febvre will do all that he judges necessary for the well-being and advantage of His Majesty's service.'[26] Little by little, the *Trésoriers généraux de France* were placed again under the authority of the *intendants*.

The *Conseil* having brought the *Trésoriers de France* to heel, everything happened as though designed to give them satisfaction, however. An edict of 1653 suppressed the *élus*. Authorisation was in fact given to start putting the edict into effect. One of the items of Le Febvre's *com-*

mission in the Dauphiné was to put in hand the suppression of the *élus*. These last in fact had great difficulty in avoiding catastrophe.[27] This study of the financial *officiers* is very far from being exhaustive. It does not exhaust, far from it, the possibilities offered by the documents in Paris. It does not make use of provincial sources, and important local and regional studies could well be undertaken. In addition to the questions broached here, several points need to be clarified. We need to know more about the political and social ideas of the *Trésoriers de France* and the *élus*. Among the immense number of *Mazarinades* there are doubtless some which could be attributed to them. Their remonstrances, journals, letters and *mémoires* have not yet been entirely made available to us. We need to find out precisely why they were evidently unable to substitute themselves for the tax-farmers, in supplying the financial needs of the Crown; and for this we need to study the composition of their fortunes, the use their liquid money was put to, the financial operations they were involved in and the credit available to them. We need to know how effectively they fulfilled their functions in this troubled period, and whether they really deserved the reproaches levelled against them. Where they were *seigneurs*, it is necessary to clarify their relations with the inhabitants of their *seigneuries*. Finally, we need to try to determine their real role in the armed uprisings. On all these points, indeed, one might say that practically everything really remains to be done. The archives of the *Parlements*, the *Chambres des Comptes* and the *Cours des Aides*, the papers of the *Bureaux des Finances* and the *élections*, the registers of the *bailliages* and *sénéchaussées*, together with notarial and family records and contemporaneous publications in the provinces, no doubt contain treasures waiting for us; but this is not the place to examine how to make our enquiries of them.

NOTES

1 [Editor's note:] For details of the manuscript references in the *Bibliothèque Nationale*, see p. 77, footnote 1, of the original French edition of this article in *XVIIe Siècle*, Nos. 42–3 (1959).

2 [Editor's note:] For details, see p. 77, footnote 2, of the original French edition of this article in *XVIIe Siècle*, Nos. 42–3 (1959). On both the *Trésoriers* and *élus*, the author refers the reader especially to E. Esmonin, *La taille en Normandie au temps de Colbert* (Paris, 1913) pp. 38–66 and 107–33.

3 R. Mousnier, 'Etat et commissaire. Recherches sur la création des intendants des provinces (1634–1648)', in *Forschungen zu Staat und Verfassung: Festgabe für Fritz Hartung* (Berlin, 1958).

4 Request of the *Trésoriers de France* to the *Parlement*; undated, but after 13 May 1648; B.N. Lf 31 17.

5 Request of the *Elus de France* to the king and *Nosseigneurs de son Conseil*, 3 February 1648; B.N. Lf 38 9. Also, Discourse of the *Syndics* of the *officiers* of

the *Elections de France* regarding their request presented to the *Cour des Aydes*, 28 March 1654, ibid., 17.

6   Letters of the *Trésoriers de France* of 21 July and 29 October, from the *généralités* of Riom, Poitiers, Limoges, Bordeaux and Montauban.

7   Request from the *Trésoriers de France* to be called to the Assembly of the Deputies of the *Compagnies souveraines* (subsequent to the suppression of the intendants on 13 July 1648); B.N. Lf 31.

8   See Note 4.

9   Reply of the *Syndics généraux* of the *officiers* of the *Elections de France*; B.N. Lf 38 12.

10 Circular letter of the *Syndics* of the *Elections de France*, 27 April 1649; B.N. Lf 38 7.

11 L. Romier, *Lettres et chevauchées du Bureau des Finances de Caen* (1910) Nos. XXXIII, LIX, LXV, CVII.

12 B.N.ms.fr. 17387, 17389, and 17388.

13 B.N.ms.fr. 17388.

14 Request of the *Trésoriers de France* to the *Parlements*, B.N. Lf 31 17. See supra, Chapter 6, pp. 169–200, and especially p. 196.

15 Du Perron, from Alençon, 30 July 1648; B.N.ms. fr. 17388.

16 B.N.ms.fr. 7686, No. 99. Also, R. Mousnier, 'Le Conseil du Roi de la mort de Henri IV', in *Société d'histoire moderne*, I (1947) passim.
[Editor's note:] Except where otherwise indicated, all subsequent manuscript references given by the author are from B.N.ms.fr. 7686, and may be referred to in footnotes 17–30, 34, 36–7 and 42–6 of the original French edition of this article.

17 R. Mousnier, 'Etat et commissaire', in *Festgabe für Fritz Hartung* (1958).

18 Retz, *Mémoires*, ed. Feillet, I p. 324; Lefèvre d'Ormesson, *Journal*, ed. Chéruel, I p. 545, 546 and 555, note 2.

19 B.N.ms.fr. 18479, fols. 43–8.

20 P. Néron and E. Girard, *Recueil d'édits et d'ordonnances royaux sur le fait de la justice* (éd. 1720) II p. 633.

21 R. Mousnier, *La Vénalité des offices sous Henri IV et Louis XIII* (Paris, 1945).

22 *Mémoires* of the *Trésoriers de France* against the *Elus* and *Messieurs* of the *Cour des Aides*, 1649, *Séguier Papers*, B.N.ms.fr. 18479, fols. 31–32.

23 Remonstrances of the *Syndics* of the *Elections de France* to the king and *Nosseigneurs* of his *Conseil*; Reply of the *Syndics généraux* of the *officiers* of the *Elections* of the Realm to observations made by the provincial *Trésoriers de France* concerning the remonstrances of the said *Syndics*, 1649; B.N. Lf 38 19 and 12.

24 *Mémoires of the Trésoriers de France* against the *Elus*, ms. fr. fols. 31–2 and 37–8.

25 B.N.ms.fr. 18479, fols. 23 et seq. and 39 et seq.

26 B.N. K 891, *Minute d'arrêt du Conseil du Roi*.

27 B.N. Lf 38 17.

8 The French Nobility and Absolute Monarchy in the First Half of the Seventeenth Century*

PIERRE DEYON

In opposition to traditional accounts which complacently describe Riche-lieu's struggle with the *Grands*, and the endeavours of the nobility to resist the development of French absolutism, Boris Porshnev sought to establish, more than ten years ago, the idea of a common front uniting the monarchy, the *seigneurs* and the urban bourgeoisie against the lower classes in the towns and countryside. This thesis, which was without doubt too bold in its scope, has had the great merit of attracting renewed attention to the significance and frequency of the popular uprisings before the Fronde.

Certain of the objections to the theories of the Soviet historian have centred on the responsibility of the privileged groups themselves in the origins of several of the uprisings. This straightaway raises the problem of the relationship between the nobility and the absolute mon-archy, which is for ever being posed, but which is still not fully resolved. Although we know a great deal about the successive plots directed against the cardinal-ministers, we know little about the group psychology and material situation of the order of the nobility taken as a whole.[1] While awaiting the results of research in progress and the precise information it will bring as to the actual participation of the various social groups in the uprisings which disturbed the realm from 1624 to 1653, we would like to draw attention to certain particular aspects of aristocratic dis-content and protest.

I

It would be entirely wrong to suppose that the nobility was completely protected from the fiscal pressures imposed by the government of Louis

* This is a translation of Pierre Deyon's article, 'A propos des rapports entre la noblesse française et la monarchie absolue pendant la première moitié du XVIIe siècle', in *Revue Historique*, CCXXXI (1964) pp. 341–56.

XIII and the Regency. Engaged in a vast European conflict, at the very moment when a reversal of the *conjoncture* disturbed the prosperity of the realm, the monarchy was forced to increase the existing taxes, by introducing a multiplicity of new ones, by recourse to a whole host of financial expedients, and by seeking at the same time to reduce the scale of fiscal privilege. In order to study the government's financial policy, it is necessary to distinguish the *pays* which suffered the levying of *taille personnelle*† from those where *taille réelle*† was raised. In the former, taxation merely took personal status into account; whereas in the latter the character of landed estates themselves, whether they were 'noble' or 'non-noble', determined whether taxes were levied or whether their owners were exempt.

In the *pays de taille personnelle*, where noble status was probably more advantageous, successive regulations on the levying of the *tailles* sought progressively, however, to limit fiscal privilege. The edict of March 1600 ordered all tenants of ecclesiastical *seigneurs*, *gentilshommes* and other privileged persons to be inscribed on the tax rolls, 'as much by reason of their general assets as for the profits which they may have been able to make from the said farms'.[2] Regulations of 1634 and 1640 repeated this requirement,[3] and in April 1643 the *intendants* and the *Trésoriers de France*† were ordered to impose *taxes d'office*†

on those with privileges which had been revoked by the edict of 1640 . . . and on those who are the most influential inhabitants of parishes, who by their authority or by intimidation have until now been able to have themselves exempted altogether or else put down for very small amounts . . . and likewise the tenants of *gentilshommes*, the *seigneurs* of the parishes concerned, who until now have only borne few or none of the said taxes, through the power of their masters to gain them exemption.[4]

This insistence, these repetitions, speak clearly enough of the difficulties involved and of the obstacles which were regularly encountered. The solidarity of the seigneurial landowners, whether consisting of nobles or *officiers*†, to a great extent paralysed the will of the government and of its agent, the *intendant*. These renewed initiatives, however, these new decisions, brought about a whole series of enquiries, most often confided to the tax-farmers, which aroused immediate disquiet, as the *Journal of the Assembly of 1651* bears witness.

These regulations of 1634, 1640 and 1643 contained other innovations besides, which were contrary to the interests of the order of the nobility. Article 33 of the Edict of 1634 authorised nobles, ecclesiastics and other privileged persons to develop 'by their own hands only one of their estates and houses', and ordered agents and servants handling their other estates to be taxed, 'just as ordinary tenants could be'.[5] These restrictions sought to render impossible the fraudulent practice whereby certain privileged persons declared tenants to be their own domestic servants whom they then bound to themselves by secret leases. These restrictions provoked complaint throughout the nobility, and in 1643 the Estates of Normandy protested against the severities employed by the *commissaires*† in applying this measure in the administration of the *tailles*.[6] Those with privileges thought up other procedures to deflect the intentions of royal legislation and to shield their domains from taxation. They regrouped several under-developed farms under the direction of a single steward, 'putting three or four farms together, and buying up the houses of their peasants in order to pull them down'.[7] The study of noble properties confirms this evidence. In the inventory drawn up after the death of Lemaître de Bellejame, *conseiller d'Etat*†, in 1666, we find indeed the trace of more than a hundred contracts of purchase and exchange concluded between the said personage and his neighbouring peasants, and all with the precise intent of regrouping his seigneurial domain.[8] It would be easy to give further examples from family archives or notarial records, but only a systematic comparison of a large number of land maps would enable us to assess the importance of this phenomenon. It was however real enough to arouse the disquiet of the government and lead it, in 1667, to reduce the effects of its benevolence: 'abusing the permission granted to them by the Regulations of 1643 and 1664, to hold one farm in their own hands without paying *taille*, certain of them join several farms together and exploit the labour of eight to ten ploughs'.[9] The extent of exempt land in future was to be restored to the labour of only four ploughs in the case of ecclesiastical estates and those of *gentilshommes*, and of two ploughs in the case of '*bourgeois de Paris*'.

Other measures also pursued usurpers of nobility and those who had been recently ennobled. These latter were subjected to fresh enquiries and then were forced to pay for confirmation of their nobility.[10] Two edicts of 1610 and 1614 were designed to combat abuses which the *commensaux*† of the royal and princely households benefited from. These titles were widely distributed and a great number of such *commensaux* were 'solely so, for the honour'.[11] In future, however, only *officiers* who rendered actual service, and were on a salary of more than sixty *livres* and whose names were included in annual statements of accounts were to be accepted for exemption as *commensaux*.[12] These measures were in fact in line with the often expressed desires of the ancestral nobility, but their application was entrusted to tax-farmers and gave rise to 'searches' which were harmful to the nobility as a whole. In December 1634, and again in 1635, the Estates of Normandy complained of the actions taken by tax-farmers and *Trésoriers de France* who had applied themselves to the verification of patents of nobility.[13] The same complaint was still being made in 1658, by the organisers of seditious assemblies which affected Normandy in that year.[14]

In the *pays de taille réelle* there had been bitter conflicts for centuries between the various orders in regard to the *taille*, as to whether the nobility should or should not pay tax on their non-noble land. Almost everywhere, in the first half of the seventeenth century, the monarchy intervened to restrict their privileges. In Provence, a judgment of the *Parlement* in 1552 had already established the principle that all non-noble land paid *taille* whatever the status of its owner. Certain details of this decree gave rise to serious dispute, and a decision of the *Conseil du Roi* was necessary on 21 January 1625 to reaffirm the obligation resting on all inherited land consisting of tenures. Only those estates were spared whose owners could prove that the acquisition of them compensated them for fiefs which had been alienated since 1556.[15] Equally, in Languedoc, at the end of Louis XIII's reign, the essentially landed nature of the land tax was enforced, and 'no privilege could exempt anyone any longer from charges on inherited land'. The treatise on *tailles* by Antoine Despeisses, a lawyer in the *Cour des Aides*† at Montpellier, showed precisely in its 1643 edition that 'it had been thus decided' by decres of 28 April 1633 and 15 March 1634.[16]

The development of royal policy in the Dauphiné seems to have been even more direct still. Until 1639, the *nobles d'épée*†, the *nobles de robe*† and the clergy remained exempt from all taxes. The regulation promulgated by Louis XIII on 24 October of that year, however, compelled all inherited non-noble land to pay *tailles*, *taillons* and *garnisons*.[17] Finally, the new register drawn up for the *élections*† of Condom and Agen, from 1604 to 1622, included for the first time all non-noble land in the parishes, without taking into account the status of its proprietors.[18]

It is far from our intention to assert that fiscal privilege did not exist in the *pays de taille réelle*. From the fact that they possessed a number of fiefs, the nobility did not contribute to the royal taxes in exact proportion to their landed wealth. Moreover, the *seigneurs* could often have had excluded from the tax registers those tenants whom they retained in their own *seigneuries*, or those whom they could compensate with old alienations of the noble land in their family. Nevertheless, and this is, in our opinion, too often forgotten, they did contribute and probably resented the global increase in the volume of the *tailles* just as much as the other taxpayers did.[19] We can already guess the possible consequences of such a development. D'Epernon, the governor of Guyenne, certainly knew how things stood when on 25 March 1649 he wrote to Séguier: 'the nobility, and this is principally so in the *pays* where the *tailles* are *réelles*, interest themselves in the general interests of the people.'[20]

Moreover, the fiscal grievances of the nobility were not limited solely to the direct taxes. They also complained of the increase in tolls, in the *aides* and customs, of which they themselves bore their share. In 1651, the assembly of the nobility recalled that 'being subject to all kinds of *tailles* and other taxes . . . they also pay whatever is levied on merchandise.'[21] Finally, the tax of the *ban et arrière-ban*† equally aroused their discontent. Already on several occasions in the sixteenth century, the monarchy had substituted a levy to contribute toward the provision of a 'replacement' for the actual service involved in the *ban et arrière-ban*. After the failure of the 'call-up' of 1635, the government of Louis XIII renewed the procedure; and the service involved in the *ban*, as a system of recruitment, seems to have been gradually transformed in reality into a veritable system of taxation of the nobility and the possessors of fiefs.

We know from Richelieu's *Testament*[22] the exact intention of the king and his minister in this respect. They wished to recruit regular companies of light horse and *gendarmes* from the contributions towards the cost of substitutes provided by those who did not serve in person. The value and military effectiveness of these would have been infinitely superior to the feudal militia furnished by the traditional levies. But the king and Richelieu lacked time for the realisation of their project, of which only the financial aspect really materialised. The assault made in this way on fiscal privilege, however, was so serious that, in order to mask its significance, there was always a pretence made of actually preparing for a mobilisation of the nobility in real terms, which, before the opening of the campaign, would be transformed into a monetary levy. The summons of February 1639 contained stern words about 'those who lived at home in shameful idleness';[23] and Article 4 recalled the obligation of all nobles to join the companies raised by the *ban et arrière-ban*, armed, mounted and fully equipped. Some weeks later, however, at the start of the campaign, and without governmental fear of being accused of inconsistency, their service was converted into a monetary payment, and the offers of service on the part of the provincial *hobereaux*† were rejected, obstinately anxious as they were to serve in person. In 1642 the *gentilshommes* were excused personal service, on condition that they paid for the maintenance and arming of one foot soldier, and the same comedy of the summons to arms, duly annulled at the last moment and 'generously' transformed into a tax for a replacement, was played through again in 1675 during the Dutch War.[24] This was a formidable precedent. Not only did the tax amount to some fifteen to twenty per cent of the estimated revenue of the fief concerned,[25] and therefore represent a charge that was in no sense negligible, but even more serious, it carried with it a grave assault on the whole principle of fiscal exemption itself.

II

All these measures were livelily resented by a nobility whose material situation was frequently scarcely flourishing and whose income was lowered by the joint effects of war and the reversal of the economic *conjoncture* between 1630 and 1650. As with other social groups, the nobility was tempted to blame the monarchy for its family difficulties, which the reduction of seigneurial privilege and landed income represented. In such a context, the initiatives of a government in severe financial straits seemed to many merely confused and provocative, and the pursuit of the war itself seemed almost a nonsense. As yet incapable of the clear thinking which, sometimes, there has been a wish to endow them with, all social groups looked feverishly for a scapegoat, the *traitant*†, a *mazarin*, who had deprived them of the paternal protection of the king.

Family records and the account books of lay *seigneurs* are unfortunately only too rare, but a whole file of grievances and melancholy descriptions exists which shows very well the reduced material condition of a section of the nobility during the reign of Louis XIII and the Regency.

The memorandum sent to the king after the assembly of notables of 1626–7 invokes the financial distress of the entire order: 'it is in the most pitiful state it has ever been in . . . poverty overwhelms it . . . idleness renders it corrupt . . . oppression has reduced it almost to despair.'[26] An exercise in rhetoric perhaps, but in his *Testament Politique*, Richelieu confirms the essentials of it, and in several places alludes to the distress of the rural nobility.

During the Fronde, a certain number of pamphlets and *mazarinades* took up the theme. After the usual protests about venality of office and the insolence of the *robins*, the *Complaints of the Nobility against the Tax-farmers and Feeders upon the People* describes certain *gentilshommes* who have 'grown old in harness, dying in their houses without reward, constrained to crush the innocent and plunder the peasant in order to live according to their rank and quality'.[27] In the same way, 'the noble confused on the subject of money' presents us with a picaresque hero, with hollow stomach, beating the Paris pavements in search of an invitation to dinner or a loan from friends, all of whom are equally hard up: 'Heavens, what a pitiful reign is this? Must the nobility be treated so? . . . poor nobility who go the way of the times.' The protagonist of this little comedy has the merit of informing us of the origin of his own financial difficulties – his tenant has not been able to pay him what he owes him.[28] Such failure necessitated even further recourse to credit on the part of the nobility, which they had already so long abused. The institution of 'rente' cloaked mortgage loans, which were fraught with such menace for the future of the landed fortunes of the nobility. The author of a *mémoire* of 1655–7, preserved in the Colbert manuscripts, treats this problem with clarity and feeling:

> Another kind of man has risen among us . . . the *rentiers*, these ignorant and unlettered men who amass great fortunes without difficulty, without work or taking risk; great men who do nothing, who have no commerce except with notaries . . . It is they who have chased the two pillars of the State, the *gentilshommes* and the *laboureurs*†, from their ancient inheritance and who have expropriated the majority of the estates of both noble and commoner for the past one hundred and fifty years. As for the nobility, three things have ruined it: the facility with which it finds credit, extravagance and war.[29]

A moving spectacle perhaps, but one which calls, just as the previous evidence does, for statistical verification. We are only able to conjecture on all these problems, as long as we do not possess a sufficient number of studies on the development of noble property[30] and on the effects of the economic *conjoncture* on the movement of landed and seigneurial incomes.[31]

In awaiting the result of such complex enquiries, it is possible to make use of records and rolls drawn up on the occasion of the issuing of the summonses to the *ban et arrière-ban*.[32] Although these are often only a source based on estimates, they are easy to use and quickly yield interesting information. The *déclarations* which are made either verbally or in writing by the *gentilshommes* at the time of the 'preparatory muster' already provide numerous personal valuations. This *gentilhomme* recalls that he has served His Majesty for forty years, that his son is employed in the regiment of Rambures, but that to equip him he has had to involve himself in several substantial loans.[33] Another, aged sixty-five and handicapped in both arms, invokes the smallness of his resources: 'a small house covered with thatch and a walled farmyard at Boves with a hundred *livres* in the form of several rents.' He adds with bitterness that he passed his youth 'in the service of the king in which he ruined himself in body and in wealth'.[34] Another 'has consumed his wealth in service with the Piedmont regiment', but declares himself ready to respond to the call to arms 'provided that he is given the wherewithal to equip himself'; while another begs His Majesty to make him serve in person and to exempt him from paying the '*contribution*', since his estate has been burned by the Spaniards and because he can obtain nothing from his tenants.[35] But in face of this evidence, what have we to think of the *hobereau*† who invokes his sciatica, and of his neighbour who excuses himself because he is obliged, as an ancient prior *in commendam* of a neighbouring religious community, to recite his office each morning?[36] Without wishing to underestimate the revealing and representative character of these *déclarations*, it would be very difficult and dangerous to establish the degree of the fidelity of the nobility to the monarchy and the level of the provincial nobility's resources on this basis.

Fortunately, however, there are sometimes other documents which enable us to check the authenticity or false pathos of this evidence against the reassuring neutrality of figures. When we possess at one and the same time the muster-roll with the initial *déclarations* of the *gentilshommes* and the list as it became finalised after the eventual adjustments were made in the taxes to be actually levied to provide for replacements, it becomes possible to establish certain elements of a statistically representative nature of the situation of the nobility at this time. Here, for example, are the results disclosed by the records of the *ban et arrière-ban* for the *bailliage*† of Amiens from 1639 to 1675. The rolls constructed before the Fronde are very brief. They generally only mention the names of men ready to serve and of those who are already fighting in the king's armies, without giving any precise information regarding their financial position. In 1639, the particular roll for the *prévôté*† of Amiens bears only fifty-eight names, but fourteen heads of family have presented valid excuses, since their eldest sons are already bearing arms, and two of the nobles summoned have already joined their regiments. In 1642, in the *prévôté* of Saint-Riquier, the *officier* charged with drawing up the roll notes the names of six cavaliers ready to serve, together with those of four ageing valetudinarians and three *gentilshommes* already employed in the army. The *officier* involved in the same work in the *prévôté* of Vimeu gives us one hundred and one names, of which nine belong to persons already engaged in the king's armies. The roll of the *prévôté* of Fouilloy is an exception. It gives precise information about the material and financial situation of the *hobereaux* of the *pays:* four are with the army; eight can serve in the usual way, and a ninth can only do so with very poor equipment; two are declared to be 'very poor; one, merely poor; three are not very comfortably off; and there are yet three more who posses no fief and cannot serve'.[37]

The records for 1675, unfortunately rather late for our purpose, contain more numerous examples giving precise information. We find the *déclarations* of the *gentilshommes* concerned and the roll for the payment of the *contribution* for replacement duly audited by the *lieutenant-général*†. Three hundred and eighty-six nobles were constrained to appear: thirty were already serving with the king's army, sixty-two older men had served or had unmarried sons in the army; forty declared themselves incapable of contributing to the costs of their equipment and upkeep; eighteen made the most of the fact that their principal abode was not in the *bailliage*, and the majority of the others declared themselves ready to respond to the king's summons.[38] Thus a little less than a quarter of the *gentilshommes* of the *bailliage* had served, were serving or were maintaining a son in the army. It was few enough for an order vowed to the military profession; but venality of office and poverty forbade honourable service to a large number of the sons of noble families.

The final roll of *contributions* for replacements audited by the *lieutenant-général* endorses the majority of excuses put forward and includes no more than two hundred and thirty names. But it furnishes us with valuable information on the estimated level of their wealth:

Contribution (livres)	Estimated revenue (livres)	Number of Gentilshommes
40	Less than 300	89
80	300– 600	26
100	600– 900	17
150	900–1500	33
200	1500–2000	14
300	more than 2000	51

We note that at the bottom of the scale not only were some forty exempted altogether for reasons of poverty, but eighty-nine more were charged only forty *livres*, which corresponded to a total annual revenue of less than 300 *livres*. If this were not actual poverty, it was, to be sure, not a very considerable sum. At the other extreme of the hierarchy of wealth, there are fifty-one *gentilshommes* to whom an income of more than 2000 *livres* is attributed and who have to pay 300 *livres*. One would certainly like to have rolls as precise as this for the musters of 1639 or 1642, and for the same districts. Comparison between them would enable us to fix the first point on the trail of the social history of the seventeenth-century nobility. Other places, other archives may provide the lucky chance which will serve the historian's purpose. We may, in any case, state that in the middle of the seventeenth century a kind of noble proletariat existed, an inexhaustible reservoir of men to provide all the instigators of trouble; and we may state equally forcefully that the efforts at reform on the part of the monarchy occurred at a particularly unfavourable time and were likely to provoke the opposition of the privileged.

III

A large section of the French nobility felt that in threatening its privileges the absolute monarchy was violating the fundamental laws which sanctified the various conditions and hierarchy of men. Nothing is more significant in this respect than a comparison between the claims of the nobility

as they were expressed in the *cahier de doléances*† of 1614 and those
we find trace of in the assemblies of the nobility held in 1649, 1651 and
1658 and in certain of the *mazarinades*. In 1614, the efforts of the order
seem directed entirely against venality and against the *officiers de justice
et de finances*, as usurpers of noble rank. The *cahier* of 1614 claims a
monopoly for the ancient nobility of offices and charges in the king's
household, in the orders of chivalry and in appointments carrying the
greatest prestige in the *Parlements*. It also demands the restoration of
seigneurial justice and the strictest suppression of all usurpations of
nobility.

We find again, of course, in texts contemporary with the Fronde, the
same hostility toward venality, the same complaints against royal justice.
The assembly of the nobility of 1651 repeated that it was a scandal to
make members of the authentic nobility appear before commoners: 'a
prévôt or the most inferior judge in a *présidial*† daily institutes criminal
proceedings against members of the nobility . . . A simple priest may not
be judged except by ecclesiastical judges, a commoner is judged by commoners like himself; a *gentilhomme* however is judged by persons who
are not of his condition.'³⁹ Venality of office was the more unpopular in
that it provided opportunities to a great number of financiers and tax-
farmers for scandalous speculation. The nobility joined with the rest of
the country 'in its hatred for these financial harpies who exclude the
nobility from government and make them despair of ever entering the
public offices of their ancestors, because of a shameful and excessive
venality'.⁴⁰

But new grievances added themselves to these traditional complaints.
The first collective manifestation of this came in 1649, in complaints
against the privileges accorded by the Court 'to certain *gentilshommes*
and to particular families to the prejudice of the whole nobility of the
realm'.⁴¹ A union of the nobility was formed against the pretensions of
princes étrangers† and the *ducs et pairs*,⁴² while the king was begged not
to grant any future warrant or patent in this respect. This initiative on
the part of the nobility was made in direct opposition to the monarchy's
aim to overturn the traditional hierarchy of the nobility by granting
royal favours to individual members of the order. In arousing a sense of
grievance, the jealousies of certain of the great *seigneurs* awakened a
feeling of silent rancour among the order of the nobility as a whole,
against the favourites and familiars of the king. The nobility felt itself
confused and frustrated, and was unable to appreciate the need for a
more effective system for administering both Court and government. It
felt itself abandoned and neglected, to the exclusive benefit of certain
intriguers. In spite of its limited objectives and its small political significance, the union of 1649 certainly revealed a new aspect of noble
opposition.

More significant still was the assembly of the nobility held two years later in 1651. Its aims were altogether wider, its representative character more assured. If we are to judge by the letters which it addressed to the provincial *gentilshommes* and the *Journal* which the Marquis de Sourdis has left us, it placed in the forefront of its preoccupations its struggle against excessive royal taxation.[43] It called attention first of all to the difficulties encountered in raising seigneurial dues: 'The *financiers* over-charge the subjects of the nobility with immense taxes, so that being rendered thereby entirely impoverished, they have no means left to furnish their *seigneurs* with any appreciable amount of money.'[44] It is all very crudely stated, this problem of the competition between the royal and the seigneurial tax-gatherers, with both aiming to raise the maximum from peasant production. The *Journal* of the Marquis de Sourdis refers to searches made by agents of the *gabelles*, coming armed right into the houses of the nobility[45] to conduct their investigations. He reports the grievances of the *gentilshommes* of the *élection*† of Dourdan, who were being pursued 'because they have developed their estates too much by the work of their own hands and are threatened as a result with being made liable, they or their servants, to pay *taille*'; and he does not hesitate to declare that 'in regard to their property, the nobility are subject to all sorts of *tailles* and other taxes, and their estates depreciate in value to the extent that their tenants pay *tailles* . . . they themselves are still liable to serve at their own cost and in person in the *ban et arrière-ban*.'[46] The letters which were addressed at this time to provincial *gentilshommes* added a supplementary grievance to these complaints, regarding injuries occasioned by the billeting of soldiers: 'the honour of our wives and daughters, our houses, our belongings, our lives are exposed to the insolence and plunder of the soldiery.' On this last point, to which, it seems, they attached a great deal of importance, the deputies of the assembly obtained a promise from Gaston d'Orléans, the *lieutenant-général* of the realm.[47] A regulation of 4 November 1651 granted a privilege of exemption from billeting to ecclesiastics, *gentils-hommes* pursuing the profession of arms, heads of the corporations of justice and the king's representatives sitting in such courts.[48] It was to remain a dead letter, however, in the state of anarchy into which the realm dissolved in 1652.

Assemblies held in June and July at Nogent-le-Roi, La Roche-Guyon and Dreux again petitioned the king both for a meeting of the Estates General, promised a year before, and 'for remedies against the military'. It was a 'feeble recourse', they said, 'to invoke the protection of ordinances which have force today only in so far as the sword itself authorises them.' In order to assure the maintenance of order in the provinces and to put an end to the plunder by armed bands, the assemblies proposed the formation of corporations of the nobility, a suggestion which the Regent and the *Conseil*, with every good reason, hastened to ignore.[49] The same complaints were made by the organisers of the assemblies of 1658 and 1659,[50] among whom we find again certain of those who instigated the assemblies convened at the time of the Fronde. The royal *Déclaration* of 1658 describes the motives or pretexts for their concern in these terms: 'to this end, they have taken advantage of the searches we have ordered into those who have usurped titles of nobility', and have made the most 'of certain abuses committed entirely against our wishes, either during such searches or during the setting up of winter quarters and other billetings of our troops'.[51] More explicitly, a decree of the *Conseil* of 1 June 1665 provides us with a glimpse of the nature of what was happening: 'frequently, the tax-farmers and their agents have caused anxiety among true *gentilshommes*', whereas 'they have come to terms with anyone' among those who have usurped the title of nobility.[52]

It does not seem in any way exaggerated therefore to propose that the fiscal policy of the absolute monarchy in France during the first half of the seventeenth century seriously disturbed the order of the nobility, and that this could have contributed in certain cases to a temporary alliance between popular, bourgeois and noble elements against the developing fiscal policy of the king.

If this resistance on the part of the nobility ended in a major political setback, it most probably obtained certain results and satisfactions, even though at a fairly modest level. The complaints and disturbances, which lasted for almost half a century, contributed to checking the reforming intentions of the monarchy and to maintaining abuses within the system. The records of the *élections* and the *Bureaux des Finances* would furnish valuable evidence in this area. Even at this stage, the financial regulations and administrative correspondence of the first part of Louis XIV's reign suggest that, in 1685, in the *pays de taille personnelle* at least, fiscal privilege had fully maintained itself and had successfully traversed the sixty preceding years of monarchical and absolutist history without suffering too much damage. The regulation of 30 March 1673, regarding *tailles*, denounces yet again 'the everyday manœuvrings of the rich to take advantage of their influence and artifice to have themselves and their tenants relieved [from *tailles*] at the expense of the poor';[53] and in his *instruction* of 28 May 1681, Colbert is forced to admit that 'almost all, or at least a considerable number of *gentilshommes*, *officiers* and other influential persons cause the tax rolls to be drawn up in their châteaux or in their houses or under their orders'.[54] In this area of government, the effective solidarity between the judicial and financial *officiers* and the nobility, all equally seigneurial and landed proprietors, paralysed the will of the *Conseil* and the *commissaires*. The royal *Déclaration* of 12 February 1685 took cognizance of the ineffectiveness of a too frequent use of *taxes d'office* by the *commissaires* to circumvent tax evasion;[55] while a decree of 24 September 1688 of the *Cour des Aides*† referred to one final abuse perpetrated by the *élus*†: 'In order to favour their own tenants, relatives and friends' they 'send their *commissions* into the parishes with notes attached enjoining the *collecteurs* to draw up their tax rolls through the registrar of the *élection* or his clerk, by which means they are able to render themselves masters of the assessments made on the *taillables*.'[56]

Behind the façade, then, of the absolute monarchy of Louis XIV, it is justifiable to imagine these privileges safeguarded and society therefore temporarily stabilised. Such a guarantee contributed quite as much as fear perhaps to the new docility of the nobility. It was a docility in face of an authority which pursued with every severity the conspirators of 1658–9;[57] but it was also a docility toward an authority which was in itself essentially conservative[58] and, once again, incarnate in the person of a king. The government of this young sovereign, who was so 'determined never to appoint a *Premier Ministre*', and who associated the nobility so closely in the ceremonial and liturgy which he gradually organised about his royal person, appeared most probably much less fearsome than the improvised policies of the Cardinal-Ministers and the tax-farmers during the worst period of the Thirty Years War.

NOTES

1 M. Bloch, from 1936, encouraged researchers to make good this gap. See *Annales d'Histoire économique et sociale* (1936) p. 238.

2 *Nouveau code des tailles ou recueil par ordre chronologique des ordonnances, édits et déclarations*, Poullin de Viéville, 1 p. 183 art. 19.

3 Ibid., p. 277 art. 34 and p. 370 art. 19.

4 Ibid., p. 370 art. 8.

5 Ibid., p. 277 art. 33.

6 E. Esmonin, *La taille en Normandie* (Paris, 1913) p. 549; also, Beaurepaire, *Cahiers des Etats de Normandie*, III p. 106.

7 E. Esmonin, ibid., p. 226.

8 Notarial minute-book, Paris, 5 August 1666, *Etude* XC, 162.

9 *Nouveau code des tailles*, II p. 20, Regulation of March 1667. The *lettres patentes* of August 1664 had expressly authorised the procedure: '. . . And in the event of their occupying more in the same parish, they may join them and make only one out of them,' ibid., 1 p. 556.

10 *Nouveau code des tailles*, 1 p. 280 art. 1, 'Edict of January 1634 concerning the regulation of the *tailles*, carrying the injunction to impose the said *tailles* on all those who have laid false claim to exemption in the past'; also, ibid., 1 p. 362, 'Edict of November 1640, carrying the revocation of ennoblement accorded during the last thirty years'.

11 J. Combes, *Traité des tailles et autres charges et subsides* (Paris, 1598) p. 82.

12 *Nouveau code des tailles*, 1 p. 215, *Déclaration* of 8 September: 'The *officiers*

of his household and others exempt from *taille* will be taxed unless they perform actual service.' Also, ibid., p. 229 art. 25, Edict concerning the regulations relating to the exempt, June 1614.

13   Beaurepaire, op. cit., iii p. 7, Dec 1634.

14   According to the *Déclaration* of the king conveying pardon to *gentilshommes* who had participated in the assemblies of the nobility, September 1658, B.N. *imprimés*, F 5001 (185).

15   M. de Beaumont, *Mémoire concernant les impositions et les droits en Europe* (Paris, 1768) ii p. 227 et seq.

16   A. Despeisses, *Traité des tailles et autres impositions* (Toulouse, 1643) p. 86.

17   M. de Beaumont, op. cit., pp. 129–32.

18   Ibid., p. 160.

19   Which most probably did not exclude the pursuit of disputes between the privileged and non-privileged on the subject of the classification of land.

20   *Arch. Hist. du Département de la Gironde*, ii p. 39.

21   De Sourdis, *Journal de l'Assemblée de la noblesse* (Paris, 1651), Arch. Nat. K. 118, No. 24, pp. 43–4; also, B.N. Lb 37 1858.

22   Richelieu, *Testament Politique*, ed. L. André (1947) pp. 218–23.

23   *Arch. Département de la Somme, bailliage d'Amiens*, B. 334.

24   Ibid., B. 333, *Déclaration royale* of 14 May 1639; also, B. 336, letter of the king, 5 June 1642. The monarchy adopted the same procedure in 1675. After announcing a call-up for actual service, the king justified the establishment of a tax for replacement in these terms, in a letter to the *intendants* of 14 January: 'in consideration of the great expense which the muster of the *ban et arrière-ban* involves my nobility in . . . I have deemed it fitting for this reason and because of the small amount of actual service which I could draw from it . . . I have no doubt but that my nobility will be entirely willing to be excused from serving in person for so small a sum . . .' Those who obstinately asked to serve in person were finally refused. Ibid., B. 337.

25   In 1675, in the *bailliage* of Amiens, for a fief bringing in 300 *livres* and less, the contribution was 40 *livres*; from 300 to 600: 80 *livres*; from 900 to 1500: 150 *livres*; from 1500 to 2000: 200 *livres*; and for a fief with a revenue of over 2000 *livres*: 300 *livres* in contribution.

26   *Requêtes et articles pour le rétablissement de la noblesse, éd.* A. de Montluc, cited by E. Lavisse, *Histoire de France*, Vol. vi, ii p. 390. This *mémoire* also demanded the suppression of venality in the king's household, the monopoly of a part of all ecclesiastical benefices for the younger sons of the nobility, the creation of military colleges and the authorisation of the right to participate in commerce without *dérogeance*. See also, in this context, Richelieu's *Testament Politique*, ed. L. Andre, pp. 221–3.

27   Paris, 1651, B.N., *imprimés*, Lb 37 1886.

28   Paris, 1649, ibid., 930.

29   B.N. Mss 500 Colbert, 203, *fol.* 257.

30   See on this subject the notable article by J. Jacquart, based on research into land registers, 'Propriété et exploitation rurale au sud de Paris dans la deuxième moitié du XVIe siècle', in *Bulletin de la Société d'Histoire moderne, 12e série*, Nos. 15–16 *(59e année)*.

31   The series of domanial and seigneurial leases contained in notarial minute-books or private archives are useful in this context.

32   As P. Goubert has already done, *Beauvais et le Beauvaisis, gentilshommes ruraux*, p. 206 et seq.

33   *Arch. Département de la Somme*, B 333, déclaration du sieur Glisy.

34   Ibid., B 338, *prévôté de Beauvaisis, déclaration du sieur du Gard.*

35 Ibid., *déclaration de Bartolomé de Luq.*

36 Ibid., B 338, the muster of 1675, *déclaration du sieur Louis de Tercelin.*

37 Ibid., B 336.

38 An analysis of the *déclarations* gives the following figures:

Déclaration without giving details	70
Infirm or aged	18
Son in army, or long personal service, or wounds received in serving the king	62
At present with the army	30
Ready to serve	134
Residing elsewhere	18
Doubtful excuses	6
Inhabitants of Amiens, invoking privileges of the town or their own rank as *officiers de justice*	11
Too poor to equip themselves	40
Agree to pay tax for replacement	6

39 De Sourdis, op. cit., p. 43.

40 *Déclaration des prétentions de la noblesse assemblée aux cordeliers de Paris,* 1651, B.N. Lb 37 1856, p. 11.

41 *Union de la noblesse de France touchant leurs prééminences* (Paris, 1649); also, *Requête au Roi par le corps de la noblesse pour les dignités de ducs et pairs de France et les honneurs et prééminences des nobles de ce royaume,* Arch. Nat., K 118,24.

42 These problems, which were so important to Saint-Simon, were fought over once again at the end of Louis XIV's reign and during the Regency following his death.

43 Already, in 1616, the nobility of Normandy complained 'that through the process of several levies which had been made indifferently on everybody, the nobility have been stripped of their prerogatives . . . rendering them liable to charges unfitting to their rank', Beaurepaire, *Doléances de la noblesse aux Etats de Normandie,* I p. 124 (cited by E. Esmonin, op. cit.).

44 *Déclaration des prétentions de la noblesse,* op. cit., p. 11.

45 De Sourdis, op. cit., p. 2.

46 Ibid., p. 44.

47 *Lettre circulaire envoyée dans les provinces à tous les gentilshommes par ordre de l'assemblée de noblesse;* also, *Lettre envoyée sur le sujet de l'assemblée de noblesse,* B.N. Lb 37 1849 and 1859: 'If we remain silent, we shall be oppressed and have to suffer without remedy that our wives and daughters, our houses and our property, our honour and our lives remain exposed to the insolence and pillage of the military, the *prévôts,* the *gabelleurs* and *partisans* . . . If God does not inspire some legitimate means to maintain the advantages of our birth, we shall settle to pay the *taille,* we shall faithfully pay all sorts of taxes and provide the soldiers who lodge in our houses with the best possible treatment, so as to spare our wives and daughters; and we shall be forced to pay court to *prévôts, gabelleurs* and *partisans.*'

48 *Nouveau code des tailles,* op. cit., II p. 422.

49 See in particular the *Lettre circulaire à tous les gentilshommes pour leur adresser l'arrêt fait à l'assemblée de la Roche-Guyon,* B.N. Lb 37 2700; also, the letter of a *gentilhomme* on the current uprisings: 'The soldiery make no distinction between the *gentilhomme* and the peasant', B.N. Lb 37 3128.

50 See in this context the numerous letters published by P. Clément, *Lettres Instructions et Mémoires de Colbert* (Paris, 1861) I.

51 *Déclaration au Roi portant pardon aux gentilshommes,* Sept 1658 B.N. f 5001 (185).

52 An *arrêt* of the *Conseil* of 1 June 1665, suspending searches into the nobility in Normandy, cited by E. Esmonin, op. cit., p. 208. Already in 1655, the Archbishop of Rouen had declared to the king that 'the search still goes on more severely than ever into the titles of the nobility here . . . who see with anger the sleep of their dead ancestors disturbed; they sift through, for the fourth time in twenty years, the ashes of their fathers', Beaurepaire, *Cahiers des Etats de Normandie*, III p. 404.

53 *Nouveau code des tailles*, op. cit., II p. 103.

54 P. Clément, op. cit., II p. 154: 'His Majesty has received various advice that in almost all the parishes, the principal inhabitants and the rich find easy means for discharging themselves from paying *tailles* . . .'

55 *Nouveau code des tailles*, op. cit., II p. 189: '*Taxes d'office* have been introduced to maintain equality in levying the *tailles* and to oblige the richer sort and those in authority to bear their share in proportion to their capacity; but whatever care we have used to compel those we have appointed to apportion the *tailles* to continue the said *taxes d'office*, those who have found themselves subject to them have made every effort to avoid the effect of our orders and regulations, by initiating appeal proceedings in our *Cours des Aides*, where they easily obtain discharge . . . since the parishes are not in a condition to meet the expenses of a trial.'

56 Ibid., II, *arrêt* of 24 September 1688. It was probably in noting this setback that a certain number of minds in the entourage of the *contrôleur-général* came to envisage the suppression of *taille personnelle* altogether and the generalisation of a form of land tax.

57 Once more, as a result of these events, a section of the nobility could claim that the *princes* and the *grands* scarcely cared at all for their collective interest, through their making an easy settlement with the Crown and abandoning the claims of the *gentilshommes* in general. The development of a more centralised royal administration, the increased role given to the *intendants* and *commissaires*, also contributed to breaking noble solidarity, thus depriving the order as a whole of part of its cohesion and dynamic.

58 The royal authority will show great severity toward the popular uprisings of 1675 and allow attempts at seigneurial reorganisation to take their course in several provinces, although they were seriously detrimental to the interests of the peasants. See especially, in this respect, G. Livet, *L'Intendance d'Alsace sous Louis XIV*, III Chapter IV; also, P. de Saint-Jacob, *Les paysans de la Bourgogne du Nord au dernier siècle de l'Ancien Régime* (Paris, 1960) I Chapters II, III, and V, 'Les modes de possession du sol, la seigneurie, les charges paysannes'.

Glossary

Aides	Indirect taxes on items of consumption, such as meat, fish, wood and, especially, wine.
Asséeur-collecteur	An assessor and collector of *taille* (q.v.).
Bailli	A royal official with jurisdiction over a *bailliage*. Medieval in origin, the office had become almost entirely formal during the course of the sixteenth century, with the appointment of legally qualified *lieutenants* (*lieutenants généraux*, *lieutenants criminels*, *lieutenants civils*) to administer the courts of the *bailliages*. By the sixteenth century, nobility had become a pre-requisite for appointment as *bailli*, and one of the chief remaining functions of the office lay in issuing the *ban et arrière-ban* (q.v.). The equivalent official in the *Midi* was the *sénéchal*, although no absolute distinction is to be made between north and south in this respect.
Bailliage	See previous entry.
Ban et arrière-ban	The traditional proclamation issued to muster the nobility for military service. The '*ban*' was addressed to direct feudatories of the king, and the '*arrière-ban*' to their vassals. It is suggested that such proclamations were used under Louis XIII as an indirect method of taxing the nobility, by requiring them to provide for the maintenance of substitutes (see Chapter 8, pp. 237–9). Proclamations were less frequent after 1661. The last recorded was in 1697.
Banalités	Seigneurial rights obliging tenants to use the mill, oven and winepresses of the *seigneur*.
Bureau des finances	*Bureaux des finances* were created in the *généralités* (q.v.) during the sixteenth century. An edict of 1551 established the office of *trésorier général*, and a further edict of 1577 fixed the number of *trésoriers généraux* at five in each *généralité*. The number in each *bureau* increased with the growth of financial business and the development of venality during the later sixteenth and early seventeenth centuries.
Cahier de doléances	Representatives of each estate of the realm drew up a *cahier de doléances* on the convoking of *Estates General*, listing their grievances and wishes.
Cens	An annual due paid to the *seigneur* in return for land

granted on his *directe* (q.v.). Almost always paid in money, it was much reduced in value as a result of inflation by the seventeenth century.

Chambre des Comptes

The *Chambre des Comptes* of Paris and the provincial *Chambres des Comptes* evolved from the medieval *curia regis* (q.v.). Their function included the registration and auditing of taxes, and the registration of the leases for the tax-farms.

Chambre des Grands Jours

A special tribunal created from a *Parlement* (q.v.), to expedite justice in difficult circumstances, such as those arising from the chronic violence and lawlessness of the *gentilshommes* of the Auvergne in the mid-seventeenth century which led to the holding of *Grands Jours* at Clermont in 1665.

Champart

That part of a peasant's harvest due to his *seigneur* and paid in kind. It could amount to as much as a third of the harvest, but the average payment was approximately twelve sheaves in the hundred.

Chevauchée

A circuit made by an official. The term *'en chevauchée'* was often used of a *commissaire* (q.v.) out on his tour of inspection in a *généralité* (q.v.).

Coadjuteur

An assistant to a bishop, or indeed to any benefice-holder.

Collecteur

See *asséeur-collecteur*.

Commensal

An officer or servant in the royal household, or in the household of a great noble (literally, someone sharing his table). Royal appointments were much sought after, since they carried first degree nobility.

Commissaire

An official provided with a *commission* to undertake particular duties in a province. Increasingly used under Richelieu, *commissaires* became embryonic *intendants* of the later period.

Conseil de bailliage

The court of the *bailliage* (q.v.).

Conseil d'Etat

By the seventeenth century, this phrase had become the one most commonly used to describe the king's *Conseil* taken as a whole body, containing within it its various departmental sub-divisions. The phrase was also used to describe the king's *Conseil* in its administrative, as distinct from its political, competence. This was especially so in the judicial sphere, where it was sometimes used synonymously with the phrase *Conseil des parties*, or *Conseil privé*, to describe that part of the *Conseil* which exercised the private, reserved justice (the *justice retenue*) of the king, as distinct from the ordinary justice of the king which was dispensed in the 'public' courts. Since the rendering of judgement was the royal function *par excellence*, it is not surprising that the generic term *Conseil d'Etat* should still be used in the

	seventeenth century to describe the *Conseil* when it was performing that function.
Conseiller	A widely used title, covering members of the *Conseil d'Etat* (q.v.), the *Parlements* (q.v.) and lesser courts.
Conseiller aux Requêtes	A counsellor in the *Requêtes*, one of the three main *Chambres* of the *Parlement de Paris* (q.v.). Originally formed as a clearing house for requests for justice made to the king, the *Requêtes* gained the major right from 1364 to judge, as a court of first instance, civil cases brought by litigants possessing the privilege of *committimus*, which enabled them to bring their cases directly to the *Requêtes* from anywhere in the realm. This became and remained its main function.
Conseiller d'Etat	See *Conseiller* and *Conseil d'Etat.*
Conseil privé	See *Conseil d'Etat.*
Corvée	A labour due owed by the peasant to his *seigneur*.
Cours des Aides	Courts whose primary function was to try both civil and criminal cases arising from the administration of the *taille* (q.v.), the *aides* (q.v.), the *traites* (q.v.) and the *gabelle*. The *Cour des Aides* of Paris had approximately the same 'ressort' (area of jurisdiction) as the *Parlement de Paris* (q.v.). In precedence, the *Cours des Aides* would normally come after the *Parlements* and the *Chambres des Comptes* among the 'sovereign courts'.
Crue	A new or increased direct tax.
Curia regis	The original body through which the medieval king took counsel and dispensed justice.
Dérogeance	Loss of status by nobles participating in certain occupations, such as retail trade.
Directe	The 'directe'—sometimes called the *domaine éminent*—was both the authority of the *seigneur* over his land and the land over which he held that authority. That part of his 'directe' which he granted out in tenures was known as the *directe seigneuriale*. A tenant on the *directe seigneuriale* enjoyed the *domaine utile* over his tenure, that is the right to enjoy its produce, in return for fulfilling various obligations to the *seigneur*. That part of the *directe* which the *seigneur* retained and farmed either directly or indirectly was known as the *domaine proche*.
Domaine éminent	See previous entry.
Domaine proche	See *Directe.*
Domaine utile	See *Directe.*
Echevin	A member of a municipal corporation. The equivalent title in the *Midi* was often *consul*.
Ecu	A coin whose value depended on its declared value in terms of the money of account, the *livre tournois*. On the foreign

exchange market it was valued at 3 *livres* in the seventeenth century.

Election   An administrative district within a *généralité* for purposes of levying *taille*, *aides*, etc., under the jurisdiction of *élus*.

Elu   See previous entry.

Enquêtes   One of the three main *Chambres* of the *Parlement de Paris* (q.v.). Founded originally to undertake the examination of cases prior to litigation in the *Parlement*, involving written as distinct from oral evidence.

Feu   A unit for purposes of taxation. Although meaning a 'hearth', and therefore a household, the designation of '*feux*' became in time quite inexact, and their number did not necessarily correspond to the actual number of households in a community.

Généralité   The term derives from the medieval *généraux des finances*, of whom, by the fifteenth century, there were four. In 1542, Francis I established sixteen *recettes générales* for the receipt of taxes throughout the realm, each under a *receveur général*. The office of *trésorier général des finances* was established in 1551 (see *Bureau des finances*). Subsequently, the number of *généralités* increased, becoming twenty-three by the mid-seventeenth century. The fiscal division of the *généralité* became, significantly, the basic administrative unit of the *ancien régime*.

Grand 'Chambre   The senior *Chambre* of the *Parlement de Paris*.

Grand prévôt   An official with jurisdiction over members of the Court.

Hectare   An area of approximately two and a half acres.

Hobereau   A provincial nobleman, often of limited means.

Huissier   A court bailiff.

Justicier   The traditional title of the king *qua* dispenser of justice.

Laboureur   A prosperous peasant-farmer.

Lettre de cachet   A letter issued personally by the king, containing orders to an individual, or regarding a particular case of which the king himself was taking direct cognizance.

Lieutenant-général   *Lieutenants-généraux* were appointed from the sixteenth century to assist and supervise the function of provincial *gouverneurs*. At a lower level, *lieutenants-généraux* were appointed to the *bailliages* (q.v.).

Lit de justice   A *lit de justice* was held when the king attended the *Parlement de Paris* (q.v.) in person to enforce registration of his edicts, on the theory that by his presence he resumed the authority which he ordinarily delegated to the public courts. In the other *Parlements*, a *prince du sang* (q.v.) was often delegated to attend for this purpose.

Lods et ventes   Important seigneurial dues charged at the time of the transfer of tenures, either by inheritance or sale.

Maître des requêtes   One of an important group of lawyers originally appointed to deal with pleas for justice to the king. Their main function in the seventeenth century lay in the *Conseil* itself, in the work of the *Conseil privé* (q.v.). *Intendants* were frequently chosen from among this élite *corps* of lawyers. Their expert knowledge of the effects of royal legislation made them a likely choice for establishing the ultimate administrative link between the *Conseil* and the provinces, through the office of the *intendant*.

Métairie   See following entry.

Métayage   Land held on the basis of sharing its produce between the peasant *métayer* and the landowner, who frequently supplied seed and stock. The land so held was a *métairie*.

Métayer   See previous entry.

Méteil   A mixed crop of wheat and rye.

Mouvance   A subinfeudated fief.

Noble d'épée   A member of the *noblesse d'épée*, the nobility of the 'sword', who were, either in fact or in their own consideration, heirs of the traditional, 'ancient' nobility, which performed military service as feudatories of the king. Its relationship to the *noblesse de robe* (q.v.) is currently debated. (See Chapter 1, pp. 16–20.)

Noble de robe   A member of the *noblesse de robe*, whose nobility derived from office in the higher appointments of the judiciary. (See Chapter 1, pp. 16–20.)

Officier   Someone holding office through purchase in the judicial and financial administration. There is no really satisfactory English translation.

Parcours   The right enjoyed by neighbouring communities to pasture beasts on each other's 'common' land, during the period of *'vaine pâture'* (q.v.). It was a major impediment to agricultural improvement.

Parlement de Paris   The *Parlement de Paris* evolved out of the medieval *curia regis* (q.v.). Although formed to undertake appellate jurisdiction arising from the increased demand for royal justice in the late medieval period, and although its judicial function was to remain primary, it carried with it, genetically, an imprint of the comprehensive nature of the royal authority itself. Its registration of royal edicts, together with its claim to discuss them and remonstrate concerning them, and, at need, delay registration, gave the court a political function and quasi-legislative involvement.

Originally, the *Parlement de Paris* had jurisdiction over the whole realm, but with the increase in litigation and the gradual agglomeration of provinces under royal control in the late medieval period, *Parlements* were created at Toulouse (1443), Grenoble (1453), Bordeaux (1462), Dijon (1477), Rouen (1499), Aix-en-Provence (1501) and Rennes (1553). Although these were 'provincial' *Parlements, par excellence*, it is important to realise that, in the seventeenth century, the jurisdiction of the *Parlement de Paris* still extended over some forty per cent of the realm, and that the privilege of *committimus* enabled cases to be initiated there from the whole realm. The *Parlement de Paris* was therefore the most important royal court, both in its authority and its prestige. The claim of the *Parlements* that, as 'sovereign courts', their judgements were 'without appeal', brought them into conflict with the *Conseil* in the early seventeenth century, when the 'sovereignty' of the crown was increasingly expressed through *commissaires* (q.v.) armed with powers to 'evoke' cases away from the ordinary courts and to over-ride the ordinary processes of justice.

Parlements   See previous entry.

Parties casuelles   Sale of office was administered through the *bureau* of the *parties casuelles*, formed by Francis I from 1523.

Partisans   Tax-farmers.

Paulette   An annual tax introduced by Sully, in 1604, at the suggestion of the tax-farmer Paulet. By paying it, an office-holder was assured of the inheritance of his office within his family or by his legatee. Prior to 1604, inheritance had depended on the survival of an office-holder for at least forty days following his making the bequest. The *Paulette* simply abolished the forty day rule, and thereby facilitated and reinforced hereditary tenure of office.

Pays d'élections   Provinces sub-divided into *élections* (q.v.) for purposes of tax-administration. These provinces were for the most part without Estates and made up the core of monarchical France. No rigid distinction may however be made between *pays d'états* and *pays d'élections*, since some *pays d'élections* retained their *états*—Auvergne and Normandie indeed until the mid-seventeenth century.

Pays d'états   Provinces with Estates, i.e. assemblies periodically convoked to represent the estates of those provinces. The most important in the seventeenth century were those of Brittany, Languedoc, Burgundy and Provence.

Premier-Président   The chief justice of the *Parlement de Paris*, nominated by the king. Being non-venal, the nomination was always revocable. After the King and Chancellor, the *Premier-Président* was the senior law-officer of the realm.

Président   A presiding judge in any court, but especially in the *Parlements* (q.v.).

Présidial   One of the courts, the *présidiaux*, created by Henry II in 1551, to relieve the pressure of appeals to the *Parlements* (q.v.) from the *bailliages* (q.v.). In certain cases, they also served as courts of first instance.

Prévôt   An official serving as judge and administrator at a level of responsibility normally below that of the *bailli* (q.v.). The *prévôtés* maintained the peace of towns and conducted the primary business of local government. In Paris, however, the *prévôté* had the competence and authority of a *bailliage*.

Prévôt des marchands
The chief officer of the municipal administration of Paris, nominated by the king.

Prévôt des maréchaux
The *prévôts des maréchaux* were constituted under Francis I, as military personnel rendering summary justice in cases of banditry and highway robbery. They served as a force to police and maintain the peace of provincial France.

Princes du sang
The immediate princes of the royal blood.

Princes étrangers
Princes of sovereign houses at the French court, such as those of Savoy and Lorraine, and including the Rohan and Bouillon families.

Procureur-fiscal
The representative of the *seigneur* in a seigneurial court. Concerned primarily with protecting the fiscal interests of the *seigneur*, he administered the levying of seigneurial dues.

Quartenier
An officer responsible for the maintenance of order in a *quartier* of Paris. Originally elected on a restricted franchise, the *quarteniers* were, by the seventeenth century, nominees of the king.

Quintal
A weight approximately equivalent to one hundredweight.

Receveurs généraux
Officiers in charge of the provincial *recettes générales*. (See *Généralité*.)

Receveurs particuliers
Officiers responsible for the initial receipt of *taille* from the *élus* (see *Election*) before transmitting it into the hands of the *receveurs généraux* (see previous entry).

Rentes
Loans made by individuals to the state.

Requêtes
See *Conseiller aux Requêtes*.

Seigneurie
The area over which a *seigneur* exercised his authority. (See *Directe*.)

Sénéchal
See *Bailli*.

Sénéchaussée
See *Bailliage*.

Taille
The major direct tax of the monarchy, of great complexity and variety in its incidence and administration. In the provinces where *taille personnelle* was levied, it fell on the peasantry for the most part, according to the amount for which they were personally assessed. In these provinces the nobility were exempt as regards their personal possessions and the land they directly cultivated (the *domaine proche*, q.v.), up to an amount which varied from one area to another. In the provinces where *taille réelle* was levied, it fell on 'common land', that is non-noble land, and was paid by whosoever held it.

Taxe d'office
A tax imposed by a *commissaire* (q.v.) on his own personal assessment. Levied in cases where either under or over

	assessment was suspected, *taxes d'office* were intended to make the tax-system more equitable.
Traitants	Tax-farmers who formed *traites* (in this context simply treaties, agreements) with the state for the collection of an indirect tax.
Traites	Customs charged on goods crossing either the external or certain of the internal provincial frontiers of the realm.
Trésoriers de France	See *Bureau des finances.*
Vaine pâture	The right of the inhabitants of a *seigneurie* to pasture beasts on the 'common' lands, which included, among other areas, fields after harvest and the fallow land. It inhibited agricultural improvement. (See *Parcours.*)

Select Bibliography

This select bibliography is intended to assist students wishing to read further in the areas of French seventeenth-century history discussed in this collection of extracts and articles. Works which relate to the subject of more than one section have been cross-referenced accordingly.

A GENERAL STUDIES

(1) Esmonin, E. *Etudes sur la France des XVIIe et XVIIIe siècles* (reprinted articles, etc.), Paris, 1964.

(2) Forster, R. and Greene, J.P. '*Introduction*', *Preconditions of Revolution in Early Modern Europe*, London, 1970, pp. 1–18.

(3) Goubert, P. *The Ancien Régime: French Society 1600–1750*, London, 1973 (translation by S. Cox of Vol. I, *L'Ancien Régime*, '*La Société*', Paris, 1969). Vol. II remains untranslated (see following entry).

(4) —— *L'Ancien Régime*, Vol. II, '*Les Pouvoirs*', Paris, 1973.

(5) Koenigsberger, H. G. 'Dominium Regale or Dominium Politicum et Regale: Monarchies and Parliaments in Early Modern Europe', Inaugural Lecture, King's College, London, 1975.

(6) Mandrou, R. *La France aux XVIIe et XVIIIe siècles* (Nouvelle Clio), Paris, 1967.

(7) —— *Louis XIV en son temps* (Peuples et Civilisations), Paris, 1973.

(8) Méthivier, H. *Le Siècle de Louis XIV* (Que sais-je? series), Paris, 1962.

(9) —— *Le Siècle de Louis XIII* (Que sais-je? series), Paris, 1964.

(10) —— *L'Ancien Régime* (Que sais-je? series), 6e édition, Paris, 1974.

(11) Mousnier, R. *Les XVIe et XVIIe siècles* (Histoire générale des civilisations), Paris, 1954.

(12) Pagès, G. *La Monarchie d'Ancien Régime en France de Henri IV à Louis XIV*, Paris, 1928.

(13) —— *Les Institutions monarchiques sous Louis XIII et Louis XIV*, 'Les Cours de Sorbonne', Centre de Documentation Universitaire, Paris, 1961.

(14) —— *Les Origines du XVIIIe siècle au temps de Louis XIV, 1680–1715*, 'Les Cours de Sorbonne', Centre de Documentation Universitaire, Paris, 1961.

(15) Prestwich, M. 'The Making of Absolute Monarchy', in *France: Government and Society*, ed. J. M. Wallace-Hadrill and J. McManners, London, 1957, pp. 105–33.

(16) Rabb, T. K. *The Struggle for Stability in Early Modern Europe*, Oxford, 1975.

(17) Ranum, O. and Ranum, P. *The Century of Louis XIV*, New York, 1972 (selected documents, with introduction and commentary).

(18) Rule, J. C. (ed.) *Louis XIV and the Craft of Kingship*, Ohio, 1969.

(19) Shennan, J. H. *Government and Society in France, 1461–1661*, London, 1969.

(20) Tapié, V. L. *La France de Louis XIII et de Richelieu*, Paris, 1952 (trans. D. McN. Lockie as *France in the Age of Louis XIII and Richelieu*, London, 1974).

B PARTICULAR STUDIES

(21) Asher, L. *The Resistance to the maritime classes: the survival of feudalism in the France of Colbert*, Los Angeles, 1960.

(22) Bitton, D. *French Nobility in Crisis, 1560–1640*, Stanford, 1969.

(23) Bluche, F. 'L'origine sociale des secrétaires d'Etat de Louis XIV (1661–1715)', *XVIIe Siècle*, Nos. 42/43, 1959 ('Serviteurs du Roi'), pp. 8–22.

(24) Bourgeon, J.-L. 'L'Ile de la Cité pendant la Fronde: étude sociale', *Fédération des Sociétés hist. et arch. de Paris et de l'Ile de France*, 13, 1962.

(25) Buisseret, D. J. *Sully and the Growth of Centralised Government in France, 1598–1610*, London, 1968.

(26) Church, W. F. *The impact of Absolutism in France—under Richelieu, Mazarin and Louis XIV*, New York, 1969.

(27) Dent, J. 'An Aspect of the Crisis of the Seventeenth Century: the Collapse of the Financial Administration of the French Monarchy (1653–1661)', *Econ. Hist. Review*, 20, 1967, pp. 241–56.

(28) —— *Crisis in Finance: Crown, Financiers and Society in Seventeenth-Century France*, Newton Abbot, 1973.

(29) Franklin, J. H. *Jean Bodin and the Rise of Absolutist Theory*, Cambridge, 1973.

(30) Grassby, R. B. 'Social status and commercial enterprise under Louis XIV', *Econ. Hist. Review*, 1961, pp. 19–38.

(31) Hartung, F. and Mousnier, R. 'Quelques problèmes concernant la monarchie absolue', *10th Congress of Historical Sciences, Rome, 1955, Relazioni, IV, Modern History*, Rome, 1955.

(32) Knecht, R. J. *The Fronde*, Appreciations in History series, Historical Association, London, 1975.

(33) Kossmann, E. H. *The Fronde*, Leiden, 1954.

(34) Labatut, J.-P. *Les Ducs et pairs de France au XVIIe siècle: étude sociale*, Paris, 1972.

(35) Littlejohn, G. M. 'An introduction to Lublinskaya', *Economy and Society*, I, 1972, pp. 57–64.

(36) Lublinskaya, A. D. *French Absolutism: the crucial phase, 1620–1629*, trans. B. Pearce, Cambridge, 1968.

(37) —— 'The contemporary bourgeois conception of Absolute Monarchy', *Economy and Society*, I, 1972, pp. 65–92.

(38) —— 'Popular masses and the social relations of the epoch of abso-

lutism: methodology of research', *Economy and Society*, ii, 1973, pp. 343–75.

(39) Mandrou, R. *Introduction à la France moderne: essai de psychologie historique, 1500–1640*, Paris, 1961.

(40) Meuvret, J. 'Comment les Français du XVII siècle voyaient l'impôt', *XVIIe Siècle*, Nos. 25/26, 1955.

(41) Moote, A. L. *The Revolt of the Judges*, Princeton, N.J., 1971.

(42) —— 'The French Crown versus its judicial and financial officials, 1616–1683', *Journal of Modern History*, xxxiv, 1962, pp. 146–60.

(43) —— 'The Parlementary Fronde and seventeenth-century Robe solidarity', *French Historical Studies*, ii, 1962, pp. 79–82.

(44) —— 'Law and Justice under Louis XIV', *Louis XIV and the Craft of Kingship*, ed. J. C. Rule, Ohio, 1969, pp. 224–39.

(45) Mousnier, R. *La vénalité des offices sous Henri IV et Louis XIII*, Rouen, 1945 (reissued Paris, 1971).

(46) —— 'Comment les Français du XVIIe siècle voyaient la constitution', *XVIIe Siècle*, Nos. 25/26, 1955.

(47) —— 'Quelques aspects de la fonction publique dans la société française du XVIIe siècle', *XVIIe Siècle*, Nos. 42/43, 1959 ('*Serviteurs du Roi*'), pp. 3–7.

(48) —— 'L'évolution des institutions monarchiques en France et ses relations avec l'état social', *XVIIe Siècle*, 1963, pp. 57–72.

(49) —— 'Problèmes de stratification sociale', *Introduction* to *Deux Cahiers de la noblesse pour les Etats Généraux de 1649–1651*, ed. with introductions by J.-P. Labatut and Y. Durand, Paris, 1965, pp. 9–49.

(50) —— 'French Institutions and Society, 1610–1661', *New Cambridge Modern History*, Vol. iv, 1970, pp. 474–502.

(51) —— 'The Fronde', *Preconditions of Revolution in Early Modern Europe*, London, 1970, pp. 131–59.

(52) —— 'The Social Structure of the Kingdom of France', *Peasant Uprisings in Seventeenth-Century France, Russia and China*, London, 1971, pp. 3–31 (translation by B. Pearce of *Fureurs paysannes: les Paysans dans les révoltes du XVIIe siècle (France, Russie, Chine)*, Paris, 1967).

(53) —— *Social Hierarchies: 1450 to the Present*, London, 1973.

(54) Pagès, G. 'Autour du "Grand Orage": Richelieu et Marillac, deux politiques', *Revue Historique*, clxxix, 1937, pp. 63–97.

(55) —— 'La vénalité des offices dans l'ancienne France', *Revue Historique*, clxix, 1932, pp. 477–95.

(56) Parker, D. 'The Social Foundations of French Absolutism, 1610–1630', *Past and Present*, No. 53, 1971, pp. 67–89.

(57) Ranum, O. *Paris in the Age of Absolutism*, New York, 1968.

(58) Rowen, H. H. 'Louis XIV and Absolutism', *Louis XIV and the Craft of Kingship*, ed. J. C. Rule, Ohio, 1969.

(59) Russell-Major, J. 'The Crown and the Aristocracy in Renaissance France', *American Historical Review*, lxix, 3, 1964.

(60) Salmon, J. H. M. *Society in Crisis: France in the Sixteenth Century*, London, 1975.

258   *Select Bibliography*

(61)   Treasure, G. R. R.   *Cardinal Richelieu and the Development of Absolutism*, London, 1969.

C   ECONOMIC AND SOCIAL REFERENCES
Reference Section A: (3) and (4).
Reference Section B: (21), (22), (24), (28), (30), (36), (37), (38), (49), (52), (56) and (60).

(62)   Baehrel, R.   *Une Croissance: la Basse-Provence rurale (fin du XVIe siècle—1789)*, Paris, 1961.

(63)   Bloch, M.   *French Rural History: an essay in its basic characteristics*, trans. J. Sondheimer, London, 1966.

(64)   Bondois, P. M.   'La misère sous Louis XIV: la Disette de 1662', *Revue d'histoire économique et sociale*, 1924, pp. 53–117.

(65)   Carrière, C.   'La draperie languedocienne dans la seconde moitié du XVIIe siècle: contribution à l'étude de la conjoncture levantine', *Hommage à E. Labrousse*, Paris, 1974, pp. 157–72.

(66)   Delumeau, J.   'Le commerce extérieur français au XVIIe siècle', *XVIIe Siècle*, Nos. 70/71, 1966, pp. 81–105.

(67)   —— *et al.   Le mouvement lu port de Saint-Malo, 1681–1720, bilan statistique*, Paris, 1966.

(68)   Deyon, P.   'La production manufacturière en France au XVIIe siècle et ses problèmes', *XVIIe Siècle*, Nos 70/71, 1966, pp. 47–63.

(69)   —— *Amiens, capitale provinciale: étude sur la société urbaine au XVIIe siècle*, Paris, 1967.

(70)   Goubert, P.   *Beauvais et le Beauvaisis de 1600–1730*, Paris, 1960 (published in abridged form as *Cent Mille Provinciaux au XVIIe siècle: Beauvais et le Beauvaisis de 1600 à 1730*, Paris, 1968).

(71)   —— 'The French Peasantry of the Seventeenth Century: a regional example', *Past and Present*, No. 10, 1956 (repr. in T. Aston (ed.), *Crisis in Europe, 1560–1660*, London, 1965, pp. 141–65.

(72)   —— 'Recent theories and research in French population between 1500 and 1700', *Population in History*, ed. D. V. Glass and D. E. C. Eversley, London, 1965, pp. 457–73.

(73)   —— 'Le régime démographique français au temps de Louis XIV', *Histoire économique et sociale de la France*, ed. E. Labrousse *et al.*, Vol. II, 1660–1789, Paris, 1970, pp. 23–54.

(74)   Jacquart, J.   'La Fronde des Princes dans la région parisienne et ses conséquences matérielles', *Revue d'histoire moderne et contemporaine* 7, 1960, pp. 257–90.

(75)   —— 'La production agricole dans la France du XVIIe siècle', *XVIIe Siècle*, Nos. 70/71, 1966, pp. 21–46.

(76)   Labatut, J.-P.   'Situation sociale du quartier du Marais pendant la Fronde parlementaire, 1648–1649', *XVIIe Siècle*, No. 38, 1958, pp. 55–81.

(77)   Labrousse, E., *et al.   Histoire économique et sociale de la France*, Vol. II, 1660–1789, Paris, 1970.

(78)   Lemarchand, G.   'Crises économiques et atmosphère sociale en milieu urbain sous Louis XIV', *Revue d'histoire moderne et contemporaine*, 14, 1967, pp. 224–65.

(79) Le Roy Ladurie, E. 'History and Climate', *Economy and Society in Early Modern Europe: Essays from Annales*, ed. P. Burke, London, 1972, pp. 134–69.

(80) —— *Histoire du climat depuis l'an mil*, Paris, 1967 (trans. by B. Bray as *Times of Feast: Times of Famine: a history of climate since the year 1000*, London, 1971).

(81) —— *Les Paysans de Languedoc*, Paris, 1966 (trans. J. Day as *The Peasants of Languedoc*, Urbana, 1974, from French paperback edition, 1969).

(82) Merle, L. '*La métairie et l'évolution agraire de la Gâtine poitevine de la fin du Moyen Age à la Révolution*, Paris, 1958.

(83) Meuvret, J. 'Le commerce des grains et des farines à Paris et les marchands parisiens à l'époque de Louis XIV', *Revue d'histoire moderne et contemporaine*, 1956, pp. 169–203.

(84) —— 'Demographic crisis in France from the sixteenth to the eighteenth century', *Population in History*, ed. D. V. Glass and D. E. C. Eversley, London, 1965, pp. 507–22.

(85) Mireaux, E. *Une province française au temps du Grand Roi: La Brie*, Paris, 1952.

(86) Morineau, B. 'Flottes de commerce et trafics français en Méditerranée au XVIIe siècle', *XVIIe Siècle*, 1970, pp. 135–71.

(87) Mousnier, R. 'Etudes sur la population de la France au XVIIe siècle', *Bulletin de la Société d'Etude du XVIIe Siècle*, No. 16, 1952, pp. 527–42.

(88) Pillorget, R. 'Les problèmes monétaires français de 1602 à 1689', *XVIIe Siècle*, Nos. 70/71, 1966, pp. 107–30.

(89) Reinhard, M. and Armengaud, A. *Histoire générale de la population mondiale*, Paris, 1961, pp. 122–35.

(90) Roupnel, G. *La ville et la campagne du XVIIe siècle. Etude sur les populations du pays dijonnais*, Paris, 1922 (rev. ed., 1955).

(91) Saint-Jacob, P. de 'La Bourgogne rurale vers 1685', *Les Paysans de la Bourgogne du Nord au dernier siècle de l'ancien régime*, Paris, 1960, première partie, pp. 3–170.

(92) Sée, H. *Histoire économique de la France*, I, 1942.

(93) Venard, M. *Bourgeois et paysans au XVIIe siècle: recherches sur le rôle des bourgeois parisiens dans la vie agricole au Sud de Paris*, Paris, 19757.

(94) Wolfe, M. 'French Views on Wealth and Taxes from the Middle Ages to the Old Regime', *Revisions in Mercantilism*, ed. D. C. Coleman, London, 1969, pp. 190–209.

D THE FOLLOWING WORKS ARE USEFUL REFERENCES FOR INSTITUTIONAL HISTORY

Reference Section A: (5), (12), (13), (14), and (19).

Reference Section B: (22), (28) and (41).

(95) Charmeil, J.-P. *Les Trésoriers de France à l'époque de la Fronde*, Paris, 1964.

(96) Doucet, R. *Les Institutions de la France au XVIe siècle*, Paris 1948.

(97) Hurt, J. J. 'The Parlement of Brittany and the Crown, 1665–1675', *French Historical Studies*, IV, 4, 1966, pp. 411–34.

(98) Marion, M. *Dictionnaire des Institutions de la France au XVIIe et XVIIIe siècles*, Paris, 1923 (repr. 1968).

(99) Mousnier, R. 'Le Conseil du Roi de la mort de Henri IV au gouvernement personnel de Louis XIV', *Etudes d'histoire moderne et contemporaine, Société d'histoire moderne*, I, 1947, pp. 29–67.

(100) 'Etat et commissaire: recherches sur la création des intendants de 1634 à 1638', *Forschungen zu staat und Verfassung: Festgabe für Fritz Hartung*, Berlin, 1958, pp. 325–44.

(101) —— *et al. Le Conseil du Roi de Louis XII à la Revolution*, Paris, 1970.

(102) Shennan, J. H. *The Parlement of Paris*, London, 1968.

(103) Zeller, G. *Les Institutions de la France au XVIe siècle*, Paris, 1948.

(104) Wolfe, M. *The Fiscal System of Renaissance France*, Yale, 1972.

E POPULAR UPRISINGS IN SEVENTEENTH-CENTURY FRANCE
Reference Section A: (16), (17) and (20).
Reference Section B: (38), (51) and (56).

(105) Beik, W. 'Magistrates and Popular Uprisings in France before the Fronde: the Case of Toulouse', *Journal of Modern History*, 46, 1974, pp. 585–608.

(106) Bercé, Y.-M. *Histoire des Croquants: études des soulèvements populaires au XVIIe siècle dans le sud-ouest de la France*, 2 vols, Geneva, 1974.

(107) Bernard, L. 'The French State and Popular Uprisings under Louis XIV', *French Historical Studies*, 1964, pp. 454–74.

(108) Boissonnade, P. 'L'administration royale et les soulèvements populaires en Angoumois, en Saintonge et en Poitou, pendant le ministère de Richelieu (1624–1642)', *Bulletin et Mémoires de la Société des Antiquaires de l'Ouest*, 2e série, XXVI, 1902.

(109) Degarne, M. 'Etudes sur les soulèvements provinciaux en France avant la Fronde: la révolution du Rouergue en 1643, *XVIIe Siècle*, 1962, pp. 3–18.

(110) Foisil, M. *La révolte des Nu-Pieds et les révoltes normandes de 1639*, Paris, 1970.

(111) Gately, M. O. *et al.* 'Seventeenth-century Peasant Furies: some problems of comparative history', *Past and Present*, No. 51, 1971, pp. 63–80.

(112) Jacquart, J. *La crise rurale en Ile-de-France, 1550–1670*, Paris, 1974.

(113) Le Roy Ladurie, E. 'Révoltes et contestations rurales en France de 1675 à 1788', *Annales*, XXIX, 1974, pp. 6–22.

(114) Mandrou, R. *Classes et luttes des classes en France au début du XVIIe siècle*, Florence, 1965.

(115) —— 'Vingt ans après, ou une direction de recherches fécondes: les révoltes populaires en France au XVIIe siècle', *Revue Historique*, CCXLII, 1969, pp. 29–40.

(116) Mousnier, R. *Lettres et mémoires adressés au Chancelier Séguier, 1633–1649*, 2 vols. Paris, 1964.

(117) —— 'La Révolution dite du Papier-timbré en Basse Bretagne en 1675', *Actes du 92e Congrès national des Sociétés savantes, Strasbourg et Colmar, 1967*, Paris, 1970, pp. 325–57.

(118) —— *Peasant Uprisings in Seventeenth-Century France, Russia and China*, London, 1971 (translation by B. Pearce of *Fureurs paysannes: les Paysans dans les Révoltes du XVIIe siècle (France, Russie, Chine)*, Paris, 1967).

(119) Pillorget, R. ' "Les Cascavéoux": l'insurrection aixoise de l'automne 1630', *XVIIe Siècle*, 1964, pp. 4–30

(120) —— 'Essai d'une typologie des mouvements insurrectionnels ruraux survenus en Provence de 1596 à 1715', *Actes du 92e Congrès national des Sociétés savantes, Strasbourg et Colmar, 1967*, Paris, 1970, pp. 359–82.

(121) —— *Les mouvements insurrectionnels de Provence entre 1596 et 1715*, Paris, 1976.

(122) Prestwich, M. Reviews of B. Porshnev, *Les soulèvements populaires en France avant la Fronde de 1623 à 1648*, and of R. Mandrou, *Classes et luttes des classes en France au début du XVIIe siècle*, in *English Historical Review*, LXXXI, 1966, pp. 565–72.

(123) Salmon, J. H. M. 'Venal office and Popular sedition in Seventeenth-Century France: a review of a controversy', *Past and Present*, 31, 1967, pp. 21–43.

(124) Westrich, S. A. *The Ormée of Bordeaux: a revolution during the Fronde*, Baltimore, 1972.

Index

Index

(Numbers in italics refer to the notes)

268   *Index*

French monarchy—*continued*
early modern period, 2, 3, 4, 12, 13, 21;
comparison with English monarchy, 4,
5; comparison with Spanish monarchy,
4, 5, 8; conflict between 'traditional'
and 'absolutist' constitutions in early
modern period, 7; federal structure of,
8; international wars and financial difficulties of, 9, 10, 11, 33, 41, 46, 185;
difficulty of raising credit, 11, 43; relationship with nobility, 16, 45–8, 51–3,
231–43 *passim*; a monarchy 'above
class', 24, 92, 163; 'sword' values of,
25, 45–8, 50–2; concept of constitutional legality fundamental to, 34–5;
always to some extent *tempérée*, 41;
influences of Fronde on policies from
1653, 43–55; aristocratic nature, 48;
constitution stabilises during early
personal reign of Louis XIV, 56–8, 243;
Porshnev on importance of development of national state by, 88; Thierry
on, 92; Pagès on, 95–5; Porshnev on
Mousnier's concept of '*une monarchie
tempérée*' via venality, 96; constitutional challenge of Fronde, 181–7; *see
also* 'Administrative monarchy'; 'Administrative revolution'; 'Bourgeois
historiography'; Feudal-absolutism;
'Feudalised bourgeoisie'; Financial administration; *Officiers*; Venality
French Revolution: Marxist theory of
origins, 78; a 'bourgeois revolution',
78–9, 92, 97, 100, 139; *see also*
'Bourgeois historiography'
French Wars of Religion, *see* Wars of
Religion
Fronde: long-term significance of, 2, 37,
42; policies of monarchy after, 2, 43–
55; origins of, 4, 11, 15, 16, 23, 36–7,
74, 181–97 *passim*; degree of 'victory in
defeat' of, 7, 40, 41; popular uprisings
before, 13, 22–4, 73–4, 78–102 *passim*,
125–7; leadership of *Parlement de
Paris* in, 17; constitutional position of
Fronde parlementaire, 35, 38–40, 181–
7; fears of renewal after, 37, 41–2;
failure of leadership in, 38, 193; princes
in, 38–9; a 'failed bourgeois revolution'?, 78, 103, 125–7, 130–3, 137;
Porshnev on bourgeoisie and, 125–33
passim; *see also* Climate; *Elus, Journées révolutionnaires*; Mousnier, R.;
Officiers; *Parlement de Paris, Parle-*

mentaires; *Paulette*; Porshnev, B.; *Tré-
soriers de France*; Venality
Fronde des princes, see Fronde
Fronde parlementaire, see Fronde

Gabelle, 47, 241
Gaston d'Orléans (1608–60), 22, 32, 33,
170, 188, 195, 207, 241
General enquiry (1664), *see enquête
générale*
Généralités, 10, 55, 56, 95, 201, 206, 210,
213, 216
German Princes, 32, 33
Germany, 5, 22, 32, 33, 37, 88, 103
Gentilshommes: grievances, 18, 162, 240–
1, 244 *n.26*, 245 *n.43* 47, *and* 49; 'gentilhomme tradition' in French seventeenth century, 31; oppression by, 52–3;
indebtedness of, 69; and popular revolts, 75, 145–9, 152–3, 156–8; and *ban
et arrière-ban*, 235–6, 237–9; *see also
Noblesse; Noblesse d'épée*
'*Gentilshommes de plume et d'encre*', 45,
162
Gloire, 25, 75
Goldmann, L., 41
Goubert, P., 2, 17, 26, *58 n.7*, *60 n.60 and
61*, 65; on French population, 27,
69; on seventeenth-century 'economic
crisis', 28–9; France mid-way between
Venice and Holland economically, 31;
on Louis XIV and nobility, 46
Gouverneurs, 8, 51, 52, 99, 138
'*Grand Siècle*', le, 64; 'legend of' according to Porshnev, 80, 86, 87, 88, 89,
90, 94, 97
Grands, 36, 38, 149

Habsburgs, 4, 5, 11, 22, 32, 36, 37, 42,
88, 164, 189, 202
Hanotaux, P., 125
Hauser, H., 29
Henry II, king of France (1547–59), 10,
11, 12
Henry IV, king of France (1589–1610), 5,
12, 13, 14, 15, 21, 22, 64, 114, 118, 203
Hobsbawm, E. J., 2, 31, *58 n.2*
Holland, 114, *see also* Netherlands; Dutch
economy
Hôpitaux-généraux, 49
Huguenots, 14, 20, 21, 22, 31, 84

Intendants: correspondence on popular
uprisings, 23, 73, 75, 83–6, 99, 144–60
passim; Richelieu and, 33; attack on